THE
WITCH
DOCTOR
OF WALL
STREET

THE WITCH DOCTOR

A Noted Financial Expert Guides You Through Today's Voodoo Economics

OF WALL STREET

Robert H. Parks, Ph.D.

 Prometheus Books

59 John Glenn Drive
Amherst, NewYork 14228-2197

Published 1996 by Prometheus Books

00 99 98 97 96   5 4 3 2 1

Library of Congress Cataloging-in-Publication Data

Parks, Robert H.
    The witch doctor of Wall Street : a noted financial expert guides you through today's voodoo economics / Robert H. Parks.
        p.   cm.
    Includes bibliographical references and index.
    ISBN 1–57392–018–5 (alk. paper)
    1. Securities industry—United States—Corrupt practices. 2. Stockbrokers—Professional ethics—United States. 3. Money—United States. 4. Business ethics—United States. 5. Political ethics—United States. 6. Monetary policy—United States. I. Title.
HG4910.P36   1996
332.6—dc20
                                                        95–43776
                                                        CIP

Printed in the United States of America on acid-free paper

Contents

Preface

A Walk Down Wall Street

> The savage, it is true, has his experts, his medicine men, who by chant or howl, by sacrifice or incantation, attempt to cajole the destroying force. The capitalist world also has its experts, its economists.
>
> John Strachey, *The Nature of Capitalist Crisis* (1935)*

Medicine Man? Witch Doctor? Call me what you will; I owe the very title of this book to John Strachey. I am a Wall Street economist, a practitioner of the dismal science for a quarter century. Reflecting on medieval demonology, I had initially thought to title this book "Mephistopheles on Wall," because Mephistopheles is composed in equal parts of Devil Pressure, Demon Insecurity, and Satan Selfishness, the embodiment of the Unholy Trinity on Wall Street as they twist and distort the best of economic and financial theory and data.

Let's begin on a bright note at Broadway and Wall Street. A magnificent cathedral stands there in all its majesty. Look up at the gothic spire topped by the cross. Now look down, and read the sign:

TRINITY CHURCH
Chartered 1697

I first spotted this sign in 1972, and was startled to see this person's name in big letters:

---

*New York: J. J. Little and Ives Company, p. 7.

15

The Rev. Robert R. Parks, Rector

"Odd," I thought, "I wonder if he is a relative." It turned out he was not, but I decided to meet Rector Parks. Since I lay claim to some expertise in the material world, and he to the spiritual, I thought the two worlds should get together. When we finally met, I said: "Why don't we combine our understanding of the material and spiritual worlds? Let's co-author a book on Wall Street. We'll title it 'Wall Street: The Clash of Money and Morality.'"

Rector Parks smiled, but that's as far as it went. It didn't matter, because as early as 1978, long before the scandals on insider trading hit the headlines, I had decided to write the present volume, which centers on the ideas Rector Parks and I talked about. We spoke of blackened ethics.

In early 1989, I (RH) asked Rector Parks (RP) about the church's brown stones:

RP: The brown stones are turning to powder. We plan to photograph and replace each stone one-by-one. We want to restore the church and retain its beauty.

RH: Too bad you can't recover lost souls as easily as you replace brown stones.

RP: Excuse me?

Just as they photographed the crumbling brown stones of Trinity Church, I tried to get clear pictures of the blackened minds of Wall Street. It isn't just outright dishonesty that stands out so starkly in the prints I developed. You can see that for yourself. You can read all about lawbreakers on Wall Street every day in the newspapers. That is not my main interest. No, my interest centers instead on the galaxy of deceptive practices, the subtle tricks and twists of argument that fall just inside the law. The regulatory authorities, I contend, look the other way at wholesale ethical malpractice, when they look at all.

A DOUBLE PLAGUE ON WALL STREET: SELF-DECEPTION AND PREACHING

Deception and trickery for the most part are not reported. Self-deception is rarely recognized. Indeed, if deliberate deception is a disease, then self-deception must be counted a plague. *The overriding message of this book is that self-deception reigns supreme on Wall Street and in the economic arena we call Washington, D.C.* A related thesis is that professional economists are too often blind, or pretend to be blind, to the awesome power of deception. Ideology dominates economic science and, with rare exceptions, professional economists on the political left, right, and middle show up as preachers, not objective scientists. Their very notion of the nature of economic human beings conflicts violently with the views of objective science and with the prospects for humanity itself, or so I argue in the concluding chapters.

Why do I concentrate on Wall Street? You know that we find deception everywhere. Deception reigns supreme in the main streets, government rows, trade association alleys, and university avenues across America. Yes, and deception has become the trademark of the polished TV evangelists who say they can save your soul for a few dollars. Still, my focus is to alert investors to the trash on Wall Street, to those who promise "Wealth without Risk" or, feigning pinpoint timing, warn of "The Great Depression of 1990" or "Bankruptcy 1995."

But why should anyone write, much less read, another book on hucksters and human greed? Have not writers aplenty exhausted the subject? No! First, much of the written material on Wall Street behavior is self-serving whitewash. Second, economists and most analysts pay far too little attention to three mind benders from the Netherworld *working as a team,* namely, *pressure, insecurity,* and *selfishness.* When these three scheme together, always in sight of Trinity Church, all hell breaks loose.

I shall introduce you to the people who walk the dark side of Wall Street, the night walkers. They come in two main categories, the *Parrots* and the *Pros:* the former are those who speak of economic and investment matters without really understanding while the latter are intellectual prostitutes. These monarchs of whitewash are the superbly trained experts who fit data and theory to predetermined conclusions in support of their own goals, not yours. Among the worst are investment bankers, Wall Street executives, and (yes) professional economists who bow to their masters.

Could it be that senior Wall Street heads were unaware of the flashing red lights on stock valuation models just prior to the Black Monday crash on October 19, 1987; oblivious to the advance furies hitting overpriced Japanese stocks preceding the crash in early 1990; deaf to the thunder threatening the collapse of junk bonds and junk stocks in the 1980s; and blind to the leading signals for five recessions during the period I have been on Wall Street (1969–70, 1973–75, 1980, 1981–82, and 1990–91)? Were these sophisticates deaf and blind? Hardly. Wall Street's executives regularly pay their economics spokesmen to manufacture sun and cheer no matter how black the outlook.

THE THEORETICAL PICKS AND SHOVELS

My all-consuming goal is to arm you with the theoretical picks and shovels necessary to understand the facts in plain English and using simple arithmetic. To do so, I must exorcise the hideous jargon and irrelevant mathematics of my fellow witch doctors. Then you can judge for yourself and not have to lean on argument by authority, which can be dangerous in the extreme. Then you can understand why professional economists, including several Nobel Prize winners, have so often fallen on defective theory. The renegade "monetarists," including Nobel Laureate Milton Friedman, fall into that category. So do the "Modiglianians" (after Nobel Prize winner Franco Modigliani) in corporate financial theory. So do modern portfolio theorists whose flawed models of risk-free returns make no sense in the applied world of finance and investment. Most important, you can use theory to identify the trash peddled as truth in many best-selling books that litter Wall Street and main street.

The characters depicted in this book are real, and any relationship to people living or dead was purely intentional. This posed a problem for me, namely, whether I should identify each by name. I decided to identify individually by name all of the good people, at least as I saw them. Under no circumstances, however, did I identify a single Parrot by name. That would have been cruel, for Parrots know not what they do. But what about the Pros? Well, the many reconstructed dialogues throughout this book presented no problem just so long as other people were present. Still, I decided not to put tags on *individuals*. (I'll let you do that.) Even so, I did identify the time, the place, and the institutions involved from the detailed diaries I kept covering the meetings I attended or hosted from 1970 to 1995.

DEDICATION AND ACKNOWLEDGMENTS

I dedicate this book to all who studied economics, finance, and investment in my classes at the Wharton School of the University of Pennsylvania and the graduate business schools of the City University of New York, as well as Lehigh, Rutgers, and Pace universities; many of my fellow Wall Streeters, including some outstanding economists; the investment experts who work with the brokerage firms on the "sell" side of Wall Street; investment experts on the "buy" side of Wall Street; the media, mainly WOR, WMCA, and WCBS on the East Coast; Cable CNBC-FNN and KWHY (L.A.) television; the press; and government officials and institutional investors who attended the investment forums, luncheons, and dinners I hosted.

My dedication includes Robert H. Thouless, a psychologist and logician, who wrote *How to Think Straight* for the expert and the layman in easy-to-understand language. It includes Dr. Saul Sands, a caustic critic of mainstream economics; the faculty at Swarthmore College; Dr. Charles Raymond Whittlesey of the Wharton School of the University of Pennsylvania; and my colleagues at Pace University, especially Finance Professors Verne Atwater, Lou Altfest, Clarke Johnson, Gerald Pollack, Barney Seligman, and, most important, Dr. Maurice Larrain for his pioneering investigations into chaos theory and the financial markets.

Many investment officers offered valuable suggestions, especially Paul Travia, Jr., Daiwa Bank Trust Co.; George Livingston, American Express; Steve Lewins, Gruntal & Co.; Dick Pike, Chancellor Capital Management; Jim McGonigle, Jamison, Eaton & Wood; and David Wray, Sun Life of Canada. My thanks go to my Pace MBA students, especially the sage criticisms of Robert Brown, Alexander Keck, Tom Mansley, Richard Maresca, Mario Pisano, and Tom Weissmann. My deepest thanks are reserved for Steven L. Mitchell, Editor-in-Chief of Prometheus Books. He taught me more than I had ever imagined about how to write clearly and precisely.

I owe a special debt to a few Wall Street economists who encouraged me to write (and finish) this book. They have my sympathy. Why? Well, just a cursory review of Appendix A makes clear that a Wall Street economist must have a very thick skin and must expect to be ridiculed for bad calls. It goes with the job. Even so, all investment strategy involves forecasting, whether conscious or unconscious, thorough or sloppy. Since no one has accurate knowledge of the future, economic seers are bound to go astray. With that in mind, I've included my wayward forecasts, along with the good ones, for the years 1970 to 1995 (Appendix A: History of Forecasts and Controversy).

Finally, my debt extends to Inta and our children, Karen, Robert, and Alison; and my mother and father. They taught me far more than practitioners of the dismal science about the chains that bind economics to ethics. Nevertheless, some readers may be displeased or even infuriated with a book designed for the expert and the layperson alike. Still, one cannot and should not try to please everybody. Strunk and White put this ethical precept beautifully in their *Elements of Style*:

> The whole duty of a writer is to please and satisfy himself, and the true writer always plays to an audience of one. Let him start sniffing the air, or glancing at the Trend Machine, and he is as good as dead, although he may make a nice living.

Yes indeed.

RH

Part One

Forecasting Theory, Practice, and Malpractice

1

Baptism of Fire

duPont, Glore Forgan & Company

Second Witch:	Fillet of fenny snake,
	In the caldron boil and bake;
	Eye of newt and toe of frog,
	Wool of bat and tongue of dog,
	Adder's fork and blindworm's sting
	Lizard's leg and howlet's wing,
	For a charm of powerful trouble,
	Like a hell-broth boil and bubble.
All Three Witches:	Double, double toil and trouble;
	Fire burn and caldron bubble.

William Shakespeare, *Macbeth,* Act IV, Scene I

Fenny refers to fens, or marshes; newt, a salamander; blindworm, a snake; and howlet, a small owl. I suppose Shakespeare added wool of bat and tongue of dog for flavor. I have a Witches' Brew in mind, too, one cooked up by three fiends who hang out at Wall and Nassau streets. You may have run into them. They are selfishness and its two inseparable companions, pressure and insecurity.

Economic theorists have long insisted that selfishness, alias self-interest, is not such a bad thing after all. They say that you must understand how beneficial it can be in motivating people to work, to save, and to invest in a market economy. You must realize, they say, just how individual self-interest and competition operate together to produce the goods, the jobs, and the incomes for a prosperous and free people. There's truth in all this, but that hardly suggests that we should crown selfishness a saint. Religious leaders warn us against that, but how about economists? Their harmonious view overlooks what happens when selfishness, pressure, and insecurity conspire as a team. Listen to the shrieking and incantations of this Unholy Trinity as they tend to their fiery cauldron:

Boil and bake	Too much confidence.
Stir in	Too little knowledge.
Throw in	Craw of hog, diseased from selfishness.
	Heart of dove, ruptured from pressure.
	Bowel of chicken, shriveled from insecurity.
Sprinkle lightly	A Shredded Rabbit of Regulation
Chant and Howl	Glory be, we worship thee:
	Selfishness, Pressure, Insecurity,
	In the caldron, we see the fall
	Of triple, triple troubled Wall,
	Of triple, triple troubled Wall.

What precisely has this gang from the Netherworld thrown into the caldron? Let's try to answer the question by retracing our steps. See the building diagonally across the street from Trinity Church, on the southeast corner? That's One Wall Street, my address when I first came to this financial Mecca in late 1968. It was then called the Irving Trust Building. Now big letters identify it as the Bank of New York. I know the building well because it was the headquarters of duPont, Glore Forgan & Company, the second largest investment banking and securities firm in the world—at least it was until the firm filed for bankruptcy.

I was duPont's chief economist. At first I reported to Research Director Phil Loomis, then later to Executive Vice President Mort Meyerson. Meyerson received his orders from Chairman Ross Perot, the very same billionaire who was to rise to political prominence in the 1992 presidential election. Perot struck me as brilliant, though he could not swim in the turbulent Wall Street currents. His troubles on Wall also signaled failure as a candidate for president of the United States. We'll see why when the Texas Tornado turns his fury on me (see chapter 2), and again when he joins company with confused fiscal extremists in (see chapter 13) and muddled protectionists in (see chapter 23). But first we must meet some one else.

On the south side of Wall Street, just a hundred steps from Trinity Church, is the New York Stock Exchange. Across Wall Street from the Stock Exchange is 26 Wall, the Federal Building. That's where we'll meet George.

There he stands so very high on the steps of Federal Hall. I mean, of course, George Washington. This proud and imposing warrior took the oath as the first president of the United States on this very site, April 30, 1789. It says so on the plaque. Every time I walk past George, I can almost hear him whisper: "Father, I cut down that cherry tree. I can't tell a lie." Did he really say that? Are George's ethics shaped by the rector of Trinity? I don't know. What I do know is that Wall Streeters pay little attention to George as they hurry by. They avoid looking into his eyes. Or am I just imagining it? I'm reminded of what the famous nineteenth-century author Charles Dickens wrote:

> I have known a vast quantity of nonsense talked about bad men not looking you in the face. Don't trust that idea. Dishonesty will stare honesty out of countenance any day in the week if there is anything to be got by it.*

Charles Dickens and George Washington were among the first to alert me to the night walkers on Wall Street. I first ran into them as chief economist with Francis I. duPont & Company (1968–71). Phil Loomis hired me in November 1968. It was shortly thereafter, when duPont merged with Glore Forgan, that it became second in size to Merrill Lynch, the thundering herd on Wall Street. I was proud to be with a major house, to be its chief economic spokesman. I was secretly excited about my business address at One Wall Street. I soon learned that zero is but a touch away from one.

Please bear with me, for I must discuss subjects that may be foreign. I must explain at length just how I arrived at forecasts on a case-by-case basis from 1970 into 1995, starting with duPont (see Appendix A). I must do so despite the warning Epictetus gave twenty centuries ago against making "frequent and disproportionate mention . . . of [your] own doings [because] other people do not take the same pleasure in hearing what has happened to you as you take in recounting your adventures."† Good advice! Even so, I must recount and record my "adventures" and the detailed "doings" of others, which ran from the hilarious to the explosive to the tragic. I must do this to familiarize you with the analytical tools, the picks and shovels indispensable to forecasting, and to document how night walkers twist theory and data, often unconsciously, to fit their hellish ends. Sound theory and data, then, are the two keys we need to unlock the secret files of the night walkers. Nothing else will do.

---

*Tyron Edwards, *Useful Quotations* (New York: Grosset & Dunlap, Publishers, 1934), p. 137.

†Quoted in *The Social Philosophers: The World's Great Thinkers* (New York: Random House, 1947), p. 267.

* * *

Let's begin with the 1969–70 recession, my baptism of fire on Wall Street. In the August 1969 issue of *Investment Values for Today,* duPont's master research publication, I wrote that, "The slowdown has actually begun, that a slide of the economy through the first half of next year is probable." I grew progressively worried, insistent, and loud about impending recession. The press, to my surprise and delight, published my comments in full (see Appendix A, Forecast 1). The plummeting leading indicators and extremely tight Federal Reserve policy would lead to severe recession, I argued, and that's what happened. The economy peaked in December 1969 and headed sharply downhill until November 1970, the low point or so-called nadir of the recession. Now we must explain why the signals for recession were strong, why the consensus proved blind to these very signals, and why my forecast of recession so enraged duPont branch managers that they demanded my resignation. This last point is critical to the deception that runs through Wall Street. What were the recession signals? Let's go quickly through the leading indicators.

RECESSION SIGNALS

Falling Capital Investment Commitments

The leading indicators, the advance orders and contracts that signal a rise or fall in business spending for equipment, machinery, and plant, were down, way down. Forward investment commitments were way off, too. These are the contracts for direct placements, that is, the privately placed loans that large institutional lenders (for example, life insurance companies and corporate pension funds) make to large business borrowers. The purpose may be to provide financing for the construction of a shopping mall, a hotel, or a manufacturing plant. Prudential Insurance Company, for example, would "commit" itself to make money available to manufacturing corporations, construction companies, or others at interest rates and other lending terms decided upon at the time the contracts were made. The funds would actually be paid out, or "taken down" over months, even years.

New commitments were dropping fast, and commitments made earlier were being canceled. The life insurance companies suddenly found themselves short of cash. As the Federal Reserve reduced the reserves it provided to the banking system, this cut into the supply of loanable funds, and market interest rates soared since more and more borrowers were seeking less and less money. Life insurance policyholders learned that they could borrow against their own insurance policies at fixed, low rates of interest. They did just that. The overcommitment by life companies to provide loans to business clashed head-on with a predicted cash flow that was drying up. To get the cash to honor those forward investment commitments that had not already been canceled by the borrowers themselves, the life insurance companies were forced (a) to sell their own investment holdings at substantial losses and (b) to borrow from the banks at high interest rates. This unfortunate situation featured poor forecasts of interest rates and even worse money and investment management, both of which are par for the insurance industry.

Contrary to their image as lenders only to the highest quality borrowers, life insurance companies are poor money managers who direct a large percentage of their loans and investments to low-rated and risky sectors of the economy. I learned this when I worked as research director for the Life Insurance Association of America, now the American Council of Life Insurance, a powerful trade association. As we shall see, after the failed savings and loan associations and the default of junk-bond financed companies, life insurance companies stand next in line for trouble. I said in 1970 to Phil Loomis that forward investment commitments, data not then generally familiar to business forecasters, were falling "like cannon balls from the sky."

Falling Advance Signals for Construction and "Durables"

Construction contractors have to get building permits before they can start construction of new houses, whether single family or apartments (multifamily). The number of permits sought and the number of "starts" registered were falling, foreshadowing a decline not only in housing construction but also spending for furniture, appliances, refrigerators, and other durable consumer goods (defined to last three years or longer). Contracts for commercial and industrial building contracts edged ahead until December 1969, then they plunged as well.

Profits, a leading signal of the overall economy, were falling as costs speeded ahead of prices. Money and credit growth was contracting in response to a tightening Federal Reserve policy. The rise in interest rates began to cut into both consumer and business spending, signaling a prospective fall despite the data showing an advance in current spending. Because consumer spending represents about two-thirds of gross national product (GNP), the retrenchment ahead in consumer demand was critical to the outlook. The array of advance or leading indicators, then, was down.

The Government's Index of Leading Indicators

The leading indicators are not infallible, as we shall see. Even so, I noted in early 1970 that the official composite index of twelve leading indicators* prepared by the Department of Commerce had started falling in April 1969. That turned out to be eight months before the economy itself peaked in December 1969, then plunged into recession. The top series of Exhibit 1–1 (at the end of this chapter) depicts the fall in the leading composite index eight months before the economy peaked. Take a look. The area within the vertical lines in the exhibit represents the recession period, December 1969 to November 1970.

I was lonely; it seemed that almost nobody agreed with me. DuPont's own analysts were bullish. My bleak views did not set well with them, which became a source of friction. The registered representatives (RRs), that is, the stockbrokers serving the individual or "retail" public, were upset, too. They revered me when I was bullish, but now openly criticized me for allegedly hurting their sales. (Who among their clients are going to buy stocks if I'm forecasting an impending downturn in the economy?) I was aware of only two other economists on the street forecasting recession: Sam Nakagama of Kidder Peabody and Gary Shilling of Merrill Lynch. The three of us made up the troublemakers of Wall Street. I am convinced that Gary lost his job for forecasting recession, and I know that I barely survived.

MISLEADING SIGNALS: THE COINCIDENT INDICATORS

Just about everybody else, on the street and off, seemed oblivious to the threat of recession. How could so many people have been so wrong? The grand and sunny consensus insisted that the available data for the economy were expanding nicely. Employment, income, production, and trade sales (retail and wholesale) were chalking up new highs, they said. Indeed they were. Most of these series, which the Commerce Department classifies as *coincident* indicators, rose briskly almost to the very point of recession. Payroll employment continued to advance even after the overall economy started downhill (see Exhibit 1–1).

What was wrong? Coincident indicators seldom provide reliable clues to the future. Instead they show what the economy is doing now. More precisely, they reflect the recent past because the data are released with a lag, often two

---

*These include new orders for durable goods, new contracts for plant and equipment, stock prices, building permits, and the broad money supply known as M2, to name a few.

or three months after the fact. That includes data on gross national product and gross domestic product, the quintessential coincident indicators.

REAR-VIEW-MIRROR INDICATORS

The coincident indicators, in short, are "rear-view mirror" indicators. They tell where you have been, not where you are heading. So, be wary of those who say, for example, that the prospects for the economy are bright because jobs and incomes are strong, or because industrial production and retail sales are rising. That type of commentary, though widespread even today, is supported neither by sound theory nor by history. For a parallel, consider the weather man. How much confidence would you place in a meteorologist who forecast blue skies for the weekend just because the sun shone brightly on Thursday? Economists have a lot to learn from meteorologists. Remember this the next time you see press reports on the coincident indicators, arguing that because jobs and incomes are up, a rise in spending must follow.

I'll dramatize my caution on the coincident indicators by way of an exchange I had when working as an economist with General Electric Company a decade earlier. Two of my fellow economists and I (RH) met with GE's top manager of the economic and industrial forecasting group. I'll call him TM. The year was 1960:

TM: I see that the three of you have come up with almost the same forecast numbers for gross national production, gross national expenditures, and gross national income. Your statistical residuals [the differences in the estimates for the three series] are less than $2 billion. That's a good cross-check for accuracy. Congratulations.

RH: Wait a minute. These are identities. Gross national production *is* gross national expenditures, which is gross national income. There are some adjustments for inventory and foreign trade, but one is the other. For every 50-cent candy bar produced and sold, 50 cents shows up as output, 50 cents as consumer expenditures, and 50 cents as income, chopped up into wages, salaries, rents, profits and interest. The identity of output, spending, and income for (1) consumption also holds for (2) investment and (3) government, the three components of GNP. That's the arithmetic of national income accounts.

TM: Yes, but the three of you arrived at the three sets of estimates independent of each other. Right?

RH: We did? We lunch together every day. Our arithmetic on GNP is consistent, but that's no reason to think that our forecasts are on track.

TM did not take kindly to my remarks. The key lesson here, straight from
General Electric, is to beware the coincident indicators. But what about the
lagging indicators such as current business spending on plant and equipment, commercial and industrial loans, and many prices and interest rates?
Well, they're even more misleading. The lagging index typically heads higher
and higher for many months after the economy has fallen into recession; it
rises even as the economy falls. Moreover, the lagging index may continue to
fall for many months after the start of economic recovery; it typically falls
even as the economy rises. You can see that in the third series from the top in
Exhibit 1–1. Like the coincident index, the lagging index isn't much help either. Would economic forecasts be more accurate and useful if we were to
consider the relationship (the ratio) of the coincident to the lagging index?
This is a favorite of the *Wall Street Journal*. Note that the ratio of coincident
to lagging indicators leads recession by between twenty-seven months and
one month. If this is any indicator of how useful this ratio is in forecasting the
economy, the the Commerce Department should scrap it as useless. We need
indicators that will give us signals we can act upon to head off recession, inflation, or what have you. Clearly this ratio watching won't help us.

I shall review other forecast rules later, but note here the most important
but least observed rule in forecasting. It is to give top priority to the initial and
the lagged effects of government policies, including Federal Reserve policy.
Look at what the government does, not what it says it does. In the 1969–70
experience, government policy was one of excessive economic restriction,
and it was signaling—with a short time lag—a terrible economic storm. The
storm was coming despite the coincident sun that still shone bright and strong.

By now you must have concluded just how I would rank policy, the forward indicators, and the coincident and lagging statistical series in trying to
look into the future. Here are the grades I give these statistics:

Government Policy, Initial Impact	A+
Government Policy, Lagged Impact	A+
Forward Indicators, Broadly Defined	A
Official Commerce Leading Index Gauge	B–
Coincident Indicators	C–
Lagging Indicators	F
Ratio of Coincident to Lagging Index	F

WAILING AND SCREAMING AT FRANCIS I. DUPONT

I was convinced that the economy was already in recession, and happy that I should get so much press. I felt useful and important in alerting the firm to the dark clouds just ahead for the economy, profits, and especially the stock market. DuPont's clients would be ever so grateful that we got them out of the market in time. The firm's top investment officers would be thankful, too, for they had substantial amounts of money under management in their own account. I thought the investment banking department would be pleased as well. They could alert their clients to defer or hold off buying new stock issues. The risk of a market fall was too great. On and on I dreamed about the good job I was doing.

I woke up fast to my own self-deception. In January and February of 1970 branch managers (BMs) telephoned me from across the country to complain, to whine, to moan, to threaten. I was astonished and bewildered at the fury directed my way. They were infuriated with the press reports, and screamed that my negative views undermined their sales efforts. They had no interest in reviewing data, theory, forecast signals, or any other matter that could be useful in appraising whether I was right or wrong on the outlook. This is typical of the calls I received:

BM: Parks, how do I sell stocks with you around? My clients come into my office and push the news headlines in my face. There you are, on the front page, forecasting a recession, damning the stock market.

RH: Yes, that's true. That's what I thought I was paid to do, to call it as I see it.

BM: Look, *Doctor* Parks, our own analysts don't agree with you. My RRs are complaining about your forecasts, all this damned publicity you get. Where are the other economists forecasting recession? What recession are you talking about?

RH: Orders and order backlogs are collapsing. The government is imitating a boa constrictor. Since when would you listen to the RRs for a forecast? Our analysts are focusing on the firms they follow, but their microanalysis does not catch the big picture. The overall picture is deter. . . .

BM: Microwhat? Seventy analysts can't all be wrong. Talking with you is a waste.

I longed to return to Wharton, where I was respected by students and faculty and secure in my teaching post. But my days and nights turned quickly to ones of anxiety and fear.

Someone should have reminded me of the messenger who brought bad tidings to the king and lost his head as a result. What hurt me most was the foul language, the discourtesy, the ridicule, the threats. I wasn't used to any of that. My heartbeat speeded up, I had trouble getting my breath, and I was sweating bullets. Pressure and insecurity were getting to me in the full light of day. Selfishness whispered that perhaps I should soften my views, that maybe I should "shade" my forecasts to protect myself, my job, and my family. "Shade?" That means to tilt or slant to the bright side to accommodate my employer, no matter how bleak the actual outlook. It's a nice word, a common but generally unspoken word on Wall Street, and a euphemism for deception.

I don't want to give the impression that all economists shouting bad news suffer as a result. Nor does everyone deliberately and consciously shade, though many more do unconsciously. Chronic bad-news bears, who are invariably wrong on their extreme predictions, cannot be accused necessarily of shading. They have other problems. I would include among the persistent pessimists the following:

Dr. Downturn, Gary Shilling
Dr. Death, Al Wojnilower
Dr. Doom, Henry Kaufman
Dr. Gloom, Martin Feldstein

We will meet them later in our review of the blockbuster recession of 1981–82 in chapter 6 and elsewhere.

AT THE CIRCUS WITH DRS. GALBRAITH AND RINFRET

The winter of 1970 was a bitter one for me. I had never before been criticized so harshly by so many for doing what I thought I was supposed to do. My job was to forecast, and to be persuasive about it. In reflecting on this, a capital idea occurred to me. It dawned on me that a debate between two prominent economists could dramatize the whole question of whether there would or would not be a recession. As moderator, I would be able to get my two cents in, though indirectly, by pressing the two economists to review government policy, the forward indicators, and the coincident and lagging series.

But who could attract the most attention from the investment community? For a truly explosive match, I decided to engage two nationally recognized economists capable of economic acrobatics, with me as ring master, and the press in attendance. Two prominent figures immediately came to mind: Dr.

Pierre Rinfret, the unequivocal, eloquent, confident, and supremely polemical head of Rinfret Boston Associates, Inc., an economic counselling firm; and Dr. John Kenneth Galbraith, the iconoclastic, lucid, assured, and uncommonly blunt professor of economics at Harvard University. What volatile gladiators they would make, considering that both were very outspoken. To my delight they accepted my invitation to debate at the Century Plaza Hotel in Los Angeles in May 1970.

I realized, of course, that as moderator, I would not be able to advance my own views. Even so, I counted on the press to interview me after the debate so that I could get my views across. As it worked out, Dr. Rinfret (PR) speeded the whole process with some verbal fireworks before the debate began. This is how I recall his exchange with me in my hotel room. Later he talked with the press shortly before show time:

PR: Listen, Robert. There ain't gonna be no recession. I'll eat my hat if there's a recession. Anyway, you're the moderator. Make sure you stick to that. Right? I'm the one debating Galbraith, not you.

RH: Of course. I wish you well. May the best man win. We have 1,200 institutional investment officers, the press, and others who will be attending this afternoon.

(My phone rings.)

RH: It's the press, a reporter from *California Business*. He would like to interview you.

(The interview lasted fifteen minutes. Dr. Rinfret became livid, and loud.)

PR: I'm through. He wants to talk to you now.

RH: No. Remember, I'm the moderator. That would not. . . .

PR: Get on the phone. You're not moderating anything now. We've got almost an hour. Maybe you can wake that reporter up. Take this phone.

I didn't fully realize what had happened until days later, when I read these words in the May 29, 1970, issue of *California Business*:

Rinfret was here recently to take part in a forum on the economy and money rates. . . . With him on the platform were John Kenneth Galbraith and Robert Parks. . . . Rinfret (said) there's been no recession to date because of signs of increases in the *economy, personal income,* and *disposable income* ("which are at all time records"), *retail sales, construction,* and *total employment.* When the reporter suggested he thought all or most of these indexes were down, Rinfret shot back: "Like hell. I stand on the figures through March, all at record levels. The difference is you're a newspaperman and I'm an economist." Parks of duPont, listening in on Rinfret's comments, (said) *sensitive financial flows, inventories, profitability, investments, all forward indicators,* have been trending down the past six to twelve months. "This doesn't suggest to me the recession that never was is over," he added. (Emphasis added)

I highlighted in my press release the coincident indicators stressed by Dr. Rinfret, and the forward indicators in my comments. The highlighted words dramatize a key lesson at this point, presented to you directly from the Century Plaza Hotel in the heart of Los Angeles, with Pierre on stage. It's worth repeating in bold letters:

Constrictive government policies and plunging forward indicators signaled recession despite the bright and shining coincident indicators cited by Rinfret. The coincident indicators, not Galbraith, felled Rinfret.

To be fair to Dr. Rinfret, I would make just two points. First, we all make blunders trying to look into the future, and Rinfret's overall forecasting record is not at issue here. Professor Galbraith was also not impressed with Rinfret's misguided emphasis on the coincident indicators, and he made this clear during the debate. Second, Rinfret has scored knockout punches too in debating and forecasting, even outfoxing a famed renegade "monetarist" and Nobel laureate in economics (see chapter 11).

I must document in the pages ahead how the Federal Reserve, the Treasury, and the consensus of economists repeatedly and chronically were misled by their focus on the coincident indicators. Don't we ever learn? For now, though, let's turn to a meeting I had with Phil Loomis in February 1970, *before* the great debate of May 1970. I reviewed the Galbraith-Rinfret circus first, I remind you, to clarify how misleading the coincident indicators can be. I had to convince Phil too. That chronicle is next, along with the fireworks and the death of a hairy mammoth on Wall.

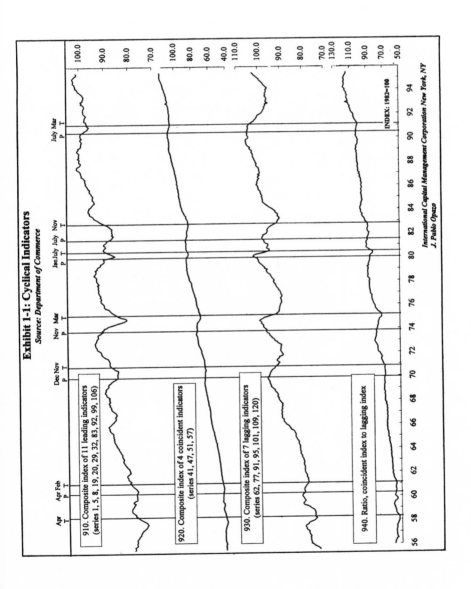

Exhibit 1-1: Cyclical Indicators
Source: Department of Commerce

910. Composite index of 11 leading indicators
(series 1, 5, 8, 19, 20, 29, 32, 83, 92, 99, 106)

920. Composite index of 4 coincident indicators
(series 41, 47, 51, 57)

930. Composite index of 7 lagging indicators
(series 62, 77, 91, 95, 101, 109, 120)

940. Ratio, coincident index to lagging index

INDEX: 1982=100

International Capital Management Corporation New York, NY
J. Pablo Opazo

Exhibit 1–2: Business Cycle Reference Dates

BUSINESS CYCLE EXPANSIONS AND CONTRACTIONS

Business cycle reference dates		Duration in Months			
				Cycle	
Trough	Peak	Contraction (trough from previous peak)	Expansion (trough to peak)	Trough from previous trough	Peak from previous peak
December 1854	June 1857	......	30	......	......
December 1858	October 1860	18	22	48	40
June 1861	April 1865	8	46	30	54
December 1867	June 1869	32	18	78	50
December 1870	October 1873	18	34	36	52
March 1879	March 1882	65	36	99	101
May 1885	March 1887	38	22	74	60
April 1888	July 1890	13	27	35	40
May 1891	January 1893	10	20	37	30
June 1894	December 1895	17	18	37	35
June 1897	June 1899	18	24	36	42
December 1900	September 1902	18	21	42	39
August 1904	May 1907	23	33	44	56
June 1908	January 1910	13	19	46	32
January 1912	January 1913	24	12	43	36

December 1914	August 1918	23	44	35	57
March 1919	January 1920	7	10	51	17
July 1921	May 1923	18	22	28	40
July 1924	October 1926	14	27	36	41
November 1927	August 1929	13	21	40	34
March 1933	May 1937	43	50	64	93
June 1938	February 1945	13	80	63	93
October 1945	November 1948	8	37	88	45
October 1949	July 1953	11	45	48	56
May 1954	August 1957	10	39	55	49
April 1958	April 1960	8	24	47	32
February 1961	December 1969	10	106	34	116
November 1970	November 1973	11	36	117	47
March 1975	January 1980	16	58	52	74
July 1980	July 1981	6	12	64	18
November 1982	July 1990	16	92	28	108
March 1991		8		100	
Average, all cycles:					
1854–1991 (31 cycles)		18	35	53	[1]53
1854–1919 (16 cycles)		22	27	48	[2]49
1919–1945 (6 cycles)		18	35	53	53
1945–1991 (9 cycles)		11	50	61	61

(Source: Department of Commerce and National Bureau of Economic Research)

Explanatory Notes for Exhibits 1–1 and 1–2. The peak (P) and trough (T) of each business cycle appear on the top of the chart in Exhibit 1–1. The composite index of leading indicators peaked eight months before the onset of the 1970 recession. The recessions of 1973–75 and 1981–82 each lasted sixteen months, as shown in Exhibit 1–2, first column. The coincident composite index of production, income, employment, and sales gave no warning of recession. The lagging index includes such indicators as bank lending rates, unit labor costs, commercial and industrial loans, and the consumer price index for services. They typically continue to rise for months after the economy sinks into recession, and fall for a while after the economy begins to expand from recession.

2

Death of the Hairy Mammoth on Wall Street

"Nobody ever saw a dog, the most sagacious animal, exchange a bone with his companion for another. . . . It is not from benevolence, as the dogs, but from self-love that man expects anything. The brewer and the baker serve us not from benevolence, but from self love."

"The wise and virtuous man is at all times willing that his own private interest should be sacrificed to the public interest."

Who do you think made these two statements, the second in apparent contradiction with the first? Why, it was none other than the so-called father of economics, Adam Smith (1723–1790). Confused? Well, we're all confused about the exact nature of economic activity.

Smith equated economic man with a dog in his *Lectures on Justice, Police, Revenue and Arms.** That's rough language. But in chapter 3 of his *Theory of Moral Sentiments,* Smith had second thoughts, reasoning that the human heart would, after all, dominate the dog in us. The benevolent "inhabitant of the breast," he said, could be counted on to govern a person's vile "passions." Later, in his masterpiece *The Wealth of Nations,* Smith had third thoughts about the nature of economic man. He replaced the heart with a hand, the "invisible hand" of competition, the controlling force for good. The hand of an angel on earth?

---

*In S. H. Patterson's *Readings in the History of Economic Thought* (New York: McGraw-Hill Book Company, 1932), p. 45.

Instead of a benevolent inhabitant of the breast, Karl Marx wrote of "the most violent, mean and malignant passions of the human breast, the furies of private interest."* So, the same human heart turns out to be benevolent for Smith, but mean for Marx. What about the hand? Marx considered the invisible hand of self-love under competition all too visible, unclean, and productive of violence within and wars among nations. He saw it more as the hand of the devil.

My conviction is that the inhabitant of the breast is neither a power for good, as Smith suggested, nor a force for evil, as Marx proclaimed. I would look for good and evil in the brain. But analogies *standing alone* destroy straight thinking.

THE HAIRY MAMMOTH:
DUPONT, GLORE FORGAN & COMPANY

There is one parallel in the suspect practice of social anatomy that I do consider eminently suitable. I have in mind the hairy mammoth of Wall Street, duPont, Glore Forgan & Company. Recall that the economy peaked in December 1969, but nobody had by February 1970 any coincident data to confirm outright recession. "Recession, what recession?" I was repeatedly asked, with a bit of ridicule thrown in. That was the problem I faced in meeting with Phil Loomis (PL), duPont's research director. Here's my reconstruction of that encounter:

PL: Robert, why do you want an emergency meeting? What's this all about?

RH: Phil, I am getting telephone calls, mainly from the branch managers. They are upset, and some insist that I be fired. They are furious with my forecast of recession. They don't like the press I'm getting on that. They say it undermines their business. Your analysts are upset with me, too. They're good at what they do—maybe the best team on Wall Street. But they are looking at their own companies, their own industry. They are oblivious to recession. Their profit numbers are absurdly high.

PL: You have been crying recession since the August 1969 *IVT* (*Investment Values for Today*). But the latest data still show an expanding economy with jobs and incomes higher. How about that?

RH: Yes, GNP and jobs were reported up, but these so-called coincident data don't tell you where the economy is headed. They never have. So, I may

Capital, Vol I, p. 15.

be a couple of months early. Big deal. No one can pinpoint timing. But the forward indicators, from investment commitments to housing starts to factory orders, are plunging. Federal Reserve policy is constrictive and rising interest rates are ripping into consumer and capital spending. All this signals a downturn, a severe recession, if we are not already in one. Recession will clobber the cyclicals and conglomerates.*

Phil, your analysts are pushing the cyclicals and conglomerates at precisely the wrong time. These stocks are ripe for a dive. The merger mania is evaporating before our eyes. The defensive stocks, like the foods and drugs, are headed down, too. That includes the interest-sensitive stocks.† Birds of a feather flock together in a downdraft, at least in the early stage of recession.

You know that you lose less money with the defensive stocks "relative" to other stock groups, but that strategy makes little sense if they all fall down together. You should ask your analysts to cut their earnings estimates. They should be recommending a shift across the board out of stocks. That includes the cyclicals, the conglomerates, the defensive, and the interest-sensitive stocks. "Relatives" can kill you in a bear market.

Phil, let me tell you a story about a frog. . . . *(I had a Professor at Wharton who was forever lecturing us about a frog. He often said: "Assuming a swamp environment, a frog is fit and I am not." His point was that everything is relative, that absolutes don't count. It seemed to me then that he was overstating his case. I came to distrust that frog. I distrust it all the more now, considering how both the buy side and the sell side of Wall Street love to measure investment performance. Thus, if the market should fall 10 percent, and an individual money manager is down 6 percent, he could then call himself a winner. He would have chalked up superior performance relative to others. I call that frog-like analysis, slippery and wrong. When tallying the numbers, absolutes do count!)*

PL: I'm not interested in frogs. What do you want?

---

*The cyclical stocks include those in the steel, paper, chemical, and other basic industries, those that respond sharply to cyclical swings in the overall economy. Conglomerates, a favorite word then, are large corporations formed by the merger of a number of companies in unrelated industries.

†The interest-sensitive stocks are first cousins to good bonds, such as high-grade utility stocks. In recession, quality bonds rise in price as interest yields fall to make more money available for borrowing. Since interest-sensitive stocks are supposedly fairly good substitutes for bonds, you could expect these stocks to fare relatively better in recession than the stock market as a whole. Interest-sensitive stocks and the defensive stocks would be expected to fall relatively less than the stock market in a major recession, but they would still fall.

RH: I'd like to review the whole array of cyclical indicators with you. They shout recession, recession with a capital "R." If I can convince you of that, then maybe I could get you to call an emergency meeting with the entire staff. I am outnumbered. You have seventy bullish analysts, a couple of frog-like strategists, and just one bear economist. I think I must be in a bad dream. They should be cutting their profit estimates. They should be switching their clients from stocks to high-grade bonds.

PL: Be realistic. You can't expect investors, especially institutional ones, to get 100 percent out of stocks. Also, the RRs are afraid they will starve selling bonds to retail buyers. Commissions on bonds are minuscule compared with those paid on stock trades. Bond investors sit forever on their bonds. They don't trade, and commissions go to hell. Anyway, your argument is that we're in recession here and now. Right?

RH: Yes, the whole thrust.

PL: OK, now tell me about those telephone calls?

RH: The branch managers like the idea of having a professional economist, but they want to turn me into a cheerleader, a huckster. They want good news, nothing but good news. Your image is at risk, too.

PL: How's that?

RH: For one thing, our August 1969 issue of the *IVT* is inconsistent. The same holds for the December issue. My lead article warns of recession ahead, but the individual analysts follow this up with profit estimates that are heavenly. One contradicts the other. It's laughable. Phil, I'm always happy to get criticism if it's backed up with data and analysis. But I'm not going to shade to the bright side to please your branch managers, your analysts, or anybody else. Shading would backfire to hurt all of us, apart from being dishonest.

PL: You've been loud about that. You're also catching flak from the fixed-income group. Did you know that? You have everybody in long bonds, but long rates head up, not down as you forecast. Anyway, you say we're in recession here and now. Well, here I am. So go ahead, convince me if you can. Take your time.

(We then reviewed for over two hours the arguments and the data signaling recession and why a falling economy and lower inflation would push interest rates down again, much along the lines outlined in chapter 1.)

PL: OK, that's enough. We'll get this straightened out.

Phil had put together one of the best research teams in the country, including thirty-five fundamental security analysts, five technical analysts, nine portfolio strategists, and five institutional research analysts, among others. They totaled seventy not including me. They served 101 branch offices in the United States and abroad. Quite a mammoth firm, you must agree. So, what was the problem?

THE PROBLEM: THE BOTTOMS-UP APPROACH

One problem was that the analysts were looking at the wrong data. The consensus focused on the coincident data, namely, income, production, employment, sales, and GNP. These rear-view mirror indicators cannot tell you where the economy is headed. DuPont's analysts made a comparable error with a different twist. They were looking at company data. They pored over financial statements of individual companies focusing on costs and revenues, and evaluated the competitive position of the company to see if it was gaining or losing ground relative to its competitors. They analyzed the company's stock, trying to determine whether the market was currently pricing the stock too low or too high relative to earnings and dividends. Their attention was on detail, on thirty or forty industries, on some two hundred individual companies. They worked independently of each other, and no one had the slightest idea of what the other was doing.

This narrow, microeconomic focus had to backfire. You can't use microscopes to capture the big picture, the macroeconomic view. The analysts were simply blind to critical developments taking place in the overall economy. They were blind to massive economic forces at the top of the economy, so to speak, and how these forces work down through the economy on individual industries and companies. They were working from the bottom, and never caught sight of the top. Without the big picture, all the little detailed photos aren't worth much. Worse, they can be misleading. That's the way I put it to Phil. This is the way I put it to you: Remember the *Titanic*? Remember the detailed analysis of the micro experts. They noted that this great ship, then the largest and most luxurious in existence, had a double-bottomed hull divided into sixteen watertight compartments. They stressed that four of these could be flooded, and still not prove a danger to the ship's buoyancy. The ship was said to be perfectly safe, unsinkable. But this British luxury liner did sink to the bottom of the sea on its maiden voyage, April 14–15, 1912. It ran into a macro force, an iceberg.

My point was simple: the overwhelming fury of recession showing up in the big picture was about to destroy the happy projections of the individual analysts. Fortunately, Phil saw that big economic iceberg. He called for an emergency meeting that included all the company and industry analysts, the portfolio strategists, the technicians, the equity (stock) and bond specialists, and key officers. I led off the meeting, reviewing again everything that I thought was pushing the economy into a severe recession. To my consternation and disappointment, there were no questions, no arguments.

This time Phil was my ally, not my adversary. He gave what I thought was the lecture of his life. He demanded that every analyst cut his earnings and dividend projections unless they had the forward data (orders, contracts, for example) to support their glowing projections. They all cut their estimates. Phil goes down in my book as a man of courage and integrity. Phil as research director was forever at war with duPont's investment banking group, as my reconstruction of this exchange shows:

RH: Company X is headed for trouble. You know that.

PL: Yes. I have made my views known.

RH: Then why is duPont lined up to underwrite (sell) X's stock in a new offering. That makes no sense.

PL: Investment banking will push anything they can get away with, anything for a fee. The stock is a dog.

RH: Recession could also murder the offering price. The financing could flop. The timing is wrong. Right?

PL: Yes. Banking wants my endorsement anyway. They won't get it. I won't push it (recommend the stock).

RH: They must despise you. Phil, be careful.

ECONOMIC STRIKEOUT AT DUPONT

Phil was replaced as research director by a new director, then another, and another, and another, and yet another in rapid and chaotic succession. Each came out by the same door he went in, and I could never be sure to whom I was supposed to report. Political in-fighting and back stabbing was the rule of the day. I ended up taking most of my orders from Mort Meyerson, duPont's new chief acting for Ross Perot. Time had run out for duPont. I realized by mid-1970 that duPont was headed for a financial strikeout. That was one forecast I hit right on the button. Here are three strikes that put duPont out of the game:

Strike One, Recession: The 1969–70 recession was an easy call, as I noted. A giant economic iceberg collided head-on with duPont. It chilled and killed commission income for the firm, both for the retail and the institutional brokers. New issues of corporate securities, stocks and bonds took an icy dive, and with it underwriting fees. Trading losses mounted. Salaries and bonuses were slashed. Talented star performers deserted duPont. Key customers deserted the firm.

Strike Two, The Paper Blizzard: While revenues slipped, costs soared. One monumental problem afflicting duPont and other brokerage firms was the inability to process and clear millions and millions of stock transactions. On this test, the cumbersome duPont proved to be among the most inefficient. In those days stock certificates had to be physically handled and "delivered," that is, sent to the buyer or held for the buyer by his broker "in street name." They were mishandled and often not delivered on time. "Backlogged" trades, as they were called, soared. Stock certificates were stacked up in piles up to the ceiling in the duPont "cage" at One Wall Street. They jammed the cage in total disorder on the desks, under the desks, in various trays, and in every nook and corner. The cage was supposed to be a restricted area. In fact it was open to many officers and others who had no business being there.

Certificates in many cases were never "delivered" to their rightful owners. They were "lost." Lost? All of them? Well, all kinds of certificates were floating around, including "bearer" instruments, that is, "unregistered" instruments, such as corporate and municipal bonds. They "belonged" to the "bearer." The owner's name wasn't on record anywhere, a fact that crooks just adored. Bearer bonds commanded a premium price in the market, over and above the prices of comparable registered securities. Anyone could sweep them up with broom and dustpan, sell them for cash, or pledge them for a bank loan, no questions asked!

In the movie *Black Orpheus* there is a scene in which Orpheus tries to find his lost love, Eurydice, by searching through the hall of records. There were huge piles of papers, the thousands-upon-thousands of certificates, each representing an individual soul, stacked up perilously in the hallways and in the vast chambers, blown up and down the massive circular staircase, and pushed around from one corner to the next by the caretaker with his big broom. Well, that classic masterpiece reminds me of the paper blizzard that hit duPont. The big difference is that those pieces of paper blowing around were worth a lot of money. They were swept up, but unlike the scene in *Black Orpheus,* they were also swept away. I suspect a lot of souls were swept away in the process.

H. Ross Perot: White Shirts and Secret Agents

Strike Three, The Fall of Napoleon on Wall Street: An entrepreneur is one who organizes and manages a business for profit. On Wall Street, it also means recognizing that most of the assets of any securities firm are its individual producers, its entrepreneurs. Ross Perot failed to see that. Worse, he strangled entrepreneurship even as he personally checked to see that everyone wore a white shirt. That in itself invited rebellion among the employees. While his mandate about white shirts was silly enough, some of his directives were hilarious (or tragic if you happened to be one of Perot's targets for the day). For example, branch managers reporting for work found their offices locked with their personal belongings piled outside the door. Often that was the first and last notice they received of dismissal.

The truly comical events centered on Perot's secret agents, the people he recruited from his Dallas, Texas, firm, Electronic Data Systems (EDS). These EDS agents imitated prospective customers. They would telephone, for example, and ask duPont branch managers what the duPont logo or company trademark meant. If the manager didn't know, he risked being fired.

Perot's secret agents got on my tail. They checked on my presentations before the RRs, city by city, in the United States and abroad. The meetings usually ended with a reception. I eventually realized that wherever I went, a well-dressed young man with black socks, close cut hair, and the ever-present white shirt, was there with me. At one point I had a brief exchange with one of these agents:

RH: Please give my best to Meyerson and Perot. Tell them to take you off my tail.

SA: How did you know?

RH: Your hair, black socks, white shirt. Your inconspicuousness was conspicuous. You all look like clones from the same EDS womb.

Perot championed individual initiative but eventually became the little Napoleon of Wall Street. What a paradox. How anti-Smithian! I had submitted my resignation to duPont in preparation for joining Eastman Dillon (later known as Blyth Eastman Dillon). Ross Perot (RP) flew to New York, unknown to me, and upon his arrival I found myself summoned to Meyerson's office. This was the first time I had ever met Perot. He greeted me, smiled, then hugged me and picked me off my feet. As I recollect, this was the substance of our brief chat:

RP: You have always been away, traveling, whenever I came to New York. It's a pleasure to meet you finally.

RH: The pleasure is mine.

RP: Let me get to the point. Mort tells me you want to resign. Forget that. I'm going to make you the richest economist in the country.

RH: I resigned two weeks ago, and won't break the commitment to·Eastman Dillon. But thanks for the compliment.

RP: You're a traitor! Traitor!

Traitor? Yes, "traitor," Perot screamed, turning in a split second from courtesy and calm to enraged fury. Traitor! That's a harsh word, one used in a state of war. Indeed, the whole scene in the final days of duPont, Glore Forgan & Company struck me as a battlefield. Field lieutenants from the branch offices tried to get me discharged. They would have succeeded if it had not been for Phil Loomis. When Ross Perot took over, chaos and wholesale desertion became the rule. Internal fighting accelerated as casualties mounted. Phil was shot down, and a whole succession of research directors were executed (figuratively speaking, of course). The battlefield chaos ended, predictably, when duPont filed for bankruptcy. I was lucky to escape from the field early, though at the price of having Perot brand me a deserter, a traitor forever.

I often wondered whether Perot had hurled the word *traitor* on others. I decided to find out. A senior portfolio manager at duPont, now a chief investment officer of a major firm and my client, put it this way: "Robert, you may have been the first, but Perot labeled me a traitor, ditto for my partner and for an institutional salesman. You know them, but I believe others were also involved. We quit despite Perot's pleading."

FROM THE DUPONT FIRE TO THE BLYTH-EASTMAN-DILLON FRYING PAN

We'll return later to examine Perotnomics in our critical analysis of trade, fiscal, and tax nostrums. For now, let's continue this unhappy narrative in which I managed to infuriate senior officers of Blyth Eastman Dillon (BED).

Actually, my first years at BED were happy ones. I traveled throughout the United States and the world, and had nothing but good news to bring to BED's clients, its branch managers, the retail and institutional salesmen, investment bankers, and others. I felt almost revered. They loved to hear their chief economic spokesman argue the case for a long and vigorous expansion. I did just that, for the forward data in the fall of 1971 signaled a bright economic future (see Appendix A, Forecast 2). With renewed confidence, I had almost erased from my mind the enraged duPont managers who wanted me fired for forecasting recession. Confidence helped me to exorcise pressure and insecurity, the inseparable fiends of Wall Street.

Alas, by the fall of 1973 the economic storm clouds turned black once again. I worried about the increased risk of an economic downturn that would exceed in severity any recession since that of the Great Depression of the thirties (see Appendix A, Forecasts 4 through 9). I warned of a "maxi-recession," and that's what took place. My words angered senior officers at BED. "No, not again," I wondered. Was this duPont, Glore Forgan & Company all over again—from one bad dream to another?

3

Mephistopheles on Wall Street

Blyth Eastman Dillon & Company

> [The] vulgar dispute concerning the *degrees* of benevolence or self-love, which prevail in human nature, [is] never likely to [be resolved]. There is some benevolence, however small, infused into our bosom; some spark of friendship for humankind; some particle of the dove kneaded into our frame, along with the elements of the wolf and the serpent.
>
> David Hume, *Principles of Morals* (1751)

Hume (1711–76) tells us that humans are made up of the dove, but also the wolf and the serpent. But it's a waste of time, he argued, to try to measure the relative importance of good and evil in human nature, at least with any precision. Hume's *Morals,* published in 1751 and available to Adam Smith, did not dissuade Smith from assigning more weight to the good (the heart) than the evil (the dog) in humans. Smith eventually dropped that exercise. A "vulgar" exercise, declared Hume.

Vulgar? Does the heart dominate the dog in humans, as economist Adam Smith asserted? Does the lamb overwhelm the boar in us, as Ralph Waldo Emerson (1803–82) contended in his beautiful essay "Compensation"? We will address that bewildering and enormously complex question, among others, in the final chapter. Meanwhile, we must first try to decipher what humans are by tracking what humans do. On that count, I am reminded of the wooden horse the Greeks gave the Trojans. Virgil (70–19 B.C.E.) tells us in Book II of the epic poem *The Aeneid* that Greek soldiers were hiding inside its hollow interior. When the Trojans pulled their gift horse inside the walls of Troy the soldiers jumped out and overcame the surprised defenders. Some gift! "Whatever it is, I fear Greeks even when they bring gifts," Virgil declared.

Have we become more trustworthy, more benevolent since the days of Virgil, twenty centuries ago? I don't know, but I suspect Virgil would agree with my updated admonition, at least as it applies to the night walkers of Wall Street:

> **Beware the night walkers on Wall Street even when they bring gifts. Composed more of wolf and serpent than dove, they ring out the truth when the skies are sunny but repress the truth when the skies turn black.**

WOLVES AND SERPENTS

In tracking what humans do, what I witnessed firsthand at duPont, Glore Forgan & Company was hardly encouraging. Indeed, I have run into night walkers everywhere during my past one-quarter of a century on Wall Street. But I encountered none so despicable as those at Blyth Eastman Dillon, which has since become Paine Webber.

As you might have deduced, it was not until late 1973, when the economic outlook began to grow dark, that these night-walking creatures came out in force. We shall meet them momentarily. But first let me introduce you to Dr. Theodore Eck, chief economist of the Standard Oil Company of Indiana. I interviewed Dr. Eck (TE) for the April 1979 issue of Pace University's *International Newsletter*:

RH: Dr. Eck, with inflation and interest rates up in the sky, and the risk of a sustained shutdown of Iranian oil, what would you say now is the probability of U.S. recession?

TE: Robert, the risk is certainly higher today than it was prior to the shutdown of Iranian oil. A number of the same conditions exist today as existed in 1973–75. We cannot afford to repeat the mistakes made in 1973–75.

But repeat them we did. I grew convinced that world central bankers were reacting irrationally to the decision of the Organization of Petroleum Exporting Countries (OPEC) to jack up the price of oil. They were overreacting to the problem of inflation, much as they did in 1973–75. Central bankers, I then argued, were tightening money and credit growth and pushing interest rates extremely high—a perfect prescription for worldwide recession. I shall fill in later the meaning and the details of what I then called monetary overkill. Suffice it to note here that growth of the nominal money supply, whether narrowly or broadly defined, fell sharply. Worse, the absolute level of real (inflation adjusted) money plummeted through 1974. Two killers, then, simultaneously strangled real buying power. The first was inflation. The second was the excessively restrictive policies of the Federal Reserve.

DIALOGUE OF THE INSANE

To see what I mean by restrictive policies, let's first slip unnoticed into an emergency meeting of world central bankers, including representatives of the Federal Reserve. The time is late 1973, immediately after the Arab oil embargo was declared. The exchange depicted here is a reconstructed composite based on the discussions I have had with Federal Reserve, International Monetary Fund representatives, and World Bank officers who spoke informally in the many forums I hosted for them and institutional investors. Now, you won't find in any central banking transcript the plain language used here. No, central bankers speak in an obscure and suffocating jargon. Even so, that does not subtract from the insane thrust of their arguments once translated into plain English. So, listen in to this odd exchange between central bankers (C1, C2, etc.) of major oil-importing nations:

C1:   We called this emergency meeting because the big oil exporters are ganging up on us. They number only fifteen or so, but they control production and pricing of most of the oil produced around the world. Oligopolists* in white sheets have doubled the price of oil. Each of us is a heavy importer of oil. We have no immediate substitute for oil. What can we do?

C2:   What can we do? Well, we have to import oil to survive, to run our factories, heat our homes, propel our trucks and buses and automobiles. We can try to reduce our consumption of oil, but we can only go so far. Even if we can cut the number of barrels of oil we import by 10 percent

---

*Oligopolists are defined as a small number of large producers who account for a large percentage of total industry output. This gives them market power to cut output. They are able to jack up prices, at least in the short run.

or 20 percent, a price boost of 100 percent would still mean soaring oil bills. Our import bill in dollars would skyrocket. That means a big trade deficit with OPEC.

C3:   Yes, the demand for oil is inelastic, or relatively insensitive to prices in the short run. We can't cut oil consumption enough to offset the huge rise in prices, not overnight. Over the longer-run we can conserve on oil, find new sources of oil to increase supply, find substitutes for oil. But we need time.

C4:   We don't have much time. Oil is priced in world markets in U.S. dollars, and paid for in U.S. dollars. We have to get the dollars to buy the oil, and we are already critically short of dollars.

C5:   Gentlemen, let me summarize. We must tighten monetary policy immediately. We have to . . .

restrict money growth
raise interest rates
restrain domestic spending
slow our economies
cool demand and inflation
get our own internal prices down
become more competitive in world markets
stimulate our exports
earn more foreign exchange to get the dollars to buy the oil to keep
our economies humming.

C6:   Yes, we must constrict, we must restrict.
We must deflate before it's too late. We must cool internally to export externally,
to earn the mark, the franc, the pound
to get the dollars, to get the oil, to keep us sound.

All: Of course, we must constrict, we must restrict
We must deflate, before it's too late.

The thrust of this dialogue of the insane is fact, not fiction. You will be introduced to specific characters in the following chapters, but let's first analyze the economic fallacy behind the dialogue. What was wrong with their proposed solution to dramatically higher oil prices? Try answering these three questions:

1. How is this dialogue linked with one of the oldest fallacies in eco-nomics, the *fallacy of composition*? The fallacy of composition sim-ply means that what may be true for the individual need not be true for the group, that what may be true for one need not be true for all.

2. What would likely happen to income, production, and employment at home, and to foreign trade, if all of the major oil-importing nations were to shift simultaneously to severe monetary restriction?

3. Is it even possible for the oil-importing countries to increase their net exports (exports less imports) to each other so that each of them could earn the foreign exchange to get the dollars to buy the oil?

Let's take question 3 first, since it is the easiest. Is it even possible for the oil-importing nations to increase their net exports to each other? The way I have worded this gives away the answer: Of course not! The arithmetic of trade tells us that the major industrial nations, with few exceptions, were net oil-importing nations. They traded in the main with each other. Increased ex-ports for one meant increased imports for another. Total exports had to add up to total imports within the same group, and total exports less total imports add up to a net zero for the group. Now, how did world central bankers manage to overlook this accounting identity, this mathematical truism?

Their arithmetic was bad enough, but their economics was worse. This takes us to question 2; the likely impact of worldwide monetary restriction. Once again, the point is that an individual nation, acting alone to restrict de-mand and spur exports, might well succeed in earning the foreign exchange needed to get the oil. But what happens when all nations restrict simultane-ously? In that case, you have monetary policy involving the drying up of credit, soaring interest rates, and—with a lag—a collapse of spending, pro-duction, employment, income, and world trade.

This takes us logically to question 1: What happens when each nation re-stricted to improve its economy? Why, they all fell down together. Individual restrictive economic policies led not to global improvement but world col-lapse. Now, how did world central bankers miss that simple fallacy of com-position?

Compounding matters during this period of soaring oil prices, other com-modity prices exploded as well. Droughts, earthquakes, and floods sent food prices higher. Wheat prices climbed swiftly in the wake of large shipments of U.S. grain to what was the Soviet Union. Also, the anchovies swam away. An-chovies? Yes, they are a source of fertilizer, and the shortage of this tiny fish contributed to rising world commodity prices. So, even the meteorological gods worked for our undoing. But overreacting human gods were most at fault. Central bankers strangled credit and money growth in 1973–74 even as inflation zapped real buying power.

Central bankers learned little from their 1973–75 experience, it seems, for they tightened far too much in the aftermath of the second oil shock to produce the 1981–82 recession. They did it again in 1990–91, pushing the industrial world into its third post-World War II global decline (see Appendix A, Forecasts 21–24, 61–67). Don't central bankers learn from their mistakes? As a general rule, no.

THE SERPENTS AND WOLVES OF WALL STREET

Let's return now to the 1973–75 recession and Blyth Eastman Dillon & Company. Following David Hume, consider this four-point knockdown of an economist by sundry serpents on the street.

Count One, an Omen Amid Sun and Celebration

On October 6, 1972, Research Director Jim MacMeekin informed me that Todd Arno, an econometrician whom I had hired as my key assistant, was promoted to assistant vice president. We celebrated. Everything seemed to come up roses, including bright prospects for the economy. But unknown to me at the time, Blyth would soon remove Jim MacMeekin, the man who had hired me. The firm replaced him with a new research director, one who had problems with the most elementary of economic and investment concepts. We'll call the new director HJ. Later I said to Jim MacMeekin (JM):

RH: HJ has an understanding of economics, finance, and investments that approaches zero asymptotically (gets closer and closer, but never actually touches zero).

JM: That's for sure. By the way, he didn't especially care for your criticisms of his research reports. Be careful.

Count Two, Mephistopheles on Wall Street

A strange thing happened on October 7, 1972. My wife and I heard Boito's opera *Mephistopheles* at Lincoln Center's New York State Theater in New York City. Dr. William Freund (WF), chief economist of the New York Stock

Exchange, and his wife joined us as our guests. We had dinner after the opera and here's the gist of our table talk:

RH: Dr. Faustus sold his soul to the devil. What's new?

WF: What do you mean?

RH: I told you about my experience at duPont. Someday I'll write all this down and call it "Mephistopheles on Wall Street." What were the whistles all about when Mephistopheles rolled all over the stage? Were they leading indicators, a warning of some kind?

WF: Robert, you're not blowing any recession whistles now. You're fairly optimistic, from what I read about your forecasts. That should not cause you any trouble.

RH: Who's worried now? The skies are bright, and I'm optimistic. I feel revered, even loved.

Later this exchange followed with my wife (I):

I: You liked *Mephistopheles.* Are you really going to write something for publication starring "Mephistopheles on Wall Street"? Will investors know who you mean?

RH: Why not? I'll explain who this devil is. I'll argue that the negativism and sour outlook of Mephistopheles is not of this world. The U.S. economy is actually in pretty good shape. Bill Freund was right when he said I should have no trouble now. But even as an optimist, I still get offers to sell my soul.

I: Sell your soul? Has Mephistopheles gone to your head?

RH: Look, the approach is usually so subtle, so discreet, so sick. But not always. Remember those women I told you about? I mean the prostitutes some institutional reps planted in my room; or the expensive leather goods another group of reps wanted me to take; or the enticements of branch managers to go to this city or that to meet with their pet institutions. I have an invitation now to go to Hawaii, again.

I: That sounds more like heaven than hell.

RH: You realize that the institutions I visit send big commission business to Blyth in payment for my presentations. Sometimes I meet with the chief investment officer, and on occasion his entire staff. The institutional rep gets a cut of that commission flow. So, if I'm optimistic and correct on the markets, the reps make out like gangbusters. That's the heaven you talk about. But if I'm pessimistic, they avoid me like the plague. They want an optimistic hawker, but with the Ph.D. in economics to look legitimate. They don't want someone knocking the economy and killing their sales, their stock commissions.

Count Three, Recession Signals

As it turned out, I didn't have to wait very long for new recession signals. Once again I began to worry aloud about recession. I first made my concerns explicit on November 24, 1973 (see Appendix A, Forecast 4), about one year after attending the opera, when I was in high spirits. That forecast spelled trouble for me, but I didn't appreciate it at the time.

Count Four, Trouble Over the World Bank

I thought I would catch a big client for Blyth Eastman Dillon. With that in mind, on Friday, March 8, 1974, I visited Dr. Yoon Park, chief economist for the World Bank. My goal was to see if Blyth could get involved more directly in helping the World Bank to manage its fixed-income investments, that is, its bond and note holdings. That would have brought a lot of trading business to Blyth. Little did I know that my meeting would spell trouble ahead.

On returning from the World Bank in Washington, D.C., I received a call to meet with one of the very senior officers of Blyth. Let's call him BS. What follows is the substance of that meeting.

RH: You wanted to speak with me.

BS: Yeah, for two reasons. You're headed for trouble. Why didn't you show up at the Washington office? You were supposed to address the RRs and the managers there.

RH: But I called two days in advance, and canceled. I was invited to make a presentation to the World Bank. Dr. Yoon Park, its chief economist invited me. I told the DC branch manager that this would be a great opportunity for us to compete for some of the World Bank business.

BS: You're way off base. Our business is overwhelmingly retail business. Understand that? Look, get this straight. You take your orders from me.

RH: Yes sir.

BS: Let me get to the real reason I wanted to talk with you. What's this I hear about a "maxi-recession"? Look at these lousy headlines. You are quoted all over the press saying we're going to be hit with a maxi-recession. What the hell is that? You've got every branch manager in the country calling me. How did the press get hold of this?

RH: The press called me. They always do. You know that. Also, editorial mails all my reports to the press.

BS: Yeah, but why in hell did you say we're headed for a maxi-recession? Whoever heard of that? Look, you are our biggest prospecting tool for the retail RRs. They use your reports. But you are now frightening them out of their mind. Why this maxi-recession crap?

RH: Oil prices have shot up. This cuts buying power. Worse, it looks now as though central banks around the world are preparing to strip away money growth and raise interest rates to fight inflation. This will cripple buying power, spending power. The forward indicators are crashing. I called our institutional clients and warned them of just that. They have to be alerted to the . . .

BS: Cut it. I don't want an economic lecture. I just told you our business is retail. Ninety percent retail! Get that. You are killing that business.

RH: I didn't know I had that much power.

BS: Don't get smart. We made you First Vice President and Chief Economist. You're supposed to be a partner with us in this firm.

RH: I'm doing my best. What do you want? If you don't agree with the forecast, then tell me, but explain why. I'm always willing to listen. Nobody has prescience.

BS: Press what? I've had enough of this. Kill that maxi stuff.

RH: But that would be shading.

BS: What?

RH: Shading, slanting, twisting the truth. That would be dishonest.

BS: Don't you understand? I'm ordering you to tone down your pessimistic forecast. I don't care whether it's right or wrong. I don't want to hear of any maxi-recession again. Understand? Get out of my office. Get out!

I understood all too well. The branch managers were screaming at BS, and BS was screaming at me. I understood also that I was being asked, once again, to shade, but this time the request was anything but subtle. So what was I to do? I refused to be paid top money as a hired gun for Blyth. Maybe lawyers can get away with arguing either side of any issue without being condemned as morally corrupt. They admit to being hired guns, at least most of the lawyers I know. That's their public image, too. But I could find no moral justification for acting as a non-admitted hired gun. So, while making absolutely certain the press was notified, I switched my forecast from that of a *maxi-recession* to a *mini-depression.* That was my reaction to this most venomous of serpents on Wall Street. David Hume would have understood.

The emerging recession, which got underway in December 1973 and bottomed in March 1975, proved to be extremely painful for Blyth's officers, its RRs, and for me. I note just two unhappy postscripts here:

The Trouble in Corporate Finance

Blyth officers in the investment banking division—suddenly and with no explanation or apology—stopped inviting me to meet with them and their corporate clients at the elegant India House. I had gotten used to having lunch with them and their clients, the chief financial officers of major corporations across the country. I always looked forward to it because I felt I could make a real contribution. The India House, just above Harry's on Hanover Square, Wall Street's most famous watering hole, was renowned for superb service and great food. I missed dining there. I noted in my calendar that my last meeting with corporate finance was on Tuesday, March 5, 1974. That figured, for I had become a full-blown pessimist by then.

It didn't take me long to figure out what was going on. I learned that I had already crippled an equity offering by arguing at one meeting that the risk of early recession could knock any new stock issue to the ground, that the proposed offering should be scrapped, or at least postponed. That cost Blyth a bundle in fees. I discovered also that the fixed-income division was angered over my suggestion that they advise their corporate clients to postpone underwritings (sales) of any long bond issue, that they should wait for lower interest rates. It made no sense for corporations to borrow at high interest rates and "lock" themselves into ten- or twenty-year bond maturities—or so I argued. Wait? That word wasn't in Blyth Eastman Dillon Company's vocabulary. Their motto had always been: A fee in hand is worth two in the bush. Phil Loomis would have understood.

The Firing of the Newly Minted Registered Representatives

On Monday, March 25, 1974, I lectured, as was customary, to the graduating class of RRs. They were recruited by Blyth, trained by Blyth, and then as a rule shipped all over the country to the branch offices. But this time was different. This time these bright and eager newly minted RRs were fired, almost all of them before the year was out. Recession, falling commission volume, a drying up of corporate underwritings, and, most important, incredible mismanagement from the very top saw to that. Dismayed and dejected, and rejected for what I'm convinced were my pessimistic forecasts, Blyth gave me my walking papers in July. Though I should have seen it coming, it was still a surprise. Gary Shilling, who suffered the same fate in 1970 when Merril Lynch let him go, was the first to call me. That helped ease the pain.

TRINITY CHURCH VERSUS
THE UNHOLY TRINITY FROM HELL

Were the loud whistles and Mephistopheles' antics in rolling around the stage leading signals, omens I should have taken seriously? I can't be sure, but I perceived his misery to be a warning to me not to sell my soul to Wall Street. Maybe I was lucky, though, considering who this beast is.

Just who is he? I view Mephistopheles as one-third pressure, one-third insecurity, and one-third selfishness, the Unholy Trinity of Wall Street. These demons infect the best of us as they hypnotically seize our minds, often without our knowing it. Of course! That makes it easier for Wall Streeters to rationalize deception and outright dishonesty in all its dimensions. One thing for certain, the rector of Trinity Church faces an immense challenge in coping with this master mind bender from the Netherworld.

Part Two

Political and Economic Theory, Practice, and Malpractice

4

Night Walkers in Washington, D.C.

The 1973–75 Maxi-Recession

Man, proud man! dressed in a little brief authority,
plays such fantastic tricks before high heaven as make
the angels weep.

Shakespeare*

Authorities in power played fantastic tricks that backfired to produce recessions in 1973–75, the first half of 1980, in 1981–82, and in 1990–91. And the whole world wept. The focus in this chapter will be the 1973–75 "maxi-recession," but the parallels relating all four slumps will be noted.

What were the common ingredients in each recession? There were several, but I shall argue that the most important was that of the destabilizing actions of central bankers, including the Federal Reserve. The Fed is supposed to constrict credit and money growth to fight inflation in an economy that is expanding too fast, and to provide stimulation in a weak economy to ward off recession. In other words, it is supposed to follow *countercyclical* policy. Instead, it repeatedly overstimulated as inflation soared, then overrestricted in the name of fighting inflation to produce recession. The Federal Reserve engaged in what is called *procyclical* policy, which made matters worse. Why? Incredible but true, the best and the brightest in authority implemented policies that were based on the worst monetary and fiscal theories.

To document the blunders both in theory and in practice let's meet the

*From *Measure for Measure*, quoted in *Bartlett's Familiar Quotations* (Boston: Little, Brown & Company, 1980), p. 228.

men of authority at the Federal Reserve. We'll also meet the inept officials of the executive branch of government, the Treasury, the Council of Economic Advisers, and sundry other government and private economists, including monetarists, supply siders, expectation theorists, and the best known of Wall Street's fixed-income seers. Here's our advance playbill in four acts:

Act I: The 1973–75 Maxi-Recession
President Gerald Ford (1974–75) and Federal Reserve Chairman Arthur Burns
The Classical Preachers: Greenspan, Seidman, and Simon

Act II: The 1980 Recession and Boom
President Jimmy Carter and Federal Reserve Chairman Paul Volcker

Act III: The 1981–82 Mini-Depression
President Ronald Reagan and Chairman Volcker
The Monetarist Preachers: Jordan, Kudlow, and Sprinkel
Supply Side Ruler and Court: Roberts, Entin, and Johnson
Four Bond Bears: Braverman, Kaufman, Nakagama, Wojnilower

Act IV: 1990–91 Recession and Ensuing Growth Recession
Presidents Bush and Clinton, and H. Ross Perot
Classical Preacher Alan Greenspan and Federal Reserve Money "Hawks"
Supply Siders, Monetarists, and Expectation Theorists
"Blue-Chip" Consensus Forecasters of the Dismal Science

Though I'll concentrate in this chapter on Act I, let me set forth the key conclusion relevant to all four acts:

Proud men dressed in brief authority repeat the same mistakes over and over. They try to explain away identical mistakes over and over. They dance.

DANCING AUTHORITIES IN THE 1973–75 RECESSION

Gerald Ford became president in 1974 while Dr. Arthur Burns was Chairman of the Federal Reserve System. Now, have you ever wondered where President Ford got his key policy suggestions? He got them from Burns and from the *classical preachers.* We'll start our chronicle with the preachers, namely, Alan Greenspan, then Chairman of the Council of Economic Advisers; L. William Seidman, Ford's political and economic adviser; and William Simon, Secretary of the Treasury.

The classical preachers resuscitated a fierce free-market theory from the classical economists, a theory that dealt with long-run trends in the economy. In a nutshell, the classical preachers argued that by stimulating savings and bringing interest rates down, the result would promote both business investment and long-term economic growth. They stumbled in their efforts to apply long-run classical solutions set forth in the eighteenth century to the short-run cyclical problems of the twentieth century. That was bad enough. Worse, they persuaded the president of the United States to implement policies that proved to be a perfect prescription for recession. Actually, the overly restrictive polices of the oil oligopolists induced me to start worrying in print about recession as early as November 1973 (see Appendix A, Forecast 4). Thanks, though, to the antics of the classical preachers, I became progressively bearish in the spring and summer of 1974. I posted this irreverent attack on September 16, 1974:

> Mr. Ford [should] pay more attention to the weakening forward indicators of demand and less attention to his new economic advisers. We wonder whether Mr. Ford, Mr. Simon or Mr. Greenspan may not be gearing policy to fight the wrong economic war with the wrong weapons at the wrong time.*

While I omitted including L. William Seidman in that release, I more than made up for it by hosting a forum for him (WS) and thirty-five institutional investment officers during the fall of 1974 in Boston, just off the Boston Commons. What follows is a portion of the proceedings of that meeting:

RH: Thank you for an excellent presentation. As host, I get the first question. The Ford administration has a legitimate concern, of course, in getting high inflation down. With that in mind, you have passed out *WIN* buttons, an acronym for Whip Inflation Now. Your objective is to get consumption spending down. You ask consumers to tighten their belts. My question has to do with timing. Are you not worried that the WIN program is being introduced too late? The fall in the economy now underway makes clear that demand is evaporating fast.

WS: Look, our problem is inflation. We have to get inflation under control. We have to cut government spending, but the public must do their

---

*Mr. Ford and the New Intellectuals, Advest Institutional Services, September 16, 1974, p. 3.

share, too. The public has to consume less and save and invest more from their salaries and wages. Yes, they must tighten their belts. This will slow inflation, get interest rates down, and generate the private saving to finance new investment in plant, equipment, and new technology. Our goal is to get production up, and inflation and interest rates down. We must beat inflation here and now. That's WIN.

RH: But you have three depressants all working at once. The Fed is squeezing the life blood from the economy. Commodity inflation is zapping buying power. *WIN* would further depress consumer spending, which is already headed downhill. It seems to me that total spending is falling even as we hold this meeting. If history is any guide, falling demand should shortly lead to slower inflation. After all, consumer prices are mainly *lagging* indicators. They tend to weaken *after* the economy starts to fall. Right? So aren't you and Alan Greenspan and President Ford risking [a] policy . . . that would make the ongoing recession even deeper?

WS: Recession? What recession? Let me make this plain, Mr. Parks. That's your view, not ours.

Mr. Seidman made that plain enough. He and his associate classical preachers asked the public to cut its gluttonous consumption to get savings up, inflation and interest rates down, investment and output up, and all this would produce happiness and joy for all. We could put their born-again message into a simple equation. But let's first explain our terms:

C = CONSUMPTION   Consumer spending from current income, which returns money to the income stream.

S = SAVING   Current income not spent, a withdrawal of income from the income stream, by itself a depressant to the economy.

I = INVESTMENT   Business investment spending, an injection of money into the income stream—by itself a stimulant to the economy.

R = INTEREST RATES The Price of borrowing money.

Here is the cause-and-effect logic of the resuscitated classical preachers:

$$-C \text{ means } +S, \text{ which causes } -R \text{ which causes } +I$$

Translated, this means a cut in consumption from current income, the same thing as a rise in saving from current income, would cause interest rates to fall, which in turn would cause investment spending to rise. The rise in investment spending would offset the fall in consumer spending, and pave the way for a more productive and less inflationary economy. Clear? It should become clear soon.

Jumping ahead a bit, in the 1990–91 recession and ensuing growth recession, for example, Fed Chairman Greenspan argued in essentially the same way. Just cut government spending and the Federal deficit, he argued, and the economy would blossom. (Substitute G [government spending] for the C in our earlier cause and effect scheme.) Well, it didn't work in 1973–75 and it didn't work in 1990–91. We'll return to the 1990–91 experience, but first let's complete our review of the folly and farce of 1973–75.

In listening to Mr. Seidman, I felt I was almost subjected to the declarations of the most famous of all French economists, Jean Baptiste Say (1767–1832). I'll merely note here two of Say's propositions. First, remembering our discussion (in chapter 2) of the rough identity of gross national expenditures, gross national product, and gross national income, Say said as much over a century ago in his groundbreaking economic essays. Second, since spending for production simultaneously generates income in equal amount, Say wrote, then it follows that the income generated—the wages, salaries, profits, interest, and rents—would enable people to buy all the goods produced. The buying power would clear the markets.

Indeed, asked Say, how could we even get into a recession just so long as current income matched current output? The flow of current income (buying power, or demand) had to be exactly equal to the value of current output (supply). Supply created its own demand, or so Say declared. We know this now as Say's Law. We also know that while Say's economic arithmetic was brilliant, his economic analysis was defective, especially for short-run or cyclical analysis. The Great Depression of the 1930s put an end once and for all to Say's Law. Production of goods soared ahead of final consumption demand, and the economy collapsed under the weight of inventory buildup.

Why didn't Say and most other classical economists worry about recessions? Some did worry, including David Hume and David Ricardo, but they represented exceptions to the classical rule. Most of the classicists, as we have just explained, believed that the magic of freely fluctuating interest rates would rule out any deficiency in total demand. Indeed, the equilibrating force of interest rates in stabilizing the economy at full employment was the centerpiece of classical economic doctrine. Relevant to Seidman's argument, all we had to do to get investment up would be to get consumption down. The miracle of lower interest rates would see to that.

Now, I don't recall one single word from Greenspan, Seidman, or Simon that would explicitly link their professed policies to the old and more extreme classical economists. But that's beside the point because they argued in almost identical ways. To be sure, the classical preachers did not fall into the error of confusing identities with analysis, as Say did. But they did fall into error in arguing that automatic and beneficial forces were at work to keep us out of recession. They made two big mistakes, as I then saw it:

First, the classical preachers geared up to fight the wrong war. President Ford's WIN program was designed to blunt excess demand, but that demand was no longer the problem. By the time WIN could kick in and be effective, the natural market forces had changed the game. The problem was now one of inadequate demand, of a generalized deficiency of demand, of major recession. Second, these three preachers tripped over the assumptions underlying classical economic theory. The classical economists assumed (1) flexible wages, (2) flexible prices, (3) flexible interest rates, and (4) adjustments in saving and investment to restore equilibrium in a purely and perfectly competitive economy *over the long run*. Their assumptions matched their theory *for long-run trends*. But the preachers distorted classical theory beyond recognition by confusing long-run trends with short-run cyclical fluctuations. Count for yourself their theoretical and applied errors in mixing up one time period with another:

1. Flexible Wages

According to classical theory, wages were supposed to drop in a softening economy. The lower wages would mean lower costs, thereby inducing employers to step up their hiring, which, in turn, would ward off outright recession. The problem with this view is that wages are often a matter of contract with highly organized unions, even as other markets weaken from recession. Indeed, in 1973–75 wages continued to advance despite falling sales and production, thereby reducing or eliminating profits. With output and productivity falling, labor costs per unit of output continued to rise sharply for months after the economy entered the 1973-75 recession (see Exhibit 4–1).

2. Flexible Prices

According to classical theory, prices were supposed to fall in a softening economy, again given enough time. Lower prices were supposed to stimulate consumer and business spending, which would also work to ward off recession. But prices proved to be rigid, too, in the 1973–75 cyclical downturn.

"Power blocs" raised prices by cutting or curtailing output. OPEC was then the prime example, but other oligopolists exercised market clout, too, including the farm sector and key industries like steel and automobiles. Government itself worked against cyclical price flexibility through a wide range of subsidy and price support measures. So, instead of falling, prices continued to advance well into recession. That was true, for example, of consumer prices for services (see the bottom line in Exhibit 4–1). As you can see in the Exhibit, consumer prices for services and six other economic indicators continued to rise even as the economy fell. They follow rather than lead cyclical fluctuations in the overall economy. That's why the Commerce Department tags them as *lagging* indicators.

3. Flexible Interest Rates

Classical theory looked upon freely fluctuating interest rates as the centerpiece of its model underlying long-run adjustments. With a drop in consumption, lower interest rates would supposedly stimulate investment and thus offset lower consumer demand. But interest rates, especially bank rates, also proved to be notoriously uncooperative for short-run swings, as in the 1973–75 recession. Short-term rates soared well into the recession (see Exhibit 4–1). Long-term yields on Treasury and corporate bonds actually ended up higher at the end of the recession than at the beginning. We'll return to an explanation of interest rates as lagging cyclical indicators later in our examination of "Reaganomics." Suffice it here to note that, contrary to popular belief, rates of interest often follow rather than lead fluctuations in the overall economy.

4. An Automatic Flow of Saving into Investment

What about the idea that lower consumption (or lower government spending) would quickly produce higher private saving, which would reduce interest rates, which would in turn produce higher investment spending? Again, that may make sense to classical theorists, but it's nonsense for cyclical analysis. For example, given the rise in the unit cost of goods and services and the rise in interest rates well into the 1973–75 recession, what do you think happened to profits and business expectations for profit? What do you think happened to investment spending? That's right. Predictably, profits and investment spending collapsed.

To repeat, much of the statistical data on costs, prices, and interest rates are *lagging* cyclical indicators. They are even more misleading in forecasting cyclical swings than are the *coincident* indicators such as income, production, employment, or gross domestic product (see chapter 1). So, never take the lagging indicators as evidence of where the economy is heading cyclically. Don't parrot the classical preachers.

Let's document our case further by way of Exhibit 4–1, in which each of the series plotted is identified by the notation *Lg*, for laggers. The first of these letters refers to the timing at business cycle peaks, the second to the timing at business cycle troughs, and the third to the timing at all turns, i.e., an average of peaks and troughs combined. The *P* and *T* at the top of the exhibit refer to the cyclical peak and trough, respectively. In plain English, these series typically continue to rise after the economy has fallen into recession, and continue to fall after the economy has begun to recover from recession.

The lagging indicators remind me of the guy who shouts "Watch out for the ball!" after it's already hit you on the head. How in the world could the classical preachers have overlooked such an elementary rule of forecasting?

KEYNES AND MARSHALL ON THE CLASSICAL TRIPLETS

What I have said here is hardly new. The renowned economist John Maynard Keynes (1883–1946) said all of this and much more many years ago in *The General Theory of Employment, Interest, and Money* (1936). His masterpiece ripped into classical theory. As far as I know, the classical preachers never uttered a kind word for Keynes. That's understandable, for they detested Keynes's unsparing attack on naive interpretations of classical theory. Keynes argued that you cannot leave expectations out of your analysis. If prices, for example, were expected to fall, this could induce consumers to postpone spending, to wait for lower prices. Employers might wait, too, for lower wage rates before hiring. Far less understandable to me is how the preachers could have ignored one of their own, the great neoclassicist Alfred Marshall (1842–1924).

Marshall warned in his *Principles of Economics,* published in 1890, that if you kill *final* consumer demand, you risk killing *derived* business demand. For example, if you depress the demand for automobiles, you risk depressing the derived demand for machine tools, equipment, and the assembly plants necessary to produce automobiles; the derived demand for rubber, steel, and plate glass, and the capital investment in real productive facilities needed to produce these materials; and the derived demand for engineers, designers, and even economists. In short, if you restrict consumption (with the goal of increasing savings), you may restrict investment. Cutbacks in government spending for (say) military goods can also clobber the derived cyclical demand for investment in the defense industries and the derived demand for a wide range of labor, including newly minted Ph.D. physicists from MIT.

A TALK WITH ARTHUR BURNS

Let's meet Dr. Arthur Burns, then chairman of the Federal Reserve Board. He had earlier offered me a job as executive director of the National Bureau of Economic Research when he was its president. I decided not to accept, because I worried, as you might guess, that his authority would clash with my unbridled skepticism of those in power.

Don't misread me. I always had great respect for Dr. Burns, especially his pioneering studies on business cycle theory. Still, that does not change my opinion of Dr. Burns's actions as the head of the Federal Reserve. I met with him (AB) in his Washington office toward the end of 1974, late in the afternoon and very late in the recession then underway. I had brought with me three institutional investment officers. He was gracious and charming, but I shall never forget this short exchange:

RH: Dr. Burns, we understand why you are so concerned with curbing inflation. But it seems to us that continued Fed restriction runs the highest risk now of turning this massive recession into an outright depression.

AB: Robert, you have three problems. The first is interpreting the past. The second is analyzing the present. The third is forecasting the future.

That was precisely the criticism I was then directing against the classical preachers. Fortunately, the Fed did switch just in time to a highly expansionary stance. It pumped up bank reserves and the money supply (which we will detail in later chapters). I anticipated that, as of January 1975, and this turned me into a "guarded optimist" (see Appendix A, Forecast 9). Still, I am puzzled to this very day why Dr. Burns kept arguing before the Congress, as late as August 1974, that the economy was still growing.

HAYWIRE MONETARY AND FISCAL POLICIES

The policy errors made in the 1973–75 recession were but a prelude to the monetary and fiscal policies of the late 1970s and the recessions of 1980, 1981–82, and 1990–91. We'll move first to the bizarre 1970s and the 1980 recession in chapter 5, then in chapter 6 to the haywire policies under Reaganomics in 1981–82. Hold on to your seats.

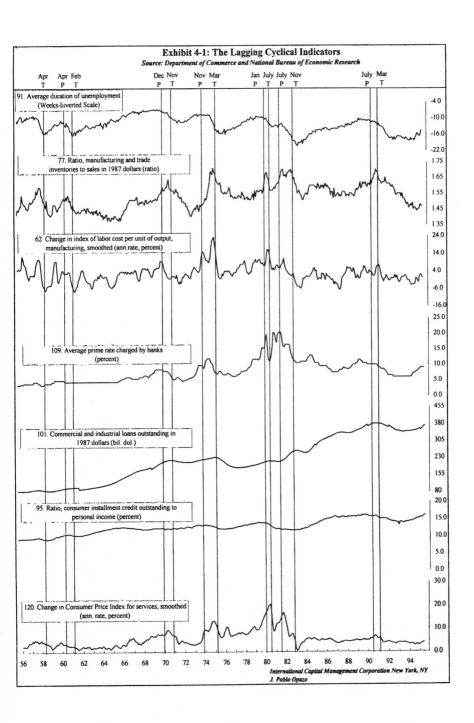

Exhibit 4-1: The Lagging Cyclical Indicators
Source: Department of Commerce and National Bureau of Economic Research

91. Average duration of unemployment (Weeks-Inverted Scale)

77. Ratio, manufacturing and trade inventories to sales in 1987 dollars (ratio)

62. Change in index of labor cost per unit of output, manufacturing, smoothed (ann.rate, percent)

109. Average prime rate charged by banks (percent)

101. Commercial and industrial loans outstanding in 1987 dollars (bil. dol.)

95. Ratio, consumer installment credit outstanding to personal income (percent)

120. Change in Consumer Price Index for services, smoothed (ann. rate, percent)

International Capital Management Corporation New York, NY
J. Pablo Opazo

5

President Carter, Chairman Volcker, and Haywire Monetary Economics

Forecast accuracy guaranteed—or your money back. Take a subscription to *Blue Chip Economic Indicators* at absolutely no risk: if you're ever dissatisfied with the quality of forecasts and economic analysis you find in *Blue Chip Economic Indicators,* you may cancel and we will send you a refund for the full subscription price.

Form letter addressed to Robert H. Parks
dated January 1989

Nobody can guarantee the accuracy of forecasts, much less guarantee the accuracy of currently reported economic statistics subject to later and often drastic revision. The sales brochure sent to me reads "CONSENSUS FORECASTS, THE ACCURACY ADVANTAGE." What about that? Well, a consensus forecast is nothing more than the average of the projections of a group, in this case the forecasts of GNP and other economic indicators of some fifty participating Blue Chip economists. But the average economist, bless him or her, is reluctant to walk out on a pessimistic limb alone. So, the consensus can be skewed to the bright side. Again we find pressure, insecurity, and selfishness dominating consensus thinking. Listen to their entreaty, at least as I would write it:

Look, shade to the bright side. If the entire pack of economists is optimistic, don't, for heaven's sake, walk way out on a limb as a pessimist. If you're wrong, that could cost you your reputation, even your job. But if you're in the pack, you'll still be in good company, respected. Who could fault you? Remember that

74

people will judge you relative to the pack, and that's an absolute truth. Stay close to the pack. Play it safe. You're only human.

Yes, economists are only human, so it's understandable that they can err badly and often. As just indicated, they seriously understated the 1973–75 recession; were caught flat-footed in failing to spot the fall in the economy in the first half of 1980; and missed completely the recession that struck with fury in August 1981. They forecast a rise in real GNP of 2.2 percent for 1982, but it plummeted a whopping 2.5 percent. Call that, if you will, a guaranteed forecast inaccuracy. A decade later the consensus was far too late in identifying Federal Reserve constriction in 1990, the resulting 1990–91 recession, the subpar growth into 1993, disinflation, and the plunge in interest rates. The Fed and Iraq's Saddam Hussein spooked the consensus of economists (see Appendix C).

With such poor performance in 1973–75, 1980, 1981–82, and 1990–93, why did the Blue Chip economists perform so poorly? That's an important question because the press and key government agencies give prime attention to the Blue Chip reports. To repeat, shading was always a factor in Blue Chip bias on the upside. But I shall argue that poor theory, the mother of bad policy, was more important. Poor theory dominated the 1973–75 slump (Act I). Poor theory was an underlying factor in the most incredible blunders of the late 1970s and the recession in the first half of 1980 (Act II, the focus of this chapter). Poor theory was at the heart of Reaganomics and the 1981–82 recession (Act III, which we will take up in chapter 6). I submit that the three acts together could easily be turned into a smash Broadway tragi-comedy starring folly, farce, and failure.

I worried silently about a repeat of the 1973–75 global decline, then worried out loud in an international conference I set up at Pace University in 1979. I labeled the forum, appropriately, "The Risk of Global Recession." That title brought ridicule my way, but I had become accustomed to ridicule. It goes with the job.

Even so, I was not alone in my fears. We have already met oil economist Ted Eck of the Standard Oil Company of Indiana, who warned of comparable risk (see chapter 3). Besides Ted Eck, the three experts who impressed me the most for their unshaded views were a central banker, a professor, and a novelist. Let's meet them, for they are relevant to our chronicle. The first is Darryl Francis, president of the Federal Reserve Bank of St. Louis. He was my guest on March 3, 1977, for a forum I hosted for institutional investors. The second is Dr. Charles Kindleberger, Ford Professor of Economics at MIT. I interviewed him for the May 1978 *International Newsletter* at Pace

University in New York City. The third is Dr. Paul Erdman, economist and author of the best-selling book *The Crash of '79*. He was my guest at a forum I hosted in New York City on March 20, 1979, for money managers. Let's listen now to their insistent comments, made long before the recession of 1981–82 hit suddenly and with devastating force, starting with Darryl Francis (DF) in March 1977:

RH: Darryl, what worries you the most?

DF: Robert, our policymakers are playing a dangerous game, the way they always play it. I see no evidence yet that the stop-go policies of excessive stimulus followed by economic overkill have been abandoned.

RH: By policymakers, you include the Fed itself. You have been loud as an insider in your criticism of Federal Reserve policy. Has this caused any problems for you?

DF: I have my critics within the Fed.

That was an understatement. I dubbed the courageous Darryl Francis Mr. Money M1. Let me explain. M1 is money narrowly defined to include mainly currency, demand deposits, and other "checkable" deposits at commercial banks and elsewhere. Mr. Francis was one of the most eloquent spokesmen of "monetarism," a strange branch of monetary theory that focuses on fluctuations in the money supply (M1) as the crucial variable impacting the economy, prices, and interest rates. The rigid monetarists, whose ideology always dominated their science, never made sense to me (see chapter 11). Mr. Francis was an exception, a scientist at heart. For one thing, he always questioned authorities in power who did not pay homage to the relevant data and sound theory. I liked that about him. Also, he was on track in his monetary analysis and forecasts even as other Fed officials at the top of the hierarchy bumbled and stumbled. He infuriated them with his caustic views as an insider, as one of their own.

Now let's listen to Dr. Kindleberger (CK) in May 1978:

RH: You have written another book, *Manias, Panics and Crashes*. . . . What crashes are you looking for now?

CK: Assuming a recession, I would expect that some of the big international banks would be forced to roll over their loans, to reschedule their credits (postpone interest and principal repayments). They would incur sizable losses.

RH: Where would the problem loans be? What countries?

CK: Brazil, South Korea, Zaire, Peru, Turkey, and Mexico, among others. Mexico would be a giant problem.

We shall return to Dr. Kindleberger later in our review of stock market theory, practice, and malpractice. Listen now to Dr. Paul Erdman (PE) in March 1979:

RH: Is your crash to take place this year, in 1979? Or did you mean that more in a fictional sense?

PE: More in a fictional sense. . . . [I also foresee] a true crisis in the classical or Kindleberger sense.

RH: Paul, will the world move into global recession?

PE: Yes, more severe than 1973–75.

Prescient enough for you? Neither Eck nor Francis nor Kindleberger nor Erdman pretended to pinpoint the exact timing of worldwide recession. But all four looked for worldwide recession, one that would outclass 1973–75. Most important, they spelled out in detail, and correctly, the factors that would bring on global recession.

ACT II: THE 1980 RECESSION AND BOOM

With that gathering economic storm so well documented, we now move directly to Act II, starring President Jimmy Carter, Chairman Paul Volcker, and the chairman's yes men, mainly those at the Federal Reserve Bank of New York. The key point to keep in mind is that the Fed, Carter, and the Congress managed (mismanaged) to push consumers and business into a borrow-and-buy binge through highly expansionist and inflationary policies in the late 1970s, until 1979. In July 1979 Carter offered the Federal Reserve chairmanship to Paul Volcker, who accepted. Volcker, a professional economist, had considerable experience in both commercial and central banking. Volcker wasted little time, and announced in October 1979 that henceforth the Fed would "target" steady and moderate growth of money. The Fed said it would abandon "targeting" of interest rates.

Targeting? What's that? Briefly, targeting rates in the late 1970s meant that the Fed provided the reserves to permit lenders to expand credit and money at a fast pace in an attempt to keep interest rates down. (I will have

more to say about targeting in later chapters.) But the attempt backfired because fast money growth produced boom and inflation and higher interest
rates. Fed folly induced me to forecast "a post-election blowoff in interest
rates as the Fed is forced to restrict . . . and recession in 1981" (see Appendix
A, Forecast 21).

Keep in mind that the Fed has several objectives. It wants economic
growth fast enough to produce maximum output and employment, a stable
price level, and a stable and sound dollar in world markets. These goals can
often conflict. For example, economic growth that is too rapid can generate
inflationary pressures, which, in turn, can push the dollar down in exchange
markets.

How does the Fed influence economic activity? It does so by expanding
or contracting the supply of credit and money and by raising or lowering interest rates. For example, if the Fed wants to slow down the economy to reduce inflation, it may reduce the reserves it provides to the financial system,
which would slow growth of credit and money, which would slow the economy and total spending, which would slow inflation. If the Federal Reserve
should constrict too much, however, it could shove the economy into outright
recession. Indeed, as we shall see, the Fed repeatedly overstimulated and
thereby produced inflation, then overrestricted and produced recession. We
shall explore the details of monetary theory, monetary mechanics, and actual
Federal Reserve operations as we proceed, but let's focus here on the mechanics of Fed targeting.

Let's track targeting round-by-round as I reported it in 1977 and 1978 (see
Appendix A, Forecasts 14–17). Now, what follows would be unbelievable if
it were not true. Let's call it ludicrous but true. Let's concentrate on the following circle, which at the time I called idiocy circle number one:

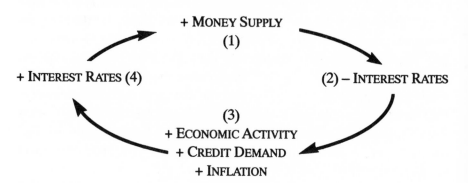

+ MONEY SUPPLY
(1)

+ INTEREST RATES (4)   (2) – INTEREST RATES

(3)
+ ECONOMIC ACTIVITY
+ CREDIT DEMAND
+ INFLATION

Track this monetary idiocy, starting from (1) clockwise:

1. + MONEY SUPPLY: The Federal Reserve tried to keep interest rates from rising too much. It was concerned that its policy should not choke off economic expansion. So it shoved reserves into the banking system, and speeded the growth of credit and money with the aim, it said, of keeping interest rates from rising above its expressed target.

2. – INTEREST RATES: Interest rates declined temporarily in response to the huge influx of money and credit engineered by the Fed. Monetary economists call this the *Liquidity Effect.*

3. + INFLATION: With a short lag, inflation speeded up in response to the liquidity infusion and the rapid and excessive expansion of money and credit. The total effective demand for goods and services speeded ahead faster than effective supply, thereby fueling demand-pull inflation. Economists now call this lagged or deferred impact of rapid money growth on inflation the *Fisher Effect,* after famed economist Irving Fisher.

4. + INTEREST RATES: With a short lag, interest rates rose in response to sizzling economic activity, rising loan demands, and the accelerating inflation set into motion by the Fed itself. Inflation and expectations of accelerating inflation induced lenders to protect themselves by raising interest rates, by demanding that an "inflationary premium" be tacked onto interest rates. The lagged rise in interest rates was also part of the lagged Fisher Effect.

(1) + MONEY SUPPLY: The Federal Reserve tried to keep interest rates from rising too much. It was concerned that policy should not choke off economic expansion. So it shoved reserves into the banking system and speeded . . .

Wait a minute! We are back to (1), where we started. By pouring in reserves and money in the futile attempt to keep interest rates down, within the Fed's targets, the actual outcome was to produce a roaring economy and push interest rates up, far above its targets. That made a bad situation worse, an inflationary situation even more inflationary. The word to describe Fed policy here is *procyclical,* an antonym for countercyclical. Instead of stabilizing economic activity, which is supposed to be the number one function of a central bank, the Fed did the opposite. The Fed *destabilized,* but it will never tell you that.

I was often called upon to explain Fed policy on WOR radio and television. Obviously I couldn't go through the explanation just noted here for millions of listeners and viewers, most of whom had little understanding of monetary theory. I said on August 22, 1978, in response to a call from the *Wall*

Street Journal: "The Fed has a tiger by the tail, and the probability that it can live with fast money growth will approach zero in the next six months" (see Appendix A, Forecasts 16 through 21, especially 16).

I had another parallel in mind, admittedly exaggerated. I compared the United States with Brazil, arguing that the Federal Reserve was inflating the money supply much as Brazil was. That worked. Everybody seemed to understand that Brazil was running the money printing press at lightening speed, and that the flood of money led to a buying frenzy, soaring prices, and sky-rocketing interest rates. Excessively easy money produced high interest rates, not low rates. Call the 1977–79 targeting, if you will, the uphill run of the tiger. The same uphill targeting characterized the second half of 1980, again fueling inflation. I put it this way to Rudy Ruderman on the *Wall Street Journal Weekend Report,* which aired October 3, 1980: "Rudy, the U.S. economic recovery will be choked off by a credit crunch. It will be brought on by the Fed restricting (the) explosion in the money stock." Anyone could have predicted it. Just remember the first rule in gauging monetary policy: Excessively easy money produces inflation and higher, not lower, interest rates. Let's put the rule in bold letters:

Never take the level or direction of current interest rates, considered alone, as a reliable gauge of current monetary policy. Always distinguish between the immediate and the lagged effects of monetary policy.

THE DOWNHILL RUN

Let's turn back briefly now to the *first* half of 1980 and the *downhill* run of the economy. By that I mean the futile attempt by the Fed to target rates higher, which backfired to produce recession and plunging rates. Remember, "targeting" interest rates was supposed to have been banished in October 1979. The Fed declared so, insisting that it would instead target money, i.e., promote moderate and steady growth of money. It did no such thing. Instead, it strangled credit and money growth. It was procyclical.

The telltale evidence of Fed strangulation was there for all to see, but they had to look. Narrowly defined, the M1 money supply virtually collapsed. So did M2, a broad money aggregate defined as M1 plus mainly time and savings accounts and certain money market funds. See for yourself the plunge in both M1 and M2 in 1979 and well into the early months of 1980 (see the top two lines of Exhibit 5–1). To make matters worse, the Fed—to my consternation—instituted direct controls designed to curb consumer borrowing and spending as late as April 1980, long after the economy had begun to fall. So, direct Fed constriction came on top of monetary constriction, a hard signal for economic contraction. That's like administering a depressant to a weak and failing person who desperately needs a stimulant.

What about the Fed's own words? It said it was tightening to keep interest rates from falling too far and too fast. The Fed said repeatedly that it didn't want interest rates to drop too much and (a) lead to excessive short-term capital flows abroad (which we will touch on later), and (b) lead people to think that it was weakening in its resolve to bring inflation under control by cutting interest rates too much and too fast.

Wait! The fall in interest rates was in no sense evidence of easy Fed policy. No, rates plunged in *lagged* response to monetary constriction that produced recession. Once again, Fed officials and others were identifying the *current* level of interest rates with *current* Fed policy, this time mistaking falling rates as evidence of an ease. That violated, again, the first rule in gauging monetary policy. Put it this way: the most popular measure of monetary policy, *the direction and level of current interest rates,* is also among the most defective.

So, targeting interest rates in the first quarter of 1980, well into recession, takes us directly to idiocy circle number two. All you have to do is reverse the signs of idiocy circle number one. I have done that here, and have filled in the appropriate explanations once again of Fed procyclical policy. In this case, the Fed managed to shove an already weakening economy into recession. Here is the idiocy circle in the early months of the 1980 recession.

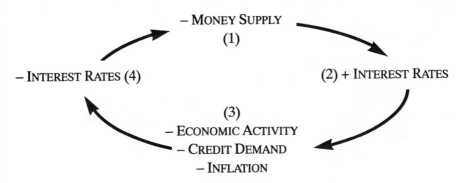

Let's track the circle, starting with (1) and moving clockwise:

1. – MONEY SUPPLY: The Federal Reserve tried to keep interest rates from falling too far and too fast. So it stripped monetary reserves from the banking system, and constricted the growth of credit and money.

2. + INTEREST RATES: When the money and credit was removed from the system, interest rates rose momentarily, in a fleeting fashion, in response to the huge liquidity drain and the reduced supply of credit and money engineered by the Fed. This, again, was the initial liquidity effect.

3. – INFLATION: With a short lag, however, inflation fell in response to the drying up of liquidity and the swift and excessive contraction of money and credit. The total effective demand for goods and services plummeted below effective supply, thereby pushing price inflation down. This again was consistent with the lagged Fisher Effect.

4. – INTEREST RATES: With a short lag, interest rates also fell in response to plunging economic activity, falling loan demands, and slower inflation set into motion by monetary overkill itself.

(1) – MONEY SUPPLY: Seeing the interest rates falling, the Fed thought it hadn't constricted the supply of money and credit enough to equalize supply (available money) with demand (willing borrowers). The Fed, in an attempt to keep interest rates from falling too far and too fast, stripped more reserves from the banking. . . . Sound familiar? Yes, we're back to (1) where we started, still in a circle.

Let's continue this chronicle: The Fed reversed course again, abruptly, in the second quarter of 1980. You can see that shift in Exhibit 5–1, with both M1 and M2 suddenly rocketing higher for the balance of 1980. With the Fed now injecting massive monetary adrenaline into the economy, the result again was predictable. You guessed it: accelerating inflation and soaring interest rates. By now you can fill in the details for this third run of the Fed into early 1981, then the abrupt shift to Fed constriction, then to major recession in 1981–82.

A decade later, starting in 1991, we witnessed the fourth run of the Fed. It once again targeted interest rates with a fury by clobbering reserve and money growth. It pursued monetary overkill via targeting, which made forecasting the 1990–91 recession a piece of cake (see Appendix A, Forecast 66). Does the Fed ever learn? No.

THE DANCING FEDERAL RESERVE

Does the Fed ever admit mistakes? No! It dances around its mistakes. Consider here Fed dancing in 1981. It reported in early 1981 that it had successfully met its money growth targets for the year 1980. It did? To be sure, the *average* money growth in 1980 for the full year was not too far from the Fed's *projected* average money growth for the full year. But as we have just seen, the collapse in money in the first quarter held down the average despite booming money growth the rest of the year. Averages can certainly hide the greatest folly. At the time, I said that the Fed's math was like putting your left foot in boiling water and your right foot in freezing water, and finding the average temperature just right.

Just as weird, and intellectually insulting, whenever the Fed overshot its money growth targets, guess what it did. It raised the targets, and then measured future money growth from the new and higher targets. That's like shooting arrows way above the target, never hitting the target, puzzling over your error, but finally deciding to have the target moved higher.

That's the stuff dances are made of. That's just what happens when authorities in charge trip over poor theory and worse policy. They fast-step away from their own folly.

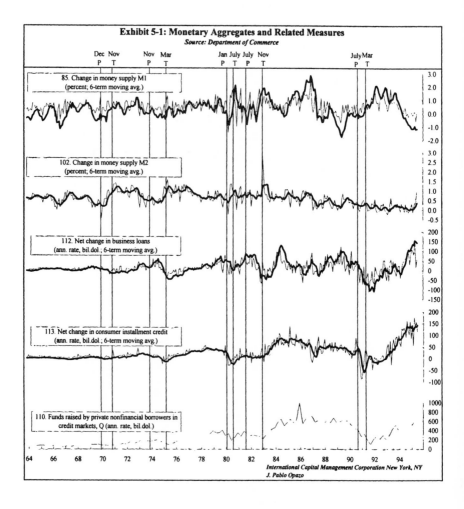

6

President Reagan, Chairman Volcker, and Haywire Fiscal Economics

> *Any graduate student would know* that you tighten money (to fight inflation) and keep the economy going with a tax cut. (Emphasis added)
>
> John Makin, economist with the
> American Enterprise Institute,
> *Business Week,* February 5, 1990, p. 25.

ACT III: REAGANOMICS AND THE MINI-DEPRESSION OF 1981–82

Let's turn now to Act III, the 1981–82 recession with Chairman Paul Volcker and President Reagan in command. The 1981–82 experience also featured bad theory in the lead, with folly, farce, and failure trailing behind—predictably.

Contrary to what Mr. Makin says in our opening quote, nothing is quite that simple, as you must know. Still, his comments serve as a perfect introduction to this chapter on Reaganomics, the fiscal-monetary program President Reagan unveiled in early 1981, which induced me to forecast a major recession on July 9, 1981. Recession struck the next month (see Appendix B). We must explain why, then note any parallels to the Republican "Contract with (on?) America" unveiled by Speaker of the House Newt Gingrich in 1995. Righteous right-wing political screaming dominated economic science in both periods (see Appendix A, Forecast 93).

Keeping in mind that President Reagan inherited a wildly inflationary economy, his game plan stood on three legs:

- Cut taxes on corporate profits and personal income.
- Cut nonmilitary spending but raise military spending.
- Tighten Fed policy to slow money growth gradually, hence slowing inflation.

We got the tax cuts. Politically, that proposal was a shoe-in. How about spending? Well, both defense and nondefense spending soared. Anybody could have predicted that. How did private economists react to the tax and spending prospects? They forecast boom, runaway inflation, and flyaway interest rates. They were wrong. How about the government "supply-side" and "monetarist" economists? They preached a rosy scenario of higher saving, higher investment, increased productivity, greater profits, slower inflation, lower interest rates, and vigorous growth of output and jobs. They were wrong, too. They also talked about "trickle down" benefits. If the well off and corporations received tax cuts, we would all benefit from a booming economy.

These were haywire forecasts. The economy in fact peaked in July 1981 and plunged for sixteen months, the worst slump since the Great Depression. How could so many have been so very wrong? Let's find out by meeting (1) my graduate finance students, (2) a crack WOR radio interviewer, (3) senior officials and economists then in charge of government mismanagement, and (4) prominent Wall Street economists who insistently but mistakenly warned of inflation, soaring interest rates, and boom.

"How could so many have been so wrong?" I (RH) fired this question at my students (S1, S2, etc.) at Pace University in the fall semester of 1981:

RH: You can be certain that total spending, nonmilitary and military, is headed higher. The tax cuts look like a shoe-in, too. With these two assumptions, here's my first question: Do tax cuts necessarily put more money into the pockets of the public?

S1:   Yes, the public would have more money left after taxes.

RH: But where do you think the Treasury will get the money to pay tax refunds?

S2:   The Treasury borrows the money?

RH: But does it matter *how* it borrows, and *from whom*?

S3: You said that the Reagan tax cuts are not being monetized (see Appendix B). That means, I guess, that little or no new money is being created. To pay tax refunds the Treasury has to borrow by selling Treasury bills, notes, and bonds.

RH: Selling Treasury securities to whom? Whom do you have in mind? Who is lending its cash to the Treasury?

S3: I guess individuals.

RH: Yes, but include also private businesses, state and local governments, and institutional investors, among others. Does that mean the money borrowed from the public at large is the same money used to pay tax refunds to the public at large? Does that put new money *in total* into the hands of the public at large?

S3: I guess not. Not if you put it that way.

RH: That's the way I put it because that's the way the Treasury is mainly financing itself. Whenever Federal spending runs ahead of tax revenues, the Treasury has to borrow to make up the difference. If it borrows money already in existence, economists call that *nonmonetized* borrowing. That means a shuffle of existing money balances. Money is shifted from one pocket to another, but with no increase in the total available money. (But how about Treasury borrowing from outside sources, e.g., foreign purchasers of Treasury bonds? We will review this in chapter 22.)

 Nonmonetized borrowing, also called *nonmonetized deficit financing,* need be neither expansionary nor inflationary. Under certain conditions, it can be contractionary and deflationary. Those conditions may exist now, as I shall argue in a moment. For now, let me repeat that nonmonetized borrowing to pay tax refunds is a shuffle. What about higher taxes to finance increased government spending? What is that?

S4: That's a money shuffle, too.

RH: Yes, if the Treasury finances higher spending from higher taxes, that money comes from taxpayers' pockets and moves into the pockets of those who get Treasury checks, another shuffle. But there are important differences. Anybody know what I have in mind?

S5: When you lend to the government, you get a Treasury bond for your money. When the government taxes you, it doesn't give you anything in return.

RH: Anything? Well, government does spend to provide services to the public, but we won't get into that issue here. You are correct, though, in noting that government spending, whether financed by taxes or by non-monetized Treasury borrowing, involves a transfer of money balances, not an increase in the total money supply. Either way, it's a shuffle of money, from the purchaser of Treasury obligations to the recipient of the tax refund. There is, however, one difference. There is a small and positive "wealth" effect from nonmonetized borrowing because the recipient of the tax refund has a higher net worth and spending power that may more than offset the reduced liquidity of the purchaser. The purchaser, you see, has given up cash (demand deposits) for a Treasury instrument. He has shifted from a completely liquid to a less liquid asset. Apart from this qualification, though, no new money creation is involved. To understand that, just track nonmonetized Treasury financing via the "T-Account" example I passed out to you (see Exhibit 6–1). The zeros noted there point up the absence of any net money creation.

Let's turn to this question: What is *monetized* deficit financing?

S6:   If the Treasury borrowed by selling Treasury securities to the Federal Reserve? The Fed would create new money in that case.

RH: Yes, that's how the Treasury defines monetization. Brand new money and buying power come into existence. But I want you to keep in mind a broader definition of monetization. The Fed can directly create money, but it can also make it possible for the private financial system to create money. For example, suppose the Treasury increases its spending through new borrowing while the Fed simultaneously cuts legal reserve requirements or provides reserves to the banks by buying Treasury securities (which we will review later). In that case, the banks would have the reserves to create new credit and money. The money creation could match or even exceed higher Treasury spending and borrowing. That's monetized financing. In plain English, that means paying for things by printing more money.

Let's apply what we have learned about monetized versus nonmonetized borrowing to the actions under Reaganomics. As you know, many Wall Street economists are forecasting that tax cuts and higher federal spending will produce boom and inflation. I think they are dead wrong. Who's right, and why?

S6:   Private consumer and business credit demands are strong. So, if the Treasury now comes to the market with huge borrowing to compete with private credit demands, I guess interest rates could soar. That could cause recession.

RH: Yes, especially when the Fed cuts off new growth of credit and money. But let's get back to interest rates. Are they going up forever? What would Professor Irving Fisher say if he were alive today?

S7: Fisher said not to confuse the initial versus the lagged effects of monetary action. Since you are forecasting recession, that would mean a fall in interest rates in the months ahead.

RH: Exactly. Though few agree with me, I think recession is already here. What could cause the recession to deepen?

S8: Crowding out. Huge government financing could displace or crowd out consumer and business credit. That could depress private spending, and worsen the recession.

RH: Yes, if the Fed does not print new money, that means the Treasury has to soak up money from the private economy, money that otherwise could be spent on consumption or new investment. That's what is meant by crowding out.

DR. DEATH, DR. DOOM, AND DR. GLOOM

S9: That's not what other economists are saying.

RH: Right! The consensus warns instead of boom and inflation from the tax cuts and the surge in federal spending. Some look for yields on long-term Treasury bonds to climb to 20 percent, maybe even as high as 24 percent. The biggest and the loudest Bond Bears are Dr. Death and Dr. Doom. Dr. Death is Al Wojnilower, chief economist with First Boston. Dr. Doom is Henry Kaufman, chief economist with Salomon Brothers. They're both friends of mine.

S9: They don't look like friends in your July *Monitor* (see Appendix B). And who's Dr. Gloom? I've heard that name, too, somewhere. Who gave them these odd names?

RH: I don't know the answer to Dr. Doom. One day, though, I was listening to Al Wojnilower lecture on the economic outlook. George Livingston, an investment client of mine, sat beside me taking notes. He wrote "Dr. Death" at the top of his notes. Later on I wrote a monitor entitled "Dr. Death, Dr. Doom, and Dr. Gloom," and the press got hold of it. I'll introduce you to Dr. Gloom later. His real name is Dr. Martin Feldstein (see Appendix A, Forecast 27 and chapter 14 on Tax Nostrums and twisted ideologues).

Look, our job is to analyze. Bond Bears, Death, and Doom could turn out to be right provided the Fed were to monetize, to roll the printing presses to finance huge Treasury and private borrowing. That combination would feed inflation, produce a boom, and send interest rates to the moon. But the Fed isn't monetizing. Quite the opposite! What's the key lesson I have tried to stress? I'll answer my own question: When anybody asks you what the effect of tax cuts and higher federal outlays will be, you must make certain that you never, but never, divorce fiscal policy from monetary policy. You must always ask how budgetary deficits are to be financed. Let's put the question on the board in big block letters:

HOW WILL THE BUDGETARY DEFICITS BE FINANCED?

Yes, always ask that question. Keeping the thoughts of my graduate students in mind, let's track step-by-step the forces culminating in the severe recession of 1981–82.

First, the tax cuts plus higher federal spending resulted in huge Treasury deficits. Second, the Treasury had to finance those deficits by soaking up money from the public at large. Fed restriction saw to that because it cut off the growth of new credit and money. Third, given the fact that the economy was already in a borrowing binge, the additional Treasury financing clashed head-on with the curtailed supply of new credit. Fourth, this clash of huge borrowing demands with the cutoff of new money and credit by the Fed sent interest rates soaring. This, again, represented the *initial liquidity effect*. Liquidity dried up, and interest rates rose, but only temporarily. Fifth, the effect of the crowding out of private borrowing and spending produced, with a lag, a major recession, a collapse of private borrowing, and a sharp decline in interest rates. This was the *lagged Fisher effect*. Sixth, the recession clobbered tax revenues, and the reported budgetary deficit ballooned to record levels. The huge increase in the debt was largely a consequence of a falling economy, one pushed down by fiscal high jinks and monetary overkill.

THE CROWDING-OUT IMPACT ON CAPITAL SPENDING

Extremely high interest rates severely depressed business spending on capital equipment. Why? It's not just that consumer spending fell or that higher interest rates meant higher borrowing charges to business. That's not the whole story by any means. No, corporate executives had the option in the fall of 1981 of investing their spare cash, if they had any left, in AAA corporate bonds at 17 percent and in long-term Treasury bonds at 15 percent. Those returns were magnificent. The opportunity cost (income foregone) by not investing in 15 percent and 17 percent bonds was unprecedentedly high, irresistible. No wonder business spending on plant and equipment collapsed. In other words, there was no need at the time to spend on plant and equipment when profit pictures were bleak, so business decided to invest its extra cash and earn high rates of interest.

Keep our step-by-step analysis in mind as we now meet Bernard Meltzer (BM) of WOR Radio. He always asked the hard but relevant questions. The ones he fired at me on Saturday, November 28, 1981, bear directly on Reaganomics. The questions he asked then serve now as an introduction to the Reagan officers in charge of the tragi-comedy of 1981–82:

BM: Robert, The Wall Street Journal quoted you as saying the worst part of this recession has just begun. What do you mean by that?

RH: The decline will prove to be severe and protracted and widespread.

BM: Is there any chance that this recession could (turn into) a depression?

RH: That chance always exists. A number of officers in the administration, particularly the Treasury, are terribly concerned that the economic decline already underway could degenerate into something far worse than [that of] 1973–75.

THE MONETARIST TRIPLETS

This takes us now to the officials in charge of fiscal and monetary mismanagement. Let's first meet the monetarist triplets. They were Dr. Beryl Sprinkel, then Treasury Under Secretary for Monetary Affairs; Jerry Jordan, a member of the Council of Economic Advisers (CEA); and Larry Kudlow, Associate Director, Office of Management and Budget. Mr. Kudlow was actually more of a supply-sider than a monetarist, always preaching the need for a tax cut no matter what the economic weather. (We'll define and expand on these terms in chapter 14 when we meet a galaxy of preaching tax-gurus.)

I hosted institutional investor forums with each of these gentlemen, and on a fairly regular basis with Dr. Sprinkel. What do you think these three were thinking about in the second half of 1981? We know what they had to say for public consumption, namely, that we should look for continued economic expansion, a slowing of inflation, a surge in investment, and other lovely developments. But that's not my question. What did they really believe?

Public Propaganda Versus Private Truth

My conviction as early as April 1981 was that the monetarist triplets were looking for recession. They talked sunshine publicly but looked for rain privately. They knew recession was at hand; at least I was convinced they did (see Appendix A, Forecast 22). How could they not have known? They had the same data I had, which shouted out the high risk of recession straight ahead. They were all familiar with the concepts of monetized versus non-monetized deficits.

I asked Dr. Sprinkel (BS) about all this after the fact, that is, after the economy had emerged from the 1981–82 mini-depression. The occasion was that of an institutional investor forum I hosted for him and other Washington officials. We had a dinner meeting in the Arlington Room of the Madison Hotel in Washington, D.C., on Tuesday, December 13, 1983. I fired this question at precisely 10:15 P.M.:

RH: Beryl, what were you really thinking in the second half of 1981 about the course of the economy? What were you saying for internal consumption among your colleagues in government? You were talking economic sunshine publicly.

BS: Look Robert, we asked the Fed to slow money growth by 50 percent over a period of several years to bring inflation under control while promoting continued economic growth. What we got instead was an abrupt and almost total freeze on money growth in a matter of months, virtually all of that in 1981. Now you can't slam on the money and credit brakes like that without bringing on a severe contraction in the economy. So what do you think I was saying for internal consumption?

The Supply-Side Ruler and Court

It's clear what Dr. Sprinkel was thinking. It's also clear that what he was thinking had nothing to do with what he was saying publicly. The same holds for the supply-side ruler and his court. The ruler was the Assistant Treasury Secretary for Economic Policy, Dr. Paul Craig Roberts. His court proteges included deputies Steve Entin and Manuel Johnson. (Johnson later became vice chairman of the Federal Reserve Board.) All were my guests at these forums. Our interest here concerns what Dr. Roberts (PR) said versus what he thought. Consider this exchange, a telephone conversation in response to his call to me on the afternoon of April 18, 1989:

RH: You remember our June 1981 forum in Washington?

PR: Not really.

RH: We met at 9:30 A.M. on Tuesday, June 2, 1981, in Treasury Conference Room 4121. You had two Treasury officers, John Auten and John Schmidt, with you. I brought along thirty-five institutional investment officers.

PR: I remember now.

RH: Remember, I asked you about the second half of 1980? I asked you why the Fed was imitating the central bank of Brazil in printing money like mad and driving inflation and interest rates higher and higher. Then I asked you about Fed policy overkill in 1981.

PR: I refused to answer.

RH: I remember. You said you wouldn't answer. Why?

PR: You knew very well that we were all under wraps not to criticize the Fed or Volcker. We were gagged.

RH: Was Volcker off track? Will you answer my question now, eight years later?

PR: Way off track. The Fed targeted interest rates in 1980, a disastrous policy. The Fed killed the economy in 1981, and supply siders took a bad rap for that.

Exception to the Rule of Shading

The one Washingtonian who was right on track in his forecasts was Dr. Robert Ortner (RO), then chief economist with the Department of Commerce. He never shaded or twisted in the countless forums I hosted for him and institutional investors over the years. But being straight and honest sometimes put him at risk. To see why, listen in on our telephone conversation of January 20, 1989. We finally got around to the mini-depression of 1981–82:

RH: You and I go back a long way, when we first taught at Wharton. Before you went to Washington, you were chief economist with the Bank of New York. You caught some flak there for just being your candid and truthful self. Right? What about 1981, when you were with Commerce? I believe you told me then that Regan [Treasury Secretary Donald Regan] was giving you holy hell.

RO: I grew worried in 1981, as you did. By early 1982, I said the economy was sinking. Regan said the economy was roaring back. The monetarists and supply-siders came up with the same Regan nonsense. Yes, Regan gave me hell.

The Thin Line Separating Truth from Deception

RH: Why do so many of your associates in Washington cross that thin line separating truth from deception?

RO: Robert, people in Washington, D.C., walk in a haze, not a thin line. They deal in unethical and dishonest activity, and don't even realize it.

RH: Does that include economists? They are best trained to spot deception in economic analysis.

RO: (laughing) Robert, if you ever finish *Witch Doctor,* which I doubt, remind your readers of what Joan Robinson [a British economist] had to say.

RH: What was that?

RO: She said everybody should study economics, or run the high risk of being deceived by economists.

THE BOND BEARS ON REAGANOMICS

Paul Craig Roberts said the supply-siders got a bad rap. That's debatable, as we shall later argue. But speaking of raps, I must lay one on the Wall Street bond bears of 1981. They really missed out. They misread Federal Reserve policy despite the overwhelming evidence of monetary overkill. To compound their error, they misinterpreted just how *nonmonetized* financing would impact the economy and interest rates. They misread and distorted, perhaps unconsciously, the very meaning of Keynesian economics (see Appendix B).

Watch out for the tax-cut and spending "multipliers," they warned. Higher government spending and lower taxes, they said, would propel private consumer and investment spending higher. That would bring with it accelerating inflation and sharply higher interest rates. Stay away from long government bonds, they screamed. Bond prices will dive. So they declared.

Poor John Maynard Keynes. He would have gagged on all this. Keynes argued in his *General Theory* (1936), *Treatise on Money* (1930), and *How to Pay for the War* (1940) that the question of the economic effects of tax cuts and higher government spending could not be answered unless you made explicit two critical conditions. The first was the level of employment of capital and labor (a matter we take up in the very next chapter). What was the second? Always inquire, he said, whether tax cuts and higher spending are to be monetized or not. If Keynes had been alive in 1981, he might well have fired this question at the big bond bears:

> Tell me, Bears, how will these deficits be financed? Will they be monetized or nonmonetized?

In summary, two killers stalked the land in 1981–82. Inflation sapped real buying power. The Fed sucked away money and credit, and forced money velocity into a freefall. The two killers, operating jointly, choked off private spending for sixteen long and dreadful months, almost to the point of depression.

"DEFICITPHOBIA," IDEOLOGICAL RAGE, AND INTEREST RATES

I hope I have not contributed to deficitphobia, the hatred of deficits. True, my main goal in this chapter is to stress that huge *nonmonetized* budgetary deficits under certain conditions can crowd out consumer and business spending, and weaken the economy. That contrasts with the widespread but mistaken view that a deficit must necessarily be expansionary and inflationary. But there are all kinds of deficits, and we will meet them in the chapters ahead: bad and good, private and public, whether in our domestic or international trading accounts. So, whatever you do, don't take the absolute size or the direction of a deficit considered by itself alone to mean anything necessarily.

Anything? Yes, that includes the impact of deficits on reported interest rates. Popular conviction has it that exploding deficits go with booms and soaring interest rates. Well, that view is seriously flawed. Take a look at the data (see Exhibit 6–2). You can see that big deficits for the U.S. government go with recessions and falling, not rising, interest rates. That was true in eight out of nine recessions of the post–World War II period, including 1948–49, 1953–54, 1957–58, 1960–61, 1969–70, 1980 (first half), 1981–82, and 1990–91. (The 1973–75 recession was the only exception, though this period came to be called the years of "stagflation.")

The *inverse* correlation of deficits and interest rates—the fact that as one goes up the other is going down—is easy to understand. Why? People lose their jobs and their incomes in recession, hence the Treasury sees its tax revenues evaporate. Government spending for unemployment insurance automatically increases. When, however, the economy is speeding uphill, jobs and incomes advance, too. So do tax receipts even as government outlays for unemployment automatically fall. Under these conditions, tax revenues tend to rise faster than federal outlays, and the reported deficits shrink. Indeed, the economy could be expanding and the reported deficit falling sharply in the face of huge and inflationary monetary and fiscal stimulation. The late 1970s were a perfect example (see chapter 13). Unenlightened politicians from Gingrich to Perot have yet to learn that the reported budget deficit is one of the very worst measures of fiscal policy. This is a matter that will command our attention in chapters 13 and 14.

What about the colossal deficits after 1982? The 1982–1990 economic expansion was the longest period of economic growth in the post-World War II years (see chapter 1, Exhibits 1–1 and 1–2). We had a vigorous recovery and chalked up the biggest cumulative deficit over these nine years in our entire history. What happened? Yields on long-term Treasury bonds fell from a peak of 15.75 percent in 1981 to below 8 percent in 1986, rebounded slightly, then fell below 8 percent again in 1991. Rates continued down, predictably, in the 1990–91 recession, with yields on long-term Treasuries falling to about 5.8 percent by October 1993. The deficit widened as interest rates came down, down, down. They went their opposite ways.

Then to the consternation of just about every money manager I know, yields skyrocketed in 1994 even as the deficit contracted from $280 billion annually in 1992 to $200 billion in 1994, and even as inflation slowed. See for yourself on the bottom line of Exhibit 6–2. Yields on 30-year Treasury bonds, for example, increased dramatically from about 5.8 percent in October 1993 to 8 percent in 1994. The *fear* of inflation frightened the market even as inflation fell, as market psychology held dominion over the fundamentals, including shrinking deficits (see chapter 7). Again, though, the deficit and interest rates went their opposite ways. In 1995, both the deficit and interest rates fell—a most unusual phenomenon!

Why the widespread confusion on the data that show, with few exceptions, an *inverse* (not direct) correlation of nominal interest rates and budget deficits? One reason is that Parrots and Pros have no use for good data and theory. They often become defensive and emotional when confronted with the facts. Some get angry. Their ideological screaming governs their good sense and makes a mockery of economic science, whether in 1981 or 1995. We'll encounter the loudest of them shortly, including Newt Gingrich and H. Ross Perot, among others (see chapters 13 and 14).

Linking Data to Theory on Interest-Rate Fluctuations

But we must first review theory in greater depth, including the theory of inflation and deflation (the theory of the fluctuation in the buying power or value of the dollar). Then we will explore both monetary theory and the theory of swings in nominal and real (inflation-adjusted) interest rates. All three are inextricably linked.

Exhibit 6–1:
Nonmonetized Tax Cuts and Nonmonetized Spending:
A Money Shuffle

	FEDERAL RESERVE		COMMERCIAL BANKS, SPECIAL DEPOSITORY INSTITUTIONS	
1. Borrowing				−DD p +T&L
2. Treasury Call	−DD r +DD t		−R	−T&L
3. Tax Refund (or Higher Outlays)	+DD r −DD t		+R	+DD p
4. Net (1+2+3)	0		0	0

1. **Nonmonetized Treasury Borrowing:** Treasury sells Treasury obligations to the consumer and business public. Buyers draft checks against their demand deposits **−DD** payable to the Treasury. The result is to reduce the demand balances of the public **−DD p** and increase the Treasury's checking account at the private commercial banking level, which shows up as an increase in the Treasury's tax and loan account **+T&L.**

2. **Treasury Call:** The Treasury shifts its account from private depository institutions **−T&L** to the Federal Reserve, which shows up as an increase in the demand deposits of the Treasury at the Federal Reserve **+DD t,** a decrease in reserves at depository institutions **−R,** which is the same thing as a decrease in the Federal Reserve's liabilities to depository institutions **−DD r.**

3. **Treasury Payment of Tax Refunds (Tax Cut):** The Treasury drafts checks payable as tax refunds which reduces its account at the Federal Reserve **−DD t,** which increases the demand deposits of the public as they deposit the tax-refund checks **+DD p,** and replenishes the reserves of depository institutions **+R,** which is the same thing as increasing the reserve liabilities of the Federal Reserve to depository institutions **+DD r.**

4. **Net Results:** *Nonmonetized* tax cuts (and *nonmonetized* federal outlays) do not put cash into the pockets of the public at large but instead shuffle money from one pocket to another. True, the recipient of the tax refund has a higher net worth that may offset somewhat the reduced liquidity of the purchaser, who has given up cash for Treasuries. But the important point to note, one almost universally misunderstood, is the shuffle.

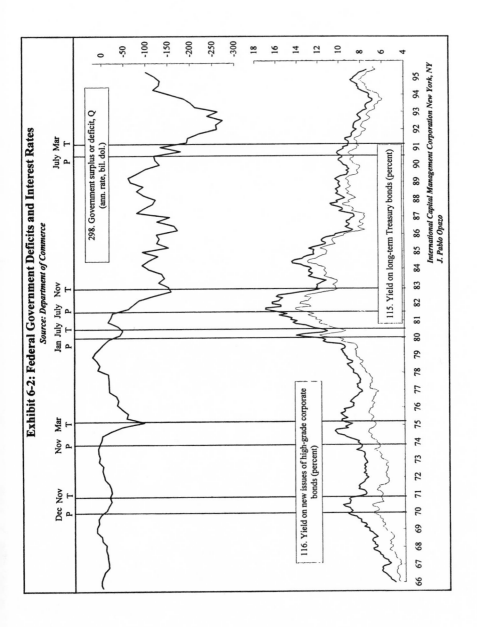

Exhibit 6-2: Federal Government Deficits and Interest Rates
Source: Department of Commerce

298. Government surplus or deficit, Q (ann. rate, bil. dol.)

115. Yield on long-term Treasury bonds (percent)

116. Yield on new issues of high-grade corporate bonds (percent)

International Capital Management Corporation New York, NY
J. Pablo Opazo

Part Three

Interest Rate Theory, Practice, and Malpractice

7

Sense and Nonsense Theory on the Value of the Dollar

> In symbols the Fisherian model [is]: $\frac{dP}{dt} =$ alpha (M– kPy), $\frac{dM}{dt} =$ beta (Pr – P) where $\frac{dP}{dt}$ denotes price change, P actual prices, Pr their fixed target level, M the money stock (and) $\frac{dM}{dt}$ its change, k the inverse of money's turnover velocity or the fraction of nominal income people wish to hold in money, y real income, and alpha and beta positive constants.
>
> *Economic Review,* Federal Reserve Bank of Richmond, May/June 1990, p. 4.

What? Can you understand this? No? Well, let's try to put it into plain language and easy-to-understand arithmetic. First, we need to explain what P, M, V, and k are. The following is an exchange with Pace graduate finance students during the spring semester of 1989. Beware the many data pitfalls and theoretical land mines:

RH: We have to review the theory of value of the monetary unit. That's the dollar in our system. Suppose the price level triples, that an index of prices climbs from 1.00 in some base or earlier period to 3.00 in the current period. What percentage price rise is that?

S1: Prices are up three-fold, an increase of 300 percent.

RH: No. Think again. If you pay $3 to buy a loaf of bread today that cost you $1 in the base period (say, four years ago), how many more dollars do you pay? Let's take bread to be a stand-in for a market basket of consumer goods. What percentage rise is that over the old price?

S1:   You pay $2 more. So I guess that's a 200 percent rise.

RH: Good. Three dollars less $1 is $2, and $2 is 200 percent of $1. That's a 200 percent increase. You could also say that current prices rose to 300 percent *of* base prices, which means current prices rose *by* 200 percent over the base prices. Don't confuse these prepositions. What happens to the value of the dollar?

S2:   It falls 100 percent?

RH: What? In that case the dollar would become worthless. Think again.

S2:   66.67 percent?

RH: Good. If a loaf of bread costs $1 in the base period and $3 in the current period, then $1 would buy only one-third of a loaf in the current period. So the value of the dollar declines *to* one-third of its original value, or falls *by* two-thirds, by 66.67 percent. Now, just as we represented prices with an index, we can do the same thing for value. When we say the value of the dollar falls by 66.67 percent, we can say it falls from an index of 1.0 in the base period to an index of 0.333 in the current period. So, a rise from 1.0 to 3.0 for an index of prices is the same thing as a fall from 1.0 to one-third of 1.0, or 0.333, for an index of value. Let's put the arithmetic on the board:

	Base	Current	% Change
Price Index	1.00	3.00	+ 200.00 percent
Value Index	1.00	0.333	− 66.67 percent

ECONOMIC ARITHMETIC VERSUS ECONOMIC THEORY

RH: Does the rise in prices by 200 percent cause the fall in the value of the dollar by 66.67 percent, or does the fall in the value of the dollar cause prices to rise? Which is cause and which is effect?

S3:   Inflation causes the dollar to fall in value.

RH: Suppose I said that I am taller than you are because you are shorter than I am. It that good logic?

S3:   Are you saying that price inflation does not cause the value of the dollar to fall?

RH: That's correct. A rise in prices is the same thing as a fall in the value of the dollar. One *is* the other. One doesn't *cause* the other. These are identical statements, though expressed in different ways. Now, what is price theory?

S3: When we find out what causes prices to rise?

RH: Yes. When you theorize, you assign cause and effect to certain variables. In our example, we want to know what can cause prices to rise by 200 percent; that is, what can cause the value of the dollar to fall by 66.67 percent? Here's a fast answer to this question:

Cause	Effect
If D > S	P rises.
	The value of the dollar falls.

What does this say? It says that if the demand for goods and services D exceeds the supply of goods and services S, this will cause prices P to rise and the value of the dollar to fall. So, if you want to explain why prices rise and the value of the dollar falls, you have to focus on the cause. That's where you'll find theory. Just looking at the effect tells us nothing about what causes prices to rise (or the purchasing power of the dollar to fall).

EX POST IDENTITIES VERSUS *EX ANTE* DEMAND AND SUPPLY

RH: How is it possible for prices to change when we know that purchases are always equal to sales?

S4: But they're not always equal.

RH: Can you imagine anybody buying a loaf of bread for $2 without somebody selling a loaf of bread for $2? Purchases and sales are always equal.

S4: But that's not true of demand and supply.

RH: You're right. Purchases and sales are always identical from an accounting or historical point of view. The economist calls this *ex post.* But people may try to purchase more goods at the current level of prices than suppliers are willing to offer to the market at the current level of prices, in which case prices rise. That's called *ex ante* demand

and supply. It's also called effective demand and supply, or just plain demand and supply. So, demand can exceed supply *ex ante*, but purchases must always equal sales *ex post*.

RH: Where can I get exact measures of demand and supply?

S5: The Department of Commerce publishes all that stuff.

RH: Suppose I said that exact measures of demand and supply have never existed and never will exist. If you can define demand for me, you already know why that's true. What are the two components of demand?

S6: Ability to spend plus the desire to do so. You have to know these two things to estimate demand.

RH: But we have only rough ideas about ability to buy. Income, wealth, and borrowing power are all important, but they don't add up to exact measures of total ability. What about desire? Economists have only the foggiest notion about how to measure desire, much less add your desire to mine. They pretend they can with their indifference curves made up of "utils" (units of pleasure) and "disutils" (units of pain). It's all so silly. Psychologists don't do much better, and they are the experts. If anybody here ever does find a way to measure demand with precision, let me know. We'll both get Nobel prizes in economics. We'd get rich overnight, too. If we knew for certain that demand will exceed supply for any given item, that the item's price would soar, then we could load up on the item and sell it later for a huge profit. That would be a sure thing, but sure things don't exist.

There's another lesson here. Never take the reported historical statistics on purchases and sales to be reliable measures of the effective demand for and supply of goods. To repeat, the reported statistics are *ex post* identities. They are not intended to show purchases made in advance of delivery (*ex ante*). These conflicting concepts will pop up again in our analysis of saving and investment, interest rates, and exchange rates. Beware. If you fail to distinguish between *ex post* identities and *ex ante* demand and supply, you risk error.

We just met two sets of identities. I now want you to meet lookalike triplets. The first of this economic trio is *gross national product* (GNP). The Commerce Department just released its estimate for gross national product for the fourth quarter of 1988. It was reported at roughly $5 trillion in nominal or actual prices. Now look at this equation:

$$MV = PT = GNP^* = \$5 \text{ trillion (4Q 1988)}$$

GNP is the dollar value of currently produced goods and services for the entire economy. MV signifies that the total amount of money (M) multiplied by the velocity (average turnover) of the money (V) is equal to total dollar expenditures for current production. PT shows that the average price (P) of current production (the average final price set for all units produced) multiplied by the physical volume of current production (T) is equal to the dollar value of current production. MV = PT is Dr. Fisher's equation of exchange. It's simply an algebraic statement of identities, MV (purchases) = PT (sales), and both MV and PT are equal to GNP. Are Gross National Product, Gross National Expenditures, and Gross National Income related?

Ss: Silence.

RH: They are one and the same, with just a couple of qualifications I'll note in a second. These are our triplets. To illustrate, for every $3 spent on a pizza pie hot out of the oven at the local pizza parlor, $3 of pizza was produced, and $3 of income was generated, and split up after taxes into wages, interest, rent, and profits. The same identity holds for consumer expenditures on new automobiles, or business purchases of currently produced machine tools, or government outlays for new fighter planes.

  What are the qualifications? Current spending may run a bit above or below current production and show up in inventory swings. Also, our trade with other nations requires that we modify our GNP accounting somewhat. If, for example, we import more than we export, then we end up spending more than we produce. But these things need not concern us here. To repeat, gross national expenditures, gross national product, and gross national income are mainly identities.

  Can we calculate the velocity of money?

S7:   You know what spending is. If you know what the money supply is, you can calculate velocity.

RH: The narrowly defined money supply, consisting of currency, demand deposits, and other checkable deposits, totaled almost $0.8 trillion on average in the fourth quarter of 1988. Economists call that M1. So what was velocity?

S7:   GNP of $5 trillion divided by $0.8 trillion?

RH: Yes. Here it is:

---

*The Commerce Department now focuses on GDP or gross domestic product.

$$V = \frac{PT}{M} = \frac{\$5 \text{ trillion}}{\$0.8 \text{ trillion}} = 6.25x$$

The 6.25x means that money turned over 6.25 times on the average. This is the "income" velocity of money, a term borrowed from British economists. You can call it production velocity or expenditures velocity since, to repeat, income, production, and expenditures are roughly equal in GNP accounting. Call it what you will, it means that one dollar showed up as spending (output or income) about 6.25 times a year. One dollar did the work of $6.25. The 6.25x income velocity of money is plotted in the top line of the exhibit I passed out to you (see Exhibit 7–1). We shall have a lot more to say about that. But let me warn you now. Don't confuse the income velocity of money with the turnover of checking accounts at commercial banks. (Demand deposits are another name for checking accounts.) Demand deposits for the major New York City banks, for example, may turn over 3,500 times a year (see Exhibit 7–2). The Federal Reserve calculates this by dividing the total dollar volume of checks drawn against deposit balances (total "debits") by the average demand deposits held. Economists call this "transactions velocity." So, $1 did the work of $3,500 for the large banks. Transactions include GNP expenditures but also bond and stock trading, purchases and sales of real estate, used autos, foreign exchange, and a lot of other things that lift total money spending far higher than spending for current production alone. That explains why the transactions velocity of money is much higher than the income (GNP) velocity of money.

Now let's return to prices, P. Let's calculate P.

$$P = \frac{MV}{T} \text{ where T is output, the same as real GNP}$$

The average price per unit is equal to the total amount of money times the velocity (turnover) of that money (total money expenditure for current production) divided by the total output of goods and services. We are not going to discuss here how T, an index of physical output (production) is calculated. The idea is what counts. The idea is simply that if you add up total money expenditures for current production, and divide by the number of units of physical production, you get the average price per unit, or P.

Let's turn now, finally, to theory. We must theorize just how M, V, and T affect P. Put another way, we have to see how M, V, and T affect the value of the dollar. Now look at this equation for late 1988 when nominal GNP approximated $5 trillion:

$$MV = PT = GNP = C + I + G = \$5 \text{ trillion}$$

If we were to analyze GNP through a Keynesian model, we would concentrate on C, I, and G. What do those letters represent?

S8:   Consumption, investment, and government spending?

RH: Yes. Remember that we are ignoring net exports here, but we will return to that later. We have to internationalize the Fisher equation to make complete sense of it. With that qualification, we can still analyze the main causal forces on U.S. price levels. How would we arrive at P, the average price of a unit of goods and services produced?

S8:   Divide MV by T. Divide $5 trillion by real output.

RH: Yes, let's show this:

$$\frac{MV}{T} = P$$

See the equal sign? That tells us that this is an identity, not a theory. To develop a theory, we have to find the causal forces operating on P. Let's do just that. What, other things being equal, could cause the price level to rise?

Causes		Effect
M+	→	P+
or V+	→	P+
or T–	→	P+

Stated plainly, fast money growth or a speeding up in spending or a reduction in the supply of goods offered to the market would together cause prices to rise, other things being equal. Dr. Fisher put it this way in his book *Why the Dollar Is Shrinking*:* "The equation thus simplified [is] MV = PT. To recapitulate, we find that the price level (P) varies: directly [in the same direction] as the quantity of money in circulation (M); directly as the velocity of its circulation (V); [and] inversely [in the opposite direction] as the volume of trade done by it (T)."

*The Macmillan Company, New York, 1914, p. 46.

Let's see whether Fisher's theoretical views are supported by the data. Try to appraise the validity of this statement, one I included in a recent examination: "Clearly, a rapid and sustained explosion of the money supply will guarantee rapid inflation. Any graduate student familiar with sound theory and history could tell you that."

S8:   The statement is wrong, at least as a generalization.

RH: You're right. The statement is supported by neither theory nor history. Textbook writers label the idea that rapid money growth must guarantee inflation as the "rigid or naive quantity theory of money." You could have guessed something was wrong from the words *clearly* and *guarantee* in the statement. Remember, these words are red flags. To see why, let's check history first. Do you recall any periods in U.S. history that contradict the statement?

S9:   In the years 1962 to 1965 we did cut taxes under President Kennedy. Also, the Federal Reserve made possible a fairly rapid growth in credit and money, but we had little inflation. That's one example. Also, we had an explosion of money in the 1982–86 period when inflation dropped. That's another.

RH: Take the 1962–65 period, one that economists sometimes call the Golden Age of Economists. We had little inflation. Here are the numbers. Consumer prices rose 1.3 percent in 1962, 1.6 percent in 1963, 1.0 percent in 1964, and 1.9 percent in 1965. But the money supply speeded ahead at a faster clip. The broad money supply, which economists call M2, was up about 8 percent a year over these years. So, how can you have fast money growth with slow inflation?

S8:   The two other "causal forces," V and T, must have offset the rapid rise in M, money.

RH: Not exactly. Velocity rose a bit to push spending even higher. But production (T) rose swiftly, too, keeping pace with the rise in total spending. As we said, M multiplied by V is total spending. You can call that roughly the effective demand for goods and services. At the same time T rose to keep pace. Call T roughly the effective supply of goods being offered to the market. So, despite the rapid rise in the aggregate (total) demand for goods (MV), we enjoyed a companion rise in the aggregate supply of goods (T). T kept up with MV. That ruled out demand-pull inflation. That's one reason price inflation was so low. Let's put this in Fisher's terms:

Cause	Effect
$\underline{MV}$ surged, but	
T surged to offset MV	Prices fairly stable.

RH: How could production rise so much, so powerfully?

S9: We had just come out of the 1960–61 recession, and had a lot of unemployment.

RH: Yes, we had unemployed labor and idle capital. So when the demand for goods recovered, business could meet the demand by putting available labor and capital to work to increase output. That meant no demand-pull inflation. Nor did we have cost-push inflation. Business could hire from a low-cost labor pool and could borrow capital at relatively low rates.

Think of the U.S. economy as a huge ocean liner. When the ship is operating at only 60 percent of capacity, the captain must still be paid his salary. That's a fixed cost. So, the captain's salary divided by the number of passengers translates into a high fixed cost per passenger. That translates into a high fixed *unit* cost. The same is true for other fixed costs like depreciation or insurance. Fixed unit costs are high when capacity utilization is low, when few passengers are on board. Also, the stewards and cooks still have to be paid even though they may not have much to do. They are called variable labor because the number of cooks and stewards hired depends somewhat on just how fully booked the ship is. You hire more workers when the ship is fully booked, and fewer when it is only partly booked. Even so, when the ship is occupied at only 60 percent of capacity, labor costs divided by the total number of passengers is relatively high. Unit operating costs are high when capacity utilization is low.

But consider what happens when demand picks up, when the ship is booked at (say) 85 percent. Presto. Like magic the unit operating costs come down. This presents us with a great paradox, almost universally misunderstood. Rapid growth of money and spending can exert a deflationary impact on unit costs, or at least slow unit cost inflation, whenever the economy is recovering from a major recession. The paradox is explained by the cost economies enjoyed as utilization climbs to more efficient operating levels—as more passengers climb aboard.

After 1965, prices and unit costs advanced swiftly. What happened to cause rapid price inflation?

S9: The Vietnam War.

RH: Yes, we waged a money printing press war. President Johnson didn't ask for a tax increase; he was afraid the voters would turn against him. The huge increase in military spending—from $51 billion in 1965 to about $80 billion in 1968—had to be financed largely through creating new money. Spending was largely *monetized,* a practice which we have seen can be highly inflationary under certain circumstances. The U.S. economy hit full employment in 1965. True, new people coming into the labor force and higher productivity can increase total output. But these are mainly long-run forces. By late 1965, then, the economy was operating full blast. There was no slack. We had to operate beyond full capacity, when unit costs tend to climb swiftly.

A second red flag was signaling inflation. The federal government had to bid scarce resources, labor, capital and materials, away from private industry. You cannot make guns and butter with the same resources. Soaring military spending increased the incomes and buying power of Americans, fueling their demands for goods, but added little to the supply of goods for civilian markets. This provided no fallout of goods for the private economy. No wonder prices soared.

The Vietnam War was no exception to the rule. Price inflation is always a major problem in war. Look at the upper-left part of Exhibit 7–3 and note the huge impact of war on inflation.

Note that the 1965–68 period of fast money growth and accelerating inflation contrasts violently with the 1982–86 period, also one of fast money growth and *disinflation,* meaning a fall in the pace of inflation. Consumer price inflation fell from a fast 9 percent in 1981 to about 1 percent in 1986. Wholesale prices plunged, too, falling absolutely in 1986. Keep in mind these two contrasting examples. Always remember to check the level of employment of labor and capital, domestic and worldwide. Always ask how much T can advance to keep pace with any given rise in MV.

PRICE THEORY IN HISTORICAL PERSPECTIVE

Remember history whenever you analyze money and prices! Beware the rigid quantity theorists: those who focus solely on money in trying to explain fluctuations in price levels (fluctuations in the value of the dollar). They focus only on money in explaining prices. They leave out velocity (V) and pay too little attention to output (T). They ignore the availability of T worldwide. They slide over the question of whether the domestic and world economies are operating way above or below capacity. No wonder their analysis and forecasts are faulty.

I don't mean to suggest for one moment that M is unimportant or doesn't matter. Money does matter, a lot. One group of monetary economists, the monetarists, have spent their lifetimes documenting that rapid money growth over long periods must be counted as a critical causal variable in explaining inflation. They deserve credit, perhaps more than any other group of economists, in warning of the inflationary dangers of excessively monetized spending. At the same time, they have persistently but mistakenly left out V and T for shorter periods of time, including cyclical movements lasting many years. We'll review the problems of the renegade monetarists later when we take up monetary theory and policy.

THE BENEFICIAL LEGACY OF IRVING FISHER

In simple English, money is important in explaining price-level fluctuations, as is velocity and the supply of goods and services. All are important. Remember always to be a *loose* quantity theorist of money, one who always includes V and T, as well as M, in your analysis and forecast. If you do, you'll avoid a host of errors in understanding swings in interest rates, the subject of the immediate chapters ahead.

A POSTSCRIPT ON THE MUMBO-JUMBO IDENTITIES OF k AND $\frac{1}{V}$

Let's return to mumbo jumbo. What did the Richmond Federal Reserve Bank mean by "k, the inverse of money's turnover velocity or the fraction of nominal income people wish to hold in money"? We must answer this question because many writers, including the press, speak of the "demand for money" rather than velocity. (British economists and the American "monetarists" often speak of changes in the "demand for money to hold" or "money demand" instead of velocity.) To understand what they are talking about, we must understand that k and V are related. Here's the relationship:

$$k = \tfrac{1}{V} = \text{The Demand for Money to Hold}$$

Still not clear? Well, why don't you join me in this exchange with my students (S1, S2, etc.):

RH: Remember that we calculated the income velocity at 6.25x:

$$V = \frac{PT}{M} = \frac{\$5 \text{ trillion}}{\$0.8 \text{ trillion}} = 6.25x$$

With velocity at 6.25 times, what would k be?

S1: You said k was $\frac{1}{V}$. So we divide 1 by 6.25.

RH: Good.

$$k = \frac{1}{V} = \frac{1}{6.25} = .16 \text{ percent}$$

This means the public is holding money equal to about 16 percent of nominal GNP. Let's show that. Look at these calculations:

$$MV = PT = \$5 \text{ trillion}$$

Since: $\frac{PT}{M} = V = \frac{\$5.0 \text{ trillion}}{\$0.8 \text{ trillion}} = 6.25x$

And: k is the inverse of V, or $\frac{1}{V} = k$

Then: $\frac{M}{PT} = \frac{M}{GNP} = \frac{\$0.8 \text{ trillion}}{\$5.0 \text{ trillion}} = 16\% = k$

    We come up with the same 16 percent: the total amount of money available divided by the total value of goods and services.

    That's the arithmetic of k. But what's the theory of k? Theory tells us that if people expect price inflation to soar, they try to get out of holding money and invest it in goods. They want to buy goods now before prices rise. They may try to buy now and sell later at a big profit. Under these conditions, we would expect the velocity of money to climb (with the large numbers of money transactions). Given a rise in velocity, what would that imply for the demand for money to hold? Before you answer the question, make the additional assumption that the Federal Reserve manages to keep the total money supply unchanged.

S2: If you want to spend money at a faster clip, then your demand for money has to fall.

RH: Yes, a *rise in V* is the same thing as a *fall in k*; one is the other. (They are inversely related.) Now, if we were fully employed and operating full blast, would a fall in k (a rise in velocity) have a greater impact on prices or on output?

S3: The effect would mainly be on prices.

RH: Yes, prices could rise even with no rise in the total money stock. Total spending for goods measured by the product MV would rise because V rises, and this could lift prices. Now what would higher inflation mean to the real purchasing power of the $0.8 trillion money supply?

S3: The real buying power of the $0.8 trillion would fall.

RH: Yes, and the public would have succeeded in reducing its *real* money holdings. Its *nominal* money holdings would remain unchanged in dollars but would fall as a percentage of the higher level of nominal GNP (to below 16 percent in our example).

We can now tackle the arithmetic and theory governing fixed income markets (chapters 8 and 9). Then we'll be able to spot with knowledge and confidence the advocates of wealth-without-risk who run wild on Wall Street (chapter 10).

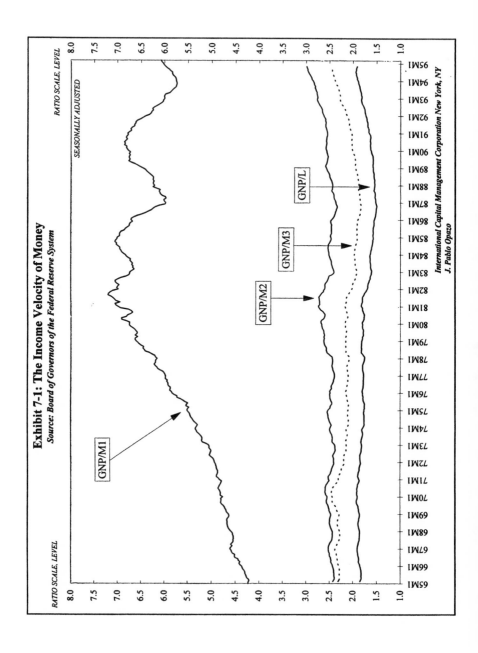

Exhibit 7-1: The Income Velocity of Money
Source: Board of Governors of the Federal Reserve System

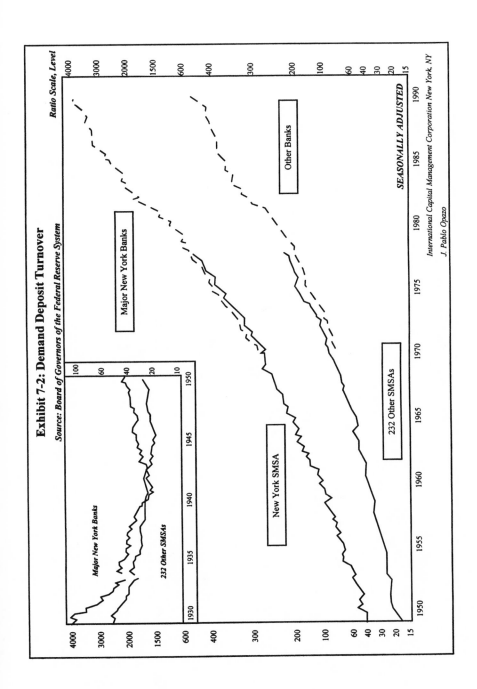

Exhibit 7-2: Demand Deposit Turnover

Source: Board of Governors of the Federal Reserve System

Ratio Scale, Level

SEASONALLY ADJUSTED

International Capital Management Corporation New York, NY

J. Pablo Opazo

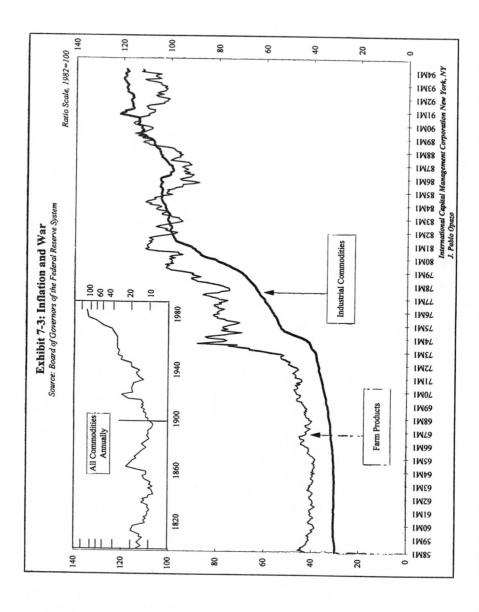

Exhibit 7-3: Inflation and War
Source: Board of Governors of the Federal Reserve System

8

The Fixed-Income Markets

Confusing Arithmetic with Analysis

> Money bearing compound interest grows at first slowly; but since the rate of increase is constantly accelerated, it becomes so fast after a while as to defy all imagination. A penny, loaned at the birth of our Savior at compound interest at 5 percent, would already have grown into a larger amount than would be contained in 150 million globes, all of solid gold.
>
> Karl Marx, *Capital*, Vol. III (1894)

Either Marx or his translator was careless because Marx assumed the rate to be a constant 5 percent. His example shows the *absolute amount* to accelerate, not the *rate*. Also, what about his estimate of 150 million globes? I suppose he used globe to mean the planet Earth (though I suppose he could have meant the small globes we have at home which children use for geography lessons). Even so, since he provided us with no data on the price of gold or the weight of the Earth (or the smaller globe), we have no way of verifying whether his calculations were right or wrong. Finally, what about "our" Saviour? I thought Marx was an atheist.

Marx's statement induced me to calculate how many dollars a penny would grow to if invested at a compound rate of 5 percent per year *from* the birth of Christ (not one year later) to the end of the twentieth century. How many years is it? Well, that's 2,001 years, not 2000. Right? That's why I multiplied 1.05 by itself 2,001 times. I did all this in seconds with my calculator (which I ask my graduate students to bring to class, always). This number popped up: 2.510657^{42}. Then I multiplied that huge number by .01 to convert pennies to dollars. This second number popped up: 2.510657^{40}. That's 2.510657 times 10 to the fortieth power, or 2.510657 with the decimal point shifted forty places to the right. Here it is:

$$\$25,106,570,000,000,000,000,000,000,000,000,000,000,000,000.$$

Can you read this number? I can't. It defies imagination. The lesson here is a simple one: Nothing grows at a constant compound rate forever. Actual growth for this world and everything in its is best described as a variant of the well known "Gompertz" curve: At birth things grow for a while at an increasing rate; next they reach a point of "inflection" to grow at a decreasing rate of increase, then flatten to a zero rate; and finally fall absolutely back to nothing, to death. That's the way things are; it's a fact of life and death. Investors often forget this, as we shall see. For now, just remember that Father Time demands that you draw the Gompertz life-death cycle not as a straight line, but like this:

PERCENT RATE OF GROWTH

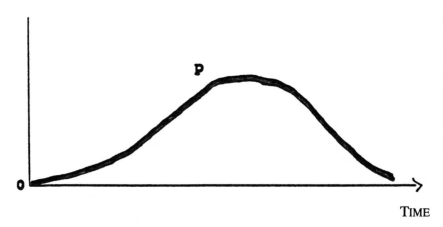

TIME

Do you see the "point of inflection" on the chart, the point I have marked with a P? That's where the percentage rate of increase stops accelerating and starts to slow. Have you passed the point of inflection?

Father Time is crucial to our analysis of fixed-income contracts. By fixed income, we mean debt contracts such as bills, notes, bonds, bank loans, and mortgages. Since every dollar borrowed is a dollar loaned, debt contracts can be called credit contracts. Debt is credit. They are identities—different sides of the same contract. Let's look into the arithmetic now of these debt (credit) instruments. The following is a classroom exchange that took place in the fall of 1981:

RH: Let's calculate what a penny would grow to in 2,001 years if invested at a 5 percent rate compounded each year. We'll break up the analysis into separate steps. Tell me first how much interest you could earn by investing one penny ($.01) for just one year at 5 percent.

S1: Multiply $.01 by .05. That gives you $.0005 interest.

RH: O.K. You started out with one penny ($.01) in principal, the original investment. You earned $.0005 in interest. So, your accumulated amount is $.0105 at the end of the first year.

$$\text{Principal} \times \% \text{ Rate} = \text{Interest for First Year}$$

$$\$.01 \quad \times \quad .05 \ = \qquad \$.0005$$

Original Principal $.01

+ Interest for First Year $.0005

= Accumulated Total $.0105

You earned $.0005 in interest for the first year. That's five ten-thousandths ($\frac{5}{10,000}$) of one dollar, or five one-hundredths ($\frac{5}{100}$) of one cent, which is one-twentieth ($\frac{1}{20}$) of one cent. Right? Now how much interest do you earn in the second year?

S1: Take the accumulated amount at the end of the first year of $.0105 and multiply by .05.

THE MIGHTY POWER OF INTEREST: FROM ACORNS TO GIANT OAK TREES

RH: Good. That works out to $.000525:

Accumulated Sum, x Rate = Interest for Second Year
End of First Year

$$\$.0105 \qquad \times \ .05 \ = \qquad \$.000525$$

and . . .

Accumulated Sum, End of First Year $.0105

+ Interest in the Second Year $.000525

= Accumulated Sum, End of Second Year $.011025

You can see that in the second year we earned (a) interest on the original penny, again in the amount of $.0005 plus (b) interest on interest, calculated by multiplying .05 by $.0005 the interest earned in the first year. That product is $.000025. That's not much interest on interest, is it? No, $.000025 is only 25 millionths of one dollar, or 25 ten-thousandths of one cent, or just one tiny piece of a penny chopped up into 400 parts (10,000 divided by 25 = 400).

(a) Interest Earned

    on Original Penny   .05 x $.01   = $.0005

(b) Interest on Interest   .05 x $.0005 = $.000025

(a) + (b) = Total Interest in Second Year = $.000525

That's enough of these calculations. I just wanted to illustrate that compounding interest on interest starts in the second year, though at a snail's pace. But it's interest-on-interest growth that leads inexorably to the rocketing numbers that numb the mind. Let's return to my original question. What would one penny grow to if invested at 5 percent compounded annually for 2001 years?

S2:   I get 2.510657 (40) on my HP 12C calculator.

RH: Now you know why we call compound interest the eighth wonder of the world. Let's reverse this. Suppose someone with an extremely high credit rating wanted to borrow money from you today at 5 percent annual interest with a promise to pay you back 2.510657^{40} dollars 2001 years from now? What would you pay today for that mind boggling pile of dollars due that far in the future?

S3:   One penny. That's the present value of that huge sum.

RH: How much would you lend to me?

S3:   Nothing. Your credit rating is too low. Nobody would lend you money at 5 percent for 2001 years.

RH: Nobody would lend me money at 5 percent, not when they can lend to the U.S. Treasury at 17 percent on ninety-day Treasury bills. *(Remember, this exchange took place in 1981, when the Treasury issued a twenty-year bond with a 15.75 percent coupon.)*

    So, we see that accumulated sum and present value are related. Let's take a more realistic, but still simple example. Governments have in the past issued bonds that have no maturity date. That means you never get the principal back. But these bonds promise to pay interest income forever. They are called perpetual bonds. Would anybody ever buy such a bond?

S3: Certainly. They would buy to get the interest stream.

RH: Good. Now, based on the following hypothetical data, how much would you pay for this perpetual government bond? Assume that you get $100 a year interest payable at the end of each year forever. Also assume that you are satisfied with a 10 percent return, and that the overall market requires a 10 percent return. Here are the data:

Contract (Coupon) Rate	10%
Promised Interest Stream	$100 a year forever
Market Rate (Required Return)	10%
Market Price	?

S4: $1,000?

RH: Good. The answer is $1,000. You can see that $1,000 invested at a 10 percent rate generates $100 interest each year, that .10 x $1,000 = $100. Though most bonds pay interest twice each year ($50 every six months in our example), for simplicity of calculation we're assuming one payment annually. So, the amount you would have to invest at 10 percent to get $100 interest a year payable at the end of each year is $1000, or $100 divided by .10. Thus:

$$\frac{\$100}{.10} = \$1,000$$

I'm also assuming a ready market for this bond. So you can always sell it on the market even though you can't get back your investment from the government. In the jargon of economists, the market price of $1,000 is the discounted value of the infinite interest stream of $100 a year discounted at the assumed 10 percent rate. Also, the 10 percent rate is often called the market rate or the current rate. It's the rate the overall market demands for lending money under similar circumstances.

The Contract Rate Versus the Market Rate

Make sure you never confuse the market rate with the individual contract rate on any one bond. We had no problem here because I assumed that the actual coupon rate on the bond is the same as that required by the market. Both are 10 percent, which would mean the bond would sell at $1000 on the market. But, assume now that for some reason the market rate of interest doubles to 20 percent. Further, assume that the same issuer has to borrow new money at the higher rate, and that the new bonds carrying a 20 percent contract rate are exactly the same quality as the old bonds with the 10 percent contract rate. What would you now pay for the old bond, the outstanding bond with the 10 percent coupon?

Contract Rate (Old Bond)	10%
Interest Stream (Old Bond)	$100 each year
Market Rate (Required Return)	20%
Market Price (Old Bond)	?

S5: It falls from $1,000 to $500.

RH: The "old" bond must be priced to yield a return competitive with that of the new bond. You can buy the new bond for $1000 and, with its 20 percent contract rate, get $200 a year interest. You can alternatively spend $1,000 for two old bonds priced at $500 each, and get $100 interest income on each of the two old bonds, for $200 total interest. Arbitragers will price the old bonds down to provide an identical return to the new bonds. Here are the numbers:

One New Bond	Two Old Bonds
Interest/Price	Interest/Price
$\frac{\$200}{\$1,000} = 20\%$	$\frac{\$100}{\$500} = 20\%$
	$\frac{\$100}{\$500} = 20\%$

Let's turn now to a different question. Did the rise in the market yield to 20 percent on the old bond cause the price to fall to $500, or did the fall in price cause the yield to rise? Which is cause and which is effect?

Market Yield on Old Bond   10%   to   20%
Market Price on Old Bond $1,000   to $500

S6:   The rise in yield caused the price to fall.

RH: Here we go again, round and round. You are in a circle. Don't you remember our discussion on price level changes and changes in the value of the dollar? We talked about identities. The same holds with interest yields and prices of fixed-income contracts. A rise in interest yields on already issued and outstanding debt contracts is the same thing as a fall in price. One is the other. It is only when we ask what pushes interest yields up (what pushes bond prices down) that we get into an analysis of cause and effect, into theory.

S6:   I don't understand. You just said that the old 10 percent coupon bond had to be priced down to $500 to yield a competitive return with the new 20 percent coupon bonds. So the higher market rate on the new bond *caused* the fall in price of the old bond. That's cause and effect, right?

RH: No, that's arbitrage within markets. The dictionary defines an arbitrager as someone who buys and sells essentially identical goods in different markets to profit from unequal prices. The law of one price tells us that identical products must command the same prices in competitive markets. In our example, two old bonds are identical to one new bond. Nobody would pay more than $500 for the old bond or more than $1000 for the new. But what about the answer to this one question I have expressed in two different ways:

Why did the market rate rise to 20 percent on the new bond?
Why did the market yield rise to 20 percent on the old bond?

Why? The answer involves theory. Here's a quick answer:

CAUSE	EFFECT
If D > S	+ Market Rate on New Bonds
where	
	(Arbitrage)
D = Credit Demand	+ Yield on Old Bonds
S = Credit Supply	− Price on Old Bonds

See that box on yield and price of the old bonds? Well, never look for theory inside the box. You won't find anything on cause and effect inside that box. Don't box yourself into circular reasoning.

CONFUSING ARITHMETICAL IDENTITIES
WITH INTEREST-RATE THEORY

All the box tells you is that yields and prices on already-issued and out-standing bonds move in opposite directions. That's the arithmetic of arbitrage, not theory. It's just as silly to say that higher yields *caused* the prices of the old bonds to fall as it is to say that the lower prices on the old bonds *caused* the yields to rise. Both statements are ludicrous. Both confuse sound theory with arithmetic identities, with arbitragers paying identical prices for identical goods.

Look for theory on the left-hand side of the cause-effect chart above. As illustrated there, the demand for credit D is assumed to have sped ahead of the supply of credit S. It was this excess of demand over supply that (a) *caused* the market rate of interest on new bonds to rise and (b) *caused* the yield on the old bonds to rise (the same thing as causing the price of the old bond to fall).

We have seen that a rise in the market yield from 10 percent to 20 percent on a perpetual bond would mean a 50 percent fall in its price, from $1,000 to $500. That's a big drop in price. Let's now consider bonds with finite matu-rities. We'll start with a short (one-year) maturity. Can anybody figure out how much a one-year 10 percent contract bond would fall in price, assuming the market climbs to 20 percent?

S7:   Not much. You have to wait only a year for your money.

RH: That's right. Let's illustrate by calculating the price of this one-year bond both before and after the market rate rises from 10 percent to 20 percent. How much would you pay today for a 10 percent coupon bond that promises you $100 in interest at the end of one year plus $1,000 in principal? Let's assume the market rate is now also 10 percent.

S7:   You would pay par, or $1,000.

RH: Of course. Let's show that by breaking up my question. First, what would you pay for the $100 in interest?

S7:   You would have to divide $100 by 1.10. That's $90.91.

RH: Good. The present value of $100 due one year hence is $90.91. Put an-other way, $90.91 invested at 10 percent for one year will grow to just $100 by the end of the year. That is 1.10 x $90.91 = $100.00. What would you pay for the principal sum you get at the end of one year?

S7:   Again, you divide by 1.10. You divide $1,000 by 1.10, and that gives you $909.09.

RH: You know the third step. We just add the two present values. Here it is:

Present Value of Interest	$(\frac{\$100}{1.10})$ =	$ 90.91
Present Value of Principal	$(\frac{\$1,000}{1.10})$ =	909.09
Total (rounded)		$1000.00

Suppose that market rates jump overnight to 20 percent, immediately after you bought the 10 percent coupon bond. What would happen to the market price of a 10 percent coupon bond with one year to maturity? Here are the results:

Present Value of Interest	$(\frac{\$100}{1.20})$ =	$ 83.33
Present Value of Principal	$(\frac{\$1,000}{1.20})$ =	833.33
Total (rounded up)		$916.67

Notice that this short-term bond fell in price to only $916.67. That's a percentage fall of only 8.33 percent. Do you recall what happened to our perpetual bond when the market rate doubled from 10 percent to 20 percent? Its price plummeted 50 percent. So, if you believed interest rates were headed up, would you invest in long- or short-term bonds?

S8: Short term. The shorter the better. Instead of buying one-year maturities, you'd be better off buying short-term bills maturing in thirty days or so. Then you could quickly reinvest at higher rates. And you wouldn't be hit with big price declines.

RH: Excellent. Let's look at what we have learned:

> The longer the maturity of any given fixed-income contract, other things being equal, the greater will be the percentage change in its price for any given percentage change in the market rate of interest.

Let's illustrate this for a ten year-bond with a 10 percent coupon. What happens to its price when the market rate rises from 10 percent to 20 percent? Here are the calculations:

PRESENT VALUE (PV) TABLE FOR A TEN-YEAR BOND
WITH A 10% COUPON

	10% Market Interest Rate		20% Market Interest Rate	
Year	PV of $1	PV of $100 Annual Interest	PV of $1	PV of $100 Annual Interest
1	$.9091	$ 90.91	$.8333	$ 83.33
2	.8264	82.64	.6944	69.44
3	.7513	75.13	.5787	57.87
4	.6830	68.30	.4823	48.23
5	.6209	62.09	.4019	40.19
6	.5645	56.45	.3349	33.49
7	.5132	51.32	.2791	27.91
8	.4665	46.65	.2326	23.26
9	.4241	42.41	.1938	19.38
10	.3855	38.55	.1615	16.15
		$ 614.45		$419.25
(a) PV, Interest		$ 614.46		$419.25
(b) PV, Principal		385.54		161.51
Price (a + b)		$1000.00	(Rounded)	$580.76

You can recognize some of the numbers in this table. For example, we earlier calculated the present value of $100 at a 10 percent market rate at $90.91. That number of $90.91 shows up at the top of the third column, directly under PV of $100. If you look now at the last column, you can calculate the market price of a ten year bond with a 10 percent coupon when market rates are at 20 percent. The present value of the interest stream ($100 a year for ten years) is $419.25. Let's illustrate how we got that number with a couple of calculations. For example, to calculate the present value of the $100 of interest due at the end of the first year, you simply divide by 1.20, which is the same as multiplying by .8333. Thus .8333 x $100 = $83.33. Similarly, the present value of $100 for the second year is the same as dividing by 1.44. The 1.44 is 1.2 multiplied by itself. Dividing by 1.44 is the same as multiplying by .6944, the present value number also shown in the table. So, $100 x .6994 = $69.44.

By making similar present-value calculations for the other eight years, you can then total up the interest column, which comes to $419.25. You could get that figure at a glance by looking it up in a table, but I wanted to make sure you understand where these numbers come from. The present value of the $1,000 principal is shown as $161.50. The sum of the present values of both interest and principal is $580.75. That's the price of the bond:

PV of Interest Stream	$419.25
PV of Principal	161.50
Total	$580.75

Notice that the ten-year bond fell almost as much as the perpetual bond. Let's calculate what would happen to the price of a twenty-year bond with a 10 percent coupon if the market rate should rise from 10 percent to 20 percent. (Prove to yourself that the answer is $513.04.) Here are the price changes with a rise in the market rate of interest from 10 percent to 20 percent:

One Year Bond	$1,000 to $916.66
Ten Year Bond	$1,000 to $580.75
Twenty Year Bond	$1,000 to $513.04
Perpetual Bond	$1,000 to $500.00

Again, you see that the longer the maturity, the greater will be the percentage price swing for any given change in interest rates. Of course, this works both ways. If interest rates should drop, bond prices will rise, and the longer maturities will rise the most in price. So, maturity is important. Even more important is the *duration of* a bond, a concept we shall return to later.

FIXED-INCOME PARROTS AND PROS:
A WOR RADIO REVIEW

You may recall that in 1981, monetary constriction and soaring interest rates "crowded out" consumer and business financing. The developments then under way signaled a blockbuster recession ahead, a prospect that turned me into a giant bull on long bonds in July 1981 (see Appendix A, Forecast 23). Not often recognized, the recession posed high risk to those who remained invested in short-term Treasury bills, money market funds, and other fixed-income contracts with near-term maturities. With that in mind, listen in to my exchange with WOR's Bernard Meltzer (BM) on Saturday November 28, 1981,* when interest rates were still close to post-World War II peaks:

BM: What would you advise my radio audience about money-market funds, Treasury bills, and other short-term money-market instruments? Treasury bills have been yielding about 16 percent, a spectacular return. Some of the money-market mutual funds are advertising even higher returns.

RH: Bernard, I was your guest a little over a month ago, on Saturday, October 24. Short-term rates were even higher then. I have the same advice now as then: *Get out!* This is no time to be rolling bills.

BM: Rolling bills?

RH: Yes, that's an expression institutional investors use. They invest in short-term bills when they expect interest rates to rise. So every few months they reinvest the proceeds of maturing bills into new short-term bills. They "roll over" their bills. You can greatly increase your investment income that way provided interest rates head higher and higher.

BM: But when interest rates are expected to head down, should investors do the opposite?

RH: Exactly. Investors should then go long. They should get out of bills. They should lock up high-yielding long Treasury bonds and corporate bonds. The recession is going to mean a sharp decline in interest rates ahead. If you are invested in long, high quality bonds, you would profit from big price advances as rates fall. But heaven help you if you stay in short-term bills. You will end up reinvesting at lower and lower interest rates. I think short-term rates are headed down from the present stratosphere to 6 percent. That will mean a massive loss of income for those who stay invested in short-term instruments. So beware the hucksters.

BM: Hucksters?

RH: Yes. Major Wall Street houses continue to push their retail or individual clients into money market mutual funds. The registered representatives or brokers (RRs) are having a field day in selling these funds. Given the spectacular current yields, that's not unlike taking candy from a baby. What an easy sell! What truly angers me is the RR pitch that short-term investments like Treasury bills are riskless. Risk is not

---

*Quoted with permission.

restricted simply to capital loss, the possible loss of principal. Risk also includes the possible loss of income, something the RR keeps quiet about. The high-yield money funds are now at high risk. If you stay in high-yielding, short-term mutual funds initially yielding 20 percent, plunging rates could reduce that return to 6 percent or 7 percent or lower. That will mean a massive loss of income. The same holds for Treasury bills. So, contrary to wide misunderstanding and unending Pro and Parrot talk, there is no such thing as a riskless investment.

BM: To be fair, you could be wrong in your forecast.

RH: Yes. I could also be charitable and assume that all of this advice from major Wall Street firms is based on their own naivete, their own lack of understanding. Yes, there are Parrots, the naive counselors. They abound on Wall [Street]. But many Wall Street houses knowingly push their retail investors into short-term money market funds at the same time that they advise institutional clients to invest in long bonds. That's discriminatory and dishonest. These are the Pros, despicable intellectual prostitutes.

BM: I have always believed that the little investor gets a bad shake from Wall Street. Wall Street RRs are salesman first and foremost. Would you agree?

RH: There are exceptions to every rule, but the typical RR is primarily a salesman, and is interested in his own commission flow. That's why he's still pushing stocks this late in the game.

BM: But the fall in interest rates would help stocks.

RH: The recession will clobber corporate earnings. Lower interest rates would help stocks, but the plunge in earnings will more than offset lower interest rates.

BM: That means investors should reduce equity holdings?

RH: They should get out of stocks, get out of money market funds, and get into long Treasuries.

We noted here just two risks of fixed-income contracts: income risk and capital (price) risk. We now turn to other key risks the Parrots and the Pros seldom tell you about.

9

Parrot Talk on Interest Rates and the Money and Capital Markets

"The cause of lightning," Alice said decidedly, for she felt
quite sure about this, "is the thunder—no, no!" she corrected herself, "I meant the other way."

Lewis Carroll, *Through the Looking Glass*

The lightning came first. The thunder followed, caused by the sudden heat-
ing and expansion of the air along the path of the electrical discharge. Right?
Well, is it also possible that heavenly forces not completely understood (the
causes) produced both the lightning and the thunder (the effects)? Am I be-
laboring the danger of confusing cause and effect? No! We have barely
scratched the surface of error in fixed-income theory. To see why, please join
me in an exchange with students and money managers. Be careful in walking through the theoretical thicket ahead.

RH: Glance first at this chart.

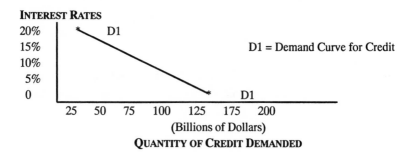

132

As you can see, the plots represent our hypothetical demand curve for credit. The vertical axis represents interest rates, and the horizontal axis the quantity of credit demanded. While the numbers are fictional, the shape of the demand curve does describe borrowing behavior. As you can see, the curve slopes downward from left to right. People generally borrow more money at lower interest rates than at higher interest rates, other things equal. Why?

S1:   Because people will demand more at lower rates than at higher rates. That's because rates are cheaper.

ARGUMENT BY DEFINITION: CONFUSING ARITHMETIC WITH THEORY

RH: Wait a minute. You used the word *because* two times. But the chart is purely descriptive: it defines what people generally do; it doesn't tell us why they do what they do. What I said and what the chart says is that people tend to borrow more money at lower rates than at higher rates. What about my question? Why is the demand curve downward sloped? My question is, why?

Ss: (Silence.)

RH: Let's narrow the question down. Why do businessmen, for example, borrow more at lower rates?

S2:   Because the lower the rate, the lower the cost, and the higher would be expected profits.

RH: Now we're getting somewhere. Businessmen treat interest as a cost of doing business. Interest payments made to attract and retain debt capital are no different from wages and salaries, rents, and the expenditures for supplies, among other costs. The lower the interest costs, other things being equal, the greater would be expected profits. Also, lower interest rates mean a lower *cost of capital* (lower required investment return) for business. A lower required investment return translates into a higher present value for a future stream of profits, and could spur additional investment. That's something we shall explore in depth when we get to stock valuation theory, practice, and malpractice. Now, what about the consumer? Why does he borrow more at lower rates?

S3:   You assigned Irving Fisher to us. He said that consumers would rather consume more now than later. If interest rates are extremely high, the consumer has to pay back more in interest if he borrows now to consume now. Also, with high interest rates, the consumer can earn a lot of interest by saving.

RH: Good. Consumers typically save more with higher interest rates, other things being equal. But other things are not always equal, as we shall see. Still, Fisher's view is that people on average tend to save more at higher rates than at lower rates; they consume more at lower rates than at higher rates. But why? I'll answer the question.

THE "PURE" RATE COMPONENT OF THE INTEREST RATE

According to Fisher, consumers demand a reward in the form of interest for deferring present consumption for future consumption. They want to be paid interest to get their money back, even when they perceive no specific risk of loss. They demand a reward for waiting, which economists dub the *pure* component of the interest rate. That's what is meant by Fisherian *time-preference theory*. A complete theory of interest involves a lot more than time preference. But for now, let's concentrate on the demand for credit. Please study this second chart:

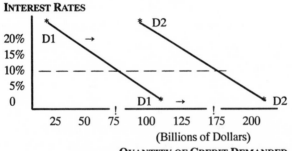

CHANGES IN THE DEMAND FOR CREDIT (SHIFTS IN CURVE)

Note that I have added a second expression at the bottom of the chart. It now reads "Quantity of Credit Demanded" and "Changes in the Demand for Credit." The two expressions sound almost identical, but they have entirely different meanings. The first expression refers to movements along the demand curve, a matter of elasticity of demand. The second refers to shifts in the demand curve, a movement of the whole curve to the left or the right. Don't confuse one with the other.

For example, suppose that the whole demand curve shifts to the right, from D1 to D2. That would mean borrowers are now willing to borrow more money at the same rate, or the same amount of money at a higher rate, or somewhat more money at somewhat higher rates. For example, they might want to borrow about $175 billion instead of about $75 billion at 10 percent, as depicted by the shift to D2.

We can see now what is meant exactly by a shift of the demand schedule to the right, which is "an increase in the demand for credit." That's a matter of definition. But let me ask now what would *cause* the demand schedule to shift to the right? What explains an "increase in the demand for credit"?

S6:   Expectations of faster inflation?

S7:   A pickup in the growth of the economy? Maybe business steps up its expansion by buying new plant and equipment, or consumers go on a spending spree. Any of these would probably result in increased borrowing.

RH: Good. Let's illustrate a shift in the demand schedule to the right but assume also that the supply schedule of loanable funds remains unchanged:

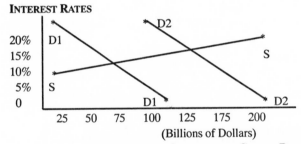

CHANGES IN THE QUANTITY OF CREDIT DEMANDED
CHANGES IN THE DEMAND FOR CREDIT

I have drawn in a supply schedule, and marked that S. Note that S slopes up from left to right, indicating that lenders are willing to lend more money at higher rates than at lower rates. That's just the opposite of the slope of demand schedules. The Federal Reserve has a tremendous influence on the supply of credit, but let's not get into that now. For now, what happens to interest rates as the demand for credit increases while the supply schedule for credit remains unchanged?

S7:   Interest rates rise. In the chart, rates look like they climb from about 12 percent to 15 percent.

RH: Yes, you can see that in the intersection of the two demand curves with the one supply curve. The intersections take place at about 12% and 15%. The chart depicts the increase in the demand for credit as a shift in the demand curve from D1 to D2. The new 15% rate is called an equilibrium rate. Any rate below 15% would mean more funds are demanded by borrowers than offered, and rates would rise to 15%. Any rate above 15% would mean that more funds are supplied than demanded, and rates would fall back toward 15%.

ELASTICITY OF DEMAND: A SNAPSHOT WITH EVERYTHING FROZEN

RH: It's extremely important to distinguish between movement along any one demand schedule, and shifts in that schedule. When you analyze any given schedule, you are taking a snapshot at one instant in time. That means income, growth, tastes, inflation, expectations, and everything else are assumed fixed, or "frozen." All the snapshot tells you is that people borrow more money at lower rates than at higher rates, other things being equal (frozen). That's demand elasticity. But a shift of the entire demand schedule means an increase or decrease in demand resulting from changes in income, tastes, growth, and so on.

A Circular Argument

RH: Would you say, other things being equal, that a huge increase in the demand for credit would lift interest rates?

S1: Yes, other things being equal, interest rates would soar.

RH: If interest rates were to soar, would this not cause a steep fall in the demand for credit, assuming all other things are equal?

S1: Yes.

RH: Then, other things being equal, the fall in the demand for credit would push interest rates back down again?

S1: Yes.

RH: So a steep decline in interest rates would, other things being equal, cause a huge increase in the demand for credit?

S1: Well . . . yes.

RH: And again, other things being equal, a huge increase in the demand for credit would lift interest rates. Isn't that what you said in answer to my very first question?

S1: I'm back where I started.

RH: I am glad you said that. Yes, you *are* in one big circle:

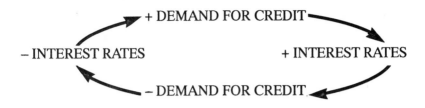

Parrot Circle: Confusing Demand Elasticity with Shifts

RH: I call this a Parrot circle, meaning that Parrots can never find their way out of the circle. To repeat: if you define an increase in the demand for credit correctly as a shift in the schedule to the right, then any increase in demand will lift interest rates to a new and higher level. Interest rates will rise to the new and higher equilibrium level, and stay there. This assumes, of course, no further changes in either the demand for or the supply of credit. So, you're out of the circle. Now appraise this statement:

> Don't worry about recession clobbering home building. Decidedly lower rates on home mortgages guarantee a rebound in borrowing for construction of new housing and related consumer spending on furniture, rugs, appliances, and other durable consumer goods.

S2: Strike out the word "guarantee." There are none.

RH: Good. What else?

S3: The demand for credit might shift to the left.

RH: Yes, but why?

S4: You could lose your job and your income in a recession. You would not be in the market for a house then.

RH: Excellent. We could show this on the chart.

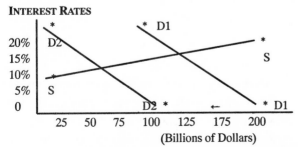

(Billions of Dollars)

CHANGES IN THE QUANTITY OF CREDIT DEMANDED
CHANGES IN THE DEMAND FOR CREDIT

Just reverse the arrows and the Ds. Here's the way we would properly read the chart: The recession-induced "decrease in the demand for credit" (shift in schedule to the left as jobs and income fall) more than offsets the "increase in the quantity of credit demanded" as a result of lower rates. The result could be a fall in home buying and building.

Parrot Circles Versus Fed Circles

RH: The parrot circle is a first cousin to the idiocy circle involved in Federal Reserve targeting of interest rates (see chapter 5). But there's a big difference. As we saw, Fed targeting of interest rates did in fact result in major disruptive fluctuations in the demand for and supply of funds, and violent swings in interest rates. These were real swings put into motion by confused central bankers who would constrict in time of weakness and stimulate in time of boom. We labeled those actions *procyclical,* which means making a bad situation worse.

      The Parrot circle, which is just as deadly, is basically a matter of confusing basic economic concepts. The Parrots fail to distinguish between demand elasticity and shifts in the demand schedule. Parrots, including many of Wall Street's forecasters, were perplexed to find that housing recovered slowly from the 1990–91 recession despite the precipitous fall in interest rates, including mortgage rates. They overemphasized the stimulus of lower interest rates and underemphasized the depressants of income and job losses. Don't you make that mistake.

Back to *Ex Post* and *Ex Ante* Concepts

RH: Let's turn now to another common fallacy. Look at the exhibit I have handed out to you entitled Total Net Borrowing and Lending in Credit Markets. You can see that total net borrowing in 1989 amounted to $971 billion. So what was total net lending?

S2:   It shows up at $971 billion, the same number.

RH: Of course. These numbers are ex post identities, which we discussed earlier (chapter 7). So don't confuse these reported data with estimates of the demand for and supply of credit in the money and capital markets. To drive the point home, look at these data from the Federal Reserve flow-of-funds account on total net borrowing by consumers, business, and governments from 1982 to 1992 (in billions of dollars):

1982	$ 519	1986	$1,228	1990	$876
1983	678	1987	986	1991	$614
1984	936	1988	994	1992	$824
1985	1,094	1989	971		

The grand total borrowed over the 1982–89 period amounted to a colossal $7.406 trillion. So, what do you think happened to interest rates over the same 1982–89 period? Keep in mind that this represented the biggest explosion in borrowing for a sustained period in U.S. history.

S3:   Interest rates went way up?

RH: Yours is the answer I receive nine out of ten times. No, they came way down. So we know that despite skyrocketing credit demand, the supply of credit must have advanced at an even faster pace. But you would never know that by looking at the *ex post* identities on net borrowing and net lending. Often these data are labeled demand and supply by Wall Street firms, with confusion being the obvious result. Don't confuse identities with supply and demand.

THE "YIELD SPREAD" APPROACH TO INTEREST-RATE FORECASTING

RH: Let's turn now to another analytical tool that can help to explain fluctuations in interest rates *when used in conjunction with other tools.* I am speaking of yield spreads and yield curves. Let's look at the difference in yields on short-term versus long-term U.S. Treasury instruments, which can be useful—if properly interpreted—in signaling the prospects ahead for the economy and for interest rates. One of the most dramatic instances occurred in 1981. Interest rates soared across the board in 1981, and short-term rates climbed higher than long-term rates (Exhibit 9–1). What should private investors (lenders) have done then?

S4:   Lenders should have locked up yields on long bonds while the yields were super high.

RH: Yes, but what about borrowers? What should corporate borrowers have done?

S4:   Borrow short term.

RH: Of course. Private borrowers should have been extremely wary of locking themselves into twenty- or thirty-year corporate debt with interest rates at 17 percent and 18 percent. Many businesses strapped for cash resorted instead to borrowing through the commercial paper market. Smart arbitragers borrowed short-term money, invested the proceeds in long bonds, and enjoyed huge price gains on the bonds once interest rates did fall. So, if interest rates are sky high and expected to fall, what do you ideally do?

S5:   Borrow short, lend long.

RH: Great. Let's examine yield curves in greater depth. Here's the way the yield curve looked in 1981:

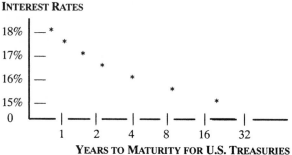

"INVERTED" YIELD CURVE IN LATE 1981

We already know that nominal interest rates in 1981 were extremely high, both short-term and long-term, and the yield curve was inverted, or downsweeping. That meant short-term rates were higher than intermediate-term rates, which were in turn higher than long-term rates. But how do market expectations and actions explain the shape of the yield curve?

S6:   The market expects rates to fall. It's looking for falling inflation and economic slowdown or recession.

RH: Yes, but you have yet to explain what determines the slope. The explanation is simple. You have to stress, consistent with the expectations theory, that the relative pressure of demand was in the short end of the market and that lenders channeled a greater supply of funds, again relatively speaking, to the long end. So, the demand and supply pressures operating together pushed short-term rates above long-term rates. Now, compare 1981 with the yield curve in the early 1930s.

UPSWEEPING YIELD CURVE IN THE GREAT DEPRESSION

INTEREST RATES

```
3% |—
                                    *
2% |—                        *
                       *
1% |—         *
        *
 0 └── |— |— |— |— | — | ——
        1  2  4  8  16  32
```

YEARS TO MATURITY FOR U.S. TREASURIES

We can see from this chart that nominal interest rates in the early years of the Great Depression were extremely low, both short-term and long-term. The yield curve was upsweeping, or rising from the southwest to the northeast part of the chart. That meant short-term rates were lower than intermediate-term rates, which were in turn lower than long-term rates. Again, consistent with the expectations theory of the shape of the yield curve, borrowers and lenders generally expected interest rates to rise. How should investors have behaved in the early 1930s, knowing in retrospect what happened? Should they have purchased short-term bills or long-term bonds?

S6:   Short term. You didn't want to get locked into long-term bonds, not if you expected rates to go up. You would have preferred to "roll your bills," as they matured, into higher and higher yields as rates rose.

RH: Excellent. And how about borrowers?

S6:   Corporations should have borrowed all they could have, and long term.

RH: Exactly. As borrowers, they should have locked in long-term money at low rates. Money was cheap. So, if rates are deemed low, and expected to rise for a sustained period, what do you do?

S6:   Borrow long, lend short!

RH: So, the prescription then, in the 1930s, was just the opposite of what you ideally would have done in 1981. These two instances represent two extremes in U.S. financial history. Again, you can see that expectations help to explain the shape of the yield curve. The relative pressure of borrowing in the 1930s was in the long end of the market. At the same time, lenders were channeling a greater supply of funds, again relatively speaking, to the short end of the market. The two forces working together helped to explain the upsweeping yield curve, with long rates above short rates.

Sometimes expectations are way off the mark. Like the stock market, the fixed-income market can be wrong! I'll note several examples here. In the late 1970s and early 1980s, as we know, interest rates soared far beyond market anticipations, and far beyond that signaled by the upsweeping yield curve. One major group of financial institutions failed completely to anticipate the sharp rise in interest rates. They got into deep trouble. Do you know who I have in mind?

S7:   The savings and loan associations and savings banks.

RH: Exactly. They are also called thrifts. They had invested long and borrowed short. But then, calamity of calamities, interest rates shot up across the board, and climbed to record levels by 1981. Short rates climbed more than long, and the yield curve inverted. Their cost of funds, the interest they had to pay depositors, climbed higher and higher, and then exceeded the incomes they earned on their mortgage portfolios. That spelled massive red ink. Depositors pulled their money out of the thrifts, and invested instead in high-yielding money market instruments, like Treasury bills, and in the money market funds. Do you remember what that was called?

S8:   Disintermediation?

RH: Yes. That's a mouthful. The thrifts suffered a hemorrhage of red ink, and many ended up in bankruptcy. At the time, I referred to the mortgage portfolio of the thrifts as icebergs, meaning that most of their portfolios were under water. With the swift rise in interest rates, the market value of the iceberg mortgage portfolios sank way below the book value of the mortgages, and below even the claims of depositors. To repeat, thrift managers failed completely to anticipate that yields would soar (possibly due to inflationary government policies) and that the yield curve would—horror of horrors—invert.

Let me turn now to my second example, and lighten this conversation. On July 9, 1981, I sent a report to all of my institutional clients recommending that they make massive commitments to long prime bonds (Appendix B). I was convinced we were headed for recession, and pointed out the inversion of the yield curve. So, what happened?

S7:   Rates went up instead?

RH: Yes, across the board. The entire yield curve shifted upward. I was a couple of months early in timing, and some of my institutional clients were upset. Fortunately, for me at least, yields did fall swiftly by late 1981 and 1982, and long-bond prices soared. Even so, let me stress that nobody can time exactly just when rates may turn. The yield curve may help you to look ahead *provided that market expectations are correct.* But you can never be sure because the yield curve is nothing more than an echo of the expectations of the overall market. *The market can be wrong and the market can be early.*

S7:   Where did you go wrong?

RH: I was a little early. I underestimated the spillover of the inflationary fury into the recession. Also, credit demands soared beyond my expectation. Business had to borrow in the short-term markets as sales evaporated and inventories piled up. Still, the fundamental and advance factors at work—e.g., excessive Federal Reserve tightening and fast weakening of the forward indicators—persuaded me that recession lay straight ahead (see chapter 6). That's what I forecast, and that's what happened.

The 1990–93 Consensus Strikeout on Yield Curves

Let's turn now to a most incredible period of subsophomoric interpretation of yield curves, namely, the period from late 1990 to October 1993. We are all fallible in peering into the future, but I did find it amazing that so many of the biggest and the brightest and the best could have been so wrong for so long. Over this entire period the curve was upsweeping, accurately reflecting expectations of higher interest rates. But the expectations proved wrong. The market was wrong, dead wrong. Rates collapsed instead of rising (see Exhibit 9–1). The Fed was wrong in shouting wolf on inflation, and the giant consensus of both institutional investors, corporate controllers, and economists on Wall Street and Washington was far off base (see Appendix A, Forecasts 64 through 83).

How could so many have been so wrong for so long? The answer is that they understated the great credit and money implosion (contraction) of 1990–93 and the lagged but powerful disinflation (the slow pace) of that implosion. They understated capital, credit, monetary, and fiscal constriction and the lagged disinflationary impact of that constriction. They understated fiscal and monetary constriction abroad, and its lagged impact on lower inflation and interest rates. They grievously misread the meaning behind steeply upsweeping yield curves. Yes, the upsweeping yield curves in 1990, 1991, and 1992 did precisely reflect the expectations of fixed-income managers of accelerating inflation and higher interest rates. But those expectations proved wrong, dead wrong, at least until October 1993.

Then all hell broke loose. From October 1993 into mid-1994 yields skyrocketed on long bonds both here and in other major industrial nations, bankrupting many investors. They soared despite continued disinflation and weak growth abroad in response to extreme fears of inflation. The Fed, I argued repeatedly, helped to fan inflation fears by its repeated wolf-call warnings. Fed Governor Wayne Angell was the worst of the lot on this score. Then in 1994, the Fed lifted short-term rates with the idea that long-term rates would come down. Their bet was that the market would interpret its actions as counter-inflationary and that long rates would cool down. Instead they soared. Inflation fears dominated 1994 even as actual inflation slowed. In contrast, the disinflation fundamentals dominated in 1995, and interest rates fell.

There are two lessons worth repeating from this chapter. The first is to be wary of consensus expectations. The second, a theme running throughout this book, is to recognize that there has never been and there never will be a single and consistently reliable economic indicator of the future. That includes yield curves. They can deceive, too, a fact of life that has yet to be documented in the refereed journals of finance or even in the most recent textbooks on investments and the money and capital markets. Yes, just as the market can be wrong on stocks, it can be wrong in the fixed-income markets, too. Why? Well, one problem is the inability of anyone to separate psychology from fundamentals, especially for short-run swings. We'll have a lot more to say about just what "fundamental" means when we review stock valuation models for the United States and Japan (chapters 16 and 17).

We turn now to best-selling books on how you can get rich without taking risk. With the theoretical tools we have developed, we should now be able to identify the hucksters, including economists, who say they can exorcise pressure and insecurity from your dreams. Really?

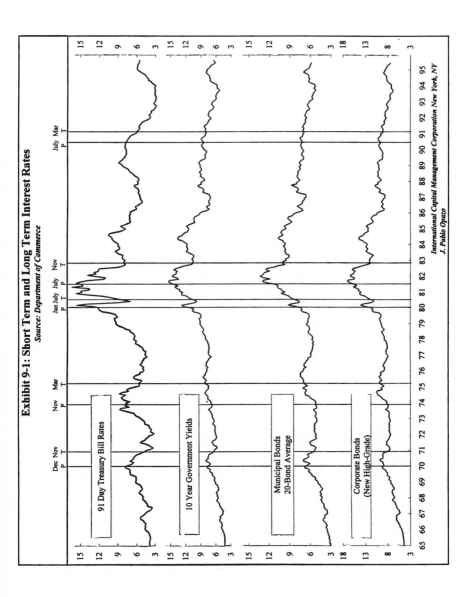

Exhibit 9-1: Short Term and Long Term Interest Rates
Source: Department of Commerce

10

Anatomy of Interest Rates

Huckster Hash on Wealth without Risk

> Thirty-Four Dishonest Tricks Which Are Commonly Used
> in Argument, with the Methods of Overcoming Them . . .
> (29) *Ambiguity, vagueness, or meaninglessness in the terms
> used in the argument.* Dealt with by continually demanding
> explanation until the terms become clear, or by proffering
> such explanation yourself and asking your opponent if that
> is what he means, then going over the argument again with
> the terms clarified. With a persistently confused thinker
> this remedy may be useless; nothing will drive him to think
> clearly. The only remedy is not to argue with him.
>
> Robert H. Thouless, *How to Think Straight,*
> *The Technique of Applying Logic*
> *Instead of Emotion* (1947)*

Before meeting the wealth-without-risk intellectual harlots, we must brush up
on the theory of fixed-income contracts. We must brush away the ambiguities
attached to financial jargon. So, please join me in this exchange on the fixed-
income cobwebs of the mind, on the meaninglessness of terms described in
Thouless's "Dishonest Trick Number 29." Keep in mind that the following
conversation with graduate finance students took place in the fall of 1987:

RH: Risk is everywhere and always. That's true for long-maturity corporate
     junk bonds, at one extreme, and short-term U.S. Treasury bills, at the

---

*New York: Simon and Schuster, p. 178.

other. Eleven types of risk found in fixed-income contracts must command our attention. Count them: credit risk, inflation risk, capital risk, reinvestment risk, liquidity risk, marketability risk, pure-rate risk, call risk, event risk, prepayment risk, and exchange-rate risk. I warn you that analysis in the fixed-income area is universally sloppy. The terms are slippery. So hesitate before you answer my questions. Beware the traps ahead.

Let's look at the real rate first. Nominal (or market) rates are in current dollars. Real rates (which are lower) are nominal rates adjusted for inflation. The link between nominal rates and real rates is the inflation rate. In the examples that follow, be alert to the difference between past and expected rates of inflation. Using past rates of inflation is no option. Focus on the expected rate of inflation if you want to avoid needless error. Also, always ask yourself whether you agree with the market's expectation. The market can become wild, irrational; you might have the better judgment based on good data and sound theory. Sound theory is a must, which is one reason we reviewed the fundamentals of economic forecasting (see chapters 1–3) and interest-rate forecasting (see chapter 9).

The examples we shall pursue are extreme. If you get into the habit of thinking in extremes, you'll see that the underlying principles are easier to understand. Let's illustrate. Consider this extreme hypothical example, which assumes purely hypothetical data: *Assuming actual and expected inflation at a 100 percent annual rate and a required real return of 3 percent, what would you demand as a minimum nominal contract rate on a one-year bond priced at par, at $1,000?*

S1:   The rule is that you must add to the real rate the expected increase in inflation. So, a 3 percent real return plus 100 percent inflation is 103 percent. You need a 103 percent coupon.

RH: No. I said to be careful. I warned you.

S1:   The text says to add the inflation rate to the real rate to calculate the nominal rate.*

RH: Yes, and your text also says that's a rough answer. In our example it is way off. Why?

Ss: (No Response.)

---

*David Kidwell, Richard Peterson, and David Blackwell, *Financial Institutions, Markets, and Money* (New York: The Dryden Press, 1993), p. 140.

DEFLATING BOTH PRINCIPAL AND INTEREST

RH: Let's show that the 103 percent nominal rate is too low. First, glance at these numbers:

	Principal	Interest (103%)	Total
Current Dollars	$1,000	+ $1,030 =	$2,030
Price Index (Current)	2.0	2.0	2.0
Deflated Dollars	$500	+ $515 =	$1,015

Remember our earlier discussion on converting nominal dollars into inflation-adjusted dollars (see chapter 7)? All we did was divide nominal dollars by the appropriate price index. Economists call this procedure *deflating,* which measures just how much a nominal dollar will buy in real terms once inflation is taken into account. We'll use 1.0 as the price index for the base period and 2.0 for the current period, one year later, to represent 100 percent annual inflation. In our exhibit, we have assumed also a 103 percent coupon. We'll calculate the real interest return by deflating the moneys we get back on the bond for both principal and interest. You see that we get back in deflated dollars only $1,015, just $15 more than our original investment of $1,000. That's a 1.5 percent return, not 3 percent. Right?

S1: Yes. The text ought to junk the rough formula.

RH: I agree. The correct answer is a 106 percent coupon:

	Principal	Interest (106%)	Total
Current Dollars	$1,000	+ $1,060 =	$2,060
Price Index (Current)	2.0	2.0	2.0
Real Dollars	$500	+ $530 =	$1,030

You can see that you get back $1030 in real dollars for a 3 percent *real* investment return over your initial investment of $1,000. To get a 3 percent real return you need a 106 percent (not 103 percent) rate with 100 percent inflation. Here's the correct formula:

$$
\begin{array}{ccccccl}
N & = & R & + & I & + & IR \\
106\% & = & 3\% & + & 100\% & + & (100\%)(3\%) \\
106\% & = & 3\% & + & 100\% & + & 3\%
\end{array}
$$

I don't expect you to memorize any formulas, but I do expect you to understand. In this case, the correct required coupon of 106 percent is the sum of the required real rate R of 3 percent plus the inflation rate I of 100 percent plus IR of 3 percent. Now, what is IR?

S2: The inflation rate times the required real rate.

RH: Yes, we can't leave IR out. It's easy to see that you must recover your principal and get back additional dollars to offset the loss of real buying power of principal from inflation. But you must also get back your interest and the additional dollars to offset the effect of inflation on interest, which is IR. You can see that in these data:

$1,000 to recover principal in nominal terms
+ $1,000 to offset inflation impact on principal
+ $30 to recover nominal interest of 3 percent
+ $30 to offset inflation impact on interest (IR)

The formula $N = R + I + IR$ holds no matter what the time span involved. Prove that to yourself by assuming a two-year contract with 100 percent inflation each year. Now let's broaden this analysis. Here are two examples from recent history. The first takes place in 1981. Do you remember what the top coupon was on a long Treasury bond?

S3: 15.75 percent. You mentioned it often enough. Inflation was soaring, just when President Reagan took office.

RH: Yes, we reviewed that period earlier (see chapter 6). I had forecast recession in July 1981, and tried to get anybody who would listen to load up on long Treasuries. That experience is a good case study of the importance of the expected rate of inflation. The point is that the expectations of the consensus were far too high. Let's illustrate with a long Treasury bond then yielding 15 percent. With a 3 percent required real return, what was the implied inflation rate? What did that imply for a consensus expectation of inflation?

S3: Well, the expected rate of inflation would be about 12 percent. The real rate of 3 percent plus inflation add up to the 15 percent market yield. Roughly, as you say!

RH: Roughly, as I said. Actually, the rate calculated as an approximation and the rate calculated exactly are close in this instance. It's only when inflation soars *à la Brazil* that you get into big differences. Even so, for somebody making investments in millions of dollars, a fraction of a percentage point can be important. If you really demanded a 3 percent required real return and expected 12 percent inflation, your required nominal rate would be higher, at 15.36 percent. (Prove that to yourself.) Now, what's the wild card? It's not the difference in the rough and the more precisely calculated real rate.

S4:   The wild card is expected inflation. It can be far off.

(Yes indeed. To see just how far off, let's jump in time from the 1980s to exchanges I had in the 1990s.)

RH: We know now that consensus expectations of inflation in 1980 and 1981 proved to be far too high. Also, the real rate calculated as the nominal rate less current inflation was too high, far too high. Current inflation, to repeat, may have little to do with future inflation. Many economists in 1981 forecast that interest rates on long Treasury bonds would rise above 20 percent. They looked for boom and accelerating inflation. Instead we got recession followed by disinflation and plunging rates. Consumer price inflation fell from 12.5 percent in 1981 to 1.1 percent in 1986, averaged about 4.5 percent in 1987–89, and about 3 percent by 1993 into 1995. Yields on long Treasury bonds fell below 8 percent by 1986–87, and below 6 percent by mid-1993.

Market Psychology Versus Fundamental Theory and Data

RH: In late 1993 and 1994, though, market psychology and fear of inflation took over. Rates soared, bankrupting some financial institutions, even as the fundamental disinflationary forces remained firmly on track. Yes, economic forecasters and money managers were bombed out in 1994. In 1995, though, the fundamental disinflationary forces regained dominance over misplaced inflation fears, and long-term interest rates resumed their fall.

Over this entire period from late 1990 well into 1995 I counted and forecast five false alarms on inflation. Repeated but temporary spurts in commodity spot and futures prices frightened bond traders and fixed-income money managers with resulting sharp but short-lived advances in rates. All the while, to repeat, the comprehensive indexes on consumer inflation were trending down, down, down. Fear dominated fundamentals and, like schools of fish, bond traders changed course violently and abruptly and repeatedly in response to just about every irrelevant economic statistic. Darwin said man came from the sea. Yes, bond traders are his proof.

REAL RATES: THE LESSON FROM THE 1930s

RH: Let's turn now from fish to interest rates in the Great Depression. Were they low or high? Again, I caution you. Think before you answer.

S7: Low.

RH: Real rates?

S7: I guess I meant nominal rates were low. Prices were falling in many years of the depression. According to our formula, that would mean high real interest rates.

RH: Yes. Nominal interest rates for prime borrowers in the private markets were low, at 3 percent to 4 percent, and even lower for the U.S. Treasury. Even so, who in the private economy would borrow at (say) 4 percent to buy real estate or commodities expected to fall by (say) 10 percent in price over the next year? You still have to pay back the loan plus interest of 4 percent. Add to the 4 percent the 10 percent loss on the property. You lose 14 percent *roughly,* but 15.556 percent precisely: Here are the common-sense calculations:

	Borrow	*Pay Back*
Nominal Dollars	100	104
Price Index	1.0	0.9
Real Dollars	100	115.556

Now let's link common sense to our not-so-frightening formula with the help of sixth-grade algebra:

$$N = R + I + IR$$
$$N - I = R + IR$$
$$N - I = R (1 + I)$$
$$R = \frac{(N - I)}{(1 + I)}$$
$$R = .04 - (-.10) \text{ divided by } 1 + (-.10)$$
$$R = .14 \text{ divided by } 0.9 = .15556 = 15.556\%$$

If your income should fall even more than prices, then you are hurt even more as a borrower. Yes, many businessmen and even economists argue that real rates are pure academic fictions. They simply don't understand. Corporate graveyards attest to that. What are the other elements of risk in interest rates?

S8:   You listed capital and reinvestment risk.

RH: Yes, the risk is potentially huge for long Treasury bonds, and even for short-term U.S. Treasury bills. Anyone who bought long bonds in the late 1970s lost heavily as interest rates soared into 1981, and long bond prices plummeted. Both recently issued and current outstanding bonds plunged (see chapter 7). At the other extreme, anyone who stayed invested in Treasury bills, for example, in 1981–83 or late 1990 to late 1993 would have suffered a massive loss of income as interest rates plummeted in reaction to slow economic growth and continued disinflation (see chapter 9, Exhibit 9–1). Money managers I know who stuck with bills after late 1990 in some cases lost their clients, then their jobs. To repeat, there is no such thing as a risk-free investment instrument. *Even U.S. Treasury bills cannot protect you against risk of loss!*

NONSENSE TEACHING IN ACADEME

RH: Who knows, maybe modern portfolio theorists in academe, including many at Pace University, will some day get around to recognizing this basic truth. They still persist in talking about risk-free returns. The "capital asset pricing model," for example, assumes risk-free returns (see chapter 21). Modern corporate financial theory following Franco Modigliani and Merton Miller (MM), two Nobel prize winners in economics, still persist in talking about risk-free arbitrage. This is all so ludicrous, so damaging to sound money management (see chapters 18 through 21 for a discussion of this model). So, remember that when you take your next course in investment theory. Remember, too, that not one of the fifty institutional clients I counsel either understands or has any use whatsoever for the capital asset pricing model or MM corporate financial theory.

Now let's look at liquidity risk next. What's that?

S5:   You may not be able to sell your asset quickly or easily.

RH: And close to the current market price. Liquidity and immediate marketability are close concepts. Liquidity risk is minimal with U.S. Treasury securities. You can sell quickly, even in huge volume, and very close to the quoted current market prices you get from your broker. That's because the market itself is active, broadly based, and extremely competitive. No individual private seller can *normally* exert a significant influence on the market as a consequence of his own purchases or sales. (In updating this exchange, I must stress the word *normally* given the widely reported Salomon Brothers scandal in 1991 over their role in rigging the market for Treasuries fresh in mind.) Even so, the U.S. Treasury securities market still stands as the most liquid, the safest, and the most competitive of fixed-income markets. In contrast with the U.S. Treasury securities market, the market for corporate low-grade, high-yield, "junk" bonds is often paper thin. They can be illiquid (see chapter 21). Now, answer this question: Is there any other source of liquidity other than sale?

S5:   If the contract matures tomorrow or next week, it's more liquid than one maturing fifty years from now.

LIQUIDITY VERSUS VOLATILITY AND RISK OF LOSS

RH: Good. You may also be able to borrow against your securities. That's yet another source of liquidity. Be careful, though, that you don't confuse liquidity with risk of loss. Treasury bonds, for example, can be sold close to the current market. Even so, you could easily end up selling at a loss, at a price far below your purchase price. So, never identify even a very liquid instrument with a loss-proof instrument. One is not the other by any means. *You can suffer big losses on perfectly liquid investments.*

Liquidity and the Fallacy of Composition

RH: Also, remember that a seller's liquidity (cash for securities) is the same as the buyer's illiquidity (accepting securities for cash). The seller's increased liquidity is at the expense of the buyer's increased illiquidity (his ability to translate securities into cash). Only the Federal Reserve can create new and incremental liquidity for the market as a whole. Put yet another way, never identify the individual with the market. To do so is to commit the oldest of fallacies, the fallacy of composition. We'll return to and expand upon the concept of liquidity when we review monetary theory and the stock markets (see chapters 15 through 17). For now, just remember that any net increase in liquidity for the overall market must come from the Federal Reserve when it increases the money supply.

　　　　O.K., now what is the pure rate of interest?

Ps: (Silence.)

RH: The pure rate is that rate the lender demands independently of any specific risk. Why?

S7: For *waiting* for your money, as Fisher put it. You want to be rewarded
for saving, for foregoing present consumption. This is his theory of time
preference.

RH: Yes, we discussed that earlier (chapter 9). If you are persuaded to wait,
you want to be rewarded. But something else is involved here. The pure
rate is extremely volatile. Does anybody know why?

Ss: (Silence, total and complete.)

RH: The answer is that the pure rate responds to changes in the overall demand for and supply of funds in the money and capital markets. Let's
illustrate this. In a recession private credit demands generally fall while
the Federal Reserve typically pumps up the supply of credit, and the result is a fall in the pure rate of interest. In an expanding economy, especially as you get near the tail end of a boom, credit demands move up
rapidly while the Federal Reserve generally restricts the supply of ·
credit, and the result is a sharp rise in the pure rate of interest.

S9: I still don't understand. How do you measure or separate out movements in the pure rate?

RH: You can't, at least not with any precision. In fact you can't see, touch,
taste, or even smell the pure component of an interest rate. But it exists!
Let me tell you a strange but true story that may help to clear this up.
While doing research for my doctoral thesis at Wharton, I chose as my
subject the Treasury securities markets. I pored over the data comparing prices of Treasury bonds to the prices of low- and medium-grade
corporate bonds of roughly the same maturities. I discovered something
bewildering, and in conflict with everything I had ever read. I was
taught that low-grade corporate bonds were more volatile than Treasury
bonds, or so my Wharton colleagues argued. That was "obviously" and
"clearly" true, or so every single textbook and journal article stated. But
with few exceptions, I found the opposite to be the case over most of
the period from 1945 to the late 1950s. Yields (prices) on Treasury
bonds moved over a wider percentage range than on low-grade corporate bonds.*

You must admit that it sounded logical to argue that Treasuries
should be more stable than low-grade corporate bonds, given compa-

---

*Robert H. Parks, "Income and Tax Aspects of Commercial Bank Portfolio Operations in
Treasury Securities," *The Journal of Finance,* March 1958.

rable *maturities. Durations* are another matter, as we shall shortly see (Exhibit 10–1). Logical or not, we have learned that when data contradicts theory, then one must be an imposter. The data were checked, double checked, triple checked. So I had to find an explanation, a good theory, to match the data. Now, you try to do the same. Any ideas?

S9:   Investors don't think of U.S. Treasury bonds as being subject to the credit risk we spoke of earlier; low-grade corporate bonds include both the pure rate risk and credit risk.

RH: Excellent. In a sense, Treasury bonds have more of the pure rate component in their yields. In the case of low-rated corporate bonds, the pure rate component and the credit risk component often move in opposite directions, and one may partially offset the other in the determination of total yield. It's these opposite and offsetting movements that are the key to our answer.

Let me give you an example. In a recession, yields on Treasury bonds would fall in response to a fall in the pure rate. Yields on high coupon bonds issued earlier would fall the most as their prices soar (see chapter 7). The fall in the pure rate would also push yields down on low-grade corporate bonds. Even so, the rise in perceived credit risk would brake or partially offset the fall in the pure rate component in corporate yields. Similarly, in the expansion phase of the business cycle, yields on Treasuries would rise with the rise in the pure rate. Yields on low-grade corporate bonds would also rise to include the rise in the pure rate, but the reduction in perceived credit risk in an expanding economy would again brake or check the rise in the overall yield on low-grade corporate bonds.

In sum, violent fluctuations in yields in the pure rate can act with full force on Treasury bonds, but there may be offsets on corporate bonds. This led me to label Treasury bonds as "inherently unstable," a conclusion itself in violent conflict with then existing thinking. Also, the Federal Reserve conducts its open-market operations in Treasuries with the aim of stabilizing the economy. The result, paradoxically, contributes to the inherent instability of Treasuries. In a sense, whatever the Federal Reserve touches becomes unstable. It deals in Treasury obligations (and some agencies) almost exclusively in its market operations, as we shall see.

There were exceptions to the rule of greater fluctuations in prices of Treasuries than in low-rated corporate bonds, particularly after the late fifties. For example, in the extremely tight credit markets of 1981, yields on low-grade corporate bonds soared more than yields on comparable maturity Treasury bonds. Recession fears led to an increase in perceived credit risk at the very time the Fed restricted the supply of credit, which pushed up the pure rate. In this case the two components of yield were working in the same direction on low-grade corporate bonds. Their yields rose more than yields on Treasury bonds. There are other major exceptions to the rule, especially for "junk bonds," which we shall consider in due course.

THEORY, PRACTICE, AND MALPRACTICE: MONGREL DOGS VERSUS CATS

How did you fare in that exchange? Well, let's consider just one example here of the applied side of good theory. The example I have in mind has to do with CATS. Our review of CATS, which are extremely volatile zero coupon bonds, should shed further light on the dimensions of risk, especially capital and reinvestment risk. Let's see why.

In the weeks just preceding Black Monday, October 19, 1987, I had suggested that investors sell DOGS and buy CATS. By DOGS I meant dangerously overpriced gung-ho stocks. Later we shall analyze various stock valuation models to see why I thought stocks were wildly overpriced. Our interest here is CATS. By CATS I meant certificates of accrual on Treasury securities. So, why were long CATS then so attractive? That's the question I fired at my graduate finance students in early October 1987. The subject was the assigned October 7 and 14, 1987 monitors damning DOGS and extolling CATS (see Appendix A, Forecasts 38, 44, and Appendix D):

RH: What is a CAT?

S1:   A zero coupon bond. There are no coupons or interest payments. The bond is sold at a huge discount. The buyer receives nothing until it is redeemed at maturity, at par. Then he is paid the principal (par or face) amount in full, usually $1,000.

RH: Good. A zero coupon bond is just the opposite of an infinite income bond, a bond with no principal but a promised income stream to infinity. We discussed these infinite income (or perpetual bonds) earlier (see chapter 8). Can anybody tell me why I have fallen in love with CATS?

S2:   You think stocks are overpriced and bonds underpriced? Are you looking for a big drop in interest rates, which would mean an increase in bond prices?

RH: Yes, and CATS should be an immediate beneficiary if the stock market should dive, as I expect. You could see frenzied buying of CATS for three reasons. First, long CATS are extremely attractive because they have a high "pure-rate" content in being backed 100 percent by Treasuries. Second, I expect the Fed to shift to an expansionary stance. That would drive the "pure" rate lower. Third, long CATS are zero coupon bonds, which means they are the most sensitive debt contracts you can find. A fall in their yield could send CATS jumping over the moon.

Long CATS (with maturities beyond ten years) are by nature wi. and volatile, as the simple mathematics of CATS will bear out. Let's i lustrate. What would you pay now for $1,000 you get back in the yea 2017? That would approximate a thirty-year CAT. *(Remember that thi. exchange took place in late 1987.)*

With a yield of 10 percent, which is now close to the rates on long CATS, the present value of $1000 due in thirty years and discounted at 10 percent translates into a price of $57.31. If the market yield falls just to 9 percent, the market price would jump to $75.37, or by 31.5 percent. Here are the calculations, ignoring brokerage fees, and compounding annually:

Yield	10%	9%	
Price	$57.31	$75.37	+ 31.5% Price Rise

FIXED-INCOME MATHEMATICS AND A THEORY FOR SPOTTING HUCKSTERS

Let's expand now on the mathematics and the theory of CATS, which will serve as a preface to the hucksters in the fixed-income markets. We'll start with the concept *duration.* Suppose you buy a long bond just before interest rates soar and remain at much higher levels. Assume also a flat yield curve, meaning that short-term, intermediate-term, and long-term rates are all equal. You might then kick yourself because the price will have plummeted. The bond would be priced at a discount over its life, until maturity. On the other hand, you might gain some satisfaction from knowing that you can reinvest the coupon income at higher rates over the life of the bond. Under these assumptions, answer this question: Is there some point in time before maturity at which the higher income from reinvestment will just offset the capital loss incurred on sale? Yes. It's the point of duration (see Exhibit 10–1 for an arithmetic example of duration).

Put another way, duration in a rough sense tells you how long *on average* it takes to get your money back. In the case of zero coupon bonds (often referred to as "zeros," you get back every dollar at maturity. So duration and maturity are identical for zeros. For a coupon bond with the same maturity, you get the principal back at maturity, but you also get income over the life of the bond. That means the average life of a coupon bond is shorter than for a zero. Assuming identical maturities, you get back your money earlier with the coupon bond. Let's contrast the price behavior of a thirty-year Treasury 10 percent coupon bond with that of a thirty-year CATS, assuming again a 1 percent decline in market yield:

YIELD	PRICE (THIRTY-YEAR CATS)	PRICE (30-YEAR 10 PERCENT COUPON)
10%	$57.31	$1000.00
9%	75.37	1102.74
	(+31.5%)	(+ 10.3%)

As you can see, a fall in the market yield from 10 percent to 9 percent means a 31.5 percent price rise for the zero coupon bond, but only a 10.3 percent price rise for a thirty-year Treasury 10 percent coupon bond paying $100 interest each year and $1000 principal at maturity. So, with any assumed fall in yield, CATS give you the biggest swing in price. Interest rates did decline sharply after Black Monday into early 1988. So, purebred long-duration-zero-coupon CATS jumped obediently over the moon. That meant investors who bought long CATS at the peak of interest rates (lows of bond prices) just prior to Black Monday could have sold in early 1988 and realized large capital gains. Many institutional investors did just that. CATS also soared from 1990 to 1993, which explains why we fell in love again with these wild beasts (Appendix A, Forecast 63) and once again in 1995 (Appendix A, Forecast 94).

Wealth without Risk: Pure Huckster Hash

Wait! There's another side to CATS. Never forget that while CATS can fly to the moon, they can also crash back to earth. Your friendly broker may have neglected to tell you that. Since there is no interest or coupon income to reinvest on zeros, the return is fixed for the life of the bond. Your broker may advise you to buy long CATS to avoid reinvestment risk, to "guarantee" that you will have the money to finance your children's college education. "Cage those twenty-year CATS," he shouts. What about that?

Well, maybe yes and maybe no. We know that what goes up can also come down, that the timing of any investment is crucial. Long CATS can cost you dearly under the assumption that you lock up these wild beasts just before a major rise in interest rates. That was the case, for example, from 1986 to early 1989 (chapter 9, Exhibit 9–1) and from October 1993 to mid–1994. Long CATS and long STRIPS (zero coupon bonds backed by Treasuries) collapsed in price. If you then had to sell to meet (say) emergency needs for cash, you would have suffered a big loss. Long CATS, then, are hardly suitable to meet unexpected emergency needs for immediate cash. We also know that long CATS can represent your very worst investment under the assumption that inflation soars beyond the nominal yield you have locked up. So, CATS can be dangerous to your health. Long CATS with a principal sum due way out in the future would collapse with an unexpected acceleration of inflation. So would long coupon bonds, but not as much.

THE QUINTESSENTIAL HUCKSTER, PRO, PARROT?

With our review of fundamental analysis, I cannot resist introducing you to C. J. Givens who, in my judgment, has written the very worst (best?) treatise of its kind. How does this title catch you: *Wealth without Risk, How to Develop a Personal Fortune without Going Out on a Limb.** I caught sight of *Wealth without Risk* one day when walking past a bookstore on Broadway, near Wall Street. "Incredible," I said to myself. I walked in and took notes, but did not buy the book. Heavens no! Consider here Givens's "objectives," the first of which he pens on page 300: "Earn a safe 20 percent per year with no commissions in a liquid investment." A safe 20 percent percent? Wow!

I read as fast as I could, out of breath. On page 319 I found his secret to wealth: "If you purchased your shares at $10.00 each (100 shares for each $1000 you invested), and the share price increased over the next six months to $12.00 per share, you have made a 20% profit on your money." *If?* Of course! It's all in the arithmetic. But wait. His 20 percent calculated profit "over the next six months" works out to a 44 percent annual return, compounded every six months. Isn't that right? Thus 1.20 x 1.20 = 1.44. Strange.

Then I skipped back to page 286: "Time your investments in stocks, bonds, and money market instruments to safely average 20 percent+ per year." *Safely average 20 percent plus per year?* Ignore the split infinitive. Ignore the 20 percent return. Why? The answer is that he has an even better alternative.

---

*Simon and Schuster, New York, 1988.

So, consider this get-rich-quick-with-no-risk alternative I found on page 353: "Invest in discounted mortgages for a guaranteed 30 percent return." *A guaranteed 30 percent return?* That's better. His arithmetic is on page 355.

Skipping breathlessly and eagerly ahead, I came across this gem on page 358: "Your outside risk when buying discounted mortgages is that the mortgagor won't make the payments and you may have to foreclose on the property to protect your investment—not a problem if you plan effectively." Risk? *Risk on a guaranteed return?*

Thanks, Mr. Givens. I had in mind quoting two dozen best-selling financial writers in this chapter, but you saved me the trouble because I can use your advice as a proxy for the best (worst). Some of the most ludicrous things are said in ways that are so easy to spot. So, is Mr. Givens (1) Parrot, (2) Pro, (3) Huckster, or (4) a reliable expert on how to make a lot of money fast with no risk? You decide. I invite you to check one of these four options.

Let's summarize our thesis on risk in the fixed-income markets. Your two options are always the present and the expected future, never the past. Moreover, you must make future judgments for every type of risk, including the eleven categories I listed at the beginning of this chapter. (We analyzed seven so far, discussed the prepayment horrors for investors in mortgages in Exhibit 10–1, and later we will analyze call risk, event risk, and exchange-rate risk.) Put another way, you must forecast! There is no other way.

Your forecast can range from sloppy and careless to one showing great care and deliberation, along with professional, honest assistance. Even with the best analysis, however, your forecasts may go awry. So, what about guarantees? There are none.

In the following three chapters we will shine our theoretical search beams on the "monetarists" (chapter 11); next on a motley collection of gold bugs, monetary cranks, and assorted pecuniary nuts (chapter 12); and then on their first-cousin fiscal and budgetary parrots and pros (chapter 13). As we shall see, they all wilt under bright lights.

Exhibit 10–1: A Technical Note on Duration*

Assume a five-year bond with a coupon rate of 8% but priced to yield 9%. Here is the present value (PV) of the bond and weighted present value (WPV), i.e., weighted by the year (W) the future sums are to be received:

YEAR	FUTURE SUMS	x	PV FACTOR AT 9%	=	PV	x	W	=	WPV
1	80	x	.9174	=	73.39	x	1	=	73.39
2	80	x	.8417	=	67.34	x	2	=	134.68
3	80	x	.7722	=	61.78	x	3	=	185.34
4	80	x	.7084	=	56.67	x	4	=	226.70
5	80	x	.6499	=	51.99	x	5	=	259.96
5	1000	x	.6499	=	649.90	x	5	=	3,249.50
			(Rounded)		961.10				4,129.57

Here is the duration of the bond, defined as the present value of the interest stream and principal sum divided into the total time-weighted present value:

$$\text{Duration} = \frac{\text{Total Time-Weighted Present Value}}{\text{Total Present Value}}$$

$$\text{Duration} = \frac{\$4,129.57}{\$961.10} = 4.2967$$

$$= 4.3 \text{ years}$$

DURATION AND ELASTICITY

Duration is a better index of price volatility than maturity. Moreover, one can link elasticity, the percent change in price to any given percent change in yield, to duration. To show this, assume that the market rate falls by 100 basis points, from 9% to 8%, and the price rises to par, to $1,000. The percent change in price is roughly the product of duration with a negative sign (–4.2967) multiplied by the change in yield (–1%) over 1 + the initial yield (1.09). As shown here, duration (D) is negative, reflecting the opposite changes in yields and prices:

---

*Before you read this exhibit be sure to review the theory and mathematics of fixed-income contracts in chapter 8.

$$\text{Percent Change in P} = -D \quad x \quad \frac{\textit{Change in Yield}}{\text{1 Plus Beginning Yield}}$$

$$\$38.90/\$961.10 \quad = -4.2967 \quad x \quad -.01/1.09$$
$$4.0\% \quad = -4.2967 \quad x \quad -.009174$$
$$4.0\% \quad = 4.0\% \text{ approximately}$$

Thus, a fall in yield of 1% from 9% to 8% means a rise in price of about 4%, from $961.10 to $1000. The increase in price of $38.90 is 4% ($38.90/$961.10 = 4%). The duration number comes in handy as a rough approximation, for the higher the number (the longer the duration), the greater would be the percentage swing in price for any given change in yield to maturity. (We can show this with a thirty-year zero coupon: where maturity is duration, a fall in yield from 9% to 8% would send the price of the zero soaring *roughly* 30%. You can get the results from the formula [above], any good calculator, or simply by reading the values from a present value table.)

So, if the holding period of the bond matches duration, both at about 4.3 years, a rise in interest rates would mean a fall in the price of the bond but higher incremental income on the reinvestment of coupon income. The higher incremental income would mostly offset the lower price at 4.3 years. Similarly, if interest rates should fall, the higher bond price would roughly offset the lower reinvestment income at the point of duration. The realized yield at duration roughly matches the initially computed yield to maturity.

Let's take another example, an extreme example, to show how a realized capital gain (loss) at duration just offsets lower (higher) income from reinvestment as interest rates fall (rise). Assume you bought a 20% coupon thirteen-year Treasury bond at par with $100 interest payable every six months (twenty-six payments). The duration of this bond is a little over five years. Then assume that market interest rates drop to 10% across the board on all maturities (a flat yield curve) and stay there for thirteen years. That would mean at duration the bond still has eight years (13–5) to maturity. So, if your holding period roughly matched duration at five years, the bond would be priced at duration at about $1542.

The $1,542 is the present value discounted at 5% of $100 every six months for eight years (16n on your calculator), which is $1,083.78, plus the present value of $1,000 due at 5% in eight years (16n), which is $458.11. That's dandy, for you sell at a premium of about $542 over par at duration ($1,083.78 + $458.11 – $1,000). But wait! Remember that your interest stream of $100 can be reinvested only at the lower rate of 10% annually, not 20%. So, your next step is to calculate the future value (accumulated sum) of $100 interest every six months for five years (10n) at 5% each period. The future value works out to about $1,258. Now add the proceeds from the bond sale of $1,542 and the accumulated interest income of $1,258, and you get about $2,800. Your final step is to calculate what rate of return (IRR) equates a future receipt of $2,800 five years (10n) from now to an initial outlay for the bond of $1,000. I did that on my calculator and got 10.84%, or 21.7% annually. Even with this huge swing in rates, the realized return *roughly* matched the initially computed yield to maturity of 20%.* Here's the arithmetic:

(a) PV of $100 every six months (16n) at 5%	$1,083.78
(b) PV of $1,000 principal (16n) at 5%	458.11
(c) Total	$1,541.89
(d) FV of $100 every six months (10n) at 5%	$1,257.79
(c) + (d) Grand Total	$2,799.68

(e) IRR that just equates FV of $2799.68 to PV
   of $1000 for five years (10n)..10.84%
   (annualized, or 10.84 x 2)..21.7%

Query: What would have been the realized yield if you had held the bond to maturity rather than duration? The answer is only 14.4%, far below the 20% initially computed yield. The calculations are easy. Calculate first the future value of $100 payments for 26 periods at 5% (not 10%) per period, which is $5,111.35. Add to $5,111.35 the $1,000 principal due also in 26 periods, for a total of $6,111.35. Now calculate what rate equates $1,000 to $6,111.35 for the 26n periods away. Answer: 7.2% per n, a 14.4% annual rate.

DURATION CHANGES AND MORTGAGE PREPAYMENT HORRORS

Now that we have the concept duration in our kit of tools, you can join me (RH) in this exchange with institutional investor clients (IC) on July 15, 1994:

IC: Collateralized mortgage obligations (CMOs) collapsed.

---

*With *huge* swings in yields, the formula $\%P = -D \times \left(\frac{\text{Change in Yield}}{1+\text{Beginning Yield}}\right)$ produces large errors.

(CMOs are securities against which mortgages are pledged, including government backed, insured home mortgages. The cash stream from borrowers is passed on to investors. Wall Street often slices up the interest from the principal on CMOs, and sells them as separate contracts.)

RH: Investors counted on interest rates falling, and on early prepayments. So, they bought principal-only CMOs at discounts. They expected to get back their principal at par, and quickly, which would have meant a big yield (see chapter 8).

IC: But interest rates rocketed instead. That itself meant knockdown prices. Worse, homeowners decided not to prepay, but to hold onto their mortgages. Horror of horrors, Robert, duration lengthened at the same time market rates shot up. Many CMOs skidded in price 30 percent, even more.

What can we say finally about duration? Well, duration does not guarantee a maximum return and does not rule out the eleven categories of risk we counted. No, duration is but a rough hedge against interest rate swings, other things being equal. That's all. Take note, Mr. Givens.

Part Four

Monetary and Fiscal Theory, Practice, and Malpractice

11

The Renegade "Monetarists"

Their Problems with Monetary Theory

> [The dispute was over] a live squirrel . . . clinging to one side of a tree trunk; while over against the tree's opposite side a human being was imagined to stand. This human witness tries to get sight of the squirrel by moving rapidly round the tree, but no matter how fast he goes, the squirrel moves as fast in the opposite direction, and always keeps the tree between himself and the man, so that never a glimpse of him is caught. [The question is] *does the man go round the squirrel or not?* He goes round the tree, sure enough, and the squirrel is on the tree, but does he go round the squirrel?
>
> William James, *Pragmatism* (1975)*

What's your answer? Every time I have presented James's question to people, the answers were split right down the middle, half saying yes and half saying no. I have witnessed this spectacle a hundred times or more in my classrooms, and occasionally in forums I have hosted for businessmen. What's wrong?

The problem here is precisely the problem we wrestled with in earlier chapters. In this case, until we agree on a definition for "go round," the arguments are bound to become sterile, emotional; the disputants are condemned to run in circles around the proverbial tree. As James made clear, the answer to his question is yes if we define "go round" to mean the human circles an area in which the squirrel is located, and no if we define "go round"

---

*Cambridge, Mass.: Harvard University Press, p. 27.

to mean the human moves to the left side of the squirrel, then to his backside, then to his right side, then to his front to complete the circuit.

Parrots are notorious for flying around in circles. That's true for the gold bugs, monetary cranks, and assorted pecuniary nuts we are about to meet. They become hopelessly lost because they confuse definition with theory. While one would expect this from average nonprofessionals, it's less understandable when the same malady afflicts trained professional economists with doctorates from prestigious universities. The "Chicago" monetarists fit that mold.

Just what are monetarists? I call them preachers, a highly educated sect of ideologically crazed monetary economists who have become infamous for bad theory and even worse forecasts. They have failed to pay even elementary attention to logic and scientific method in economics. This is admittedly a severe indictment, but one I intend to document with the help of data, theory, professional logicians (including Thouless), and the monetarists themselves. To be sure, the renegade monetarists deserve some credit for popularizing the linkage of money growth to economic activity and price levels, but this was hardly new to trained monetary theorists. Fisher said as much, and with the necessary qualifications, long before the monetarists arrived on the scene. Let's compliment the monetarists, too, for stressing the idiocy of targeting interest rates (see chapter 6), and for their research on monetary overkill as a major factor in the economic contractions of 1920, 1936–37, and the Great Depression of the 1930s. Milton Friedman and Anna J. Schwartz reviewed a mountain of historical data to support their conclusions in *A Monetary History of the United States, 1867–1960.** They worked hard to compile the data, run countless regressions, and calculate a galaxy of correlations. For this they are deserving of our thanks.

They deserve our applause also for integrating monetary and fiscal theory and policy. They persuasively argued that unless we always analyze how government outlays are financed, whether through taxes, monetized borrowing, or nonmonetized borrowing, we get absolutely nowhere in analyzing the impact of fiscal policy on the economy. We thank them for that even though many other economists had long before alerted us to the need for coupling monetary and fiscal analysis.†

Most important, the monetarists deserve immense praise for their tracking of stop-go Fed policies, with excessive stimulation that itself fueled inflation, followed abruptly with excessive tightening that produced recession and falling interest rates. The Fed repeatedly shifted from monetary adrena-

---

*Princeton, N.J.: Princeton University Press, 1963, pp. 690–91.

†Abba Lerner is one outstanding example: *Economics of Control* (New York: Macmillan, 1959).

line to monetary codeine, all the while contributing to violent cyclical fluctuations in the post-World War II era. Fed constriction, which I repeatedly tag as monetary overkill, was a major factor in the recessions of the post-World War II era. Just glance at this doleful history:

Fed Policy Constriction	What Followed?:	
(1) 1948	1948–49	Recession
(2) 1953	1953–54	Recession
(3) 1957	1957–58	Recession
(4) 1960	1960–61	Recession
(5) 1969	1969–70	Recession
(6) 1973–74	1973–75	Recession
(7) 1980	1980	Recession
(8) 1981–82	1981–82	Recession
(9) 1990	1990–91	Recession
(10) 1994	1995	Real GDP slowed from 5.1 percent in the fourth quarter of 1994 to 1.1 percent in the second quarter of 1995, then bounced up to 4.2 percent in the third quarter.

Do you see any correlation here? Is it possible that the Federal Reserve is recession prone? Is it possible that by concentrating unduly on its monolithic devil of inflation that it pushes us repeatedly into recession? Well, it's precisely Federal Reserve policy mismanagement that induced me to forecast recessions (see Appendix A, 5 through 9) as a Wall Street economist. They were fairly easy calls based on the lagged factor of policy constriction. (Alas, I forecast six of the last five recessions, worrying out loud that my call on Black Monday would likely produce recession. There was none, for reasons I set forth in Appendix A and in chapter 15.)

FROM PRAISE TO CAUSTIC CRITIQUE

With all that praise, let's get back now to a detailed critique of the monetarists's blunders in theory and in application. We have already met a few monetarists, including Beryl Sprinkel, Jerry Jordan, and Darryl Francis, and the quasi-monetarist Lawrence Kudlow (chapters 5 and 6). Shortly we shall see Dr. Friedman in action in an institutional investor forum I hosted in his honor. Except for Dr. Schwartz, all were my guests in roundtable meetings and forums I hosted for them and senior investment officers. Listening to the monetarists argue, I must confess, was far more exciting than poring through their research papers and books. Listening to Friedman and Sprinkel was not unlike sitting in on a religious revival meeting. Dr. Sprinkel once told me he started out to be a preacher. I believe he succeeded. In any case, their histrionics always put me on my guard. I'm forever wary of eloquent preachers who permit, consciously or not, ideology to dominate science.

Their eloquence aside, it is monetarist literature that bothers most. It includes the odd tracts of Alan Meltzer of Carnegie-Mellon University; Carl Brunner of the University of Rochester; Erich Heinemann of the Wall Street firm of Ladenburg Thalmann, formerly with the *New York Times*; and Leif Olsen, the former head of a monetarist staff of some eighty at Citibank. This literature includes the pronouncements of the monetarist-manned Shadow Open Market Committee, a self-appointed committee set up to track and appraise the doings of the Federal Reserve. True to its name, the Shadow shed little light in resolving the problems and contradictions of monetarist theory.

NOMINAL M1: THE FIRST ICON

A little history can help us in our appraisal. This takes us back to the first god of the monetarists, or M1, now a deposed god. I must document their romance with M1 because the monetarists, including Dr. Friedman, would like us to forget just how intense and insistent they were in courting their first love. Sprinkel, for example, swore allegiance to M1 in his first major book, *Money and Stock Prices.** He defined M1 on page 10 as "private demand deposits subject to check and cash." He reaffirmed his faith in his 1971 work titled *Money and Markets, A Monetarist View,* in which he defines M1 on page 32 as "the public's holdings of coin, currency, and demand deposits in banks."†

What about Friedman? Well, he wrote an introduction to Sprinkel's *Money and Markets* in which he praised his prized pupil to the sky for his understanding of money, for his devotion to M1. But M1, predictably, proved to be a defective god because it failed to meet the test of good theory. My early conviction on that count led me to make this forecast: "The fate of the Chicago school will not be a happy one."‡ That was an easy call. I continued to track

---

*Homewood, Ill.: Richard D. Irwin & Co., 1964.

†Homewood, Ill.: Richard D. Irwin & Co.

‡"The Trouble with M1," *Banking, Journal of the American Bankers Association,* November 1970, p. 57.

the monetarists, and concluded that they would not learn from their mistakes.*
They learned very little. Worse, they became defensive and quick to anger.

Let's be specific. Monetarists suffer from four serious problems. First,
they reason in circles by confusing definition with theory. Second, they mistakenly rely on static rather than dynamic theory. Third, they hold to bad theory in the face of data that persistently contradict their analysis and their projections. Fourth, they fail to control their evangelical fervor, which subjects
them to the charge of ideological dominion over scientific method.

Monetarists Confuse Definition and Theory

Let's illustrate the definitional fallacy as applied to what is meant by "money."
As I indicated, for many years economists defined money as being chiefly
made up of (a) *commercial bank demand deposits* (checking accounts) and (b)
currency in circulation, with demand deposits representing the bigger part. I
highlighted commercial bank demand deposits to stress that other financial institutions were legally barred until the 1970s from holding demand deposits.
Currently, the thrift institutions also provide demand deposits. Other checkable deposits such as negotiable order of withdrawal (NOW) accounts and
automatic transfer of savings (ATS) accounts are currently available in all depository institutions. Monetary economists make the obvious point that the
government or the central bank could create money, including demand balances, currency and coin. There is no confusion there. Nor does anyone question that it was the central bank that had the power to create legal reserves for
the commercial banks, which in turn made it possible for the commercial
banking system to create credit and money by a multiple of its legal reserves.
So, without sacrificing precision, I can put my criticism of the early monetarist thesis on M1 as follows:

The Monetarist's Major Premise:	Demand deposits are the principal component of some money.
The Monetarist's Minor Premise:	Only commercial banks can provide demand deposits.
My Conclusion:	So what?!

Just as apples and oranges satisfy our demands for fruit, so do different
kinds of money satisfy our working and theoretical definitions for money. Restricting money to mean demand deposits (and currency) leaves too much out

---

*"Monetarist Mania," Standard & Poor's *CreditWeek,* April 29, 1985, p. 1.

of the monetary picture. The monetarists leave out of the picture something critical to sensible thinking about money. They omit all kinds of money balances other than demand deposits (and currency) that can and do perform the functions of money. Definitions are not arguments. They have no content. They don't tell us anything. The monetarists then fall into the trap of error-by-omission. Both fallacies are tied in with the problems they have with "static" theory.

Monetarists Rely on Static Theory

We must distinguish between static and dynamic theory. Now, I could show you pages of mathematical formulas and the impossible jargon economists use to make this distinction. To do so would serve no useful purpose. There's a much easier way to get the idea across. Consider a parallel here. Assume you had four or five photographs of yourself in various activities in that week you spent away from home, away from your mate. Assume that your mate were to rely solely on those photographs to analyze what you had been doing. That's static analysis. Contrast the few photographs with a continuous and uncut motion picture of everything you did that week away from home. That's dynamic analysis.

We can see how tough a job historians face in trying to uncover what really took place over past centuries. They have photographs of sorts, including fossil imprints, and even these are few and far between. What they need is a motion picture. Historians have to rely instead on static analysis, the equivalent of analysis through a limited series of instant snapshots. Static analysis also lies at the heart of monetarists's theoretical error. I'll explain with reference to a puzzle I first ran into in the 1960s. What puzzled me at the time was the contradiction between the increase in commercial bank demand deposits outstanding, on the one hand, and the much faster advance in commercial bank loans and investments on the other. How could that be, I pondered? In answering the question, we can only touch on the mechanics of the creation of credit and money here, but I can make my key point. Let's put this in three steps:

1. When commercial banks make loans or acquire investments, they simultaneously create demand deposits (checking accounts). One is the mirror image of the other.

2. So, other things being equal, the increase in commercial bank assets (loans plus investments) should roughly match the increase in commercial bank demand balances.

3. But in fact assets shot far ahead of demand deposits, the principal component then of the narrowly defined money supply. What happened? That's the mystery.

What happened is that simultaneously with the *creation* of demand deposits, a lot of people were *converting* either newly created or already existing demand deposits into higher-yielding savings and time deposits. These two operations, creation and conversion, were taking place simultaneously. Let's illustrate this process. Just suppose $1,000,000 of loans are made and that $1,000,000 of demand deposits are created as a mirror image of the loan expansion. Now suppose that the demand deposits created are then circulated through the banking system as checks are drawn in payment for goods and services. Assume also that holders of demand balances decide to convert $600,000 of their demand balances into time and savings deposits at the very time the banking system is creating new loans and deposits by $1,000,000. Now, try to answer these questions:

1. *How much money in the form of demand deposits is in fact created?* The correct answer is $1,000,000, the mirror image of the $1,000,000 creation of loans.

2. *What is the increase in demand deposits outstanding?* The correct answer is $400,000. True, $1,000,000 of demand deposits are created, but $600,000 of demand deposits are simultaneously converted to a secondary or broader money in the form of time and savings deposits, which some economists call "near-money." That leaves only $400,000 of demand deposits outstanding of the $1,000,000 created.

3. *What's the origin of time and savings deposits?* They owe their life to the initial creation of demand deposits, and then the conversion of demand deposits to a broader money form.

This gets us back to the problem with M1, the narrowly defined money stock. The monetarists kept insisting on tracking the rise in M1, the narrowly defined money stock *outstanding*. Notice that I have highlighted *outstanding*. Why? In our example, if you were to take two photographs, one at the beginning and one at the end of this whole process, you would find that total demand deposits outstanding increased only $400,000. But we know from our motion picture that $1,000,000 of demand deposits were in fact created (which matches the $1,000,000 rise in loan assets). So, did bank robber Willie Sutton walk off with $600,000? Of course not: $600,000 of demand balances were merely converted into a broader form of money.

Maybe this note I wrote on chameleon money will help you to see the importance of distinguishing between narrowly and broadly defined money:

> The (monetarists) pay far too little attention to: the creation of demand deposits; the rise in expenditures based on credit and demand deposit creation, and the accompanying circulation of demand deposits within the financial system; and the conversion of newly created or already outstanding demand deposits to time and savings deposits which are included in the broader monetary aggregates of M2 and M3.
>
> M1 should be called chameleon money. Chameleons do not cease to exist because their color changes. Only their appearance is altered. Similarly, the conversion of money to one of the broader money aggregates does not contradict the fact that money was created in the first instance. It is this very process of creation and conversion that underlies the unprecedented growth of credit and money since mid–1982 . . . [a veritable] monetary explosion.*

The monetarists have trouble also with velocity, especially with what I have dubbed the circuit velocity of money. You can think of the circuit velocity of money as an update of Fisher's notion of velocity. The key difference lies in the circulation of money within the consolidated financial system. What's important and magical is that the faster circulation of money narrowly defined (demand deposits) within the consolidated system of financial institutions brought into being new credit, new lending and investing power, and new money creation very broadly defined to include fund liabilities (near-moneys). We saw that, for example, in the period just prior to Black Monday. The explosive expansion of the funds then reflected the speedup in the circuit velocity of money (as was the case also in 1990–94). The opposite took place for several quarters after Black Monday as investors liquidated their fund holdings. You can track such money flows via simple accounting records (see Exhibit 11–1).

Let me note the economic observations on the period 1961–65 as one more example of bad monetary theory based on static analysis. Not only the monetarists but also other monetary economists were screaming at the time that the Fed was pursuing a highly restrictive policy. The proof of tight money, they said, lay in (a) the fall in excess reserves and (b) the rise in member bank borrowing from the Federal Reserve. They were wrong. But before I attempt to explain the data, let me first present you with an analogy.

I had the job of getting the idea over to investment officers in countless luncheons that monetary policy in the early 1960s was easy, not tight. That's when this martini analogy came in handy:

Imagine a gentleman at the bar over there. Assume he has a martini in front of him, and that the martini glass is full. Assume that when we next look in on the same gentleman two hours later, we find him at the bar and we see that the glass is still full. What conclusion can we reach on the basis of these observations, these two photographs? How many martinis has he consumed in two hours?

They got the point. We need a motion picture, not photographs, to check the flow. Now let's apply the martini analogy to our monetary problem. True, net free reserves, or excess reserves less borrowing for the commercial banking system, did fall from almost $0.5 billion in 1961 to a negative amount in early 1965, when borrowing exceeded excess reserves. (When borrowing exceeds excess reserves, the negative net amount is referred to as "net borrowed reserves.") The monetarists had this right. But just about every other economic statistic contradicted the notion of tight money. As the Fed shoved in reserves, the banks expanded their loans and investment holdings, and this in turn increased deposits subject to reserve requirements. The two took place simultaneously, with *excess* reserves evaporating almost as quickly as the Fed provided them. A motion picture could have caught the flow of events.

The monetarists have devoted enormous attention to comparing the degree of liquidity of this or that type of money outstanding. I call this "after-the-fact analysis," a static and sterile way to conduct monetary analysis, one in which monetary theorists still find themselves ensnared. I quickly tire of hearing, for example, that currency and demand deposits are more liquid than large time certificates, even more liquid than long Treasury bonds, and far more liquid than the farm house someone owns in Kansas. (With equity home-ownership mortgage loans and an automatic line of credit, even this seemingly "illiquid" example is suspect.)

Monetarists and other monetary economists should have been focusing all along on the creation of credit and the companion creation of money and near-monies in the first instance. That's what is crucial when accounting for the violent swings in the money and capital markets, for inflation, for interest rates, and for real output. They should have paid secondary attention to the final form money takes, and primary attention to the creation of money by the consolidated financial system, not solely the commercial banks (Exhibit 11–1). They didn't. Instead, they put last things first, a priority consistent with flawed theory.

Monetarists Are Blind to Relevant Data

Consider just two instances here of monetarist blindness to the relevant data:

1. Misreading of V and T in 1981–87

In 1981–82, monetarist reassurance of no recession flew in the face of the mini-depression that got under way in August 1981 (chapter 6). They left out the precipitous fall in rascal V, the velocity of money. Their excuse for this fatal omission was that financial innovations distorted M1 and M2, and the velocities of these money supplies. That's a dance, a lame excuse, one even the Federal Reserve Bank of St. Louis rejected.* Could it be that the St. Louis Fed, a bastion of monetarism, has finally seen the error of its ways? Possibly. How refreshing that would be!

What truly killed the monetarists was the mid-1982 through 1987 period, when credit and money expanded rapidly. The monetarists kept screaming wolf, year after year, insisting that rapid monetary expansion would bring with it a massive acceleration in inflation. Instead, we experienced disinflation, a major slowing of inflation. Where did they go wrong this time? Remember Fisher's equation, $\frac{MV}{T} = P$? Well, for one thing they left V out of their calculations as money velocity continued to fall. The slide in V partly offset the explosion in M. For another, they left out the vigorous rise in T, or output. The surge in the effective supply of goods and services reflected in part the higher utilization of labor, capital, and materials. Vast unemployed resources existed as a legacy of the 1981–82 recession, and the available surplus helped to boost output and keep unit costs down. Also, foreign countries stepped up sharply their exports to the United States. We got "T" not just from China, but from virtually the whole world.

There's a lesson here. We must never identify T to mean domestic output only. We have to internationalize Fisher's equation of exchange. We have to scrap monetarist "reduced equation" forecast models that (a) focus on changes in the domestic money stock and (b) treat foreign fluctuations in money, output, prices, interest rates, or even velocity as *exogenous*. There are no *exogenous* causal forces in an intensively competitive global economy linked together with instant means of communication. The word should be scrapped.

---

*Review, Federal Reserve Bank of St. Louis (July-August 1990), p. 51.

2. Monetarists Misread the Reserve Data in 1990–93

The monetarists tripped over the monetary base again, and badly, in the period 1990 to 1993. The monetary base is an apples-and-oranges gauge composed of legal reserves plus currency. The problem is that when currency is drawn from the banking system and put into circulation, the effect is to reduce high-power legal reserves dollar-for-dollar. That's what happened. The resulting "external drain" crippled the lending and investing power of the financial system by a multiple of the reserves stripped away, even as the reported monetary base rose rapidly. Moreover, a good part of the rise in the monetary base represented higher legal reserve requirements. The higher requirements reflected the shift of depositors from time and savings deposits, which were nonreservable, to checkable accounts in M1 subject to a 10 percent reserve requirement. The external drain of currency into circulation and the higher reserve requirements largely explained why total credit (loans plus investments) and the broad money stock M2 moved ahead so slowly in 1990–93. If the Fed had wanted to, it could have provided more reserves to speed money growth. It chose not to do so because of its obsessive and mistaken fears that inflation would accelerate.

Not only did the monetarists mistakenly take a rapid rise in the monetary base to mean accelerating inflation, but they misread badly the rise in narrow money M1 as being inflationary during this period. It wasn't. No, the rise in M1 reflected the shift of funds from time and savings deposits to checkable accounts. That shift came in response to the precipitous plunge in short-term interest paid on these deposits. Monetarists and others could have easily avoided being fooled. All they had to do was to check the asset side of the balance sheet of the banks and other financial intermediaries. If they had, they would have found anemic growth of loans plus investments. That meant, in turn, anemic growth of broad money M2.

So what's new? M1 was always defective. For most of the postwar period, the rise in M1 *understated* monetary stimulus. In 1990–93, however, M1 grandly *overstated* Fed largesse (despite the renewed though modest recovery in both M1 and M2 after April 1993). How did I know this? Easy! I just tracked the asset side of commercial banking balance sheets, which advanced ever so slowly (Appendix A, Forecast 75).

Monetarist Philosophical and Political Bias

The University of Chicago has long been associated with the training of economists as monetarists. But the "Chicago school" of economics existed long before the monetarists came on the scene. It long searched for a simple rule of government participation consistent with free markets. It wanted a minimum of authority and ideally a simple economic rule or mechanism that would operate automatically and efficiently, and be consistent with individual freedom, a democratic government, and maximum economic progress. Who could oppose such beautiful goals?

I need not detail the Chicago philosophy. Instead, I'll simply list a few of the automatic systems that economists have revered through the years, including several dear to the Chicago school:

The Gold Standard. It didn't work (see chapter 12).

The Real Bills Doctrine. Otherwise known as the commercial loan doctrine or the productive credit theory, the idea was to match money growth with growth in short-term, self-liquidating commercial paper. By matching money growth to output, it was argued, we could expect to see stable prices. But they left out rascal V. By stressing the quality of credit, the banking system was supposed to be made liquid, safe, and profitable. But this heavenly view left out the need for quantitative limits on credit. They left out a lot more, but that need not concern us here.

Matching Money Growth to Population Growth. I called this the copulatory theory of money in a lecture I presented before The Conference Board in New York City. A dollar a baby? Ludicrous!

The Bills Only Doctrine. The Fed should restrict its open-market operations to short-term U.S. Treasury bills. The idea quickly died, and is hardly worth discussing here.

Constant Growth of the Money Stock. Put the Fed on an automatic pilot, or so Friedman argued repeatedly. That would be preferable to government control, he said. But I would argue that "automatism" is a preposterous notion in view of the history of a highly volatile V and an erratic T. Also, what are we to use as the automatic money pilot? A resuscitated and defunct M1? An adjusted M2? The monetary base? An altered and corrected index of total adjusted reserves? Who knows? One thing we do know is that the monetarists will cook up brand new automatic pilots in the years ahead. They will never give up. That's one forecast I hit right on the button almost a quarter-century ago:

The Chicago school of monetarists (are) like the alchemists of old in that they seek that which cannot be found. They search for a single and consistently reliable monetary indicator that will tell them where the economy is going or explain where it has been regardless of the decade or even the century under explanation. [But] no such indicator exists now, and never will.*

FRIEDMAN AND RINFRET AT THE CIRCUS

I promised to introduce you to the monetarist king, Dr. Friedman himself. So, let's listen in on an exchange between me and Dr. Friedman (MF) shortly after a debate (held at the Plaza Hotel in New York City on May 23, 1972) he participated in with Dr. Pierre Rinfret for which I served as moderator:

RH: Why did you ridicule Pierre? Why did you bluff on the current data on orders, contracts, and other forward indicators? Pierre tracks these data. You don't.

MF: You're entitled to your opinion. I did not bluff, and I did not mean to ridicule. On a related matter, Mr. Parks, you should get your facts straight. Read my monetary history. I never did argue that M1 was a reliable indicator. Also, as moderator you should keep yourself out of the debate. Remember that next time.

RH: Dr. Friedman, I meant no offense. I only meant to alert you to the feedback from our guests. Actually, most of the feedback was good. I thought you were eloquent, organized, insistent, confident. You spoke fervently. Did you ever consider the ministry as a profession?

MF: Why do you ask?

---

*"The Trouble with M1," *Journal of the American Bankers Association* (November 1970), p. 105.

Exhibit 11–1: The Circuit Velocity of Money*

| | Commercial Banking System | | Mutual Funds | |
	Assets	Liabilities	Assets	Liabilities
(1)		− SD i + DD i		
(2)		− DD i + DD mf	+ DD mf	+ MFS i
(3)		− DD mf + DD s	− DD mf + I	
(4)		− DD s + DD v		

(1) Individual **i** shifts from saving deposit **− SD i** to demand deposit **+ DD i** in expectation of purchasing mutual fund shares **MFS.**

(2) Individual i purchases mutual fund shares **+ MFS i.** When check is cleared, the demand balances of the individual at the commercial banks fall **− DD i,** the liabilities of the mutual fund to the individual increase by the amount of the mutual fund shares **+ MFS i,** and the demand deposit of the mutual fund at the commercial banking level increases **+ DD mf.**

(3) The fund manager purchases investment instruments **+I** via drafts on his demand deposits at the commercial banks, and this shuffles demand deposit ownership from the fund **− DD mf** to the sellers of the investment instruments **+ DD s.** The instruments may be newly created or outstanding Treasury bills, commercial paper, stocks, or other contracts depending on the type of fund.

(4) The seller **s** of investment paper, public or private, then drafts checks payable to a vendor of goods and services **v** shuffling demand balances from the seller **− DD s** to the vendor **+ DD v.**

Source: From Several Money and Capital Markets Monitors, 1987–94

*I dubbed this money shuffling (1) through (4) the *circuit velocity of money.* Any speedup in the circuit velocity of money, which brings with it a companion creation of new lending power and money very broadly defined to include fund liabilities, can be stimulative, and *vice versa.* Prior to Black Monday, for example, the explosive expansion of the funds reflected the speedup in the circuit velocity of money. For several quarters after Black Monday the fall in the circuit velocity of money and fund liquidations meant a tighter Fed policy than captured by the official reserve data. An even greater quickening in circuit velocity materialized in the years 1990–93, as investors rushed into bond and stock funds in response to plunging interest rates. With rates soaring in 1994, velocity could slow once again. In any case, the Fed should not leave rascal V out of its sight.

12

Gold Bugs, Monetary Cranks, and Assorted Pecuniary Nuts

> It is claimed for gold that it keeps slovenly currency systems up to the mark. . . . So long as a country continues to adhere to a gold standard, there is force in this. But experience—an experience covering much ground and subject to scarcely any exceptions—shows that, when severe stress comes, the gold standard is usually suspended. There is little evidence to support the view that authorities who cannot be trusted to run a nationally managed standard, can be trusted to run an international gold standard.
>
> John Maynard Keynes, *A Treatise on Money* (1930)*

The monetarists, like proponents of the gold standard, have great faith in monetary mechanisms that are supposed to work automatically and with a minimum of government control. They adore simple rules and despise bumbling authorities, which is understandable. Even so, monetarist "automatism" rests on flimsy theory. As we have seen, time and time again the monetarists tripped over their mechanistic systems because they tripped over theory (see chapter 11). Gold bugs, the subject of this chapter, fare even worse theoretically and practically. Their automatic pilots don't work either.

---

*Cambridge, England: The Royal Economics Society, 1930; 1971, p. 267.

HEADLINE NEWS: GOLD BUG
KNOCKS OUT WALL STREET ECONOMIST

My first encounter with a gold bug came as a shock. One happy morning, August 20, 1973, to be exact, I picked up the *Wall Street Journal* as usual and started to read. What do you think startled me? Of all things, my résumé was on the first page! It was there along with that of gold bug Harry Schultz. There I was, pitted in battle against Schultz. He presumably floored me with a knockout punch, or so it appeared to me on first reading. Reporter Al Malabre stressed that the price of gold had soared since I had written "King Gold Is Dead" years earlier. Since Schultz was a gold bull, Malabre asked the relevant question of the paper's readers: Who should you have listened to, Parks or Schultz, the thoroughly trained economist or the unwashed gold bug? That was his question. Wow! I called Al Malabre the moment I regained my senses:

RH: Who should you have listened to? Al, my attack centered on gold in the central banking system. I was not interested in where the price was headed, up or down. You know that. I've always called gold a speculative gamble, not an investment. It's in the same class as Las Vegas. I sent you my report on gold years ago. You kept it in your files all these years? Anyway, King Gold was dead then. He's still dead.

AM: Bob, I don't disagree with you. My comments on the price of gold were meant to be tongue-in-cheek.

Tongue-in-cheek? My phone rang nonstop that morning. I was anxious to see how others reacted to the article, especially Blyth Eastman Dillon's institutional clients. At the time, I was the firm's chief economist (see chapter 3). I was incensed that the gold bugs, whom I had dubbed the quintessential non-intellectuals of finance, would now have the last laugh. But the people who telephoned me that morning said I was too sensitive, that it was all in fun. Years later, in 1982, business writer Peter Brimelow observed in *The Wall Street Gurus* that "[Malabre's] purpose was not to disparage Parks."*

That was long ago. Let me explain now why I had believed for many years, long before Malabre's ace reporting in 1973, that gold was indeed dead as a central bank mechanism. I'm convinced, moreover, that "King Gold" should be renamed "Pauper Gold." To see why, consider a three-punch critique on gold bugs. The exchange serves to update my profound disrespect

*Alexandria, Va.: Minerva Books, 1988.

for "commodity" theorists of money, or those who mistakenly equate the value of money with its commodity content or backing. The commodity normally involved is gold, hence the term *gold bugs*.

The First Punch: Irrelevance of Gold to the Value of the Dollar

First, please join me in this typical exchange on gold, one I have had many times with students, RRs, institutional clients, even assorted monetary cranks. This particular discussion took place on Monday afternoon, May 8, 1989, with some feverish gold bugs (B1, B2, etc.) working as RRs with the securities firm of Moore & Schley. Try not to walk into the traps I set for them:

RH: You say that gold could help the dollar? How is that?

B1: The dollar has no backing now. Gold could do wonders.

RH: Suppose all of our official gold stock were "to back the dollar," to use your words. The official U.S. stock is now $11.1 billion and . . .

B1: That's all? I thought it was a lot more than that.

RH: The $11.1 billion is at the official price of $42.22 per fine troy ounce.

(The official price dates back to the early 1970s, but it has no relevance today since the publicly traded commodity market establishes the daily price of gold.)

B1: Yeah? That's crazy. The market's a lot higher than that.

RH: Yes, you're correct. The market price for gold is now about $378 per ounce (Exhibit 12–1). We can calculate the market value, too, as you suggest. Just divide $378 by $42.22. That gives us a ratio of the market to the official price of 8.953 times. To get the market value we just need to multiply 8.953 times $11.1 billion, which is a little over $99 billion. So let's say all of our gold valued at market is about $100 billion. Does that sound right to you?

B1: Yeah, that's what I said. That's a different story. You should have done that in the first place.

RH: You have any idea what GNP is running, as last reported?

B2: No. What's that have to do with gold?

RH: GNP in current dollars is currently running at about $5 trillion on an annual basis. If we divide $5 trillion by 365 days in the year, our daily GNP would run $13.7 billion. We produce $13.7 billion of goods and services in just one day.

B2:   So what!

RH: Make just one more calculation. Divide the $100 billion of gold by $13.7 billion daily GNP. That gives you about 7.3 days. In other words, our entire official gold stock valued at market is worth a little more than seven days of GNP. Seven days! Seven days to live.

B3:   You miss the point. Gold has advantages you overlook.

Second Punch: The Myth of Convertibility

RH: You want to shift the subject? Are we finished with the subject of the value of gold? What are the other advantages?

B3:   Our money could be convertible into gold. That would force government to behave. Those bums in Washington wouldn't be able to print money and spend like there's no tomorrow. They're debasing the dollar, destroying our system. We need to make our money convertible into gold to preserve its value.

RH: What dollars would you make convertible? Look at this Federal Reserve release on money. The narrowly defined money stock is made up mainly of demand deposits and currency. It now is almost $800 billion. That's called M1. But the more broadly defined M2, which includes time and savings deposits, is about $3 trillion; and M3 about $4 trillion. Which of these moneys would you make convertible into gold?

B3:   M1.

RH: Why exclude small savings and time deposits included in M2? Why exclude certificates of deposit?

B3:   I have to think about that.

RH: Yes, think about that. Are you married?

B4:   All of us are married. Why do you ask?

RH: Ever make a promise to your wife you know in advance you can't keep? Just imagine the trouble that could cause? If you make a promise you cannot keep, you are just asking for trouble. Isn't that correct?

B3:   What does that have to do with anything?

RH: A lot. By insisting on convertibility, you're making a promise you cannot keep. I don't have the slightest idea what money you want convertible into gold. But with our gold stock of $100 billion at market, and M1 alone at $800 billion, any promise of convertibility would have to be a fair-weather promise. What happens in stormy weather is that payment in gold is suspended. That's why the gold standard is called a fair-weather standard. Even the threat of a "run" on gold could bring suspension. So, if you didn't want gold, you could get it, and if you wanted gold, you couldn't get it. Ha! That's fair weather.

B3: You're off track. Convertibility would force governments to behave. It would force governments to discipline themselves. There would be no runs.

RH: Do you really believe Presidents Bush, Reagan, Johnson, Nixon, Franklin Roosevelt, or Theodore Roosevelt, or the Congress, could have been disciplined or locked in by some rule on gold? I can't find any evidence historically for government discipline under gold. What you find are violent economic fluctuations and financial crises under gold. Gold itself is an extremely volatile metal. Just look at this exhibit on gold prices (Exhibit 12–1). The only thing I know of that jumps around more than gold are the gold bugs themselves. If you believe a simple rule like gold convertibility will guarantee discipline, brother, you have unbelievable religious faith. Hallelujah!

Gold bugs have no interest in relevant data or sound monetary theory. That's why it's easy to lead emotional and loud bugs into traps with just a few leading questions.

Third Punch: Fallacy of the Commodity Theory of Money

This takes us now to an amazing story about the commodity theory of money. One version of the theory argues that the value of the monetary unit, our dollar, is dependent on its gold backing. You know better. Even so, please join me in this exchange with graduate students (S1, S2). Use the theoretical picks and shovels Professor Irving Fisher gave you in his famous equation of exchange MV = PT (see chapter 7). They're perfect for squashing commodity theorists.

RH: Please write down these three propositions I'm about to dictate, and then tell me what you think is wrong. Keep in mind also that we are talking about an extraordinary event that actually took place. I have in mind the U.S. dollar devaluation against gold in 1935. You might be interested some day to read the countless pages of testimony commodity theorists and gold bugs made before the Congress. Here are the three statements in the form of a syllogism I distilled from thousands of pages of Congressional transcripts:

1. The value of the dollar is dependent on its gold content.

2. The price level is inversely related to the value of the dollar.

3. To get the price level up (the value of the dollar down), we should raise the price of gold.

Now keep in mind that we raised the price of gold from $20.67 an ounce to $35 an ounce, effective January 1, 1935. The rise in the price of gold translated into a devaluation of the dollar in terms of gold, meaning a reduction in its gold content. The gold content fell from almost $\frac{1}{21}$ of an ounce to $\frac{1}{35}$ of an ounce. According to Professor George F. Warren of Cornell University, an adviser to President Franklin Roosevelt, the devaluation of the dollar would produce a substantial rise in prices of goods and services. He convinced Roosevelt and the U.S. Congress of that. Remember, this was a time of depression. The objective was to stimulate the economy by getting the overall level of prices higher. But what happened to the general level of prices in January 1935?

S1: I don't believe prices changed much, if at all.

RH: That's right. The dollar devaluation had precisely zero impact on the general price level. Nothing happened. Consumer prices trended up a bit from their lows in 1932 into 1937, then receded. But you would be hard pressed to see any influence at all from the highly advertised devaluation of the dollar. Why? What was wrong with Warren's plan to get the overall price level higher? As a hint, keep in mind that you had to turn in your gold at the old price. You got $20.67 an ounce, not $35 an ounce. The government gave you currency or demand deposits for your gold.

S3: That means there was no rise in money outstanding?

RH: Right. Negligible. What about velocity and output?

S4: They didn't change either.

RH: So what happened to prices?

S4: Nothing, because nothing happened to M, V, or T.

RH: Since M, V, and T are the three determinants of prices, nothing happened to prices. But something else is wrong with the statements above. What is it?

Ss: (Silence.)

RH: Not a word from anyone? Well, let's highlight just one word in the list:

1. The *value* of the dollar is dependent on its gold content.

2. The price level is inversely related to the *value* of the dollar.

3. To get the price level up (the *value* of the dollar down), we should raise the price of gold.

   Now, any thoughts?

S4: The word *value* is used in two different senses.

RH: Of course. That's the problem. Have I not warned you about argument by definition? In this case, one word is used for two different meanings. Would you explain?

S4: Value is taken to mean, first, what the dollar would exchange for in gold. That's its meaning in statement 1. Then you switch to the second meaning of value in statement 2. The second meaning is what the dollar will buy in general, for all goods and services.

RH: So, the problem with Professor Warren, the Congress, and the administration lay in a confusion about the single word *value*. Yes, the value of the dollar dropped relative to gold. Yes, the price of gold was raised. One price went way up. But the value of the dollar, which we know is the reciprocal of the general price level, was unchanged in terms of what it could buy in goods and services. Nothing happened to the general purchasing power of the dollar because nothing happened to the prices of haircuts, your rent, your telephone bill, or what you paid for a gallon of gasoline or a dozen bananas.

   So, Warren and his fellow gold bugs confused the price of gold with the general level of prices for all goods and services. It's as simple as that. One single price, the price of gold, was mixed up with an index of prices paid for all goods and services. Professor Warren was a professor of agricultural economics. He should have stuck to his corn and beans.

GOLD AND THE DAUGHTERS OF THE AMERICAN REVOLUTION (DAR)

RH: Let me tell you another true story. Some years ago the Daughters of the American Revolution (DAR) insisted that we count our gold. We did, and it was all there. At the time, one astute economist—I believe it was Paul Samuelson—said that we could throw all of our gold into the ocean and, if we didn't tell anyone, it wouldn't have made any difference to the value of the dollar. I'll go him one better. We could have told everybody, and it still wouldn't have made any difference, except for perhaps a very short-run flutter. Remember, all of our gold is worth only a week or so of production as measured by GNP.

S5: But what about gold in international trade? Aren't you forgetting about that?

RH: No. We'll get to the major forces that influence currency exchange rates later. The amount of gold we hold is hardly a major force.

FISHER AND SMITH INCORPORATED: PESTICIDE FOR GOLD BUGS

RH: Don't take my word for it. Read Adam Smith. Smith had it right in 1776 in his *Wealth of Nations*. The value of a nation's money is not determined, he wrote, by its gold backing or convertibility into gold. No. That's the nonsensical commodity theory of money. So what does determine the value of money? The value of a nation's money, he said, is dependent on its ability to produce goods and services (not gold) and to sell goods and services (not gold) competitively in domestic and world markets. His focus, like other classical economists, was on production. That's the T in the Fisherian equation of exchange $\frac{MV}{T} = P$.

  We can update Smith with Irving Fisher by saying that the value of a nation's currency is determined by its ability to produce (reflected in T) and the management or mismanagement of fiscal, monetary, and international affairs (reflected in MV). So, the value of the dollar is but the reciprocal of P, the price level. If we could only explain and predict with precision the behavior of M, V, and T for the United States and for every other major nation, then forecasting the value of the dollar in world currency markets would be simple, too. But such prescience would put us in the same company with Peter Pan in Never-Never Land.

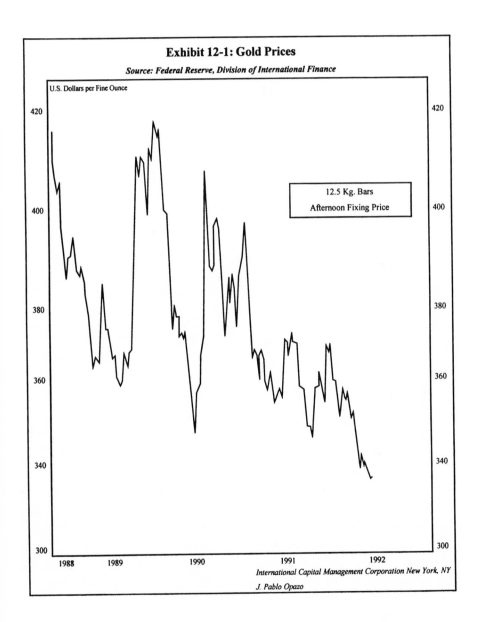

Exhibit 12-1: Gold Prices

Source: Federal Reserve, Division of International Finance

U.S. Dollars per Fine Ounce

12.5 Kg. Bars
Afternoon Fixing Price

International Capital Management Corporation New York, NY

J. Pablo Opazo

13

Fundamental Fiscal Theory

An Antidote to Fallacy and Folly

> The reason, then, for our rational confidence that the sun will rise tomorrow is not the fact that it has risen in the past, but our belief that what we have repeatedly observed are manifestations of the workings of natural laws. To assert the general proposition that future S's will be P, or that all S's will be P, simply on the grounds that a finite number (however large) of S's has been observed to be P, is to take an irrational and indefensible step.
>
> David Mitchell, *An Introduction to Logic* (1970)*

Mitchell warns us against "the fallacy of simple enumeration, or naive induction." True, his example of the sun may seem extreme to you, at least on first reading. It did to me. You expect the sun to rise tomorrow, and tomorrow and tomorrow and with the very highest probability. So do I. Even so, Mitchell has a point in warning against those who construct strong theory on weak data, even in sciences such as astronomy. That warning is far more applicable to the less exact social sciences like economics.

Taking Mitchell's advice, we must always be wary of anyone, whether philosopher or president, who makes loud claims on just a few observations of the data. Before we meet noteworthy fiscal crackpots who do just that, we should brush up on our fiscal theory, most particularly taxing, spending, and

---

*Garden City, N.Y.: Doubleday & Company, Inc., p. 204.

debt management theory. Let's join my graduate students of finance as we continue our discussion in chapter 6 on fiscal crowding out:

RH: You remember our discussion of crowding out under Reaganomics? Crowding out brought on a mean recession in 1981–82. What happened?

S1: The tax cuts and expenditure hikes were not monetized (not financed by the creation of new money). The Fed constricted money and credit, and this clashed with huge consumer and business demands for credit on top of a surge in federal borrowing. Tight money crushed private borrowing. That's crowding out.

RH: Yes, Treasury deficits and Fed overkill displaced private borrowing and spending. Now, just suppose that instead the Fed had gone to the opposite extreme. Suppose it had fully monetized the tax cuts and the increase in federal expenditures in 1981–82 by running the money printing presses at high speed. Suppose it had also monetized the rise in private borrowing. What then?

S2: Inflation and boom. Interest rates would have soared. You said Drs. Doom, Death, and other bond bears at the time thought fiscal stimulus would produce a booming economy (see Appendix A, Forecast 23; Appendix B.) I guess they expected the Federal deficits to be monetized.

RH: The big bond bears left the Fed out of their calculations. Let's shift now to another extreme case, the Great Depression of the 1930s. If you wanted to stimulate the economy by cutting taxes and increasing Federal outlays, what would you have done as head of the Federal Reserve? Would you have monetized the resulting deficits, or would you have run nonmonetized deficits, that is, borrow from the public at large? Which course would you have recommended to get out of depression?

S3: Monetize. The Treasury would want to finance the deficits with newly created money.

RH: Yes, monetized financing increases the money stock and total money spending power. Nonmonetized borrowing shuffles money from the buyer of Treasury obligations to the Treasury, then to the public, but would not increase the total money supply or total "cash" in the pockets of the public at large. So, nonmonetized deficits are hardly a recipe for fighting a depression. Take another extreme. How would you have financed World War II?

S4: Tax as much as possible. That's a shift of money and buying power from the private sector to the government. To the extent the government has to borrow, it should borrow from the public, which is also a shift in buying power. It should not monetize deficits in war. Printing a lot of money in wartime would be inflationary. With a lot of money in circulation but with little to buy, prices would rise as demand increases.

Fiscal Policy According to E-Bond Salesman Bob Hope

RH: Excellent. Remember the E bond drives in World War II? Remember Dorothy Lamour and other Hollywood stars. They traveled the country selling E Bonds. Actor and comedian Bob Hope was one of America's top salesmen of Series E savings bonds during World War II. The United States then had big advertisements for E bonds, nonmarketable Treasury savings bonds. Big government posters showed an army truck with one wheel missing. The caption read:

BUY E BONDS. DON'T LET THIS HAPPEN.

That was a bit deceptive: can you imagine our having lost the war because we couldn't afford wheels for army trucks, or motors for fighter planes? Before that would happen the Fed could have printed all the money it needed to finance the deficits. With defense spending and money incomes soaring, that would have been inflationary. The reason behind the E bond drives was to mop up the incomes of the public, curb private spending, and fight inflation. The savings bond drives represented nonmonetized financing. Let's go to another extreme. What's the Keynesian recipe to fight recessions and depressions?

S5: The opposite. Cut taxes, increase spending, and monetize the deficits.

RH: Yes, all this sounds familiar by now. These policy prescriptions are identified with what economists call Keynesian *demand management* theory. We shall turn shortly to see what Keynes himself had to say, and analyze also the criticisms of demand management theory by a strange group of economists called *supply-siders*. But first let's explore what others have said on these matters.

I'll begin with a question on *fiscal thrust.* The Conference Board, a large association of business firms, for many years popularized fiscal thrust as a useful measure of fiscal stimulus. To illustrate, suppose we were to cut taxes by $75 billion and raise Federal outlays by $100 billion. The Conference Board would then define fiscal thrust as the sum of the two, expressed here in billions of dollars:

$$\text{Tax Cut} + \text{Increase in Spending} = \text{Fiscal Thrust}$$
$$\$75 \quad + \$100 \quad\quad\quad\quad = \$175$$

What do you think? Do we have $175 billion of fiscal stimulus that would thrust the economy higher?

S6: Looks right to me. As you said, you cut taxes and increase spending to stimulate the economy.

RH: I must have been talking to myself when we reviewed the monetary and fiscal policies of 1981–82.

S5: We cut taxes in 1981 and 1982, spending went way up, and the deficit soared. But we went into recession.

RH: Correct. Why was that?

S5: The deficits were not monetized. The Fed strangled the economy with extremely tight money. That was crowding out. Because the government wasn't creating money to pay its debt, it had to borrow from the public at large. Massive Treasury borrowing soaked up the funds in the private economy that otherwise might have been spent on consumption or investment.

RH: Good. The Conference Board might well scrap its notion of fiscal thrust. It leaves monetary policy out of the picture. So, don't conclude necessarily that deficits must be stimulative, or even inflationary. Keynes had a lot to say about this. I asked one of you to report on Keynes's *General Theory* (1936); I also assigned his *How to Pay for the War* (1940) to one of you. Tell us what Keynes had to say relevant to demand management. We'll start with the *General Theory*.

S6: Keynes said the economy was operating far below full employment in the 1930s. His remedy was to run deficits, and to monetize the deficits.

S7: His short book titled *How to Pay for the War* dealt with fiscal and monetary policy in World War II. Keynes said he would cut nonmilitary spending and raise taxes. He had some kind of forced saving scheme to help finance spending in World War II.

RH: You are both right about Keynes. Let me read this from Keynes's *General Theory*:

If the Treasury were to fill old bottles with banknotes, bury them at suitable depths in disused coal mines which are then filled up to the surface with town rubbish, and leave it to private enterprise on well-tried principles of laissez-faire to dig the notes up again . . . there need be no more unemployment and,

---

*New York: Harcourt, Brace and Company, 1936.

with the help of the repercussions, the real income of the community, and its capital wealth also, would probably become a good deal greater than it actually is. It would, indeed, be more sensible to build houses and the like; but if there are political and practical difficulties in the way of this, the above would be better than nothing.*

That's one side of Keynes. In 1936 he was the big spender. But he was the opposite in *How to Pay for the War* just four years later. Let me read to you two short passages on his proposal for forced saving:

The first provision in our radical plan is, therefore, to determine a proportion of each man's earnings which must be deferred;—withdrawn, that is to say, from immediate consumption and only made available as a right to consume after the war is over. . . . That part of the earnings and other income of the public to be deferred under this plan would be placed to the credit of its owner as a blocked deposit at $2\frac{1}{2}\%$ compound interest.†

So, in addition to taxes, it's 100 percent clear how Keynes would finance war spending. He would tax heavily. How would he borrow?

S8:   As nonmonetized. I guess he was afraid of inflation.

RH: Yes, nonmonetized! The forced saving plan meant nonmonetized sales of government obligations to the public at large. He wanted to soak up purchasing power to counter inflation. That's the other side of Keynes. It appears that John Maynard Keynes and Bob Hope had something in common. They both believed in nonmonetized borrowing in time of war to fight inflation. In that sense, they are in the same league with inflation-killer Paul Volcker, that is, the Paul Volcker of 1981–82. We must classify all three as inflation fighters in these critical periods in U.S. history.

    In sum, Keynes would always ask what the circumstances were before offering counsel on fiscal and monetary policy. He would drain in time of flood, and irrigate in time of drought. Pardon the analogy, and excuse my repetition, but what I have just said stands in violent contrast with the abused and stereotyped image the typical businessman has of this extraordinary economist. He thinks of Keynes as a 100 percent big spender for all seasons, for all times.

    I think you have the essence of my remarks on fiscal thrust. As bad

---

General Theory (New York: Harcourt, Brace and Company, 1936), p. 129.
†*How to Pay for the War* (New York: Harcourt, Brace and Company, 1940), pp. 10 and 44.

as the measure is, there's another that's even worse. It's the reported budgetary deficit. Does anybody know why?

Ss: (No response.)

RH: Here's a clue. The problem with the reported deficit, the one you always read about in the press, is that it is affected by cyclical fluctuations in the economy. Any ideas?

S6:   When we go into recession or depression, tax revenues dry up. That causes the deficit to increase.

RH: Right! Big deficits go with recessions like ham goes with eggs (chapter 6). The point is that a swelling deficit automatically goes with a sinking economy. People lose their jobs and their incomes, and the Treasury sees its tax revenues evaporate. Under these conditions, the reported deficit largely reflects recession; it may not be evidence of fiscal stimulus. Don't confuse the two. On the other hand, when the economy is speeding uphill, jobs and incomes advance, too. So do tax receipts. Under these conditions, tax revenues may tend to rise faster than Federal outlays, and the reported deficit may shrink. In those circumstances the shrinking deficit may reflect an expanding economy. Indeed, the economy could be expanding and the reported deficit shrinking even in the face of huge monetary and fiscal stimulation.

Let me dramatize this. In 1978 I took thirty-five investment officers with me to Washington to meet with Dr. Nancy Teeters, who was then the chief economist of the House Budget Committee. (Later she became the first woman on the Board of Governors of the Federal Reserve System. She's quite a lady, and a superb economist.) I was worried over the risk of accelerating wage and price inflation. I expected consumer price inflation to move up to 10 percent and higher by the end of 1978. It did. And what do you think was happening to the reported budget deficit in 1978? It was contracting, and almost went into balance. Now how could that be? The answer was that the shrinking deficit reflected an overheated economy, one in which incomes and tax receipts were rising. Both fiscal and monetary policies were highly expansionary and inflationary.

That's the message I wanted to send to my institutional investor clients. Nancy Teeters did that for me. When I asked her what she was projecting for the budget deficit, she responded with this gem: "If inflation heats up much more, I'll predict a budget surplus." What did she mean?

S7:   Just what you have been saying. She meant that high and rising money incomes would push people into higher income brackets? Tax receipts could climb quickly.

RH: Exactly. *Bracket creep,* as it was called, meant that inflation lifted money incomes, and higher incomes pushed taxpayers into higher tax brackets. Keep in mind also that our meeting took place before President Reagan took office. Tax rates in 1978 were then higher across the income scale, and progressive, meaning steep rises in marginal tax rates for the higher incomes. Also, as inflation accelerated, government tax receipts tended to advance faster than government outlays. Dr. Teeters stressed that tax receipts tended to kick in quickly with accelerating inflation, while Federal expenditures tended to rise with a lag of about one year.*

     My meeting with Dr. Teeters was in 1978. What about now, 1989? Is there any chance now that high inflation could push us into surplus?

S9:   Wouldn't the tax cuts and spending increases of recent years under President Reagan work against that?

RH: To some degree. But you should know that the rise in social security tax rates largely offset the cut in other tax rates. When you combine the two you don't get lower tax rates for most of us. Any other ideas?

S9:   Slow economic growth, which we now have, would rule surpluses out.

RH: How right you are. Anything else?

S9:   The interest burden.

RH: Yes, the huge Federal debt brought with it colossal interest charges, the so-called service charge on the national debt. Let me read you these numbers reported by the Council of Economic Advisers. They say interest expense in fiscal 1993 totaled $199 billion, or 14 percent of total Federal expenditures of $1,425 billion. Interest expense represented 71 percent of the 1993 consolidated deficit of $281 billion. That huge interest translates into payments (receipts if you own Treasuries). It's a "transfer" expense, largely funded by new borrowing, a legacy of the Great Depression, World War II, nine recessions after 1945, the Korean and Vietnam Wars, Reaganomics, Bushnomics, Congressional spending, and S&L bailouts.

     Economists seldom speak of budget surpluses any longer, even

---

*She repeated these exact words in a telephone call to me on October 23, 1990, twelve years after our meeting in 1978.

under conditions of full employment. Instead, they keep projecting budget deficits. Maybe you can see now why the reported deficit must be the very worst indicator of fiscal policy. It's the most popular but the very worst. So, how can we better measure fiscal policy?

Ss: Something called the full-employment deficit?

RH: Yes. Economists have rough measures that try to separate the impact on the reported deficit of (a) tax and expenditure changes from (b) cyclical fluctuations in the economy. We have to disentangle the impact of fiscal policy on the deficit from the influence cyclical fluctuations in the economy may have on the deficit. That's easier said than done.

Let's explain the meaning behind the full-employment surplus or deficit. Just what is that animal?

S6: It's defined as the surplus or deficit that would exist at full employment. You're supposed to ask what tax revenues and expenditures would be if we reached full employment with any given tax and budgetary policies.

RH: Not bad. The idea is very simple. In the early 1960s Dr. Walter Heller, then the president's chief economist, made the point I have been stressing. Heller argued in *The Economic Report of the President* for 1961 that fiscal policy could not be gauged by looking at the reported deficit. True, the deficit ballooned in the recession of 1960–61 as the economy sank into recession, but you couldn't take that, he argued, as evidence of fiscal stimulus. He then asked what the Federal accounts would be if we were ever to get at full employment. His answer is that we would be in surplus. But he doubted that we could ever get to full employment unless we cut tax rates. So, a nasty paradox was involved here. High income tax rates, he argued, were acting as a fierce *fiscal drag* that would keep us from ever reaching full employment. What did Dr. Heller mean by fiscal drag?

S3: As the economy tended to expand, tax receipts would climb even faster, and depress private spending?

RH: Yes. Heller argued that the Federal sector would drain away too much spending power. His conviction was that extremely high tax rates worked against our ever getting out of the recession of 1960–61. His solution was to cut rates, and to *monetize* the cuts. The notion of fiscal drag was novel at the time, and controversial.

ACTUAL VERSUS "FULL-EMPLOYMENT" OR "STANDARDIZED" DEFICITS

RH: Let me illustrate just how misleading the actual deficit numbers can be. For example, in the 1981–82 recession the reported total deficit rose sharply in 1982 while the full-employment deficit, also called the standardized deficit, barely budged, then turned stimulative in 1983. (The 1983 full-employment deficit rose to $106 billion, *and it was largely monetized.*) The standardized deficit is designed to adjust for cyclical fluctuations as they impact both government spending and government receipts. For example, jobs, incomes, and tax revenues fall in recession, and the standardized deficit would add back the lost tax revenues. It would subtract the higher unemployment payments that were caused by recession. With that in mind, glance at these data from the Congressional Budget Office:

FISCAL YEAR	ACTUAL DEFICIT	STANDARDIZED DEFICIT (IN $ BILLIONS)
1980	$ 74	$ 51
1981	79	48
1982	128	51
1983	208	106

Let's analyze now the International Monetary Fund (IMF) fiscal impulse measures. They are perhaps the easiest to understand. Very simply, suppose that the IMF finds that government spending tends to rise more slowly than the growth of the economy, and that tax receipts tend to increase faster than the growth of the economy. How do you think they would classify that, as stimulative or restrictive?

S8: Restrictive.

RH: Yes. They label that as a restrictive fiscal impulse. Now suppose government spending tended to speed ahead faster than potential GNP and that tax revenues tended to lag GNP, to rise at a slower rate than the rise in GNP. How would the IMF classify that?

S8: Expansionary.

RH: O.K. What do you think of the IMF fiscal impulse measures and the standardized-employment deficits? Do you see any problem with these measures?

S9:   Neither say anything about how the deficit is to be financed, whether it's monetized or not. You said we could tell little or nothing about policy until we integrate fiscal with monetary policy.

RH: Correct. I asked the IMF when they would get around to coupling their fiscal measures with monetary measures. They said they "were working on it," whatever that means.

Let's apply now what we have learned about fiscal theory to fiscal practice. My first question has to do with the notion of a balanced budget. Some people would require that we balance the budget every year. Suppose for some reason we fell into a major recession, and tried to do just that. What would that imply for fiscal policy?

S6:   Raise taxes? Cut federal expenditures?

RH: Yes, that could risk even greater recession. At the other extreme, we just learned that we could run a surplus in a highly inflationary economy. To force balance in the budget might then require cuts in taxes and increases in spending. But that's procyclical, perverse.

S8:   But in recession, wouldn't higher taxes and cuts in consumption reduce interest rates, and stimulate investment spending?

RH: Maybe. But remember that there is no automatic mechanism that propels private spending higher with a fall in interest rates, certainly not when the economy is in a cyclical decline. You're correct in arguing that consumers and businessmen may borrow and spend more with lower interest rates, other things being equal. If people lose their jobs and income, they won't spend (see chapter 9).

A CONSTITUTIONAL AMENDMENT ON THE BUDGET?

Let's jump now to an exchange I had on March 15, 1979, with The North Westchester Branch of the American Association of University Women, whom I'll identify as P. The Dean of Pace University's graduate business school had asked me to address them on the outlook. He neglected to tell me, however, that many in the audience were ardent supporters of a constitutional amendment to balance the budget each and every year. Here's the ever-so-brief transcript following my presentation:

P: What's wrong with balancing the budget every year?

RH: Let me turn the question around. Why not balance the budget every six months, or every two years, or every five years, or every fifteen years? Why not balance the budget over the business cycle? Why not balance the budget over the long-run secular swings in the economy? I'm all for balancing the budget, but I ask what's magic about twelve months, exactly twelve months? Let's rule out any alleged accounting convenience, which could hardly be considered a major argument.

Ps: (Angry silence.)

RH: There are seventy of you here. I think a balanced budget is a good idea. I don't understand, though, why you insist on balance every twelve months.

P1:   Well, I hear that Ronald Reagan thinks it's a good idea. He could be our next president.

P2:   So does William F. Buckley, Jr. He's no dummy.

RH: I'm asking you, not Reagan or Buckley.

Ps: (Silence, total and complete. End of transcript.)

Now you know why I tagged this group (not individuals) with the letter P . . . for Parrots. I shall never forget their fever for a constitutional amendment to balance the budget every month—I meant every year. Years later in 1995 comparable delirium erupted in Representative Newt Gingrich's Contract With America. What's new?

NATIONALLY RECOGNIZED PERSONALITIES: BUCKLEY, BATRA, AND PEROT

To document and illustrate further fiscal folly and farce, let's meet three more nationally recognized personalities. They all share Newt Gingrich's penchant for turning sense into nonsense. You may recognize this trio:

- Social philosopher William F. Buckley, Jr.
- Economist Ravi (*The Great Depression of 1990*) Batra
- Businessman H. Ross Perot

1. Buckley's Babble

After meeting with the American Association of University Women, and recalling their comments on Buckley, I decided to check out just what this best-selling author, TV charmer, and revered intellectual on the political right had to say. Maybe I was overlooking something. Consider here Buckley's extraordinary (one of his favorite words) comments on federal tax and budget policies under Reaganomics. I quote from *Right Reason*:

> Sometime after the automobile was invented, it generally transpired that automobiles could not be permitted to drive as fast as engineers could make them drive. . . . So there came: the speed laws. . . . The time has come to mitigate the lure of temptation. If we had a balanced budget amendment—one carefully drawn up to take contingency into consideration—we would have the constitutional equivalent of speeding laws. How good it would be if bipartisan support could be got for such an amendment.*

What do you think of his argument? What would logician Thouless say? Thouless would probably remind us that argument by imperfect analogy should be "dealt with by examining the alleged analogy in detail and point out where it breaks down." That's as easily done as said. Buckley's speed limit could be set too low, and bring on huge traffic tieups. It's that simple. The analogy breaks down on its own. Buckley then cries out for truth in this passage:

> The *Wall Street Journal* recently poked about various studies of the effect of the reduced 1979 capital gains tax [the law reducing the tax from 49 to 28 percent]. Opponents of the proposed reduction did everything except commit satyagraha to stop Congress. Among other things they claimed the measure would cost the government, in lost revenues, $1.7 billion dollars. What in fact happened? The Treasury collected $1.1 billion more in taxes under the lower rate than the higher rate. But that isn't all. In 1969, the last year of an earlier lower capital gains tax rate, 698 stock offerings went out.†

Buckley then cites data on pages 84–85 showing that the lower the tax, the greater the stock offerings, and the greater the employment generated by business in the years through 1976.

Really? While tax revenues did rise following the tax cut, other forces were at work that could have boosted (or depressed) tax receipts for a single year. The same applies to explaining new stock issues. The point is that we simply cannot assert tax changes (as the cause) and the observed changes in tax revenues and new stock issues (as the effects). We know, for example, that tax revenues respond not only to government tax and spending changes, but

---

*(New York: Doubleday & Company, 1985), pp. 288–89.
†Ibid.

also to fluctuations in the economy itself. Economists at least try to separate out one from the other by making estimates of the standardized or cyclically adjusted budget. Not Buckley. He's content to fit the data to whatever conclusion he happens to like at the time, a fallacy Thouless classifies as proof by selected instances.

Forcing the observed data to match your wanted results can backfire. Buckley's general line of argument—that tax cuts must bolster new stock financing—would have backfired badly in the 1980s. We know that the Reagan tax cuts were not associated with any observed increase in equity financing. What we witnessed instead was a massive contraction in equity financing, and a massive increase in debt financing. The great equity *implosion* of the 1980s came on the heels of Reagan tax cuts in individual and corporate income tax rates. Many forces were at work to explain these developments, among them corporate buyout and junk-bond financing antics. All in all, the developments had little to do with the capital gains tax.

The next time you read Buckley's babble, remember to have logician David Mitchell by your side. Remember Mitchell's warning to be skeptical of anyone who concludes, reasons, implies, or infers (another of Buckley's favorite words) that just because x changes in the tax code precede y observed swings, either up or down, in tax receipts and stock underwritings, that x must therefore cause y. Keep in mind Mitchell's caution against proof by simple enumeration whenever you encounter comparable babble.

Also, be careful who you blame for big deficits. We talk and talk about balancing the budget, but in fact the last time we ran a budget surplus was in 1969. So, who's to blame? The answer is *we the people.*

Batra's Balderdash

Again, let's quote rather than paraphrase. Like Buckley, let Ravi Batra speak for himself. So, what do you think of this short piece from his pride and joy, the book he says he wrote for professional economists. It's entitled *Regular Economic Cycles* (1985).* He starts off with Jaownath Sarkar's law of the social cycle:

> Specifically, in the development of every civilization, ancient or modern, oriental or occidental, the era of laborers is followed by the era of warriors by the era of intellectuals by the era of acquisitors, culminating in a social revolution—such a social evolution is the infallible Law of Nature.†

---

*New York: St. Martin's Press.
†Ibid., p. 15.

Then Batra couples Sarkar's law, whoever he was, with a few statistics borrowed from Milton Friedman:

> Thus except for the post-Civil War interregnum, the decennial rate of growth of money crested every third decade over the past two centuries. This is an amazing feature of the U.S. economy never discovered before and it fits deftly with Sarkar's hypothesis that the dominant variable of any age follows a rhythmical pattern.*

Based on his integration of the mystical and the monetary, he then warns us of the great depression of "1990" or, depending on his mood, the "1990s." Here's his "proof," the one word I detest the most when uttered by social scientists:

> All historical patterns that I have studied point towards the inevitability of the depression of the 1990s. . . . The new depression is unavoidable. . . . Yet it is not too late. Something can still be done to escape or ease the impending crisis.†

Thank Heavens. But what? He says we must:

> Restore the tax rates prevailing before Mr. Reagan came to office, [institute] a federal property tax, and [distribute] the stock of large corporations among blue and white collar workers.‡

Now we know how to escape the inevitable.

Batra's Bastardizing of Kondratieff

Let's get serious in our appraisal of Batra. Nicholas D. Kondratieff, you may recall, was the Russian economist who identified long cycles of roughly fifty years' duration. Some economists believe that these long waves are linked with major technological developments such as the emergence of the railroads and electric power. That's legitimate enough. But how about Batra?

Batra superimposes charts of recent economic data upon past historical patterns, especially the late 1920s and 1930s, and then argues by historical analogy about future prospects. He cites a few observations of price level swings and money growth cycles going back a century or more, and then pro-

---

*Regular Economic Cycles, p. 68.
†Ibid., p. 153.
‡Ibid., pp. 160–66.

poses to tell us exactly when many interrelated variables such as income, production, employment, consumer and investment demand, exchange rates, the stock market, real estate, and prices and money are all supposed to collapse.

There are problems here, to say the least. First, Batra's conclusions are undermined by an insufficient number of "degrees of freedom." This means his forecasts of variables far outnumber his observations of the relevant data, which violates good statistical procedure and theory. Second, he trips on argument by naive induction. To do so is to commit one of the oldest logical fallacies, which is what this chapter tried to stress. Third, he revels in appeal to mystic authority, but argument by authority is weak at best and generally viewed as fallacious reasoning. These are reasons enough, even should the U.S. economy move into depression, that Batra not be given any credit for his forecast. Is Batra (1) a Huckster, (2) a Parrot, (3) a Pro, (4) a confused but well-meaning mystic, or (5) an economic scientist? You decide.

Perot's Prattle

We left Perot for last and least. What can one say of this on-again-off-again presidential contender? Well, Perot stumbles and trips on virtually all the logical traps reviewed in this chapter. Worst of all is his insistence that the magnitude of the reported deficit can be taken as a reliable indicator of fiscal stimulus and inflation. In fact it is one of the very worst. That, I remind you, is what this chapter was all about.

Postscript on the Linkage of Batra and Perot

After placing Perot and Batra in the same chapter with fiscal quacks, imagine my surprise when I read the following in the November 9, 1993, issue of the *Wall Street Journal*:

> Behind Mr. [H. Ross] Perot, the movement's leading figure is undoubtedly Pat Buchanan. In his most recent attempt to attract popular support for the movement, Mr. Buchanan has cited the work of economist Ravi Batra.

I should have guessed. We will encounter H. Ross Perot yet again in our review of Parrot-and-Pro "protectionists" in the international arena (chapter 22).

14

Taxes and the Budget

The Triumph of Self-Deception Over Scientific Method

> Man is self, and the self must be selfish. . . . Of course, we
> are told, the healthy inner-directed person will *really* care
> for others. To which I can only respond: if you can believe
> that, you can believe anything.
>
> Alan Bloom, *The Closing of the American Mind* (1987)*

Chapter 13 dealt with fiscal crackpots. We turn now to tax theory, practice, and malpractice. The focus here is not on deliberate deception, but submerged self-deception. When it comes to taxes, the unconscious mind puts its bank balance up front. Ethics and economic science sit in the back seat.

TAX IMPACT VERSUS TAX INCIDENCE

I shall try to demonstrate this in our discussion of tax *incidence*. Economists mean by incidence the final resting place or burden of a given tax. Now, be careful not to confuse *incidence* with *impact,* or the initial point of levy. For example, who do you believe pays the corporate income tax? The initial point of levy, the impact, is on the corporation. There's no debate there. But suppose the corporation can raise its prices to consumers by the full amount of the tax without reducing sales or aftertax profits. Alternatively, suppose the corporation can offset the tax by cutting wages or by forcing suppliers to

---

*New York: Simon & Schuster, p. 178.

lower their prices. In these two cases, economists say the final tax burden is shifted, either forward to consumers or backwards to labor and suppliers. Economists call this the *shifting thesis*. But if the corporation is unable to shift the tax forward or backward, then the tax would reduce corporate cash flow and aftertax profits. Economists call that the *absorption thesis*. So, is the corporate income tax shifted (either forward or backward), or absorbed, or partially shifted?

We'll explore this complex question of tax incidence, and pay attention also to the effects of both personal and corporate income taxes on the incentives to work, save and invest. Then we'll be able to understand and document just how the best and the brightest can fall victim to their own minds, to self-deception, whenever taxes enter the picture.

DELIBERATE DECEPTION VERSUS SELF-DECEPTION

Is self-deception less of a sin than deliberate selfishness at the expense of others? I don't know for sure because we can't even identify much less measure with any confidence this matter of self-deception. As Alan Bloom argues, we cannot even distinguish the selfish person from the inner-directed person who really cares for others. Even so, while self-deception may be less of a sin than deliberate deception, that doesn't make it any less dangerous to society. *Nothing is more dangerous than brilliant and highly influential ideologists who deceive themselves. Nothing is more dangerous to society than ideologists wearing blinders.*

Blinders? They are, you recall, the leather flaps on a bridle that keep a horse from seeing what is on either side. Highly respected ideologists wear blinders, too, but they are often unaware of it. That's the bad news. The good news is that, with the help of sound theory and relevant data, we can spot tax quacks wearing blinders. See for yourself in the cases we now examine of how constructed tax models collapse from the weight of their own contradictions.

Tax Models with a Powerful Trade Association

Let's start this analysis with the American Council of Life Insurance, the largest and most powerful life insurance organization in the country. When I worked as its research director in the 1960s (then The Life Insurance Association of America [LIAA]), its board of directors decided to spend some $300,000 for a study on taxes. It wanted to *prove* just how damaging high marginal income tax rates were supposed to be on the incentives to work, save, and invest. The focus was on supply-side economics, long before the supply-siders under President Reagan appeared on the scene. The LIAA commissioned economist Daniel Holland, now Professor Emeritus at MIT, to head up the investigation under the auspices of the National Bureau of Economic Research (NBER). He was to interview corporate executives to see how they might react to income taxes. That was a key objective, among others. The board took it for granted that Dr. Holland would come up with the necessary *proof.* (There's that word again.)

I was worried about the proposed study, and said so. First, I doubted that anyone would take the study seriously unless psychologists were to collaborate with Dr. Holland in these interviews. Dr. Holland was an economist, not a psychologist trained in the complex world of human motivation. I asked that a psychologist assist Dr. Holland in designing a questionnaire, in participating directly in the interviews, and in interpreting the results. The study, I thought, presented a great opportunity to integrate disciplines, a goal economists forever preach but seldom practice. The NBER, then headed by Dr. Arthur Burns, shot down my concerns and my suggestion. Too costly, I was told.

Second, and equally important, I felt sure that the results of the interviews would not support the contention of the LIAA that income taxes destroyed the incentives to work. To be blunt about it, I said they were about to throw $300,000 down the drain. They were looking for answers they would not get. The sponsors turned down my second objection too. The study went ahead.

Many years later, I decided to find out just what had happened. I asked Pace University librarian Mrs. Michelle Fanelli (MF) to help me locate the Holland study. We searched everywhere, even checking the university computer to see whether other cooperating libraries might have the Holland work. We couldn't find the study. This exchange followed on November 5, 1990:

RH: Michelle, you searched long and hard. You've checked all the LIAA publications and those of the NBER. I'll bet that neither the LIAA nor the NBER ever published the study.

MF: Why? You said it was an important study, and expensive.

Deception: Fitting Analysis to Predetermined Conclusions

RH: My guess is that Dr. Holland's conclusions displeased the sponsors of the study. I bet they shelved it. The LIAA expected Holland to demonstrate that high marginal income tax rates killed incentives. But people work for prestige, power, accomplishment, peer approval, money, among many other things. The income tax rate is far down the list in explaining efforts to work. Any introductory text in psychology would say as much. I'm convinced Holland knew that. I'm convinced he would never fit theory and data to any predetermined conclusions. I mean conclusions sought by the sponsors of the study. No, Michelle, Dr. Holland would not prostitute his mind. He's no Pro. We must find out what happened to his study.

MF: I'll keep looking. You asked me to locate Holland. He's now at MIT in Cambridge. Here's his phone number.

Tax Policy According to Dr. Daniel Holland

(I telephoned Dr. Holland that evening, Monday, November 5, 1990, at 9 P.M.)

RH: Dr. Holland, my name is Robert Parks. I met you years ago when I was research director at the LIAA in the late 1960s. I wanted to ask you about a study you then made on the effect of income taxes on corporate executives, on their incentives to work, save, and invest. I left for Wall Street before the study was completed. Do you remember?

DH: Yes. Go on.

RH: I recall you telling me that taxes seemed to have little effect in discouraging how hard top corporate executives worked. You said taxes had a minor impact, too, on the length of their vacation, their retirement plans, or the time they spent on tax matters. Of all things, I remember you telling me that many of the middle-income executives you interviewed said they would work harder as a consequence of higher tax rates. They would do so to maintain their present living standard, to get the cash to offset higher tax bills. That's what I remember of your conclusions. Am I correct?

DH: Yes, the results were generally along those lines. Some would work harder, and others would be discouraged. The interview results were mixed, inconclusive.

RH: I was not surprised. The LIAA had no interest in the results you came up with. I was convinced of that then, and am still convinced. Some of the presidents on that research committee were infuriated with your inconclusive conclusions. Did you know that?

DH: No.

RH: Let me get to the reason for my call. *What happened to your study?* I can't find it anywhere. I want to include the results in a book I'm writing on Wall Street.

DH: I believe you can find some of the research in the *1969 Proceedings of the National Tax Association.** Let me remind you that what I published in the *Proceedings* was not cleared, either by the NBER or the LIAA.

RH: I'm deeply grateful to you; I'll get the *Proceedings.*

(I did, and was no longer puzzled about his study not being "cleared." I found this devastating summary on page 456.)

> As a summary . . . most executives—eighty percent of our sample—were apparently not deterred as regards the effort they devote to their main job by the income tax.

RH: By the way, is the National Tax Association linked at all with the *National Tax Journal?*

DH: No, but I was once editor of the *National Tax Journal* for several years.

RH: I know. Did you know that you published two of my articles? One was on the incidence of the corporate income tax.†

DH: We did?

A PREFACE TO UNTANGLING THE ALLEGED DOUBLE TAX

Incidence? Let's turn now to an analysis of the incidence of the corporate income tax, especially the alleged "double tax" on corporate shareholders. So, join me in this typical exchange with students of finance:

RH: Study these illustrative data I've put on the board:

	(1)	Tax Rates	(2)	Tax Rates
Pretax Profits	$100		$100	
Corporate Tax	0	0%	30	30%
After-Tax Profits	100		70	
Personal Tax (30%)	30	30%	21	30%
Total Tax on Shareholders	30		51	

---

*Daniel Holland, "Effect of Taxation on Compensation and Effort: The Case of Business Executives," *1969 Proceedings of the Sixty-Second Annual Conference on Taxation.*

†Robert H. Parks, "Theory of Tax Incidence, International Aspects," *National Tax Journal,* June 1961.

Let's assume, initially at least, that the corporate income tax is paid for 100 percent out of corporate cash flow and earnings, that every dollar of corporate income tax leaves just one dollar less in after-tax profits. That's what economic theorists call the "absorption" hypothesis, and what ideologists often take as natural law. We're concerned here, at least initially, with just the arithmetic. Assuming 100 percent absorption, we must figure out what would be the *extra* burden on corporate share-holders of the corporate income tax.

Double Taxation Under the "Absorption" View of Incidence

RH: Assume further that all after-tax corporate earnings are either distrib-uted to shareholders or plowed back into productive assets, and that in the latter case the market price of the stock rises to reflect the plowback. Let's assume that the capital gains and the personal income tax are both 30 percent. Now, what's the *extra* burden of double taxation, even as-suming 100 percent absorption? Study these data in the column marked 30 percent for the assumed corporate tax rate:

	ASSUMED CORPORATE TAX RATES				
	0%	30%	50%	80%	100%
Pretax Profits	100	100	100	100	100
Corporate Tax	0	30	50	80	100
After-Tax Profits	100	70	50	20	0
Personal Tax (30%)	30	21	15	6	0
Total Tax	30	51	65	86	100
Personal Tax at 30%	30	30	30	30	30
Corporate Tax Shield*	0	9	15	24	30
Extra Burden of Tax		21	15	6	0

*30% x corporate taxes, which reduces after-tax corporate incomes payable as personal incomes

S1:   The extra burden is 21, not 30.

RH: Good. You can see that the difference of nine is the personal income tax actually paid of 21 (30% x 70 = 21) subtracted from the personal in-come tax you would have paid of 30 (30% x 100) if the corporate tax had been zero instead of 30 percent. Let's call the difference of 9 the double-tax shield. That means the extra tax burden of the double tax amounts to 21, not 30. The shield in dollars is calculated as the dollar amount of the corporate taxes paid multiplied by the personal tax rate, in this case 30 times 30 percent, which is 9. Now let's illustrate how the extra burden of the double tax falls, meaning the shield rises, as the marginal corporate tax rate rises. For example, with the same 30 percent personal rate, the extra burden would be 15 with a 50 percent corporate rate, and 6 with an 80 percent corporate rate. The extra tax would be zero with a confiscatory 100 percent corporate tax. Ha! In that case, there would be nothing left to tax.

The simple arithmetic here is not always obvious until pointed out. Professor Dan Holland alerted me to this tax distinction years ago in a little book he wrote for the National Bureau of Economic Research titled *Dividends Under the Income Tax* (1962).* Ever hear of Dr. Holland?

S2:   No.

RH: We'll return to Holland later.

TAX POLICY ACCORDING TO DR. MARTIN FELDSTEIN

Let's meet Dr. Martin Feldstein, a Harvard Professor of Economics, President of the National Bureau of Economic Research, and former Chairman of the Council of Economic Advisers under President Reagan. He too had some strange notions on tax incidence. So, please listen in on this exchange I had with him (MF) at a luncheon forum I hosted for him and thirty-five institutional investment officers in New York City on April 28, 1977:

MF: Let me sum up. The corporate tax absorbs corporate cash flow that otherwise would be available to finance capital formation in machinery, plant and equipment, new technology, and research and development. By absorbing cash flow, the corporate income tax cripples the rise in productivity, slows growth of real output, and raises costs and prices. The economy suffers from higher inflation, less real growth, and an impaired ability to compete internationally. Corporate shareholders pay a double tax. They're taxed first indirectly. That's because corporate income taxes reduce aftertax profits, and cut into the cash flow from which dividends are paid. They're also taxed directly on the receipt of corporate dividends. The double taxation of corporate shareholders is a major force damaging investment incentives and economic growth.

---

*A Study of the NBER (Princeton, N.J.: Princeton University Press, 1962), p. 8.

RH: Thank you very much. I have one question. You contend in your books and articles that tax *incidence,* the real burden, is shifted forward, that the consumer mainly pays the corporate tax in the form of higher consumer prices. Isn't that your position on tax incidence?

MF: Well, yes, the tax is mostly shifted forward, but . . .

RH: I'm confused. We have a double tax in the sense that the corporate tax rests initially on the corporation. That's the impact of the corporate tax. It may or may not be the incidence, the real burden of who pays. You yourself have made that distinction, and often. What am I missing? How can there be a double tax on corporate shareholders if, as you say, the tax is shifted?

MF: Well, there are other things involved here. Taxes impair incentives no matter who pays them. Taxes can raise costs and interest rates. You see that.

RH: That may be, but that's not my question.

All Dr. Feldstein had to do to get out of the box he found himself in was to make explicit the circumstances involved. For example, he could have pointed to the early post-World War II years when the United States had a seller's market, when the whole world was trying to get our goods. It was easy then to shift the tax forward. In that case, though, he could not have made a strong case that corporations were suffering from double taxation.

Better yet from his point of view, Dr. Feldstein could have noted that at the time of our meeting we were running big deficits in our trade accounts. International competition for markets had heated up, and this made it increasingly difficult to pass along tax increases into higher prices. But he didn't. Instead he tried to reconcile the irreconcilable, namely, that corporations suffer from a double tax even as they shift the tax forward to consumers. That, I submit, is an all too common example of ideology dominating science, even for the best and the brightest. Call this what it is: self-deception.

THE THEORY OF TAX INCIDENCE: INTERNATIONAL ASPECTS

Let's explain more fully this complex notion of tax incidence in an international context. I'll lean on an admittedly oversimplified arithmetic example, especially as regards elasticities of supply and demand. Let's assume that the price of an internationally traded good is, say, $10, with production costs $6, taxes $2, and normal profits $2. Now, suppose you as a domestic company were subjected to a corporate income tax of $3, and that you were subjected to perfectly competitive markets. How much could you shift? The answer, other things being equal, is $2; you would have to absorb the difference of $1. You can only charge $10. Subtract production costs of $6 and taxes of $3, and your profits are only $1, not $2. You absorb $1. It's as simple as that, a case I had argued many years earlier in the article I mentioned to Dr. Holland:

> If the differential principle as applied to business taxation is correct, then both the extent and the timing of price shifting (or absorption) of any nation is dependent fundamentally on the degree of competition faced. Short-run and long-run have little meaning out of this context. An open economy with little effective competition from foreign nations should be able to shift easily and quickly. But if competition should increase rather than decrease over time, shifting would become progressively more difficult. It would be unconvincing under these circumstances to hold, as does traditional theory, that the tax is absorbed in the short run but shifted in the long run. Just the reverse could be true, as more and more American businessmen would be quick to point out.
>
> In most careful works in taxation, the terms short-run and long-run are defined to refer to operational rather than historical time. The former abstracts from technological change and ordinarily embraces a closed system. Undoubtedly, a great deal of the confusion regarding tax incidence stems from a confusion of the operational concept with the real historical world of change and international competition.*

To repeat, Professor Feldstein could have made a fairly good case in 1977 (but not in the early post-World War II years) that corporations had a hard time shifting taxes forward. He could then have defended his thesis of double taxation. But he didn't. He danced around the question. That's what people do, whatever their education or status, when they become enmeshed in contradictions of their own making. They do an ideological dance, unconscious even that they are dancing.

A POSTSCRIPT ON IDEOLOGICAL DANCING

Our meeting apparently had zero impact on Dr. Feldstein's thinking. To illustrate what I mean, consider here his reaffirmation of the shifting thesis in a major work published a few years after our 1977 forum:

---

*Parks, "Theory of Tax Incidence, International Aspects," p. 195.

The traditional theory of tax incidence emphasized that a general factor tax is borne entirely by the factor on which the tax is levied. In contrast, this chapter shows that in the long run the burden of a general profits tax is more likely to be divided between capital and labor. This *shifting* of the tax is particularly large for a balanced budget tax change in which an increased profits tax is used to finance additional government spending. But even a differential tax change in which a profits tax is substituted for a payroll tax *is likely to be shifted by a substantial amount.** (Emphasis added.)

Shifted? Well, it follows as night follows day that to the extent the tax is shifted forward, to that same extent the corporate tax cannot be counted a double tax. You can't double count. Every dollar shifted forward weakens the double-taxation argument. Forecast: Feldstein will never abandon his view that a company pays a tax that it shifts to somebody else. To be sure, of the many forums I hosted for economists and government officials over the years, Dr. Feldstein proved to be among the best organized, the most eloquent, and the most interesting of speakers. Was he convincing? That's for you to decide. It appeared to me that Feldstein's fervor got in the way of economic science, but I can't prove that. I do feel confident, though, with this general conclusion based on the hundreds of economic forums I have hosted over the years. I'll put it in bold caps:

SELF-DECEPTION IS THE HALLMARK
OF THE CRUSADING ASCETIC.

DOUBLE TALK ON DOUBLE TAXATION

Let's insert a positive note at this point. Listen in on the telephone exchange I had years ago with a senior officer of the U.S. Chamber of Commerce in Washington D.C. I'll call him AN for anonymous:

RH: The Chamber argues in this week's *Economic Intelligence* that the corporate income tax sops up corporate cash flow. Just last month your same publication concluded that consumers paid the tax. I saw some ads of yours in the newspapers, full-page ads, also declaring that the consumer pays the corporate tax through the nose in higher inflation. What goes on here? How can you reach completely opposite conclusions every other week?

AN: Robert, I was just hired for this job. I had nothing to do with that double-talk baloney.

---

*Martin Feldstein, *Capital Taxation* (Cambridge and London: Harvard University Press, 1983), p. 409.

Part Five

Stock Market Theory, Practice, and Malpractice

15

Stock Valuation Tools

Forecasting Black Monday

> The value of any asset can be expressed as the present value of expected future cash flows discounted at a rate commensurate with the perceived risk of the asset. For common stock, the cash flows come from the expected dividend stream (to infinity) generated by the stock.
>
> $$V = \sum_{t=1}^{\text{Infinity}} \frac{Dt\,(1+g)^t}{(1+k)^t}$$
>
> where Dt = expected dividend in period t
>
> g = expected growth rate in dividends
>
> k = investors' required rate of return
>
> If dividends are expected to remain at the same dollar amount (g = 0), [the] equation reduces to $V = \frac{D}{k}$. [But] dividends may be expected to grow at some constant rate g for the foreseeable future. In this event, [the] equation reduces to: $V = \frac{D1}{(k-g)}$.
>
> William B. Riley, Jr., and Austin H. Montgomery, Jr.,
> *Guide to Computer Assisted Investment Analysis* (1982)*

Did you follow that? No? I assigned Riley and Montgomery to my graduate finance students because I thought it was one of the best texts of its kind. Even so, most of my students gave up trying to understand it. So did my institutional clients. "Too complicated," they said.

---

*New York: McGraw-Hill Book Company, pp. 56–57.

TRANSLATING STOCK MARKET
MUMBO JUMBO INTO PLAIN ENGLISH

We have to do better here. We must translate the mumbo jumbo and formulas into plain English and simple arithmetic. Only then can we understand the hullabaloo surrounding the events leading up to, for example, the crash of the U.S. stock market on Black Monday, October 19, 1987, or the collapse in the Japanese Nikkei 225 stock index in 1990. We'll proceed slowly, step-by-step to identify *bubbles,* that is, the wildly overpriced markets you are bound to encounter in your lifetime. So, please join me in this exchange I had with my students (S1, S2, etc.) in late September and the first two weeks of October 1987. Keep in mind that luck and timing were then my allies.

RH: Last week I asked you to read the October 7, 1987 *Money and Capital Markets Monitor* (Appendix D). As you know, I send the monitor to my clients, institutional investment officers. I'll give you their reactions shortly. But first we have to cover the theory and mathematics of stock valuation. Then we can apply theory to an appraisal of Standard & Poor's index for 500 stocks. I'll use the index to illustrate why I am convinced that the stock market is now overpriced.

Fundamental analysis can help to determine whether a security is overpriced or underpriced. The fundamental or equilibrium value of a security is the discounted value (present value) of all future cash receipts discounted at a required rate of return. The cash receipts for, say, corporate stock could include not only dividend income but also any gain in market price upon sale—that is, the excess of sale price over purchase price. Forecasting receipts is no easy task.

The required rate includes (1) the return available on the very highest-quality and lowest-risk security, like a U.S. Treasury note, plus (2) an additional return for any additional risk (the equity premium) associated with stocks. If the calculated fundamental value exceeds actual market value, the stock would be considered an attractive purchase, and vice versa. Appraising risk is no easy task either. Precise measures of risk do not exist even though economists and investment experts speak of risk-free returns and cite beta or the standard deviation as reliable measures of risk. They are wrong on both counts, which we shall document in due course.

Technical analysis lies in sharp contrast with fundamental analysis. Technical analysis attempts to predict future prices on stocks based on past recurring trends or patterns. The basic idea is that the future can match past fluctuations. The problem is that technical analysis rests on argument by his-

torical analogy and in its purest form is devoid of a logical theory. Logicians maintain that argument by historical analogy standing alone without any supporting theory is illogical. They are correct, a fundamental matter we document throughout this book.

S1: That means investors should sell and get out of the market?

RH: Yes.

S1: But the market has zoomed, and most of the people I know are pretty optimistic. Many investment advisory services say we are in a bull market.

RH: I know. Most of my institutional clients insist we are still in a bull market. Before we look at their arguments, and before we begin to examine the actual data for the S&P 500, we must first review fundamental valuation theory. I'll restrict all my comments to operating companies. Practitioners of finance often call operating companies *going concerns.* What are they?

Ss: (No response.)

RH: I'll give you a clue. The economist would say that operating companies are those expected to operate in the long run. What about that?

S1: They expect to stay in business indefinitely?

RH: Yes, indefinitely, as far ahead as you can see, and even further. We'll be talking about infinite time spans. As a practical matter, though, if you go out beyond fifty years, it doesn't much matter. Why is that?

S1: Who knows what will be going on in 2037? That's fifty years from now.

RH: Yes, who knows. Money due to you in the far-distant future isn't worth much now, especially if discounted back to the present at high interest rates. My key warning, though, is for you to remember that our analysis deals now strictly with the long run. We'll turn to the market- and short-run analyses later. Let's start our journey with a stock that shows no growth in dividends. We'll assume 100 percent of earnings are paid out as dividends. That's the simplest possible example.

S1: But that's not realistic.

RH: Be patient. We have to take this one step at a time. We'll build simple models, then modify our assumptions to get closer and closer to the real world. So, in our first example no earnings are invested or "plowed back" to finance growth of productive assets. Other things equal, since all earnings are paid out as cash dividends to shareholders, assets do not grow, earnings do not grow, and dividends do not grow.

CONFUSING INVESTMENT WITH REINVESTMENT

RH: We're also assuming that revenues covering depreciation are reinvested to keep assets intact. That means the machinery and equipment, for example, wear out and are replaced by the exact amount represented by the depreciation charges. So, don't confuse investment of earnings, which can finance growth, with reinvestment of revenues covering depreciation, which merely keeps assets from shrinking. To repeat, the company is assumed to remain the same size, with growth of earnings and dividends at zero. Any questions?

S1: But the company can raise new capital by selling stock, or borrowing, and put that money into assets. Wouldn't that increase total assets, and lift earnings and dividends down the road?

RH: Remember my assumption is other things being equal. We're assuming no external financing, that is, no sale of stocks or bonds to raise new capital. We're assuming no reinvestment of earnings, a form of internal financing. The only cash flows that are reinvested are revenues covering depreciation. That's internal financing too, but it just keeps you where you are, neither expanding nor contracting. Since you brought the subject up, what would happen to a company if revenues covering depreciation were distributed as cash dividends?

S1: It would contract.

RH: Yes, it would shrink away to zero over time. Suppose you expect to get $1 in dividends next year, and $1 the year after next, and so on indefinitely, as far ahead as you can see. Call this an infinite but fixed stream of dividends of $1 a year. What would you pay for $1 a year forever?

Ss: (No response.)

RH: Well, how we could go about answering this question?

S2: We need to know what the return is.

RH: Good. More precisely, you need to know what would be the minimum return demanded by well informed and logical investors. What would that be today? 2 percent, 6 percent, 8 percent, 20 percent?

S2: I don't know, but it's not 2 percent.

RH: Give me your best judgment.

S2: How about 8 percent?

THE REQUIRED RETURN ON STOCKS: k

RH: Today (1987), only 8 percent? Do you know what you can get today on AAA corporate bonds, the very highest quality corporate bonds. It's about 10.8 percent. Now that you know, would you still require only 8 percent on stocks?

S2: I guess not. I would require more than I can get on a prime bond. I would need something more than 10.8 percent.

RH: Good. You dug yourself out of that hole. Tell us how much more than 10.8 percent, and why.

S3: Stocks are junior securities, and are subject to more risk than bonds. That's why you need more on stocks.

RH: Yes, bondholders come to the pay window first. They get their interest before shareholders get a penny of dividends. Also, in the event of corporate bankruptcy, any proceeds of liquidation must be paid to the bondholders before anything is paid to the stockholders. Bondholders are the creditors. They in effect purchased IOUs from the corporation, which in turn uses the money from bonds to start up a business or to expand an existing enterprise. Stockholders, on the other hand, are part owners in the business. They have an equity interest in the corporation. There are qualifications we must make later as related to *junk bonds* and *event bonds*. Still, prime bonds are generally less risky than stocks. So, if you can get 10.8 percent on a AAA corporate bond of the highest quality, what's the minimum return you would require on stocks?

S4: I believe investment strategists would expect to get a couple of percentage points more. How about 12 percent or 13 percent, maybe even more if recession was in the cards?

THE EQUITY PREMIUM

RH: Let's say 12 percent for now because that's the required return we'll use in our arithmetic example. Also keep in mind for future reference that the 12 percent required return is labeled with the symbol k (k = 12%). Twelve percent would amount to a 1.2 percent additional return over the 10.8 percent on bonds. Does anybody know what investment officers call the 1.2 percent differential?

S5: (No response.)

RH: It's called the *equity premium.* In our example for this zero growth stock, the equity premium is 1.2 percent, or 12 percent less 10.8 percent. So, you can say that k (12%) is the return on AAA bonds (10.8%) plus the equity premium (1.2%). The 1.2 percent premium in our example is conservative. Investment strategists often look for two percentage points or more. In any event, assuming a 12 percent required return, what price would you pay for this zero growth stock?

S5: I guess you would divide $1 by .12, whatever that is.

RH: Yes, and $\frac{\$1.00}{.12}$ works out to $8.33. Seen another way, you get $1 a year in dividends by investing $8.33 at 12 percent.

$$.12 \times \$8.33 = \$1.00$$

Turn the question around: *What amount would you have to invest at 12% to get $1 a year in dividends forever?* The answer is $8.33. Thus:

$$\$8.33 = \frac{\$1.00}{.12}$$

If we translate English into the jargon of economists, the same question is worded: *What is the discounted value of an infinite dividend stream of $1 a year discounted at a cost of capital of 12 percent?* If we let D represent a fixed and constant dividend stream of $1 a year, and k the required return of 12 percent, we can solve for V, the discounted value, with this simple formula:

$$V = \frac{D}{k} = \frac{\$1.00}{.12} = \$8.33$$

Note that the formula is the same formula we used for a perpetual bond. The *discounted value* we calculated of $8.33 is the present price you would pay as a well informed and logical investor. It's also called the *capitalized value* or the *present value* of the future dividend stream. The discounted or capitalized value is the *fundamental* or *equilibrium value,* terms we'll have occasion to use again.

THE CONFUSION OVER "COST OF CAPITAL"

RH: The discount rate used, 12 percent in our example, is called the cost of capital, which means the required investment return. Our required investment return (cost of capital) is expressed here as a percentage (12 percent), or as a decimal (.12). Any questions?

S6: I thought cost of capital is what it cost you to buy capital, what you actually have to pay.

RH: Yes and no. The jargon can be confusing because cost of capital can be used in two different ways. The economist is often careless in explaining this. Suppose, for example, that the market price of our no-growth stock is $16.66, or double the $8.33 price we calculated as the logical value, the fundamental or equilibrium value. Would you pay that high a price?

S7: No. According to you, nobody would pay more than $8.33 if he required a 12 percent return.

RH: Nobody thinking straight, you mean. What would be the implied return if you did in fact pay a high market price of $16.66?

S7: According to the formula you gave us, it would be $P = \frac{D}{k}$ where $16.66 $= \frac{\$1.00}{k}$, and solving for k, you get 6 percent.

RH: Excellent. Investing $16.66 at 6 percent gives you $1 a year in dividend income. Thus $16.66 x .06 = $1. So, the discounted value of $1 a year forever, discounted at a low 6 percent, is $16.66. You can see now that if investors are willing to pay $16.66, the market must be overpriced compared with the value you have calculated as a rational and informed investor ($8.33). In this case the actual market price, or P = $16.66, would far exceed our calculated fundamental value, or V = $8.33.

That's the same as saying that the market is demanding too low a return (6%) compared with the required return of a rational investor (12%). That 6 percent, by the way, is called the *implied* or *internal rate of return,* or the discount rate that just equates the present value of future receipts to the market price. In our example, 6 percent is the discount rate that just matches the present or discounted value of future receipts, $1 a year forever, to the assumed market price of $16.66. So, what would you do if actual P at $16.66 exceeds your calculated fundamental value (V) of $8.33? That's the same as asking what would you do if the internal rate of return (6%) is below your required rate of return (12%).

S7: Sell, get out.

THE FUNDAMENTAL (EQUILIBRIUM)
VALUE VERSUS MARKET PRICE

RH: Yes. In our example, the fundamental value was only $8.33. Actual prices may fluctuate far above or far below the fundamental value, but over time actual prices tend to converge with fundamental values, assuming rational markets. So, it always pays to check actual prices against fundamental values. Never confuse the actual cost of something with its fundamental value.

S8: But in a bull market you may be speculating for a sharp rise in price. You could be a big winner.

RH: Yes, or a big loser. My point is that you should always try to distinguish between the market return (market cost of capital) and your own individual required return as an informed and rational investor (the rational cost of capital). The reason is plain enough. Markets often go haywire. The market becomes irrational, but that doesn't mean you have to become irrational. You don't have to join a crazed crowd. Stick to the relevant data. Focus on sound valuation theory. Try your very best to ignore the screams of the crowd. Once you recognize a *bubble,* in which the market (the crowd) wildly overprices a stock, you can separate yourself from it.

You can *fight the tape,* meaning you can refuse to rush in (or out) of the market with the crowd. That can save you a lot of grief because all bubbles burst sooner or later. You can't time just when bubbles break, but you can spot a bubble. That's useful to know because only gamblers or fools put their money into bubbles, whether they go long or short. Prudent and enlightened investors stay clear of bubbles.

That's enough of this exchange. We'll now apply the theoretical tools we developed in our conversation to Black Monday. Why was the market poised to crash in the weeks just prior to Black Monday? Consider this:

1. The stock market was expensive (overpriced) compared with dirt-cheap, high-quality, high-yielding bonds.

2. The stock market was overpriced because the *required* return for a rational investor lay above the *likely future return* even assuming earnings and dividends were to grow at a high rate far beyond historical experience.

This gets us back to a calculation of *fundamental* value, which lay far below actual market price. As we'll see, when fundamental is below actual, that's the same thing as saying that the required return exceeds the likely future return. I'll illustrate that shortly. But let's consider my first observation. Bonds had in fact become the arch enemy of stocks. Yields on AAA bonds, the highest quality corporate bonds, averaged a magnificent 10.8 percent in October 1987. Stock yields on the S&P 500, or current dividends divided by stock prices, had fallen to below 2.8 percent. So, bond yields exceeded stock yields by a huge 8 percent. Economists call that difference the *reverse-yield gap.* It's labeled *reverse* because for most of our history until 1959 yields on stocks generally exceeded or matched yields on bonds (Exhibit 15–1). From 1959 on, bond yields exceeded stock yields by wide margins. The low dividend yield in 1987 meant that if you were a buyer of stocks, you had to look for rapid dividend growth or price advances (capital gains) that would more than make up for the lower yield on stocks compared with bonds. The market was extremely optimistic. I was not (Appendix A, Forecast 38). The low dividend yield was a red flag.

A second red flag caught my eye, namely, the low earnings yield. Now, turn the earnings yield upside down, and you get the price/earnings (P/E) ratio. It was then a worrisome high to me, sporting a 21 multiple (Exhibit 15–2).

APPLYING VALUE THEORY TO THE STANDARD & POOR'S 500

Now we'll analyze the Standard & Poor's 500 stock index, and apply our valuation theory to the overall market. We'll drop our assumption of a $1 no-growth dividend stock and use instead the reported dividend on the S&P 500 of $8.88. We'll also assume that dividends grow at a 7.5 percent annual rate on the average for the 500 stocks included in the index. The 7.5 percent dividend projection exceeded by far the long-run performance. Here is S&P's updated record into 1993 (which I obviously did not have in 1987, just before Black Monday):

S&P 500 Percent Annual Growth:	Earnings	Dividends
1926–93	4.6%	4.4%
1950–93	5.2%	5.1%

Because I was convinced the market was overpriced even on extremely optimistic assumptions of future growth, I "leaned over backwards" and used the high 7.5 percent number. This high percentage exceeded even that of the inflationary surge in earnings and dividends in the roaring 1980s. *I wanted to be a convincing bear.* Now, let's track the calculations I made on October 6, 1987, with the help of our table (see Exhibit 15–3):

1. S&P 500 Price (10/6/87)
   P = 319.00
   The S&P 500 is an index, with 1941–43 = 100.

2. S&P 500 Dividend (Current)
   D = 8.88
   Standard and Poor's adjusts earnings and dividends to the index on a per-share basis. So, think of the dividend as $8.88 per share, and the price $319 (as of 10/6/87).

3. S&P 500 Dividend (One Year Hence)
   D   x g   = D1
   8.88 x 1.075 = 9.546
   With an assumed 7.5 percent annual growth in dividends, that meant a dividend one year ahead of 9.546.

4. S&P Dividend Yield (Current)
   8.88/319 = 2.78%
   The current dividend yield was the then current dividend divided by the current price.

5. Expected First-Year Dividend Yield
   D1/P   = First-Year Dividend Yield
   9.546/319 = 2.99%
   All returns were expected returns. With our assumed 7.5 percent annual dividend growth, the expected dividend yield for the first year was the dividend due at the end of the year of 9.546 divided by the price of 319, or 2.99 percent.

6. Assumed Annual Dividend Growth
   g = 7.5%, with g as projected annual dividend growth for an "infinite" period ahead. (We can modify this straight-line projection, as we'll see.)

7. Implie d Market Return (k)
   k   = D1/P   + g
   10.49% = 2.99% + 7.50%
   We then calculated that our implied return, assuming a 7.5 percent annual dividend growth and a dividend yield of 2.99 percent, to be 10.49 percent. The implied return, also called the internal rate of return, is that rate of return which would just equate the discounted value of fu-

ture receipts to the initial investment outlay. In this case, 10.49 percent would just equals the present value of all future receipts we projected on the S&P 500 to the initial starting price of 319. The 10.49 percent return, then, represents the required cost of capital for the overall market under the assumed happy growth projection of dividends of 7.5 percent annually.

8. The Competitive Depressant of Bonds
AAA corporate bonds yielded 10.8 percent, or in excess of the implied 10.49 percent total return to stocks on a long-run fundamental valuation basis. Also, the reverse-yield gap stood at a big 8 percent, or 10.8 percent less the 2.8 percent current yield on stocks. Either comparison suggested a big depressant to stock prices.

THE GORDON STOCK-DIVIDEND-CAPITAL-APPRECIATION MODEL

To show the common sense underlying the Gordon model (the frightening formula that attacked you at the beginning of this chapter) we must go the long way around. We'll calculate the fundamental value (V) as the present value of the dividend stream plus the present value of the stock sold after a specified period of time. In our example we have assumed a five-year holding period. We have also assumed that you, a rational investor, are not satisfied with the implied market return of only 10.49 percent. You want more. You demand a minimum 12 percent. Under these assumptions, the present value of the dividend stream worked out to $39.33, as summarized in the table and shown here:

Year	Current Dividend		Growth at g = 7.5%		Future Value		Discounted at k = 12%		Present Value
1	8.88	x	1.075	=	9.55	x	.893	=	8.52
2	8.88	x	1.156	=	10.27	x	.797	=	8.18
3	8.88	x	1.242	=	11.03	x	.712	=	7.85
4	8.88	x	1.335	=	11.86	x	.636	=	7.54
5	8.88	x	1.436	=	12.75	x	.567	=	7.23
									$39.33

The present value of the stock sold in five years is $172.80, as calculated here:

Dividend in fifth year	= $ 12.75
Dividend due one year later = $12.75 x 1.075	= 13.70
Price at end of the fifth year = $\frac{13.705}{.045}$	= 304.54
Present value at 12% of price = $304.545 x .5674	= $172.80

So, the fundamental value was calculated at $212.13:

PV of the 5-year dividend stream	$ 39.33
PV of stock sold in five years	172.80
FUNDAMENTAL VALUE	$212.13

Let's explain further the logic of the price at the end of the fifth year of $304.54. If investors had been thinking logically, they would have demanded a 4.5% dividend yield, not the actual market yield of 2.99%. The 4.5% dividend yield represented the investor's logical or required return of 12% less the assumed dividend growth rate of 7.5%. They should have been unwilling to pay more than $100 for every $4.50 of dividends, which is the equivalent of not paying more than $304.54 for every $13.70 of dividend income. Thus $\frac{\$4.50}{\$100} = \frac{\$13.70}{\$304.54} = .045 = 4.5\%$.

With the price of the stock in year five at $304.54, the next step is to calculate its present value. The answer is $172.80, or $304.54 discounted at 12% for five years. Looked at another way, $172.80 would grow to $304.54 in five years if invested at a rate of 12% compounded annually.

DIVIDENDS VERSUS EARNINGS: A RECONCILIATION

Let's explore further the logic underlying the price of a stock five years ahead. Simply put, the price five years out is the discounted value of the projected dividend stream from years six to infinity. But wait. Suppose that little or no dividends are paid even though the company is making huge earnings. Suppose that all earnings are reinvested in productive capital. What then?

This poses no problem. The maximum potential growth of earnings occurs, other things being equal, when (a) all revenues covering depreciation are reinvested to replace depreciating capital and (b) all earnings are invested, or plowed back, into new and expanded assets. In that extreme case, assuming perfect markets and no change in perceived risk or required return, the moneys plowed back into assets would show up dollar-for-dollar in a rise in the price of the stock. Assuming also no tax differences, the investor could look upon dividend receipts at the end of the year as being the equivalent of earnings plowed back into assets, and an equivalent rise in the market price of the stock by the end of the year. He could, of course, elect to sell and thereby realize a market gain. He could treat market appreciation the same as the receipt of dividend income. Put it this way:

> If all earnings are reinvested for an indefinite and extremely long period ahead, then you could treat earnings growth as a proxy for dividend growth.

At the other extreme, with all earnings paid out as dividends, then dividends, earnings, and stock prices would all register zero growth. In that case, the Gordon model would show g at zero, and a constant dividend would be valued just like a perpetual bond. In that case the model would reduce to $V = D/k$ rather than $V = \frac{D1}{(k-g)}$, where D represents the initial and constant (no growth) dividend. If, for example, dividends under the S&P 500 were to show zero growth, then a 12 percent required return would value the current $8.88 dividend at only $74, not the $212.13 we calculated assuming 7.5 percent dividend growth. Thus $V = \frac{D}{k} = \frac{8.88}{.12} = \$74.00$. (See Exhibit 15–4 for the "Modigliani-Miller dividend irrelevancy theorem" related to hucksters.)

Most corporations lie between these two extremes of 100 percent and zero plowback of earnings. For example, if 50 percent of earnings are paid out as dividends and 50 percent reinvested at a net return of 10 percent, then the stock price would presumably climb by 5 percent a year, or 50 percent times 10 percent, other things being equal. For the vast majority of corporations, then, a projection for the long run of dividend growth has already factored into it the implied degree of plowback of earnings and the implied rise in stock prices. Even so, an outside investor would still minimize uncertainty by insisting on information on plowback assumptions. *To repeat, long-range projections for dividend growth by definition cannot be made without plowback data.* Once you recognize this, and the three cases we just noted of 100 percent, 0 percent, and 50 percent assumed plowbacks, your confusion over whether to discount earnings or dividends will disappear forever. You'll never find yourself in this hopeless box faced by so many MBA or doctoral candidates (D):

RH: What receipts do you discount to determine a stock's fundamental value? Cash flow, earnings, or dividends?

D: (Deathly silence.)

It's not cash flow (see chapter 18). We can see, though, that the Gordon model recognizes capital gains as being a proxy for dividend receipts. We should really rename the Gordon model the Gordon stock-dividend-capital-appreciation model. Relevant here is the fact that the Japanese normally plow back a much larger percentage of earnings than we do. Investors there, except for the insurance companies, prefer to take their gains in capital gains rather than in cash dividends. That, considered by itself alone, would explain somewhat higher price/earnings ratios for the Japanese market than for the U.S. market. Even so, the Japanese market turned into a megabubble and crashed (see chapter 17).

A RECONCILIATION OF COMMON SENSE
WITH ESOTERIC FORMULAS

Our goal thus far has been to explain the logic underlying the Gordon formula, and to do so in plain language. That's why we took the long way around to explain valuation theory with an assumed five-year holding period. With that behind us, we can now recognize and understand the forbidding Gordon formula. Here is the monster once again:

$$V = \text{Fundamental Value} = \frac{D1}{(k-g)}$$
$$= \frac{\$9.546}{(.12-.075)}$$
$$= \frac{\$9.546}{.045}$$
$$V = \$212.13$$

The monster is not so frightening now, is it? You can recognize your old friends in the formula:

V = $212.13   That's the discounted value of the projected dividend stream.

D1 = $9.546   That's the initial dividend of $8.88 times 1.075 for annual dividend growth.

k = 12%   That's our assumed required return.

g = 7.5%   That's our projected dividend growth.

The Gordon model assumes the dividend stream to be infinite. Our example of a five-year holding period assumes the holding period to be finite. Even so, the calculation works out to $212.13 no matter how long you assume your holding period. Prove that to yourself by assuming (say) a three-year holding period but with the same format we have used in Exhibit 15–3.

We have probably tested your patience with our long and roundabout approach to the mathematics and the theory of valuation of stocks. Still, it was necessary. My own experience has been that nobody understands the Gordon formula without working through the time-consuming mathematics and basic theory.

BLACK MONDAY STRIKEOUT

Anyway you figured it, investors who stayed in the stock market in early October 1987, struck out. Count the strikes:

1. Not only was the reverse-yield gap huge (8%), but the implied or market cost of capital (10.49%) was also below the return on prime corporate bonds (10.8%).

2. The implied return (10.49%) was also below the minimum required return on stocks for rational investors (12%).

3. The fundamental value of stocks discounted at 12 percent was $212.13, or below the actual market price of $319.

Actually, strikes (2) and (3) amounted to the same thing. While the market did recover to new highs by late 1989, the question still remains as to why the crowd seemed blind to these bright red signals to cut stock holdings for bonds, at least temporarily. We'll try to answer that puzzle shortly (see chapter 16). For now, a caution is warranted, for I don't want to leave the impression that models can predict the future. What you put into your model determines what you get out of it. The caution bears on your "inputs" to the model, including the required rate of return, or cost of capital, economic and financial prospects, interest rates, the projected growth of dividends, and a host of other factors. Recall that in the Gordon model we assumed a constant percentage growth rate for dividends. But you know that nothing grows at a constant rate forever.

Do these reservations require that we junk our stock dividend model? By no means. First, we have no logical difficulty in assuming a constant percentage growth for relatively short periods of time, like five years in our example. Second, we can adjust our projected growth rates, even for short-run cyclical fluctuations of less than five years. Third, we can factor into our projections different rates of growth for different time spans. Even so, we must always remember that however reasonable and rational our inputs, investors can go wild as a herd. Models cannot digest mass frenzy.

The one giant advantage of fundamental valuation models is that they force us to forecast, to compare the present and the projected future. That's logical. It's exactly that logical linkage that made me worry about a major market correction in the months immediately preceding Black Monday. What's logical, though, may have little to do with what Wall Street does. It tends to focus not on the future relative to the present but on the present relative to the past. For example, you often read that price-earnings ratios or dividend yields are very high or very low relative to past history. Yes, such information can be taken as a possible clue to the future, as we have just seen. *Even so, never rely on rear-view mirrors alone to get a good look at the winding economic road ahead.* You must always look straight ahead. You must forecast.

Exhibit 15-1: Historical Stock and Bond Yields

Source: Courtesy of Crandall, Pierce & Company

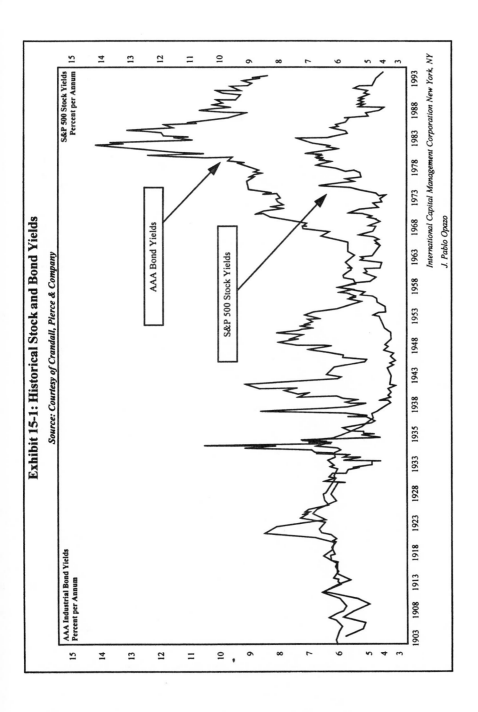

AAA Bond Yields

S&P 500 Stock Yields

AAA Industrial Bond Yields
Percent per Annum

S&P 500 Stock Yields
Percent per Annum

International Capital Management Corporation New York, NY

J. Pablo Opazo

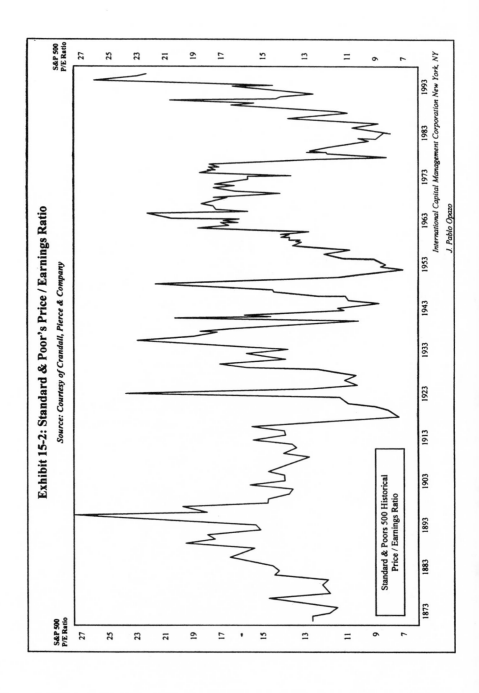

Exhibit 15-2: Standard & Poor's Price / Earnings Ratio

Source: Courtesy of Crandall, Pierce & Company

Exhibit 15–3: Stock Valuation (10/6/87) Before Black Monday

S&P 500 Price 10/6/87	P		319.00
S&P 500 Dividend (Current)	D		8.88
S&P 500 Dividend (One Year Hence)	$D1 = D \times 1.075$	=	9.546
S&P Dividend Yield (Current)	$\frac{D}{P} = \frac{8.88}{319}$	=	2.78%
Expected Next-Year Dividend Yield	$\frac{D1}{P} = \frac{9.546}{319}$	=	2.99%
Assumed Annual Dividend Growth	g		7.50%
Implied Market Return = $\frac{D1}{P}$ + g = 2.99% + 7.50%		=	10.49%

The Competitive Depressant of Bonds. The implied or internal rate of return is D1/P (2.99%) plus g (7.5%), or 10.49%. But 10.49% is below the 10.8% on AAA bonds.

The Gordon Stock Dividend Model. The required return for a rational investor would exceed the 10.8% available return on high grade bonds by an equity premium. Assume a required return of only 12% on stocks and rapid dividend growth of 7.5% a year so as not to overstate our bear case, which would mean a comparatively low 1.2% equity premium (12.0% –10.8%). Even so, the Gordon model values the market at a present value (PV) of $212.13, below the actual $319. Thus:

$$P = \frac{D1}{(k-g)} = \frac{9.546}{(.12 - .075)} = \frac{9.546}{.045} = \$212.13.$$

The logic of the $212.13 can be seen in the following example of a five-year holding period. Thus, $212.13 is the PV of the five-year dividend stream + the PV of the price of the stock sold at the end of the fifth year:

Year	Current Dividend		Growth at g = 7.5%		Future Value		Discounted at k = 12%		Present Value
1	8.88	x	1.075	=	9.55	x	.893	=	8.52
2	8.88	x	1.156	=	10.26	x	.797	=	8.18
3	8.88	x	1.242	=	11.03	x	.712	=	7.85
4	8.88	x	1.335	=	11.86	x	.636	=	7.54
5	8.88	x	1.436	=	12.75	x	.567	=	7.23

PV of the 5-year dividend Stream (sum of above)	= $ 39.33
PV of the price of the stock sold in five years	= 172.80
Fundamental Long-Run Value	= $212.13

Source: October 7, 1987, *Money and Capital Markets Monitor.*

The present value of the stock sold in five years assumes a required return for rational investors of (12%). This means a required dividend yield of 4.5%, or 12% – 7.5%, not the low implied *market* yield of 2.99%. Thus:

Dividend in fifth year	=	$12.75
Dividend due one year later = $12.75 x 1.075	=	13.70
Price at end of the fifth year = $\frac{13.705}{.045}$	=	304.58
Present value at 12% of price = $304.545 x .5674	=	*$172.80

*Rounded down from 172.83

Exhibit 15–4: The Arithmetic of the Modigliani-Miller (MM) Dividend Irrelevancy Theorem (Antidote for Hucksters)

Here is our arithmetic "proof" of the MM dividend irrelevancy theorem. It argues that, other things being equal, investors would get the same total return regardless of whether a company plows back earnings that show up in capital gains or distributes all earnings as cash dividends. Once we go through the arithmetic, you'll probably wonder why we ever brought the subject up. The principle seems all so simple *once pointed out and explained.* Even so, the failure to understand runs through the literature—both theoretical and applied—which makes a field day for hucksters. So, MM deserve our compliments for their insight. I'll never understand, though, how they could have tripped so badly over corporate cost-of-capital theory. They did (see chapter 20).

We'll use the same example developed in this chapter. Consider first the fundamental values as of October 6, 1987, for (1) the S&P 500 assuming a 7.5% annual dividend growth and (2) the S&P 500 assuming zero dividend growth:

1. The S&P 500 with 7.5% Annual Dividend Growth

PERIOD	DIVIDEND	VALUE	RISE IN PRICE	TOTAL RETURN
Present		$212.13		
End Year 1	$9.546	$228.04	+$15.91	$25.46*
End Year 2	$10.262			

*includes dividend

The fundamental value of $212.13 is the present value we calculated using the Gordon formula:

$$V = \frac{D1}{(k-g)} = \frac{\$9.546}{(.12-.075)} = \frac{\$9.546}{.045} = \$212.13$$

The total return for the first year is the sum of the dividend plus the rise in price (capital appreciation):

Dividend	$ 9.55
+ Capital Appreciation	+ 15.91
= Total Return	$25.46

2. The S&P 500 with Zero Dividend Growth

The fundamental value is the present value we calculated using the Gordon formula with zero growth. In this case use
D instead of D1.

$$V = \frac{D}{(k-g)} = \frac{\$8.88}{(.12-.00)} = \frac{\$8.88}{.12} = \$74$$

The total return for the first year, all in dividends and zero capital gain, is the number of shares multiplied by the dividend per share. The question is how many shares could you buy of the no-growth stock priced at $74 a share with $212.13, the price of one share assuming 7.5% dividend growth. Just divide $212.13 by $74, which is 2.867 shares. So, the total return for the first year is as follows:

$$2.867 \text{ shares x } \$8.88 \text{ per share} = \$25.46$$

$25.46? Of course. If you assume the investor can and does put his $25.46 to work on his own to grow at 7.5% a year, then his future total receipts will exactly match that of the growth S&P 500. The additional assumptions are that the no-growth stocks are identical to growth stocks in every way except in growth, including perceived risk and the required cost of capital (both 12%), no brokerage or other charges, and identical taxes on income and capital gains.

Having gone through all this arithmetic, don't we all feel just a bit foolish. We have been dealing, by assumption, with identical investment options all along. The trouble, though, is that unless you go through the actual arithmetic, you can overlook the importance of making all your assumptions explicit. Most people, including the best and the brightest and the most experienced investors, have never really understood the MM dividend irrelevancy thesis. They just haven't taken the time to think it through, to define exactly what they are dealing with. Until they do, the arguments on growth versus no-growth stocks will go round and round, up and down, producing sound and fury but nothing else.

The other side of dividend policy is, of course, "plowback" policy, meaning the proportion of earnings a company decides to invest in growth of productive capital. So, plowback policy is irrelevant too, *other things being equal.* (I have highlighted *other things being equal* in anticipation of the criticisms I'll get from money managers concentrating on growth stocks. I love good growth stocks.)

A Bad Mix: Dividends, Capital Gains, and Stock Hustlers

Hustlers are another matter. So, remember the MM Irrelevance Theorem the next time you bump into stock hustlers. They can argue for growth or for no-growth stocks, either way, depending on what they want to sell you. Consider these completely opposite pitches, both equally ludicrous. We'll use the same prices as in our example of $74 for the no-growth stock and $212.13 for the growth stock. Listen to these two hucksters:

> "Look, you'll be glad you ran into me. Here's a growth stock priced at only $212.13 because it's going to be paying huge dividends down the road. It's plowing back most of its earnings, and that's why the stock keeps rocketing in price. This is a real winner."

> "Look, you'll be glad you ran into me. Here's a stock priced at only $74.00, but it's paying big dividends. It's a real money gusher. The price is dirt cheap. Other stocks in this industry are priced two and three times higher. Look at these dividends, strong and steady. This is a real winner."

To repeat, the Modigliani-Miller dividend irrelevancy hypothesis (plow-back irrelevancy hypothesis) may seem obvious once stated. Still, the obvious frequently eludes us. On that count alone, I do believe these two scholars deserve credit for making the obvious clear, and useful. What is so amazing to me, though, is that they could trip so badly on basic corporate cost of capital theory. I'll get to that once we've worked through the theory and practice of the stock markets in the next chapter.

16

Monday Morning Quarterbacks on Black Monday

> Men, it has been said, think in herds (and) they go mad in herds, while they only recover their senses slowly, and one by one.
>
> Charles Mackay, *Extraordinary Popular Delusions and the Madness of Crowds* (1852)*

Charles Mackay first published his classic work on group madness in 1841. His detailed accounting of widespread investor hysteria linked with the Mississippi bubble, the South Sea bubble, and the "tulipomania" of Holland makes for exciting reading. Mackay is required reading for anybody interested in bizarre crowd behavior . . . along with Charles Kindleberger's *Manias, Panics, and Crashes*† and Paul Kennedy's *The Rise and Fall of the Great Powers*.‡ They put bubbles, panics, and life and death in perspective (Appendix H).

Let's return briefly to the unhappy events of Black Monday, and examine further the question of irrational crowd psychology. We'll begin by meeting Dr. John R. Hicks, a Nobel prize winner in economics, whom I met in New York City many years ago. He had just delivered an address before The Conference Board, a business association:

---

*New York: L. C. Page and Company, 1932 reprint of the 1852 edition, p. xx.
†New York: Basic Books, 1978.
‡New York: Random House, 1987.

240

RH: Your comments reminded me of something you had written in one of your books, *Value and Capital.** You wrote that trying to forecast and analyze on psychology alone was like "lifting yourself by your own bootstraps," that eventually the fundamentals dominate crowd psychology.

JH: You remember that? I did say that if the data contradict the psychology of the moment, and you are on sound theoretical ground, then the fundamentals will dominate sooner or later. The fundamentals invariably reassert themselves sooner than expected, when people are least prepared. But we cannot pinpoint timing.

Is it really critical to pinpoint exactly when the fundamentals will dominate psychology? No, but it is important to identify risk and reward. When data and sound theory signal danger, when they signal that risk far outdistances reward, then it's time to ignore the crowd. It's time to make your exit. In the case of Black Monday, extreme risk showed up plainly in the fundamental value of the market that lay far below actual market price. The red signals were there for all to see. (Stock valuation models also flashed bright red just before the crash of the Nikkei 225, which we'll review in chapter 17.)

GAMBLERS ON BLACK MONDAY

My conviction is that otherwise alert and astute investors became irrational in the months preceding Black Monday. They looked to each other and parroted each other, as is always the case with crowd behavior; they paid precious little attention to relevant data and theory. Many knowingly turned into gamblers but would never admit it. We'll cite some strong evidence shortly. Let's turn first, though, to a strange report of the Federal Reserve Bank of New York in its prestigious *Quarterly Review* (Summer 1988). This odd comment appears on page 5:

> . . . 71.7 percent of individual investors and 84.3 percent of institutional investors thought that the market was overvalued . . . in the period before October 1987.

This astonished me. According to the New York Fed, the great majority of "investors" stayed in the market even though they knew it was overpriced.

---

*Oxford, England: Oxford University Press, 1946.

How could that be, I asked myself? It turned out that the New York Fed survey was made after the crash, or so the Fed tells us in a footnote. That's not all. Those survey numbers of 71.7 percent and 84.3 percent give an impression of statistical accuracy that can only be depicted as hilarious. Where was the editor of this report? Here's the Fed's explanation of its findings:

> Investors . . . know that the bubble may crash and that they will not be able to get out once the crash starts, but they remain in the market because they believe— for whatever reason—there is a good probability that the bubble will continue to grow, bringing them large positive returns. These returns are expected to be higher than [nonbubble investments], and large enough to compensate them exactly for the probability of a bubble crash and a large onetime negative return."

The Fed called this thinking a rational speculative bubble hypothesis. In plain English, the Fed said you can invest in a bubble and not be considered irrational. Crowd behavior, it argued, "does not depend on some sort of collective irrationality." In short, the Fed reached the conclusion that investors were rational after all in the months preceding Black Monday.

But wait. We have a definitional problem here in distinguishing between investors and gamblers. The idea that investors prior to Black Monday were rational and sensible is, in my view, strained, to say the least. Gamblers, maybe, but not investors. Let's look at the evidence. First, we'll let the investors speak. Then we'll examine the after-the-crash arguments of the Monday morning quarterbacks.

THE INSTITUTIONAL HERD: SPOTTED OVER THE TELEPHONE

Prior to Black Monday, virtually all of Wall Street was screaming bull market, bull market! All ran together in a frenzy not unlike that of the angry bulls that once chased me across a Virginia pasture (and still remain in my dreams). But why did the great majority of institutional investors, the best and the brightest, act like crazed bulls? I was very much interested in finding out. So, in the weeks just prior to Black Monday, I made telephone calls to my institutional investor clients (C), about fifty calls in total. The following dialogue was representative:

RH: Every one of the stock valuation models is flashing red. This market is headed down. We should talk about this.

C: Robert, calm down. I looked at your calculations. They look O.K., but who knows when the bear will show up? The market is off a bit since the August high, but it will come back. This is a bull market, even though the fundamentals you cite suggest otherwise. Fundamentals aren't everything.

RH: I think the risks are extremely high. The S&P dividend yield is now 2.8 percent, but AAA corporate bonds now yield 10.8 percent. Bonds are dirt cheap. Stocks are expensive. The 8 percent reverse-yield gap is close to a record.

C: Robert, a rise in stock prices before the year is out could easily make up for the 8 percent gap favoring bonds.

RH: Sure, but speculation is feeding on itself, pure and simple. These new trading strategies on futures and cash markets are part of this mania. A prudent money manager should not be in this market, not at these prices.

C: The answer to you is sentiment, investor psychology. This is a bull market. This bull has some distance to go. I cannot afford to miss this bull market. Robert, don't fight the tape.

RH: Don't fight the tape? That's what the RRs are yelling at me. Don't fight the tape, don't fight the tape. That's all I hear.

C: You sound like you are predicting the end of the world.

RH: I am not. Still, you should get rid of your DOGS. Switch to long CATS.

C: What did you say about DOGS? Repeat that.

RH: DOGS are my acronym for Dangerously Overpriced Gung-ho Stocks. Listen, if someone bets you a lot of money that he can jump over a twenty-five foot pool filled with crocodiles, and he wins the bet, how would you characterize him? Would you call him a prudent investor, or a gambling fool? Which is it?

C: I cannot take any more of your dogs and cats and crocodiles. I've got to go a meeting.

Not all the calls went this way. Some 20 percent of my clients were as worried as I was over the fundamentals. They saw an overpriced market, and cut their holdings of stocks. But the great majority said to me, over and over: "Robert, I buy your negative fundamentals, but this is a bull market. Don't fight a bull market. I'm staying fully invested."

THE MANDATE OF INSECURITY: PERFORM OR PERISH

What struck me about these calls was the pressure to perform, the fear of being left behind in the dust. Now, it's one thing to fall down when all fall down. In that case, you may even be able to claim good performance, relative to others. It's quite another matter when you are left behind when others speed far ahead. That's when you risk losing your clients, your image, your promotion, even your job. The university world operates under the rule of publish or perish. The institutional investment world operates under the rule of perform or perish. Is it any wonder, then, that investors run wild in herds, as Mackay noted? Is it any wonder that they look at each other instead of looking at data and theory? Why do they behave this way? Why? Insecurity. Pressure. Ask veteran money manager Bodhan Kekish, President of Self Reliance Insurance Company. Bodhan put it this way to me on November 29, 1990: "The life span of a money manager is one quarter."

One quarter? Maybe that's why the crowd was starry-eyed in the months prior to Black Monday. Pressed to perform, they looked to each other for support. They routinely ignored the bleak fundamentals. They deluded themselves into thinking the investment ball had a long way yet to go. I dubbed this the "Wall of Wonder."

FROM THE WALL OF WONDER TO THE WALL OF WORRY

By late spring of 1988 the evidence became overwhelming that there was no recession, that interest rates were headed lower, and that stock prices were cheap, thanks to Black Monday's rout. The dollar had become a bargain. I became a patriotic bull, and titled the July 4, 1988, *Monitor* "Invest in America" (Appendix A, Forecast 45). But many of the precrash bulls had turned to bears. This is typical of the calls I made in late spring 1988:

RH: There is no recession. Interest rates are down. Stock prices are cheap, thanks to Black Monday. Stock valuation models flash green.

C: Robert, I accept your fundamentals. But we have a bear market. Don't try to climb that Wall of Worry out there.

Sound familiar?

THE MONDAY MORNING QUARTERBACKS

Let's turn now to the Monday morning quarterbacks on Black Monday. Let's ask the quarterbacks: Who killed the market in 1987? Who or what was the villain of the crash of 1987? I have classified their after-the-fact explanations, with some arguments contradicting others, into two classes: *bad news bears* and *bad actors.*

We can dispense with the bad news bears quickly. These quarterbacks cited the trade deficit, the budget deficit, a weak dollar, and the risk of major recession, among other items, to account for Black Monday. There is one big problem with their explanation: the bad news was overdone. There was no recession. Far more serious was the failure to see that the market was overpriced even under the assumption of good economic news. We entered, you will recall, optimistic input into our long-run valuation models. Even so, the market was overvalued.

> Stock markets can be wildly overpriced, overvalued, even in otherwise healthy economies.

Let's turn now to the bad economic actors, that is, the alleged villains of Black Monday. The Monday Morning quarterbacks singled out thirteen bad actors. Their list included (1) the despicable New York Stock Exchange specialists or market makers who failed to buy when the crowd wanted to sell; (2) the low-life corporate insiders who unloaded stock ahead of the crowd; (3) the nervous-nelly institutional traders who panicked and sold; (4) the frenzied retail investors who dumped stock provided they could get their brokers on the telephone; (5) the invisible brokers who refused to answer their phones; (6) Congressman Rostenkowski because of his bill to eliminate tax breaks on corporate junk-bond financed takeovers; (7) Treasury Secretary Nicholas Brady who said the dollar was headed south in foreign exchange markets; and (8) the boa-constrictive Federal Reserve Chairman Alan Greenspan who mistakenly pushed interest rates high.

There's more. The quarterbacks also listed (9) President Ronald (Nero) Reagan who fiddled as the market plunged; (10) the Japanese who had the unmitigated gall to dump Treasury bonds and drive interest rates higher; (11) Japanese bashers on Wall Street who parroted Treasury Secretary Brady; (12) the bumbling bankers and clearing house officials who strangled settlements on Wall Street; and (13) the portfolio insurers, index arbitragers, and programmed traders who sold stock, which pushed cash prices lower, depressed futures, pushed cash prices yet lower, and created a self-reinforcing slump in futures and cash prices.

LIQUIDITY AND THE FALLACY OF COMPOSITION

Did I leave out your favorite villain? My list is far from complete, but the longer it gets, the sillier it gets. That's the way with bubbles. What struck me as truly irrational and naive was the confidence institutional investors placed in portfolio insurance. This was supposed to provide them with protection, with liquidity. Any good student of economics will tell you that the private market cannot create liquidity. When everybody is selling at once, when everybody rushes for the escape door at once, liquidity abruptly evaporates for the group (a point the New York Fed, to its credit, does stress). Put another way, the seller's liquidity is the buyer's illiquidity in any shuffle of cash for stock. The idea that the private market itself could manufacture new and additional liquidity rests on one of the oldest fallacies in economics, the fallacy of composition.

Investors followed each other, and together they constitute the crowd. Very few paid attention to the fundamentals of risk and reward. True, the stock market did recover and move on in the years ahead to new highs, a fact of great comfort to the long-run investor. But that happy ending does not contradict the blindness of the crowd to the bright red signals for a major plunge. What is dismaying is the failure of the New York Fed to distinguish between the gambling herd and the rational investor. There's really a difference between them.

Here's my four-point summary on bubbles. First, bubbles are always accompanied by irrational group behavior and the greed and naivete of speculating Parrots. Second, the Pros, attracted to bubbles like flies to honey, fabricate any number of tricks to lure unsuspecting investors into wildly overpriced markets. Third, the Monday Morning Quarterbacks offer the silliest reasons why a burst bubble was destined to burst, though nothing was heard from them before the break. Fourth, the regulatory officials, the Ostriches, see no bubbles, hear no bubbles, and speak no bubbles (see chapter 17).

17

The Tokyo Stock Megabubble

The Role of Delusion and Deception

> Quick to admit that perfect timing isn't attainable by any-
> one, he told us: My job is to identify irrational or mania-
> cal behavior. Timing is important, but what's also impor-
> tant for a prudent investor, or someone giving honest,
> objective counsel, is to say that Tokyo is irrational. It's one
> of the biggest speculative bubbles of all time.
>
> Robert H. Parks in *Barron's,* February 15, 1988

Irrational or maniacal behavior? Well, those are the words I used in response to the questions of John Liscio, *Barron's* ace reporter. I quote myself at the outset of this chapter for three reasons. First, I want to stress that the Tokyo stock market was a bubble when John Liscio conducted the interview in 1988. Second, I want to highlight just how Ostriches, Parrots, and Pros on Wall Street abused basic theory to deny that any such bubble even existed. Bubble? What bubble, they asked. Third, I want to stress again that while nobody can ever time just when a bubble will burst, one can always use basic valuation theory to identify the existence of a bubble. That's critical because all bubbles burst.

So, what happened after our February 1988 interview? See for yourself in this chart for the Nikkei 225, including the high for December 29, 1989, and the precipitous fall to the low for 1990:

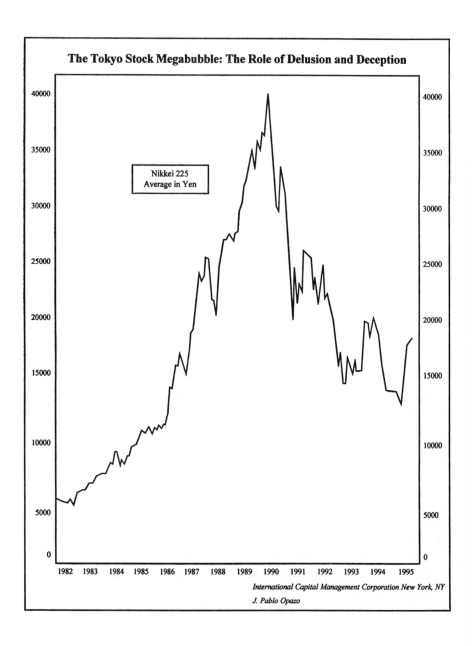

The Tokyo Stock Megabubble: The Role of Delusion and Deception

Nikkei 225
Average in Yen

International Capital Management Corporation New York, NY

J. Pablo Opazo

The Nikkei 225 soared after the interview to peak at 38,916 on December 29, 1989, then plummeted to its September 1990 low of 20,983. Thereafter, it skidded erratically to a 1992 low of 14,309 on August 18, down 63% from its 1989 peak. A dreadful crash, but foretold on the fundamentals! So, if you had bought at the time of our interview in February 1988 and sold just before the late 1989 high, you would have profited handsomely. If you had bought at the highs of early 1990 and held, you would have fared badly. With this violent history in mind, how would you classify those who committed money to the Japanese stock market over the 1988–1993 period? Were they: (1) lucky gamblers (2) unlucky gamblers or (3) irresponsible investors? Would your view change if you knew that they managed other people's money but failed to alert them to the gambling risks in the Nikkei 225. All three options seem appropriate. The fact that the market soared after February 1988 and collapsed in 1990 should be irrelevant to your answers. Irrelevant or not, consider the barbs some of my institutional clients (C) hurled my way all through 1989:

C: What about that Japanese bubble? Aren't you the guy who cried wolf in 1988? Where's the wolf? What about now? Should we get in?

RH: Long or short, it's still a bubble, a gambler's den.

Ridicule can strengthen resolve. I decided to shout out loud again, in a January 29, 1990 article for Standard & Poor's *CreditWeek*, to get out of Japanese stocks, and fast (Appendix A–58). The Nikkei 225 and the yen both obligingly tumbled, this time immediately after my warning. You can just imagine the compliments I got. But I deserved neither the ridicule nor the compliments. I had to repeat over and over again that nobody knows just when bubbles will burst. Only luck and timing can pinpoint when bubbles will burst.

Wall Street hucksters know that, too; they capitalize on the inability of anybody to pinpoint a market collapse. They capitalize also on the inability of most investors to recognize the existence of a bubble in the first place. So, capitalizing on the unknown, hucksters proceeded with confidence to twist and distort in countless ways to get you to join the gambling crowd, all the time denying the existence of a bubble. We'll shortly illustrate and document the huckster pitches. As usual, though, we must proceed in two steps. We'll begin by contrasting sound stock valuation theory with the deliberately distorted theory that found its way into the research reports of many of the premier Wall Street securities firms. Then we'll analyze the Parrot and Pro pitches, the arguments that always pop up with bubbles.

BACK TO STOCK VALUATION
FUNDAMENTALS AND THE DATA

Consider stock valuation theory first. After John Liscio interviewed me in 1988, the price-earnings ratio for the Nikkei 225 continued to climb, and shot up to seventy times earnings. That meant you had to pay 70 yen for one yen of current earnings. Two decades earlier the market traded at 12 times earnings. So, Japanese stock prices raced ahead at a far faster pace than earnings over this entire period. In seven years, 1982 through 1989, Japanese stock prices rocketed higher at a compound annual rate of about 29 percent. That alone, as you can see from the chart, should have alerted anybody to this hot air bubble.

Let's see if we can demonstrate the magnitude of this hot-air inflation. We begin by reviewing the simple mathematics of growth, of compound growth. The exercise is relevant to our analysis because a P/E ratio of 70 means that you are willing to pay 70 yen for one yen of earnings. (For simplicity, assume you bought just at the end of the year.) Assume that you expect to see earnings grow at a specified high annual rate, with all earnings reinvested. Any annuity table gives these results with 12 percent and 19 percent growth rates:

SUM OF AN ANNUITY OF 1 YEN PER PERIOD FOR N PERIODS

	1	2	3	12	15	19	20
RATE							
12%	1.00	2.12	3.37	24.13	37.28	63.44	72.05
19%	1.00	2.19	3.61	37.18	66.26	138.17	165.42

Take the 12% rate as an example, and let's calculate how we arrived at the 3.37 stream at the end of the third year:

1.00	yen received at the end of the first year
+ 1.00	yen received at the end of the second year
+ .12	interest income of 0.12 yen for one year (1.00 x .12 = .12)
+ 1.00	yen received at the end of the third year
+ .25	interest income of 0.2544 yen for two years (1.00 x 1.12 x 1.12 = 1.2544 yen less 1.00 = .2544 of interest). I have rounded the .2544 interest to .25 interest
= 3.37	total accumulated sum at the end of the third year for an annuity of 1 yen a year, with all receipts reinvested at 12% annually

THE NIKKEI 225 AND THE INDIANAPOLIS SPEEDWAY

You can see from the table that if we assume a growth rate of 12 percent compounded annually, and with no interruption whatsoever to growth, it would take only fifteen years for a starting annuity of one yen a year to grow to 37+ yen. Not bad! At 19 percent, it would take even less time, only twelve years. But there's a problem here.

In the real world, a lot can happen in twelve, fifteen, or twenty years to upset glorious expectations. The racecars that speed through the twists and turns of time face high risks of a breakdown or a crash. So, we must include time spans and speed risks into our analysis. We cannot separate speed and time from risk. As applied to the Nikkei 225, the faster the growth rate, the longer the time span, the higher must be the risk. Equally important and invariably overlooked, the greater must be the *spread of* risk over growth. That's Economics 101 in all competitive and open markets.

Let's drop the racecar analogy, and lean instead on the arithmetic of basic valuation theory. If one yen of current earnings equaled a price of 70 yen on average for a stock in this market basket of 225 stocks, how much in current yen earnings would have equaled a price of 32,000 yen? The Nikkei 225 had climbed to 32,000 by the time I got around to making these calculations. (The P/E multiple ranged from 60 to 75; I have arbitrarily used 70 here. But whether we use 70, or even go as low as 50, our final conclusion as to the existence of a big bubble is unaffected.)

What's your answer? Well, simply divide 32,000 by 70, and the answer you get is 457 yen. Now, how much would you logically and rationally pay for a yen earnings stream, starting out with 457 yen of current earnings, for a representative Japanese stock? Well, you would have to ask yourself these additional questions. What is your assumed growth rate of earnings? How long do you expect the growth rate to continue? What is your required return, or assumed cost of capital? Let's make some fantasyland assumptions, and then ask what those assumptions would imply for a P/E ratio. We'll include these optimistic assumptions in our calculations:

Assume that earnings grow for Japanese corporations at a rate that far exceeds U.S. corporate experience. We'll assume 12 percent compounded annually for Japanese companies. Here, again, are the data for the S&P 500:

S&P 500 PERCENT ANNUAL GROWTH:	EARNINGS	DIVIDENDS
1926–93	4.6%	4.4%
1950–93	5.2	5.1

The 12% should be optimistic enough.

If not, then assume that Japanese companies reinvest all earnings at a 12 percent annual rate *forever.*

Continue with this euphoric exercise by assuming that the plowback of earnings brings with it a companion rise in the market price of Tokyo stocks, which means that the investor can realize all of his gain from capital appreciation. Pleasant enough?

Now, assume that your required return or cost of capital is 8 percent. That is the number many of the Wall Street houses considered logical and rational. They took the Japanese prime bond yield, which then approximated 5 percent, and added an equity premium of 3 percent to get the 8 percent. (The approach is hardly logical, as we shall see.)

Let's get back to our original question. Given these gloriously optimistic assumptions, what would you pay? Let's plug our assumed inputs into the Gordon model to calculate fundamental value (FV), where $FV = \frac{D1}{(k-g)}$. Remember that D1 = D times assumed growth of 12 percent. We'll take earnings (E) as a proxy for dividends, which in this case is both legitimate and logical (chapter 15). Thus E x g = E1 and in our example it is 457 x 1.12. This is our result:

$$\text{Fundamental Value} = \frac{E \times 1.12}{(k-g)}$$

$$= \frac{457 \times 1.12}{(.08 - .12)}$$

$$= \frac{512}{(.08 - .12)}$$

$$= ???$$

E1 = E x 1.12; k = Required Return; g = Growth Rate

What do you get? Well, if you subtract .12 from .08 you get a negative .04. Now, if you divide -.04 into a positive number, you get a negative number. That's crazy analysis for the real world. The trouble does not lie with the Gordon formula. The trouble is that our inputs are illogical, outrageous. Put the formula aside for a moment, and let's rely on our common sense. Ask what happens if you attempt to discount future sums at a rate below the assumed growth rate. What do you get?

If you have any initial sum grow at one rate (like 12%), then discount back at a lower rate (like 8%), the discounted value of the future sum turns out to be bigger than the present sum. For example, one yen would grow at a 12% rate to 1.12 yen one year from now. If you discount that back at 8%, then the present value of 1.12 yen works out to 1.037 yen (1.12 divided by 1.08).

So, the present value of the future sum is 1.037 yen, or in excess of the present value of the immediately due sum, which is only 1.0 yen. That's good mathematics, but bad economics and crazy logic for this real world. Such mathematical calculations contradict human experience and psychology. Who would pay more for future money than for present money? Who would value a bird in the bush more than a bird in hand? With an income stream growing at 12 percent and a discount rate at 8 percent, the result would be to create a perpetually exploding economic series. You would find such a series in Crazyland, a division of Fantasyland with offices in Tokyo and New York.

So, what do we do? We do what we should have done in the first place. We either reduce the growth rate assumption, or hike the required return to reflect the high risk in the real world associated with high return. Let's hike the required return to (say) 15 percent, or only 3 percent more than the growth rate of 12 percent. The 3 percent spread of risk over growth would be generous indeed, probably too thin, given the fast growth rate being projected. What do we get then?

$$\text{Fundamental Value} = \frac{E \times 1.12}{(k-g)}$$

$$= \frac{457 \times 1.12}{(.15-.12)}$$

$$= \frac{511.84}{(.15-.12)}$$

$$\frac{511.84}{.03}$$

$$= 17,061$$

The answer is a fundamental value of 17,061, or far below the actual Nikkei average in 1988 and 1989, but much closer to its low of 20,983 in 1990. With earnings at 457, what P/E did this imply? The answer is $\frac{17,061}{457}$, or a 37.33 P/E. That's still a high P/E.

THE DUBIOUS PRACTICE OF "SHAVING" REPORTED P/E LEVELS

Many Wall Streeters said that the actual P/E on Japanese stocks was lower than 70 times because earnings were understated. Earnings had to be adjusted up, which meant reported P/Es had to be adjusted or so they insisted. Well, I could not find evidence of any grand understatement of earnings, as we shall shortly document. Even so, if we had boosted the earnings estimate, which is the same thing as "shaving" the reported P/E, the market still had to be classed as a bubble. For example, suppose we had "shaved" the P/E from 70 times to 50 times when the Nikkei 225 reached 32,000. What then? Well, that would have meant 640 yen for a representative Japanese stock in the Nikkei basket of 225 stocks, or 32,000 divided by 50. Now, let's put the 640 into our fundamental valuation formula:

$$\text{Fundamental Value} = \frac{E \times 1.12}{(k - g)}$$

$$= \frac{640 \times 1.12}{(.15 - .12)}$$

$$= \frac{716.8}{(.15 - .12)}$$

$$\frac{716.8}{.03}$$

$$= 23,893$$

This gives a fundamental value of only 23,893, far below 32,000, though much closer to the 20,983 actual low the Nikkei 225 hit in 1990. Even being generous, then, on our estimate of earnings, a bubble still occurs.

Let's return to our 37.33 P/E calculation, which I believed was closer to the truth. That high level still assumed out-of-this-world optimistic assumptions compared to the actual inflated P/E on the Nikkei 225. That was reason enough for me to tag the Tokyo market a megabubble.

One objection raised to my pessimistic view was that those looking for 12 percent growth of earnings or even higher were not looking for high growth forever, but for just a few years. Really? The moment one assumes any interruption or slowing of growth of earnings, at that moment the Fantasyland P/Es come into question. At that very moment, risk and fear intrude into the picture, which can be a telltale signal of a vastly overpriced market.

Alternatively, one could object that the required return could be put much lower, at (say) 13 percent. Let's see. If we assume a growth rate of 12 percent and a lower required return of 13 percent, what do we get? Here's the number:

$$\text{Fundamental Value} = \frac{E \times 1.12}{(k - g)}$$

$$= \frac{457 \times 1.12}{(.13 - .12)}$$

$$= \frac{511.84}{(.13 - .12)}$$

$$\frac{511.84}{.01}$$

$$= 51,184$$

A fundamental value of 51,184? No! When you project fast rates of growth of 12 percent compounded annually for an indefinite and long period in intensively competitive and troubled world markets, you must of necessity assume high risk. To repeat, the higher the growth of earnings and the longer the period assumed, the higher must be the implied risk and the spread of required return over growth. Here, the 1 percent spread (13 percent less 12 percent) would be far too low.

Basic theory soon materialized in practice, and with a fury. Interest rates in Europe, Canada, and Great Britain rocketed higher in 1989 in reaction to tightening central bank policies to fight the *perceived* acceleration of inflation. Their actions put upward pressure on Japanese interest rates (see Exhibit 17–1). So, the surge in global interest rates raised the required return on Japanese bonds, which lifted the required return on Japanese stocks, which in turn contributed mightily to the plunge in the Nikkei 225.

HIGH DECEPTION: SEPARATING GROWTH (g) AND REQUIRED RETURN (k)

One might also object that Japanese corporations normally plow back a greater percentage of earnings into growth than (say) American corporations, and this would support higher price-earnings ratios for Japanese stocks than for American stocks, other things being equal (see the chapter 15 exhibit on the dividend irrelevancy principle). But other things were not equal, and the plowback factor by itself could never have logically justified the bubble P/Es of the late 1980s. (Hucksters almost completely overlooked the legitimate plowback argument in support of high P/Es [which has limited validity] and instead advanced arguments that had little or no validity.)

This takes us to the high deception in much of the Wall Street research reports on the Tokyo stock market that now contaminate my desk. These reports generally failed to link their assumptions on required return, usually taken at about 8 percent, to their assumptions of growth in the 12 percent to 20 percent range. The more notorious of Wall street hucksters said they looked for growth rates of 15 percent to 20 percent, but they neglected to tell us for how long. You and I know that we cannot separate inseparables, not when it involves honest valuation theory. Parrots, of course, separate required returns k and growth rates g; they don't know any better. But the failure of sophisticated strategists, many with doctorates from top universities, to integrate the two must be chalked up as intellectual dishonesty. They deliberately kept k and g apart. Time and time again, the reports would, for example, discuss required returns in the first few pages, then introduce us to growth rates thirty to fifty pages later. That way they didn't have to defend their Crazyland assumptions on growth and required return.

TRASH AND LITTER ON THE TOKYO STOCK MARKET

Let's document our charges. The trash and litter on the Tokyo market blankets Deception Alley, otherwise known as Wall Street. Among the most preposterous of these tracts are the following: (1) *Global Equity Markets,* Salomon Brothers, December 1988; (2) *Assessment of the Right Price for Japanese Equities,* Shearson Lehman Hutton, February 1989; (3) *Focus on Cheap Stocks* (Part 2), Aizawa Securities Co. Ltd., February 14, 1988; and (4) *Nikko's View of the U.S. and Japanese Capital Markets,* Nikko Equity Research, March 17, 1988. This short list is merely representative. They are just among the worst I have reviewed.

Aizawa's sales pitch on "cheap" stocks, for example, would be hilarious if it were not so frightening. Nikko's hard sell involved, would you believe, an ex Federal Reserve officer. Nomura "proved"—there's that word again—that Japanese stock prices were no higher than shares on overseas markets.* One of the most extravagant tracts came from Shearson Lehman Hutton, an American Express Company. Shearson assured its clients that all was sane and logical in the Tokyo stock market with this twisted rationalization of theory and data: "All things considered, we find the Japanese market quite logical."† Quite logical? Does that mean better than logical? Shearson then followed up with this gem: "No, the Japanese market is not going to crash."‡ Crash it did.

These reports, among thirty others that clutter my office, all sang the same tune. The common refrain was that Japanese stock price-earnings ratios were not high once the proper accounting adjustments were made. Some asserted that Japanese stocks were "cheap." In addition to the accounting "adjustments" they said were necessary to compare Japanese stocks fairly with U.S. stocks, they advanced the most preposterous economic arguments to support their position. Consider here just seven of the more notorious pitches I singled out for criticism throughout all of 1989, and in January 1990 (see Appendix A, Forecasts 43, 59, 60).

The Japanese Economic Journal (March 12, 1988).

†Shearson Lehman Hutton, *Assessment of the Right Price for Japanese Equities* (February 1989).

‡Shearson Lehman Hutton, *International Strategy* (March 10, 1989), p. 2.

1. The Low-Floating Fallacy

The Pitch: Japanese stocks are concentrated in the hands of a few relatively large institutional investors. They buy, and put away, and do not sell in any way. There is little "free-float." If two-thirds of the stock is off the market, then the relevant P/E is only one-third of the free float. Thus, one-third times an assumed celestial P/E of 70 is only a moderate 23. That's not too high a P/E. This is not a gamblers' market.

Response: The arithmetic is irrelevant, and the economics rubbish. Owner-ship does not determine fundamental value. The argument smacks of the same weird rationalization for owning the "glamour" and "nifty-fifty" growth stocks in the United States in the early 1970s, just before the fall. Most important, stock prices can plummet on bad news, like a major slowdown or recession or a sharp rise in world interest rates, with little or no trading by the "low-floaters."

2. The Q-Ratio Distortion

The Pitch: Ever hear of the Q-ratio? This is the market value of a company's stock divided by the market value of its net assets, i.e., its assets less its debt. If the net asset value far exceeds stock value, which is the case in Japan, then it follows that the stock is undervalued relative to net assets.

Response: We had better give Nobel prize winner James Tobin a call on this one. He invented the Q-ratio, a familiar notion to any student of man-agerial and corporate finance. The Q-ratio was designed to answer the ques-tion as to whether one could more cheaply buy a company's stock in order to acquire plant and equipment, or purchase the physical assets outright. The point was to compare competing cost options, a relative matter. The hucksters distorted Tobin's otherwise legitimate concept. The problem is that both stock prices and the market value of physical assets chased each other higher, not unlike a tiger chasing its own tail. Put another way, both stock prices and asset values, especially real estate, climbed to highly inflated levels. So, let's re-name this distortion of Q-ratio the "Quack Ratio." It is even wackier when linked to the low float inanity.

3. The Reverse-Yield Error in International Finance

The Pitch: Japanese interest rates are relatively low. This means the total re-quired return or cost of capital on stocks, the sum of long prime bond yields plus a differential equity premium, is low, much lower than in the United States.

Response: More nonsense. The relevant reverse-yield gaps in a global market require that investors consider all fixed-income options, including high yields on corporate or government issues, wherever they exist. The argument violates *opportunity cost,* which operates in international waters. As we just noted, opportunity cost struck with hurricane force in 1989 and 1990, when interest yields in Europe and Japan soared (Exhibit 17–1). The climb in global interest rates helped, predictably, to squash the Nikkei 225 (Appendix A, Forecast 59).

4. The Monetary Miscalculation

The Pitch: Vast amounts of money are chasing Japanese stocks, and this must propel the Japanese stock market onward and upward. I was told over and over, "you can't leave out the high savings rates and the colossal flow of money the Japanese are salting away into stocks."

Response: This reminded me of comparable arguments in the United States, to the effect that rapid money growth just had to chase stocks higher. Many analysts argued that the market was "liquidity driven" just before the Fed tightened, helping to precipitate Black Monday. The argument ignores the risk that the Japanese monetary authorities, by miscalculation, could also pursue overly restrictive credit policies and kill their own economy. It ignores the lagged impact of fast and sustained money growth on inflation and interest rates (chapter 5). It ignores so much that is fundamental and basic to good analysis, that I am amazed so many people on Wall Street could have advanced such a view.

5. The Overdepreciation Hyperbole

The Pitch: The Japanese overdepreciate to reduce taxes. You have to shave their P/Es and concentrate on cash flow. Japanese stocks on a cash-flow basis are cheap compared with other stock markets.

Response: That means depreciation charged against earnings in the accounting periods ahead of us could fall, which means that earnings subject to taxes could rise. To be sure, if investment in plant and equipment were to expand onward and upward forever, this would then pose less of a problem. But who other than huckster Parrots and Pros would make that heavenly assumption? The same type of argument (and our skeptical response) applied to the view that the Japanese "over-reserve" and thereby understate earnings and potential dividends. Even more deceptive arguments on cash flow confused short-run and long-run valuation principles, which we will take up shortly (chapter 18).

6. The Cross-Holdings Delusion

The Pitch: Japanese company A holds stock in Japanese company B, and B in A, and A in C, and so on till Z. They are all very friendly and would not dare hurt one another by dumping shares on each other. Moreover, since the shares are not incorporated in the value of company assets, there exists a great undervaluation of assets.

Response: Mostly nonsense. Cross-holdings would largely "wash out" in any total valuation. Even if all the shares of Japanese companies were owned by other Japanese companies, which would entail 100 percent cross holdings, this would not add total real value for all companies combined. The "fallacy-of-composition," then, is relevant here. True, many Japanese firms value their holdings of equity at historical cost and, unlike American firms, may not "mark" to the market. Still, the crossholding argument was overdone, spurious.

7. The Unique Japanese Mentality Overstatement

The Pitch: The Japanese are different from us. They don't pay attention to fundamental valuation theory. You should not try to take American concepts of valuation and apply them to the Japanese market. You cannot use American theory to project a fall in the Japanese market.

Response: Really? Again, opportunity cost is left out of the analysis. It exercises dominion internationally, as we just saw.

A COMPLIMENT TO AN ACCOUNTANT, A STAB TO MY FELLOW ECONOMISTS

Are there exceptions to the rule of deception, whether unconscious or deliberate, on Wall Street? Fortunately yes. The standout exception in my view is the research report of Gary S. Schienemann. Gary, a CPA, set forth devastating evidence in 1988 that Japanese P/E ratios were high by any measure. He demolished as well some of the huckster arguments I have brought to your attention.* Gary called a spade a spade, and indirectly faulted my fellow economists. How refreshing!

Consider this not so refreshing exchange I had with Daiwa Bank Trust Company officers (DO) in their Rockefeller Center New York City offices on January 19, 1989. Daiwa Trust is a subsidiary of Daiwa Bank Ltd., a huge

---

*See his *Japanese P/E Ratios,* Prudential-Bache Securities, June 20, 1988.

Japanese bank, and one of my clients. Paul Travia (PT), their Senior Vice President and Chief Investment Officer, chaired the meeting:

RH: Your real estate and stock markets are bubble high. They are bound to crash sooner or later.

DO: No, Dr. Parks. You forget a big fact. If our stock market crashes, so will yours. Yes?

(A senior executive of Daiwa Bank Ltd. fired that missile at me.)

RH: The U.S. market might slide a bit from 10 a.m. to 2 p.m. the same day. Seriously, my best guess is that any decline in the U.S. market would be short lived. You could even see a buying frenzy for U.S. stocks priced at 8-to-12 times earnings, levels that are ultra cheap compared with Japanese stocks. Your overpriced stock market, your sky-high real estate prices, and even your yen are flashing *red, red, red.*

DO: NO! Your Dow fell 508 points on Black Monday, far more than our market. We recovered faster. You leave that out. You leave out our huge trade surplus. You run big trade deficits. You leave out our economic growth, faster than yours, and our inflation, slower than yours. You leave out a strong yen. You leave out a weak dollar. You leave all that out. You must agree. Yes?

BUBBLES, ALLIGATORS, AND CELESTIAL P/E LEVELS

RH: No. Stocks can be wildly overpriced even in a healthy economy. I believe that your stock market is a gamble either way, up or down. But the huge overvaluation means the odds are down, way down. Even if you bet on the market and win, I will give you my alligator analogy.

DO: Your what? Alligator?

RH: If you jump over a ten-foot pool filled with alligators to get a bag of gold, and succeed, I will call you imprudent, an imprudent gambler. Modern portfolio theorists would say your risk to adjusted return is too high.

PT: Robert, you and I are both bulls on dollar-denominated securities, at least for now. Daiwa knows that. They know that I won't put any Japanese stocks in my portfolio, not at these inflated prices.

I then brought to the attention of my Japanese hosts Charles Mackay's *Extraordinary Popular Delusions and the Madness of Crowds* and the life-and-death "Gompertz" curve. Both subjects went over like lead balloons. They were annoyed with my forecast. But luck sided with me. The Nikkei 225 climbed higher in 1989, then collapsed dreadfully in 1990. That's the way with bubbles.

BUBBLES AND OSTRICHES

Bubbles attract Parrots, Pros, and Ostriches. Ostriches? Yes, let me explain by first quoting novelist Milan Kundera's *The Book of Laughter and Forgetting* (1981):*

> They . . . came to a large fenced-in field where the ostriches were. There were six of them. All bunched together near the wire fence, they stretched out their long necks, stared, and opened and closed their broad, flat beaks. They opened and closed them feverishly, at an incredible speed, as if taking part in a debate and trying to outtalk one another, but the beaks were hopelessly mute and did not make the slightest sound.

I do believe ostriches must abound on Wall Street. Those ostriches do make sounds when they open and close their mouths. But the sounds make little or no sense. As a classic example, consider an exchange I had with a top executive ostrich of the New York Stock Exchange. We'll call him a very high level Police Ostrich (PO). The date was Tuesday, October 18, 1988. The time preceded the crash in 1990 of the Japanese stock market. The place was Pace University's Lubin Graduate School of Business in New York City. PO had talked at length to Pace faculty about Black Monday in the United States, and I asked this question:

RH: What about the Tokyo stock market, a megabubble if there ever was one? Major Wall Street houses still push investors into this market despite price-earnings ratios up beyond the clouds. They flout the know-your-customer rule. Is the stock exchange alert to this?

PO: That market has risen sharply, but the P/Es are not as high as you imply, not if you make the appropriate adjustments. You can't judge that market on U.S. valuation standards. Investors have chalked up extraordinary performance in the Tokyo market. You fail to recognize that the Japanese market is quite different from ours. Once you adjust P/Es for cross holdings, for example, Japanese stocks turn out to be reasonably

---

*New York: Penguin Books, p. 93.

priced. Are you familiar with cross holdings? You have to consider their higher depreciation rules against earnings, which understates their earnings. You must recognize that Japanese interest rates are lower than ours, that the Japanese government has much more influence in stabilizing their markets than we have, that Japanese real growth is strong while its domestic inflation is low, that their savings rates are higher than ours, that their exports are huge, that they run huge current-account surpluses while we run big deficits, that their performance in achieving high real growth of output far exceeds ours, that they motivate their work force more than we do, that they have a low level of unemployment, that they . . .

PO went on and on, opening and closing his mouth feverishly, stretching his neck to make an emphatic point. Still, no one could hear from his lips anything at all on the subject of monumental naivete, deception, and dishonesty from Wall Street in analyzing the Tokyo stock market. Not one word! Why is that?

We turn in the next chapter to stock valuation theory for the "market-period" and the "short-run" period. That analysis serves as a preface to a long-running horror show in corporate finance, one that stars bad theory and corporate financial malpractice (see chapter 19).

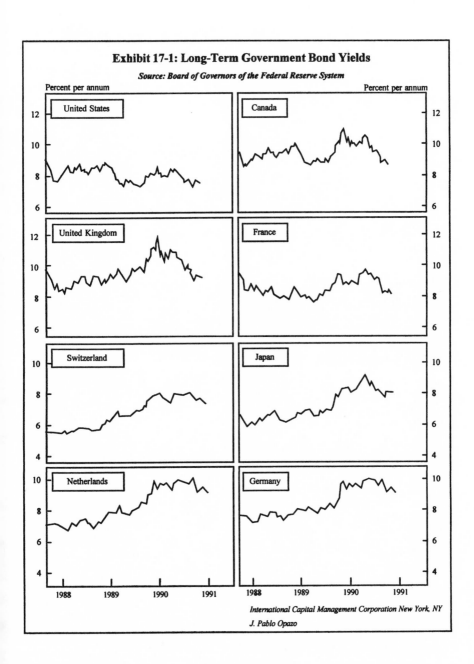

Exhibit 17-1: Long-Term Government Bond Yields

Source: Board of Governors of the Federal Reserve System

Percent per annum

Percent per annum

United States

Canada

United Kingdom

France

Switzerland

Japan

Netherlands

Germany

International Capital Management Corporation New York, NY

J. Pablo Opazo

Part Six

Corporate Financial Theory, Practice, and Malpractice

18

Valuation Muddles

A Preface to Bad Theory in Corporate Finance

> Time is the most undefinable yet paradoxical of things; the past is gone, the future has not come, and the present becomes the past even while we attempt to define it, and, like the flash of the lightning, at once exists and expires.
>
> Caleb C. Colton*

> In the long run we are all dead.
>
> John Maynard Keynes (1923)†

Mr. Colton (1780–1832) was an English clergyman, but I do believe he would have made an excellent economic theorist. He appreciated the sticky job of defining different time frames, and was alert to the error involved in mixing up one with the other. Economist Keynes was extremely careful to identify just what time frame he was dealing with. But unlike Colton and Keynes, Wall Streeters forever trip over the concept of economic time. They confuse the "market" period with the "short-run" period, and confuse both with the "long-run" period. So, we must put floodlights on these basic concepts if we are to see through the cobwebs that destroy straight thinking. If we're successful, we'll further cement our grasp of long-run stock valuation analysis. Also, we'll be in a better position to analyze the bizarre state of modern corporate financial theory.

---

*Tyron Edwards, *Useful Quotations* (New York: Grosset & Dunlap, 1938), p. 650.

†*Tract on Monetary Reform* (London: Macmillan and Company, Ltd.), p. 80; retitled *Monetary Reform* in 1971 publication (New York: Harcourt Brace and Company, 1971), p. 65.

VALUATION ANALYSIS:
SHORT-RUN SENSE VERSUS LONG-RUN ERROR

When, if ever, would it be legitimate to value corporate stock as the discounted value of the projected corporate cash flow stream rather than the discounted value of the projected net earnings or dividend stream? Think about that a moment. Remember that I have specified corporate cash flow, not earnings or dividends.

The Confusion of Earnings and Dividends with Cash Flow

As you think this through, note that I seldom get answers that make sense to this extremely important question.

The correct answer to my question is the short run. To see why, let's first construct a simplified arithmetic model. We shall make some initial assumptions, then modify them later to get as close as we can to the real world. The very first assumption is that stockholders, the equity investors, own all the assets of the corporation. There is no debt. Thus, the fundamental value we calculate for the assets should match the fundamental value of the claims of shareholders against the assets. Stock value should match asset values. Now analyze this projected income statement for our imagined corporation, with numbers in the millions of dollars:

Revenues		1,000
Variable Costs (Labor and Materials)	–	600
Fixed Costs (Depreciation)	–	100
Profits Before Tax	=	300
Corporate Income Taxes (30%)	–	90
Profits After Tax	=	210

In this oversimplified example, we have assumed that all sales are for cash and all variable expenses for labor and materials are paid in cash. If we subtract variable costs of 600 plus fixed depreciation costs of 100 from revenues of 1,000, then profits before taxes would be 300. With an assumed 30% corporate income tax rate, taxes would be 90, or 30% x 300, and profits after taxes reach 210. The 100 of depreciation assumes that the fixed plant and equipment is valued at 1,000, will last ten years, and is being depreciated on a straight-line basis at 100 each year. Assume also zero salvage value. In other words, the 100 cash revenues covering depreciation would have to be reinvested, or plowed back into new plant and equipment every year just to replace the 100 that is becoming worn out or obsolete. If the 100 of cash flow covering depreciation were instead paid out as cash dividends to stockholders, the effect would be to shrink the assets of the company. Depreciation funds paid out as dividends would mean liquidation of corporate assets.

Overstatement of the Value of Corporate Assets

This is where the fun and games begin. Let me dramatize using our hypothetical projections of revenues, costs, and profits. While the numbers are simplified here, the numerous exchanges I have had with analysts at major brokerages were real enough. One of my chores as a chief economist was to examine the analysts' research reports to be certain their projections were at least consistent with the overall economic outlook. All too often, though, I ran into analysts (A) who were hopelessly confused on the most basic of economic principles. The following typical exchange understates the problem:

RH: Your profit estimates are 210 after taxes, but you have calculated value by discounting the projected value of the cash-flow stream. Profits after taxes of 210 plus 100 of depreciation, you say, produces cash flow of 310?

A: Yes, what's wrong with that? Depreciation is just an accounting allocation of cost, not a cash outlay.

RH: That's not the point. Cash is being used to replace equipment. You can't treat 100 of depreciation as profits. Get my point?

A: I guess so.

RH: The cash flow covering depreciation disappears the moment you get it and spend it to replace worn out equipment. Now you see it, now you don't. Understand?

A: Yeah.

Yeah! The analysts often resented my interference. People don't like to be told they have mangled basic theory, no matter how diplomatic and friendly you may try to be.

The Abrupt and Unhappy Shift to the Short Run

Let's continue this exchange, but shift now to my graduate students (S) of finance at Pace University. Consider this typical discussion:

RH: Let's say that all our long-run projections fall apart, that we get into trouble. Assume that the business in question is steel. Assume that 1,000 has just been invested in specialized steel-making facilities, like a blast furnace, and that, as before, the expectation was to produce profitably. Our long-run game plan, you remember, was to depreciate plant and equipment at a rate of 100 annually over the assumed ten-year life of the furnace. For some reason, though, our sales projections collapsed immediately after we had shelled out 1,000 for the steel making facilities. The best projections we can now make appear under the short run, and they are dismal. Here are the assumed data:

	LONG RUN	SHORT RUN
Revenues	1,000	600
Variable Costs	600	525
Fixed Costs (Depreciation)	100	100
Profits Before Tax	300	0
Corporate Income Taxes (30%)	90	0
Profits After Tax	210	0

S1: Why the bad news? What happened?

RH: Perhaps we understated foreign competition and had to cut our prices as sales experienced a severe slump. Perhaps we underestimated Japanese competition. Whatever the reason, assume we can't make any profits at all. Let's examine these data. First, note that in our long-run example the depreciation cost of 100 reduces profits before tax by 100, hence reduces taxes by 30, or by the tax rate of 30 percent times 100. In the absence of the depreciation of 100, corporate profits before taxes would have been 400 instead of 300, and the tax bill would have been 120 instead of 90. You can see, then, why taking depreciation as a cost of doing business is important to business. Now suppose we make no profits, as shown under the short run. What tax break do you get then?

S1: None. No profits, no tax break.

RH: Yes, except for a possible carryover of losses for tax purposes, when you do make profits. But I'm assuming no profits, with red ink every year for ten years.

The Meaning of Short Run

RH: The economist defines short-run as that period of time in which a commitment has already been made for "fixed" capital, which means that the company has contracted fixed costs. Put another way, the 1000 outlay for the furnace is now a "sunk" investment. Like time that marches on, the purchase cannot be reversed or canceled. So, the very existence of fixed costs places us in the short-run analytical time frame. To be sure, we can either be blessed or burned in the short-run, depending on developments. In our example, it looks like we are burned by our blasted blast furnace. Ever see one?

Ss: (Silence.)

RH: Nobody? Well, it's a monstrous structure several stories high. It has no function other than that of a smelting furnace in which the fire inside the furnace is intensified by air blasts. In the jargon of economists, the blast furnace would be dubbed "immobile" capital. In contrast, a truck, for example, would represent "mobile" capital. A truck can be shifted from one industry to another, from one function to another.

Let's assume that our brand new furnace will work efficiently for exactly ten years, no more and no less, and will have zero worth after ten years. At the same time, let's agree that we shall not replace the furnace, that no reinvestment expenditures will be made over the ten years because we have decided to get out of this red-ink business once the furnace collapses. This means that our assumed short-run period is ten years, a finite span. That means the annual cash revenues covering depreciation represent a true receipt of cash that will not be gobbled up on new capital replacement outlays. Only variable costs for labor and materials are assumed here to represent cash outlays. We assume also that variable costs have fallen to 525 from 600 to reflect the lower level of production and sales in the short run. We can now prepare projected cash-flow statements for the short-run period:

SHORT-RUN ANALYSIS

Cash Flows Each Year	Close Down	Operate
Cash In	0	600
Cash Out (Variable Costs Only)	0	525
Net Cash In	0	75

So what do you do, operate or close down?

S3:   Operate. You minimize your losses that way. If you close down, you get nothing back on your investment. If you operate, you get back 75 a year. That's 750 for the ten years, or 75% of your original investment of 1,000.

RH: Good, let's state the principle on the blackboard:

> **If revenues in the short run are sufficient to cover variable costs and contribute something to fixed costs, then you operate in the short run and thereby minimize losses. But you get out in the long run.**

Let's drop now our assumptions on depreciation and on our all-equity corporation. Just assume depreciation charges are negligible. Assume also that the corporation has contracted substantial debt, and that the fixed charges of 100 are all fixed interest charges. Interest charges, you recognize, are "explicit" costs involving a simultaneous cash outlay. It is to be contrasted with an "implicit" cost like depreciation that involves no drain against revenues. So, what do you do now? Think before you answer. Here are the data:

Cash In		600
Cash Out		625
Variable Costs	525	
Fixed Costs (Interest)	100 ?	

I repeat the question: what do you do? As a hint, I have put a question mark beside the interest costs.

S4:   You have to close down because cash inflow is only 600 but cash drain is 625, made up of 525 for variable outlays for labor and materials plus 100 of interest charges. The 600 won't cover cash outlays of 625. You fold.

RH: My hint didn't work. We concluded earlier that you would operate as long as you can cover variable costs. With cash revenues of 600 and variable costs of 525, we are more than covering our variable costs. Were we wrong?

S4:   (Silence.)

RH: If we conclude we have to close down, then we have to rewrite every good text in microeconomic theory. Economists maintain that you operate in the short-run if revenues cover variable (not fixed) costs.

S5:   You said that depreciation was an implicit cost, meaning no cash drain. But interest charges are an explicit cost, and this does eat up cash flow. Maybe the text books are wrong.

RH: No, the textbooks are correct. Here's another clue. Ever hear of a financial composition (restructuring) or corporate reorganization in bankruptcy? What do you think bondholders would do in this "short-run" situation?

S6:   The court just calls in the creditors who, I guess, now own the firm. Any stockholders are wiped out. If the bondholders close down the business, they get nothing back. If they operate, they get back 75 percent of their investment. But for revenues to cover all cash outlays, the bondholders would have to agree to have "fixed" interest payments scaled back from 100 to 75.

RH: The creditors minimize their losses that way. Under reorganization, this "fixed" charge becomes "unfixed," so to speak. That's good theory, and that's the way it is in practice. That way the cash inflow of 600 would cover 525 of variable costs plus 75 (not 100) of interest. So the textbooks are correct, after all.

You operate if revenues cover variable costs and make some contribution to fixed, regardless of whether fixed costs are implicit or explicit.

If the fixed costs are interest charges, it makes sense to scale them back. One thing for certain, you will get out of this business in the long run if the new and lower projections you have made remain bleak. In the long run, no one would logically stay in a given business unless he expected to cover all costs and make "normal" profits. By "normal," economists mean just sufficient to compensate for the risk and trouble of investment.

Now we have to calculate the long-run and the short-run fundamental values of property. Let's calculate the long-run value first, then contrast that with the short-run valuation. Remember our assumptions. We assumed that net annual earnings (after taxes) were projected at $210 million, that all earnings were distributed as dividends, and that the revenues covering depreciation were instantly reinvested to keep productive capital intact. Thus we assumed a constant-sized company, neither growing nor contracting. Now also assume that you would have been satisfied with a 15 percent required return, or cost of capital. What would the fundamental value be? Here are the data:

	LONG RUN	SHORT RUN
Revenues	1,000	600
Variable Costs	600	525
Fixed Costs (Depreciation)	100	100
Profits Before Tax	300	0
Corporate Income Taxes (30%)	90	0
Profits After Tax	210	0

VALUATION: THE LONG RUN VERSUS THE SHORT RUN

S7:   You are assuming $210 million a year for an infinite time. Since this is a constant amount, with no growth, you simply divide $210 million by .15, which is $1,400 million.

RH: Yes, we can restate our conclusions for the long run in three ways, all of which mean the same thing:

1. How much would you earn each year by investing $1,400 million at 15%?
   Answer: .15 x $1,400 million = $210 million

2. How much would you have to invest to earn $210 million each year at 15%?
   Answer: $\frac{\$210 \text{ million}}{.15}$ = $1,400 million

3. In investment jargon, what is the discounted value (capitalized, or present value) of a fixed but infinite dividend stream of $210 million each year, discounted at a cost of capital of 15%?
   Answer: $\frac{\$210 \text{ million}}{.15}$ = = $1,400 million

I have used the simplest example here to calculate the value of a company in the long run, but one that has zero growth. If we had instead assumed a growth company, one that plows back its earnings, then we would have calculated a higher value for the assets than $1,400 million (chapter 15). Let's consider how we go about valuing the cash-flow stream in our short-run example. Take a look again at the data, again in millions of dollars:

CASH FLOWS EACH YEAR	CLOSE DOWN	OPERATE
Cash In	0	600
Cash Out (Variable Costs Only)	0	525
Net Cash In	0	75

S8: It's worth its net cash flow of $75 million a year.

RH: What is $75 million a year for ten years worth? What discount rate do you use?

S8: You said earlier 15 percent. That's what we used for the long-run valuation, when we discounted net earnings.

RH: But do you see any problem with using that low a rate now, for the short run?

S8: Since the company is now in shambles, and this was unanticipated, I guess risk has gone up.

RH: Yes, under the changed and dismal scene I set forth for the short-run, you would probably require a much higher return for investing in this company than under our assumed long-run conditions. Risk has gone up. For illustration, let's capitalize the net cash flow at a much higher rate, at, say, 32 percent instead of 15 percent. What do you get for a present value in this short-run case?

S6: According to the tables you passed out, the interest factor at 32 percent for a ten-year annuity is 2.9304. So the present value would be 2.9304 x $75 million, or about $220 million.

RH: If we didn't have those tables or our calculators, we could determine the value as $\frac{\$75 \text{ million}}{1.32}$ for the first year + $\frac{\$75 \text{ million}}{(1.32 \times 1.32)}$ for the second + $\frac{\$75 \text{ million}}{(1.32 \times 1.32 \times 1.32)}$ for the third, and so on through the tenth year. That's a lot of unnecessary calculation. You can see now that in the short run we can be in the red, but not yet dead. Here are the present valuations in millions of dollars:

> Long Run: Net Earnings at 15% $1,400 million
> Short Run: Net Cash Flow at 32%: $220 million

Paradox of Value Surrounded by Red Ink

RH: The short run is assumed to have hit our hypothetical company by depressing the present value sharply, from $1,400 million to $220 million. It suffered on two counts. First, the time span of receipts fell from an infinite period (long run) to a finite period of ten years (short run). Second, as is often the case, the required cost of capital soared, which means that the higher risk also knocked down the market valuation. Even so, the property still commanded value despite a sea of red ink. Remember, the principle is crucial to our later analysis of corporate financial theory and practice. Put it this way:

> Earnings and dividends may not even exist in the short run, but the assets can command great value if they can generate a net positive cash flow, even for a finite time.

The Market Period Analysis

RH: This takes us now to the market period. Let's explain again by way of simple examples. Suppose you owned a warehouse full of shirts, and had these data on unit costs and prices at the wholesale level:

Cost of Production	Present Price
$10	$8

What would you do? It costs $10 to produce each shirt but the current market is only $8. Hold or sell?

S1: Hold. If I sell now, I take a $2 loss per shirt.

RH: Well, suppose you expected the price to fall to $5 and stay there. What then?

S1: I guess I would sell right away.

RH: O.K., you changed your mind. You see now that you cannot make any logical decision by merely comparing the present with the past. That's dangerous. Logicians say that reasoning by historical analogy alone is illogical. This applies to shirts, as in our example, and it applies to that stock you bought at 30, which you failed to sell at 20 because 30 was your cost, and then the stock promptly fell to 5. You must always look at the present and the future in the market-period analysis. The present price and the future price are your only two real options. The past is not an option.

Assume now that you expect the price to rise to $12. What then?

S1: Hold, and wait for the higher price.

RH: Right. What can you say about the market-period analysis? Any principles? Any generalizations you would like to make? Remember that the market period assumes goods, in this case shirts, are already on hand. You own them. They were produced in some earlier period. Maybe your grandmother gave them to you. Maybe you produced them as a manufacturer. The key point is that you own these shirts.

S1: This means that past costs of production are irrelevant.

RH: Good. Remember that only *variable operating costs* are relevant in the short-run period. But in the market period, all past costs are irrelevant unless the past in some way can provide you with clues to the future. But all too often the past is a bad guide to the future. Are there any other costs relevant to the market-period analysis?

S: (Silence from entire class.)

RH: What about storage costs or possibly fire and theft insurance for these shirts? If you borrowed money to buy the shirts in the first place, then you must have an ongoing interest expense. All of these costs could be considered costs of holding these shirts. Economists would classify such costs as "carrying costs."

Let's specify our carrying period as one year. That is, let's assume that the present price remains unchanged for one year, then rises or falls to a given level one year later, and then remains at that new level. Consider these three different cases for the market period:

	PRODUCTION COSTS	CURRENT PRICE	FUTURE PRICE	CARRYING COSTS	DECISION?
(1)	$10	$8	$ 5	$1.00	?
(2)	$10	$8	$12	$1.00	?
(3)	$10	$8	$10	$1.50	?

What do you do?

S2: In (1) you sell immediately at $8, which means you lose $2 on production costs of $10. You end up with $8. If you had waited a year and sold at the lower price of $5, you would lose even more because the $5 less carrying costs of $1 means you end up with only $4. So to minimize your loss, you sell immediately. In (2) you hold for one year, then sell for $12. That's a gross gain of $4 over the current price, and a net gain of $3 once you subtract the $1 carrying costs. In (3) you would hold, and sell at $10 one year later. That way you clear $10 gross, and $8.50

once you subtract the $1.50 carrying cost. That's preferable to selling for $8.00.

RH: Do you all agree on Case (3)?

S3: Sounds O.K. to me.

S4: You just might be able to sell now, and reinvest the money immediately at a high rate. Like in 1981.

RH: Good. You should always evaluate any given investment against the entire range of competing investment opportunities. You must have recalled our earlier discussion. In 1981, you remember, long Treasury bonds were available at yields of 15 percent, and AAA corporate bonds at even higher yields. The "opportunity cost," or the income "foregone" in not buying these bonds and instead using your money for some other purpose was extremely high. In our third hypothetical example with the shirts, you were correct in concluding that if you had sold your shirts one year hence for $10, then you would have ended up with $8.50 once you subtracted the carrying charge of $1.50. But that's not the whole story. That $0.50 absolute return would have meant only a 6.25% return on the current price of $8 ($.50/$8.00 = 6.25%).

Common Error: Confusing Carrying Cost with Opportunity Cost

RH: Opportunity cost dictated that you would have been better off selling immediately at $8, and investing in Treasury bonds at the magnificent yields we assume were then available of 15 percent. That was a golden opportunity, even ignoring the swift descent in yields that followed, which made for huge capital gains on long bonds. Another important principle is involved here.

> If the investment opportunity cost exceeds the net return on a deferred sale, defined as the future price less the sum of the present price and carrying charges, you had better sell immediately and invest.

PARROTS AND THE MARKET-PERIOD ANALYSIS

We are all Parrots at one time or another, no matter what our education and training. Somehow other forces unpredictably dominate our thinking, and our common sense deserts us, at least for the moment. Here is a good example.

Inta (I) was one of my former students at Wharton. She was a brilliant student with a photographic mind, who got straight A's with no apparent effort. I married her and shortly thereafter resigned my teaching post at Wharton. I was hired as an economist by General Electric in Schenectady, New York. We had to move. I was agonizing over a house:

RH: We can't sell this house. It's now $3,000 below the price I bought it for two years ago.

I: Are you an economic illiterate, a Parrot? What happened to the market-period analysis? Forget your own teaching?

We sold. That made sense because the price continued down as the neighborhood deteriorated.

We have the theoretical background, finally, to consider a horror story in corporate finance. Two Nobel prize winners in economics were unwitting participants, I shall argue, in this tale of theoretical and applied failure.

19

Theory of Corporate Finance

The Antidote for Junk Bond Deception

Myself when young did eagerly frequent Doctor and Saint,
and heard great argument About it and about: but evermore
Came out by the same door wherein I went.

Omar Khyyam, *The Rubaiyat,* Verse xxx

I invite you to join me on an amazing theoretical journey that ends just where
it begins. We begin with what economists call the traditional theory of corporate finance, which has always made sense to me. That subject will consume all of this chapter. In chapter 20 we will explore the theoretical world
of Drs. Franco Modigliani and Merton Miller (MM), two university scholars
who startled the academic world in 1958 with revolutionary pronouncements.
Finally, in Chapter 21 we turn to the corporate debt explosion and equity implosion (destruction) of the 1980s. While the corporate malpractices of the
1980s were triggered by a great many forces at work, one must include in any
serious listing the legacy of defective MM valuation theory.

While this discussion will require three chapters, it has occupied me for
three decades. After all the years of work and teaching, after all the long exchanges with economists and investment officers and literally thousands of
graduate students, after serious review of these ideas with Dr. Modigliani himself (see chapter 20), and after all the arguments, I am more fully convinced
than ever of the validity of the traditional theory of corporate finance.

Exactly what were the two MM "propositions" that so shocked the academic world in 1958? The answer will come in chapter 20. For now our im-

mediate task is to set forth the basics of valuation and cost analysis that underlie traditional theory. We must understand traditional theory first. Only then can we begin to understand MM theory. This is no easy task. As a preface to an extended explanation, let's state here the key conclusions of traditional theory.

The traditional theory of corporate finance maintains that if it is initially cheaper to raise money through debt than through equity, the firm can reduce its average cost of financing, debt and equity combined, through reliance more on borrowing than on raising capital through the sale of new stock. However, if *leverage*—the ratio of debt to total funds raised—increases beyond a certain point, investors may begin to worry that the added debt raises the risk of default and bankruptcy. Their fears, their worried expectations, then, would tend to push up the cost of financing for both debt and equity.

Put another way, traditional theory argues that the firm can increase borrowing and increase net earnings per share and the market price of stock just so long as the additional earnings climb faster than the additional perceived risk by shareholders. But beyond the point of leverage where perceived equity risk speeds ahead of rising earnings, equity prices will drop. Indeed, the required returns on both equity and debt may climb swiftly with companion declines in their market prices. Prices could plummet on expectations of soaring financing costs. In short, the average weighted cost of capital (AWCC) of debt and equity would rise.

If all this isn't perfectly clear then let's explain using this exchange with graduate students in finance (S).

RH: Let's look first at the possible tax advantage leverage may provide shareholders through a simple arithmetic example. Let's track our initial analysis in Table 1 (see page 282). Assume we have two firms identical in asset size, management, product, operating income, and in every other way except for their capital structures. One is unleveraged, meaning no debt, which we shall call U. The other is leveraged, with 50 percent equity and 50 percent debt, which we'll call L. The *capital structure* in the first three lines of our table refers to the debt and equity claims, the bonds and stocks listed on the right hand side of the balance sheet. Assume a $10 par on stock, or 200 shares for U ($\frac{\$2,000}{\$10}$) and 100 shares for L ($\frac{\$1,000}{\$10}$).

Earnings before interest and taxes (EBIT) of $300 is the dollar return on assets after all operating expenses are subtracted but before any of the $300 is paid to shareholders, bondholders, or in income-tax. We have assumed a 30% corporate tax rate and an 8% pretax borrowing rate. *Consistent with the MM model (chapter 15), we have assumed that all earnings are paid out as dividends.* The purpose is merely to simplify the example. Concentrate now on net earnings after taxes for U, and after interest and taxes for L:

U: EBIT of $300   − $90 taxes = $210 Net
L: EBIT of $300   − $80 Interest   − $66 taxes = $154
Net Tax Savings for L $24

TABLE 1

| | U | L |
	EXAMPLE 1	EXAMPLE 2
BOOK VALUE: STOCK*	$2,000	$1,000
BOOK VALUE: BONDS	0	$1,000
TOTAL BOOK VALUE	$2,000	$2,000
Earnings Before Interest and Taxes (EBIT)	$ 300	$ 300
Interest (8% x $1000)	0	80
Pretax Earnings (E)	300	220
Taxes (30% Rate x E)	90	66
Net Earnings	$ 210	$ 154
Total Number of Shares*	200	100
Net Earnings Per Share	$ 1.05	$ 1.54
Cost of Equity Capital	10%	10%
Price Per Share (P)	$10.50	$15.40
MARKET VALUE: STOCK	$2,100	$1,540
MARKET VALUE: BONDS	0	$1,000
TOTAL MARKET VALUE	$2,100	$2,540

*$10 Par. So, $\frac{\text{book value}}{\text{par value}}$ = number of shares.

Net earnings per share are $1.05 for U, or $210 divided by 200 shares; and $1.54 for L, or $154 divided by 100 shares. This suggests that borrowing apparently paid off for L by increasing earnings per share. Does anyone remember what economists call corporate borrowing in the attempt to magnify the return to common stock?

S1:   Trading on equity. L borrows at 8 percent, and has to pay $80 in interest, but the interest can be deducted as a cost of doing business, and this will cut income taxes. Dividend payments to shareholders are not tax deductible.

RH: Good. Can you review the arithmetic here?

S2: The $80 interest deduction for L reduced its taxable earnings by the same $80, and this cut its taxes by 30 percent of $80, for a $24 tax savings. The tax bill for U is $90, but only $66 for L, and $90 less $66 is $24.

RH: Excellent. In our first example, then, the 8 percent pretax cost of debt results in a 5.6 percent aftertax cost, with 30 percent representing the tax rate. Thus $(1 - .30) \times 8\% = 5.6\%$. Now, just suppose the pretax borrowing rate were 10% instead of 8%. Look at the comparison:

	L(10%)	L(8%)	Difference
Earnings Before Interest and Taxes (EBIT)	$300	$300	
Interest (10% and 8%)	100	80	
Pretax Earnings (E)	200	220	+ $20
Taxes (30% Rate x E)	60	66	+ 6
Net Earnings	140	154	+ 14

You can see that at the lower 8 percent pretax rate, pretax earnings are higher by $20, but taxes are also higher by $6. So, subtract $6 from $20 to get the net gain. Now, the *extra* $14 (which is 1.4 percent of the $1,000 borrowed) is explained strictly by the lower 8 percent rate, not the tax advantage. This distinction is critical (Exhibit 19–1).

THE BRIGHT SIDE OF LEVERAGE

RH: Let's dig deeper into leverage with the help of Table 2 (see page 284). You can see in the table that earnings per share increased from $1.05 per share for U (example 1) to $1.54 for L by borrowing (example 2). That produced a parallel rise in the price of L stock to $15.40, a higher market value than the $10.50 for U. So, as long as earnings per share are expected to rise with no rise in perceived risk by stockholders, the market price of L's stock will also rise proportionately to the rise in earnings per share. Indeed, even if the cost of equity capital does rise, the price of L stock could still rise provided only that the rise in earnings per share exceeds the rise in cost. You can see that in example (3a) in table 2. Example (3a) illustrates that even with a sharp rise in the perceived cost of debt, from 8% to 10%, and the cost of equity, from 10% to 12.5%, the stock price moves up to $19.60. Who can explain the rise?

TABLE 2

Example	(1)	(2)	(3a)	(3b)
Assets (Book)	$2,000	$2,000	$2,000	$2,000
Percent Debt	0%	50%	80%	80%
Total Debt (Par)	$0	$1000	$1600	$1600
Assumed % Rise in Cost of Capital and Perceived Risk			+ 25%*	+ 100%
Cost of Debt*	0	8%	10.0%	16%**
Cost of Equity*	10%	10%	12.5%	20%**
EBIT	$300	$300	$300 ⟶	$190
Interest	0	80	160	160
Pretax Earnings	$300	$220	$140	$30.00
Taxes	90	66	42	9.00
Net Earnings	$210	$154	$98	$21.00
Shares, Par = $10	200	100	40	40
Earnings/Share	$1.05	$1.54	$2.45	$0.525
Cost of Equity	10%	10%	12.5%	20%**
Price Per Share	$10.50	$15.40	$19.60	$2.625
Mkt. Value Equity	$2100	$1540	$784.00	$105.00
Mkt. Value Debt	0	1000	1600.00	1136.00
Total Mkt. Value	$2100	$2540	$2384.00	$1241.00

*From (2) to (3a)

**Costs were 10% pretax for debt and 12.5% for equity in (3a) but the sudden fall in EBIT for the *same firm and capital structure* raised costs to 16% and 20% in (3b).

S3:   Your data show a rise in earnings per share to $2.45 from the $1.05 for U, up 133%. The 133% higher earnings exceeds the 25% rise in the cost of equity capital, which you show rising from 10% to 12.5%.

RH: Good. That means example (3a) is still illustrative of the bright side of leverage, at least for equity investors. Let's turn now to the dark side and the arithmetic in example (3b). We need to concentrate now on the impact of leveraging on *expected* financing costs.

THE DARK SIDE OF LEVERAGE

RH: Example (3b) is an extreme example, but illustrative of the extreme leverage antics of the 1980s that produced dreadful losses for millions of investors. I have tried to stress here how towering leverage can impact expectations, and cause both debt and equity costs to soar. To dramatize this, ask yourself what happens to a given company under (3a) when investors learn that a severe recession is about to strike. Suppose their *expectations* for EBIT plunge. If we assume a highly cyclical firm, EBIT could fall easily below interest charges of $160 and raise fears of default. We'll assume just for calculation that EBIT falls to $190. Remember that (3a) and (3b) refer to the same firm.

S6: With an expected EBIT of only $190, the earnings coverage of fixed charges would drop sharply. Bondholders, though, might look for worse news to come, maybe even bankruptcy. Bond prices could easily take a dive.

RH: Yes. Let's assume that the bondholders who originally paid $1,600 for their 10 percent coupon bonds in (3a) now grow suddenly worried. Suppose that the market now discounts at a higher 16 percent rate. What would the new market value be? That's easy. For a ten-year bond, the annual interest is $160, or 10% x $1,600. The present value of an annuity of $160 a year for ten years discounted at 16 percent is about $773.30. The present value of the principal sum of $1,600 due in ten years, also discounted at 16 percent, is about $362.70. So, the price would fall to $1,136 ($773.30 plus $362.70) in (3b). That's down $464 from the $1,600 shown in (3a). It could, of course, fall more or less depending on what investors believed about the future earnings coverage, about the possibility of bankruptcy.

We assumed maturities of 10 years, which was arbitrary. If debt were all short term in (say) commercial paper, then the company would immediately have to contend with higher refinancing costs that would eat into profits, and bring bankruptcy much closer. Now, what about stock prices?

S6: Stocks would dive. In example (3b) you show net earnings falling to $0.525 per share from $2.45 in (3a), resulting from the fall in EBIT from $300 to $190. Financing costs jump from 10 percent to 16 percent for debt, and 12.5 percent to 20 percent for equity. That doesn't happen overnight. Right?

RH: Well, EBIT could plunge overnight. It could fall even below the assumed fixed interest charges of $160. To repeat, though, what happens to earnings per share also depends on the maturity of the debt in the capital structure. But whatever the maturity, the key point is that debt financing costs can zoom higher, much higher. Remember, too, that debt-rating agencies like Standard and Poor's and Moody's could drop their ratings overnight. That could knock bond prices down. Future financing costs could soar, and become prohibitive. That's the way with corporations that go head-over-heels into debt. Equity investors may become rattled, and bondholders, too. So, excessive leverage can result in plummeting prices for both debt and equity.

Just what would push the cost of equity capital up to the 20 percent in example (3b)?

S7: A recession could cause trouble for a debt-heavy firm because interest payments are contractual; it could risk collapse if it fails to pay interest on time. Dividend payments to common stockholders are optional; the board of directors may decide to pass on any dividends. So, there's more risk for a firm highly leveraged, loaded with debt, especially in cyclical industries. Also, if shareholders begin to worry that the highly leveraged corporation can't make interest payments on time, they might worry about getting any dividends at all. They might dump their stock. You probably meant to illustrate that with the fall in EBIT.

RH: Of course. So, you would say that some debt might be an advantage to shareholders, as in examples (2) and (3a), but that too much debt could be disastrous, as in example (3b)?

S7: Yes. You can increase the return to shareholder by borrowing up to a point, but if you borrow too much and risk bankruptcy, the stockholders could be wiped out.

RH: Good. You have stated what economists essentially mean by the traditional theory of corporate finance. Let's illustrate what an economic slowdown or recession could do to our two firms in table 1 for U and L. Suppose a severe recession knocks EBIT down so hard for both firms, that it falls to $80:

	U	L
EBIT	$80	$80
– Interest	0	80
= Taxable Earnings	80	0
– Income Taxes (30% Rate)	24	0
= Net Earnings to Common	$56	$ 0

As you can see, the net earnings of U fall to $56. The net earnings of L fall even more, to zero. There you have another dimension of the dark side of leverage.

THE AVERAGE WEIGHTED COST OF CAPITAL (AWCC)

RH: Let's illustrate the bright side of leverage, and then the dark side via the average weighted cost of capital (AWCC). We'll use our four examples from Table 2. Example (1), you'll recall, assumes no leverage, with a 100% equity capital structure. We assumed a 10 percent cost of equity capital, earnings after tax at $1.05 per share, and the stock price at $10.50 per share. In this case, the calculation is easy:

Example (1): Unleveraged (100% Equity)

$$AWCC = \frac{\text{Net Earnings per Share}}{\text{Market Price per Share}} = \frac{\$1.05}{\$10.50} = 10\%$$

Ponder for a moment the opposite extreme.

S7: A firm with no equity and 100 percent debt?

RH: Yes. Assume also, as before, an 8 percent pretax borrowing rate and a 30 percent income tax rate, which would mean a 5.6 percent borrowing rate after tax. What do you think of that?

S8: You have a contradiction: 100 percent debt implies that the creditors *own* the firm, which would be tantamount to 100 percent equity. That makes no sense.

RH: We will return to this paradox when we review MM theory (in chapter 20). Let's turn now to the calculation of the AWCC in our example (2) of 50 percent leverage. Let's first *weight* the capital costs by the market values for both debt and equity to derive the average weighted cost of capital. So, let **Weight** represent the current market values of stock **S** and bonds **B.** Let CC represent the current costs of capital after tax for both stocks and bonds. Here's the **AWCC**:

Example (2) A 50% Leveraged Firm

		Weight	x	CC
Market Values				
$1,000 Debt $1540 Equity				
	S:	1,540	x	.10 = 154
S = Stocks	B:	1,000	x	.056 = 56
B = Bonds		2,540		210

$$AWCC = \frac{210}{2,540} = 8.27\%$$

Let's explain these numbers. If we assume that we can raise money at 10 percent through equity, and if we could raise money at a 5.6 percent net of taxes through debt, then our average cost would be 8.27 percent. The 8.27 percent is easy to understand. That is, we would have to promise to pay $210 in income each year ($154 in dividends plus $56 in interest) to raise $2,540 in capital ($1,540 through stocks plus $1,000 through bonds) via this particular mix of financing. Thus, $210 divided by $2,540 is 8.27% for this package of financing. Note, too, that if we use the market values to calculate the proportions of equity and debt, then the equity proportion works out to 60.63 percent, or $1,540 of equity divided by $2,540 of equity plus debt. It's that simple.

MARKET COSTS VERSUS MARKET PROPORTIONS

RH: Well, it's almost that simple. We must always distinguish between market rates, on the one hand, and market proportions, on the other. Suppose for example, that we wanted to raise *additional* capital beyond the $2,000 we started with, but again in *equal* amounts for debt and equity at the current market rates of 10 percent and 5.6 percent. Then the AWCC for the *incremental* capital would be the sum of the market cost of debt (5.6%) and equity (10.0%) divided by 2, or 7.8 percent. The 7.8 percent, you note, is lower than the 8.27% AWCC we first calculated. Why?

S9: You used a lower proportion of equity, at 50 percent, or below the equity proportion you calculated at 60.63 percent.

RH: So, keep in mind the distinction between market rates and market proportions. You may elect to finance incremental capital in equal proportions of debt and equity, or 25 percent equity and 75 percent debt, or whatever. It all depends on your needs and objectives, the changing relative costs of debt and equity capital, tax rates, and just how conservative or aggressive you may be. Oddly enough, the distinction I'm making here between market rates and market proportions is universally ignored in textbooks and refereed journals in corporate finance. Don't you fall into that error.

Consider now example (3a). You see there that we still get higher per-share prices despite higher costs for both debt and equity financing. Both are assumed to rise by 25 percent. That would lift the cost of equity financing from 10 percent to 12.5 percent, and lift the pretax cost of debt financing from 8 percent to 10 percent. The after-tax cost of debt, again with a 30 percent tax rate, would also rise by 25 percent, from 5.6 percent to 7 percent. Here is our illustrative arithmetic, using market weights:

Example (3a)
Assumes Increases of 25% in Costs
of Debt and Equity Capital

Weight   x   CC

Market Values
$1,600 Debt $784 Equity

S:	784	x	.125	=	98.00
B:	1,600	x	.07	=	112.00
	2,384				210.00

S = Stocks
B = Bonds

$AWCC = \frac{210}{2,384} = 8.81\%$

S9: Where did the $784 and the $1,600 weights come from?

RH: Good question. The $784 market value estimate for the stocks is taken directly from the data in Example (3a) of table 2. You see there that the earnings per share are $2.45. With a cost of equity capital at 12.50 percent, then the market value per share works out to $19.60 per share ($\frac{$2.45}{.125} = \$19.60$). With 80 percent of our capital structure in debt, that would mean 20 percent in equity. We assumed 200 shares in Example (1) of our all equity firm. So, the number of shares for our leveraged firm in example (3a) and the shift to (3b) are 20 percent times 200 shares, or 40 shares. For (3a) multiply the $19.60 price for each share times 40 shares, and you get our $784 market value for equity.

S9: How about the $1,600 weight for debt in (3a)?

RH: That's easy. I'm assuming that the firm borrowed $1600 at 10 percent on a ten-year bond in (3a). Since the market rate in (3a) is also 10 percent, the debt would be priced at par, at $1600. Let's turn now to example (3b), which takes us down the bleak-to-black implications of traditional theory. Suppose that EBIT suddenly crashes from $300 in (3a) to $190 in (3b) and stockholders become worried that it may fall even more. Keep in mind that we are focusing in the shift from (3a) to (3b) on the very same company and the very same capital structure. In that case, equity investors might now demand a minimum 20 percent return in (3b), up from 12.5 percent in (3a). Bondholders, also worried, might increase their demands for a pretax return to 16 percent in (3b), up from 10 percent in (3a). The 16 percent would translate into an after-tax cost of debt capital of 11.2 percent. What would happen to the price of the stock under our assumed deterioration in EBIT and in perceived financial returns?

S5: It would take a dive. Earnings per share are now down to $0.525. If stockholders demanded a 20 percent return on an earnings stream of only $0.525 a year, that would mean a much lower price. Are you still assuming a constant earnings stream, with no growth?

RH: Yes, that's the MM view we will examine later.

S9: In that case, the market would value the stock at $0.525 divided by the new cost of equity capital of 20 percent, which works out to a low $2.625 per share.

RH: Excellent. What about the existing bondholders? What would be the likely market impact on their holdings?

S5: You get the same downdraft. If they are going to demand a 16 percent return in (3b), up from 10 percent in (3a), then the capitalized value would fall. Bond prices would fall.

RH: Yes. Let's quantify this by calculating a rough AWCC for example (3b). Study these numbers a few minutes.

Example (3b)

		Weight	x	CC	Market Values
$1,136 Debt/$105 Equity					
	S:	105	x	.20	= $ 21.00
S = Stocks	B:	1,136	x	.112	= 127.23
B = Bonds		1,241			$148.23

$$\text{AWCC} = \frac{148.23}{1,241} = 11.94\%$$

Again, these are arbitrary assumptions because the market value of the debt already on the books depends on our maturity assumptions. Assuming again a ten-year maturity for the original nominal $1,600 of debt with a 10 percent coupon in (3a), the market value would fall to $1,136 in (3b) when discounted at the higher 16 percent rate. Here's the math:

PV* of $160 a year for ten years	=	773.32
PV* of $1,600 due in ten years	=	362.69
		$1,136.01

*Present Value (PV) factors of 10% coupon bond discounted at 16% market rate.

Assuming the firm resolved its problems, the 16 percent rate could later fall, and prices recover. Creditors might still collect all interest and their full $1,600 principal at maturity. On the other hand, a further slide in EBIT could bankrupt the firm. Also, if the debt were all short term rather than the ten-year maturity assumed here, then refinancing would immediately skyrocket for every penny borrowed. The higher financing costs could quickly chill and kill the corporation. *Traditional theory argues that you cannot separate a possibly volatile EBIT from the projected performance of bond and stock investors. It says that you cannot isolate EBIT from the* magnitude *of fixed charges, hence* expected *returns and risks.* But we will soon see that MM do just that (chapter 20).

The Bright Side Plus the Dark Side: A "U"-Shaped AWCC

RH: According to traditional theory, what would the AWCC look like if plotted on a chart? To be specific, let the horizontal axis on our chart represent leverage. So, the farther we move to the right (east) along the axis, the greater would be the ratio of debt to equity. If we take the vertical axis to plot values for the AWCC, then the farther we move up (north) along that axis, the higher would be the AWCC. What would the cost curve look like?

S5: The text says like a saucer.

RH: Yes, the four calculations we made for the AWCC with leverage at 0 percent, 50 percent, and 80 percent give us four plots. Note that I have plotted two rates at 80 percent leverage to illustrate how differences in perceived risk can impact the AWCC (see page 292). I added other plots to depict the saucer. Let's assume that the fall in EBIT also hits the unleveraged firm (1). Would its stock fall as much as that of the leveraged firm under (3b)?

THE AWCC UNDER TRADITIONAL THEORY

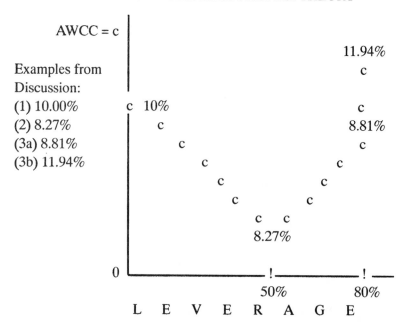

AWCC = c

Examples from
Discussion:
(1) 10.00%
(2) 8.27%
(3a) 8.81%
(3b) 11.94%

11.94%

8.81%

8.27%

10%

0

50%   80%

L E V E R A G E

S3: Probably not. If EBIT falls also to $190 for (1), then taxes would amount to $57, or 30 percent x $190. That would push net earnings down to $133, or $190 less $57. The $133 of net earnings would mean per-share earnings of $0.665, or $133 divided by 200 shares. If you discounted the per-share earnings stream at 10 percent, the price would drop to $6.65, down 37 percent from $10.50. That's a lot less than the 87 percent plunge, from $19.60 to $2.63, in (3b).

RH: Even if you discounted at 15 percent, the price would drop less than that of our leveraged firm. Even so, a 15 percent rate could easily overstate risk for the unleveraged company. On the other hand, our highly leveraged (3b) firm could easily go bankrupt with a sustained erosion of cash flow. Illiquidity can precipitate default, then bankruptcy.

MM ARBITRAGE "PROOF"

But wait. MM argue that the saucer-shaped AWCC is wrong, that traditional theory is all wet. They offer their arbitrage exercise as "proof." Proof? Yes, that's the word Modigliani and Miller use. Beware, for true scientists abhor the word. They always take their conclusions as tentative. Let's analyze this MM arbitrage "proof."

Exhibit 19–1: The Nature of the Borrowing Advantage

I asked Tom Mansley, an intellectually gifted student of finance who takes nothing for granted, to check Chapter 19 for errors and ambiguities. He found several, which I have since corrected. Consider here Tom's insight on separating the tax benefit from the lower borrowing rate:

In the beginning of the chapter, if your intent was to drive home the concept of the tax advantage rather than the lower interest rate advantage of borrowing, the example should have the same before tax cost of debt as equity (10%). You should also state that you realize that this violates certain principles (such as the equity premium), but that it is for demonstration purposes only. In your example the 8 percent cost of debt would result in an after-tax rate of 5.6 percent. Even if equity dividends were tax deductible, a 10% cost of equity would result in an after-tax rate of 7%. So, the *extra* 1.4 percent kick (7% – 5.6%) comes from the lower borrowing cost of debt rather than the tax break. You could clear up this confusion by using 10% for both the cost of equity and the pretax cost of debt, as in this example:

	U	L
Total Assets	$2,000	$2,000
Percent Debt	0%	50%
Total Debt	$ 0	$1,000
Pretax Cost of Debt	10%	10%
Pretax Cost of Equity	10%	10%
EBIT	$ 300	$ 300
Interest	0	100
Taxable Earnings	$ 300	200
Taxes (at 30%)	90	60
Net Earnings	$ 210	$ 140
Total Shares ($10 = Par)	200	100
Net Earnings Per Share	$ 1.05	$ 1.40
Cost of Equity	10%	10%
Price Per Share	$ 10.50	$ 14.00
Total Market Value, Stock	$2,100	$1,400
Total Value, Bonds	0	1,000
Grand Total	$2,100	$2,400

You can see that the $2,400 value of L is $300 greater than the identical firm, U. Why? Everything is equal: EBIT is at $300, the before-tax cost of capital is 10 percent, everything.

Well, almost everything. L pays $240 to capital (equity dividends of $140 and interest payments of $100), while U pays only $210 to capital (all in the form of dividends). The incremental $30 that L pays to capital (instead of to Uncle Sam) increases the value of the firm by $300.

This results in a benefit to the owner of the firm, the common stockholder. The firm earns $150 on every $1,000 in assets. Given a 30 percent tax rate, that translates into $105 after tax ($150 x 70%) per $1,000 of assets. The firm pays an after-tax interest cost of $70, calculated as 7% x $1,000. This means that the firm will generate extra after-tax net profits of $35 ($105 – $70) on the $1,000 in debt.*

In the case of firm L, this $35 increase in profits is spread among 100 shares of common, increasing the earnings per share by $0.35, from $1.05 to $1.40. The $0.35 increase in earnings per share and the 10 percent required return on equity result in an increase in the share price of $3.50 ($\frac{\$0.35}{.10}$ = $3.50). All compliments of the U.S. government.

That is the beauty of the tax advantage of borrowing.

Tom Mansley

---

*The $35 extra profits can be looked at another way. Consider these two statements showing the income and tax flows for (E) an all-equity capitalization of $1,000, for (C) a combined $2,000 capitalization of $1,000 equity plus $1,000 debt, and (D) the differences in sums of (C) less (E). [R.H.P.]

	E	C	D = C – E
EBIT	$150	$300	+ $150
Interest	0	100	+ 100
Taxable Earnings	150	200	+ 50
Taxes (at 30%)	45	60	+ 15
Net Earnings	$105	$140	+ $ 35

20

Flawed "MM" Corporate Valuation Theory

> In what has been called the most important paper on fi-
> nancial research ever published, Franco Modigliani and
> Merton Miller (MM) addressed the capital structure issue
> in a rigorous, scientific fashion, and they set off a chain of
> research that continues to this day.
>
> Eugene F. Brigham, *Financial Management,*
> *Theory and Practice* (1985)*

A rigorous, scientific fashion? Really? True, Modigliani and Miller (MM)
startled the academic world in 1958 by turning the traditional theory of corporate finance upside-down.† They argued that corporate leverage, the ratio
of corporate debt to equity, was irrelevant to corporate valuation and financing costs. MM propositions (1) and (2) declared:

1. *Apart from the tax deductibility of interest, leverage is irrelevant to the*
   combined market value of the firm's bonds and stocks outstanding. Leverage makes no difference regardless of whether debt is (say) one-tenth of
   equity, or ten times or even a hundred times equity.

2. *A corporation's average weighted cost of capital (AWCC) is independent*
   of leverage. That means leverage has no bearing at all on how much the

---

*New York: The Dryden Press, fourth edition, p. 453.

†"The Cost of Capital, Corporation Finance, and the Theory of Investment," *American*
Economic Review (June 1958): 261–97.

corporation has to pay on average for the mix of debt and equity capital. Thus Miller writes: "When Proposition 1 holds . . . gains from using more of what might seem to be cheaper debt capital would thus be offset by the correspondingly higher cost of the now riskier equity capital."*

MM THEORY VERSUS RATIONAL "ECONOMIC MAN"

Since Proposition 2 flows from Proposition 1, let's first focus on Proposition 1. The trouble is that Proposition 1 is itself defective. It fails to distinguish between what rational economic man can do versus what he should do. Yes, rational man *can* make money by duplicating up to a point the leveraging and value maximizing activities of others. But it does not follow that rational economic man *should* duplicate, beyond a given point of leverage, the wild antics of corporations who rush blindly and wildly into excessive leverage. Economic man is not supposed to be a borrowing fool.

> Beyond a point of excessive borrowing, the MM arbitrage "proof" contradicts the very concept of economic man operating rationally in competitive markets.

It will take me the rest of the chapter to explain and to document what is possible from what is logical. But first, I should like to introduce you to an affable and smart economist. I mean none other than Dr. Modigliani himself. I invited Dr. Modigliani (FM) to speak before institutional money managers in a forum I hosted in his honor in New York City on May 2, 1977. What bothered me was not so much his revolutionary ideas, which I suspected he had qualified and refined in his own mind. My concern lay mainly with the "Modiglianians," his devoted but confused followers who could easily fill Yankee Stadium twice over. We talked for a while immediately prior to the forum:

FM: You say that my notions of cost of capital are restricted to very special cases? That's correct.

RH: Yes, but too many university professors and Wall Street analysts misrepresent what you are driving at.

FM: They don't pay attention to the assumptions underlying the models. They include perfectly competitive markets, no brokerage charges, the

---

Journal of Economic Perspectives (Fall 1988): 100.

ability of individuals to borrow on the same terms open to business, a risk-free borrowing rate, among others. You see?

Yes, I saw. I was reminded of a similar experience. Briefly, I was a guest at a dinner party, and the hostess kept prodding me for my views on her forthcoming marriage, since I knew her and her intended husband well. I got absolutely nowhere, though, because she ruled out any discussion whatsoever of the possible impact on their marriage of such variables as money, sex, religion, or politics. She ruled out, I thought, the key variables that could be *expected* to make or break a marriage.

I have highlighted *expected,* and ask that you keep that in mind in my criticism of the MM arbitrage proof just ahead. Whether in marriage or finance, expectations can't be left out of the analysis. So, let's start with an exposition of the MM arbitrage process with a simple arithmetic example true to the MM formulation. Our earlier examples of the unleveraged (U) and leveraged (L) firms will do nicely (see chapter 19), but with one difference. We shall assume no corporate taxes, just as MM did in their first model. So, please join me in this exchange with my students (S).

RH: Have you all read the June 1958 MM article I assigned from *The American Economic Review*?

S1: Yes, but it's loaded with mathematics and formulas. It's impossible to understand.

RH: I know. The jargon and math is hideous, and I think misleading. Anyway, we have to review the MM arbitrage proof. Then you can make up your own minds.

THE STRANGE "MM" VIEWS ON THE CORPORATE COST OF CAPITAL

RH: The key MM conclusion is that the AWCC is independent of leverage under the assumption of no taxes. The AWCC curve plotted on a graph would not be "U-shaped," as in traditional theory, but would be horizontal to the base:

MM COST OF CAPITAL THEORY

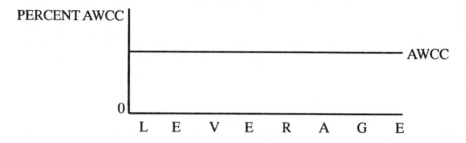

Let's track the MM arbitrage exercise via our earlier examples (in chapter 19) for an unleveraged U and leveraged L firm. Like MM, we shall assume this time no taxes:

	U	L
BOOK VALUE: STOCK*	$2,000	$1,000
BOOK VALUE: BONDS	0	$1,000
TOTAL BOOK VALUE	$2,000	$2,000
Earnings Before Interest and Taxes (EBIT)	$ 300	$ 300
Interest (8% x $1000)	0	80
Net Earnings	$ 300	$ 220
Total Shares*	200	100
Net Earnings Per Share	$ 1.50	$ 2.20
Cost of Equity Capital	10%	10%
= Price Per Share (P)	$15.00	$22.00
MARKET VALUE: STOCK	$3,000	$2,200
MARKET VALUE: BONDS	0	1,000
TOTAL MARKET VALUE	$3,000	$3,200

*$10 Par. So, $\frac{total\ book}{par}$ = number of shares.

Focus first on the unleveraged firm U. Remember EBIT? Assume that EBIT, earnings before interest and taxes, is $300. The $300 of earnings represents a 15 percent return on assets, or $300 for every $2000 of corporate assets. MM assume that EBIT is identical for both U and L, and by MM thinking, EBIT is not affected in any way by how U or L finances itself. That's true. Even so, as we saw in the 1980s, a huge interest burden before taxes can be extremely relevant to the question of the life or death of the firm during stormy weather. We'll return to this.

Concentrate now on the unleveraged firm U before arbitrage. We shall assume that $300 of earnings is all distributed as dividends to shareholders. How do we determine the total market value of U stock?

S3:   Your table assumes a 10 percent cost of equity capital and a constant dividend stream of $300 a year, which means no growth. The present value (capitalized value) of $300 a year forever would be $300 divided by .10, or $3,000.

RH: Good, you can think of this stock as not unlike a perpetual bond, one with a constant and infinite stream of income. Now examine U before arbitrage. How much would you have to invest for a 1 percent interest in U before arbitrage?

S4:   Thirty dollars. That's 1 percent of the $3,000 total of stock. That would be 2 shares (1% x 200 shares) valued at $15 per share.

RH: Now, how much would you have to invest to get a 1 percent interest in firm L before arbitrage, assuming you bought 1 percent of L's stock and 1 percent of L's bonds?

S4:   L's total stock at market is $2,200, and 1 percent of $2,200 is $22, which buys one share. L's debt outstanding is $1,000, and 1 percent of $1,000 is $10. So, $22 plus $10 is $32.

RH: Correct. And note that a 1 percent stake in U lays claim to $3 of dividends, and the 1 percent stake in L lays claim to $2.20 of dividends plus $.80 of interest income, which is also $3 in total. Let's put this on the board:

Investment:	1% of U	1% of L
	$30 for stocks	$22 for Stocks
		$10 for Bonds
Total Cost	$30	$32
Income:	$3.00 dividend	$2.20 dividend
		.80 interest
Total Income	$3.00	$3.00

You can see that it's cheaper to invest in U ($30) than in L ($32) to get the same total income of $3.00. This is the clue to MM's arbitrage, who argue that the same total income, assuming equal risk, should command the same price. What would smart arbitragers do, according to MM?

S5:   They could sell L and buy U?

RH: That's a good start, but not the whole MM proof. I'll write the Modigliani-Miller arbitrage proof on the board:

THE MM ARBITRAGE "PROOF"

Sell 1% of L stock for	$22	(1% ownership of L)
Borrow	$10	(1% of debt of L)
	$32	
Buy 1% of U stock for $30		($2 cash left over)*

Investor Position:	Before	After
	1% L	1% U
Dividends	$2.20	$3.00
Interest Paid (8% rate)	− .00	− .80
Dividends less Interest	$2.20	$2.20
*Extra Interest on $2 of extra		
cash you invest at 8% a year		$0.16

Let's review the arbitrage. First, you sell your 1% ownership in L stock for $22. Second, you borrow $10. Third, you buy $30 of U stock, and still have $2 left over. That means you're $2 ahead of the game, according to MM, which you can invest on your own at the going rate of 8 percent. Why do MM assume that you borrow exactly $10?

S6: To show that an individual can borrow, buy U, and use leverage just like L. The $10 of individual debt would be the same as 1 percent of the debt of Company L, or 1 percent of $1000.

RH: Great. This gets us to the famous MM "proof." MM argue that individual or "homemade" leverage can "undo" corporate leverages, and the arbitrage will equate the market value of the total outstanding securities of U to the market value of the total outstanding securities of L. MM assume that individuals could *and would borrow* on the same terms as L. Let's trace through the impact of arbitrage on prices and on the cost of capital of L and U. Thus, if arbitragers sell L and purchase U, market pressures would produce the following MM results:

Stock L: Price of L falls (L's yield rises).
Stock U: Price of U rises (U's yield falls).

As you can see, the prices would tend to converge, and the dividend yields diverge. Dividend yield here is synonymous with the specific cost of equity capital, which reflects the MM assumption that all earnings are paid out as dividends (which means no growth). How long would this go on? The MM answer is until the total *combined* market values of the outstanding securities of U and L were identical, which would mean also the same average weighted costs of capital (AWCC). MM tell us that this equilibrium value could take place at, say, $3,095, with the AWCC at 9.69 percent for both U and L.

This requires further explanation of the cost of equity capital, and AWCC. Now, concentrate first on the cost of equity capital for U. Since U is all equity, the calculation is easy. Arbitragers lifted the price of U from $3,000 to $3,095. With EBIT unchanged at $300, the average yield (cost of capital) fell from 10 percent ($300 divided by $3,000) to 9.69 percent ($300 divided by $3,095).

Now calculate the AWCC of L before arbitrage. Remember that we merely assumed an 8 percent interest cost on bonds, for $1,000 market value of bonds. We assumed also a 10 percent equity cost for stock, and a $2,200 market valuation based on a 10 percent capitalization rate. We want to "weight" these two rates (costs) by their respective market values.

THE MEANING OF MARKET "WEIGHTS"

S6: What do you mean by weights?

RH: We must calculate what we would have to pay on average to raise $1,000 in debt money and $2,200 in equity money at current market values. The weights in this example would be the assumed *market* values of $1,000 and $2,200. This means we would have to promise to pay $300 in total income each year ($220 of dividends plus $80 of interest) to raise $3,200 of money from the sale of stocks and bonds in the amounts indicated. This mix of debt and equity capital would have a weighted average cost of capital of 9.375 percent, or $300 divided by $3,200. Here are our results:

	WEIGHT	RATE	WEIGHT X RATE
Stocks	$2,200	.10	$220
Bonds	$1,000	.08	80
Sum	$3,200		$300

$$AWCC = \frac{\text{Sum of Weights x Rates}}{\text{Sum of Weights}}$$

$$= \frac{\$300}{\$3,200} = .09375 = 9.38\%$$

But if arbitragers forced the market value of equity down to $2095, that would be the same thing as forcing the yield or cost of equity up to 10.5 percent, or $220/$2095. Here's the AWCC of L after arbitrage:

	WEIGHT	RATE	WEIGHT X RATE
Stocks	$2,095	.105	$220
Bonds	$1,000	.08	80
Sum	$3,095		$300

$$AWCC = \frac{\text{Sum of Weights x Rates}}{\text{Sum of Weights}}$$
$$= \frac{\$300}{\$3,095} = .0969 = 9.69\%$$

The 9.69 percent AWCC for L after arbitrage ($\frac{\$300}{\$3,095}$) matches the 9.69 percent for U after arbitrage ($\frac{\$300}{\$3,095}$). The combined market value of L's securities made up of stocks and bonds is equal to the total market value of U's securities, comprised of stock. What do you think of the MM proof?

S7:   Looks all right to me.

RH: Well, let's see. Let me quote a top logician (David Mitchell, *An Introduction to Logic*):

> The truth of the conclusion is not guaranteed by logic alone. For our inference to be a sound inference and for our argument to be a proof, the premises must be true; and that they are true cannot be established by logic. But it is a truth of logic that if all men are mortal and if Socrates is a man, then Socrates is mortal.*

I'm not interested in Socrates at this moment, but I am impressed with Mr. Mitchell's comments on sound reasoning. Now consider this argument:

Premise:	If bankruptcy costs are zero in perfect capital markets, and
Premise:	Even if highly leveraged firms are subject to greater bankruptcy risk, then
Conclusion:	Highly leveraged firms can treat bankruptcy risk as being irrelevant to the AWCC.

Of course! In this example the conclusion does follow logically from its premises. But is the MM premise true? Is the idea that bankruptcy risks are zero relevant to AWCC? To answer that question, we

---

*Garden City, N.Y.: Doubleday & Company, Inc., 1970, p. 5.

must ask whether the data of the real world support or contradict the major MM premise. If the data contradict the premise, then we must conclude that the MM premise is not true, and that the inferred MM conclusion is false. Well, the data shout out that the premise of zero bankruptcy costs is false. Bankruptcy can force companies to sell assets at distressed prices, to fire valued employees, to defer maintenance of equipment, to cut research and development (R&D), and to cancel capital outlays—all of which can destroy efficiency and competitiveness, and even bring on corporate death. In short, if the MM arbitrage "proof" has a problem, it unquestionably lies in its defective premise.

EXPECTATIONS: AN ESSENTIAL KEY TO TRADITIONAL THEORY

The very *expectation* of bankruptcy may induce customers to switch to another firm. Bankruptcy fears can so frighten suppliers, who wonder whether they will be paid, that they cancel deliveries of essential materials, and cut off credit. And don't forget the lawyers. In the event of bankruptcy and liquidation, stockholders could be wiped out entirely. Little or nothing may remain after legal fees are paid, senior creditors are paid, and everybody else is paid off down to the junk bond creditors.

To the extent corporations (or individuals) do get head-over-heels in debt, you can bet that will be noticed. The rating agencies, Standard & Poor's or Moody's, will surely take notice of corporate borrowing binges, though not always in time to alert us to trouble ahead. Standard & Poor's can cut a corporate rating, and this act can trigger higher financing costs and sharply lower stock and bond prices overnight. Investors surely take notice, again not always in time to avoid serious trouble. They know that the sudden onset of recession can produce soaring yields and plummeting prices, with the highly leveraged securities hit the hardest. They know this. They expect this. Their *expectations* (there we go again) are reflected in the actual yields and prices of competing securities in the market place. That's just one reason for the huge spread in yields on junk bonds over high-grade bonds. That's precisely what one would expect from the traditional theory of corporate finance.

There's a related problem, namely, the MM reliance on argument by definition, a logical error that seems to plague economists of all persuasions most notably the monetarists (chapter 11). In the present case, bankruptcy risks are ruled out of the MM arbitrage analysis because "perfect" markets assume zero bankruptcy risks.

THE FATAL FLAW IN THE MM ARBITRAGE "PROOF"

The MM arbitrage proof has another more serious, indeed fatal, flaw. Incredibly, MM distort the very concept of economic man operating *rationally* in a competitive arena. To see why, consider the MM argument that individuals can rely on homemade leverage to "undo" corporate leverage:

> The average cost of funds from all sources will still be independent of leverage (apart from the tax effect). This conclusion follows directly from the *ability of those who engage in arbitrage to undo* the leverage in any financial structure by acquiring an appropriately mixed proportion of bonds and stocks.*

By undo, MM mean that individual and business arbitragers have the *ability to undo* (duplicate) business leverage. They *can* duplicate business leverage, and thereby equate AWCCs and total values of U and L. Yes, they can. Yes, arbitragers *can* borrow on their own, can purchase the stock of unleveraged or lightly leveraged firms, and can duplicate the profit maximizing objectives of leveraged firms. They can and would do so up to a point. Yes, arbitragers can make big bucks by riding the downward slope of the AWCC curve, a matter made explicit and clear by traditional theory.

But wait! The ride with excess debt baggage can be dangerous. There's nothing in efficient market theory to suggest that arbitragers *should* duplicate the actions of corporate officers who go off on a wild borrowing binge, who recklessly overleverage without regard to bankruptcy risks. Rational economic men would hardly be inclined to duplicate the risk positions of extremely overleveraged firms once expectations of high bankruptcy risk are admitted into the analysis. They could but wouldn't, not if they are rational.

CLOWNS EMULATING CLOWNS IN
ALICE-IN-WONDERLAND FINANCE

Nothing logically suggests that rational investors must imitate corporate borrowing fools, even if they could do so. Whether individuals (or corporations) can imitate other corporations by buying stock on high margin is far less important than whether they should do so. The *ability* to live dangerously, then, must be separated from the question of the *desirability* of living dangerously. This distinction is critical in explaining the steep rise in the AWCC curve be-

---

*"The Cost of Capital, Corporate Finance, and the Theory of Investment," p. 273. I am also giving emphasis to the words "ability" and "undo."

yond a critical point in leverage under traditional theory, but foolishly assumed away under MM theory. MM theory mistakenly separates a volatile EBIT in a cyclical economy from the size of corporate fixed interest charges, namely, expected returns and risks for both bond and stock holders. That's Alice-in-Wonderland finance. *Worse, the MM arbitrage "proof" of no rise in the weighted cost of capital despite extreme leverage and risk of failure belies the very notion of a rational and prudent economic man.*

Sound theory as well as the relevant data demand that we junk the MM hypothesis. Admittedly, my criticisms of the MM theory are harsh. But there's a good reason for being direct. I like to call a spade a spade, especially when the theoretical spade is twisted, and capable of great damage when put in the wrong hands. But I don't want to imply for one moment that my criticisms are new or original, except perhaps for my insistence that MM analysis violates the very notion of *rational* economic man.

It continues to astonish me that so many experts have overlooked for so long the fatal flaw in the MM arbitrage "proof," which dates from the MM 1958 classic. Will this homage to irrelevant mathematics and bankrupt theory ever end? I sometimes wonder, given the laurels to MM from such eminent economists or Weston, Thakor, Wall, Pringle, Harris, O'Brien, Wakeman, Woods, and Randall.* But it will end as more people recognize its fundamental error.

---

*Journal of the Financial Management Association, Summer 1989.

21

Junk Bond Hawkers and the Cash-Flow Scavengers

> Our Proposition I, holding the value of a firm to be inde-
> pendent of its capital structure (that is, its debt/equity ratio)
> is accepted as an implication of equilibrium in perfect cap-
> ital markets. The validity of our then-novel arbitrage proof
> of that proposition is no longer disputed.
>
> Merton H. Miller, "The Modigliani-Miller
> Propositions After Thirty Years" (1988)*

I am convinced that logicians would reject Dr. Miller's proof outright on three counts: it violates the rules of valid inference; it contradicts the notion of economic man acting rationally in a competitive market, and crumbles before the relevant data (see chapter 20). Even so, while Drs. Miller and Modigliani fumbled on theory, they look like supreme scientists compared with Wall Street hawkers of junk.

I shall not treat here the extent to which junk-bond practitioners have been found guilty of securities fraud, mail fraud, insider trading, manipulation of the prices of stocks, illegal "tricking" of the marketplace, and defrauding of shareholders and investors in junk securities. The press has covered these issues. My interest centers on the trash research papers, snake-oil brochures, and hawker flyers on junk bonds and junk stocks that seem just inside the law. That garbage, strewn over a street called Wall, is what this chapter is all about.

---

*Journal of Economic Perspectives, Fall.

JUNK BOND HAWKERS VISIT PACE UNIVERSITY

Let me give you an example of huckster pitches on junk, one of many I have witnessed. This took place at home base, Pace University's graduate school of business. On June 26, 1989, three trim, highly educated, and articulate officers from Drexel Burnham Lambert addressed a group of faculty and students. The visiting trio was headed up by the affable Joseph C. Bencivenga, then a Drexel Senior Vice President. He brought with him Senior Vice President Tom Arenz and First Vice President Alan Ginzberg. All three pitched in, always smiling as they punctuated their every declaration with a supporting chart or table loaded with statistics. Here's what these junk artists (JA) covered in the first thirty minutes (along with my silent notes):

JA: Corporate bond ratings define the high yield market, as indicated in this first slide:

Investment Grade High Yield (Junk Bonds)

Moody's	Aaa	Aa	A	Baa	Moody's	Ba	B	Caa	Ca	C	D
S&P's	AAA	AA	A	BBB	S&P'	BB	B	CCC	CC	C	D

Ninety-five percent of U.S. companies are high yield. The majority of rated companies are high yield. Some states have no investment grade companies. Diversified ownership (of high yield bonds) for year-end 1988 were:

Individuals	4%	Corporations	3%
Savings and loans	7%	Securities Dealers	1%
Foreign Investors	10%	Mutual Funds	30%
Pension Funds	15%	Insurance Companies	30%

High yield bonds, major investments available to thrifts—savings banks and savings and loan associations—provided risk-adjusted returns higher than that of investment grade bonds, adjustable rate mortgages, commercial and industrial loans, and fixed rate mortgages. High yield bonds have outperformed other securities. The compounded annual return, 1982-1988, was 17.9% for high yield bonds, 16.3% for high grade bonds, 15.9% for Treasuries, and 16.9% for equities (S&P 500).

RH: (Maybe we can salvage the bankrupt thrifts by compelling them to invest 100% in junk. The high returns on bonds, investment grade and junk, over the 1982–88 period reflected overwhelmingly the steep decline in interest rates and the parallel rise in bond prices. This was a period of basic growth, disinflation, and good times. But what happens to junk bonds when the economy falls into recession? They don't say, don't even bring up the subject?)

JA: Investment-grade bonds have event risk [are rated lower and fall in price in the 'event' the corporation sells junk on top of its outstanding investment grade bonds]. Event risk clobbered Allied Stores, Beatrice, RJR Nabisco, Stop & Shop, and many other high-grade bonds.

RH: (Yes, junk can infect the best. Overborrowing can lead to default with high-quality bonds that have suddenly been rated down to junk.)

JA: The U.S. is not overleveraged. Japan and West Germany have higher debt as a percentage of book value.

RH: (We are less loaded with debt than they. So, we don't have to worry about excessive borrowing? Nonsense!)

JA: Perceptions Versus Reality: High-yield bonds are less volatile; are subject to less interest rate risk than Treasuries [or] high grades; provide higher returns than equities; are subject to less event risk than high grades; and benefit from a large and liquid market. *We find value where others see nothing but risk, and we find risk where others find nothing but value.*

RH: (I can't believe these guys are oblivious to the borrowing risks now as compared with the several years after the 1981–82 recession. Then, book values of stock [corporate assets less liabilities] were far in excess of market values. Stocks were cheap, and it made sense to borrow to buy stocks priced below book or replacement costs. But the margins between book and market have narrowed, now reversed in many cases. *They completely ignore risks to junk in the event of recession.* These guys are smart, so how could they be so naive? They really believe their pitch?)

Three months after this presentation *The Wall Street Journal* reported:

JUNK MARKET'S WORST-EVER SHAKEOUT CONTINUES WITH MORE PRICE DROPS, ISSUE-LIQUIDITY PROBLEMS

Drexel Burnham Lambert Inc., by far the biggest underwriter of junk bonds, yesterday promised to upgrade the junk bonds it brings to the market. Joseph

C. Bencivenga, Drexel senior vice president and head of junk bond research
. . . (said) the record spreads in junk bond yields over Treasury issues showed
junk buyers were balking at buying inferior-quality offerings.

Junk buyers were balking, to say the least. For the year through September 1989, returns to investors from junk bonds were far surpassed by returns from almost every other sector of investment-grade bonds. Long Treasuries did especially well as inflation and the "pure" rate of interest fell. Prices of junk bonds continued downhill as individual and institutional investors retreated from the market. Many junk bond investors in no-load mutual funds switched into money market funds. Institutional investors complained that liquidity, the ability to buy and sell junk in the secondary (resale) markets, had virtually dried up.

These events should not have surprised anyone. Remember our discussion of Parrot chatter on wealth without risk, including the multiple risks on bonds such as income risk, capital risk, reinvestment risk, credit risk, liquidity risk, marketability risk, and the pure-rate risk, among others? Well, the junk bond kingdom of Parrots and Pros is notorious for such chatter. That gets me to this related question: Did our three polished and urbane visitors from Drexel, each highly educated and experienced, with strong backup in research, really believe their own pitch? I asked Pace Finance Professor Barney Seligman this question on September 18, 1989:

RH: How would you cast the Drexel triplets and their comments on junk bonds? Would you classify them as sophistic Parrots or sophisticated Pros? Which is it?

BS: Neither. They are nonintellectual Pros.

The junk-bond triplets were also blind, or pretended to be blind, to two characters running amok in the financial arena: the interest payment pac-man and the cash-flow scavenger? As we shall now see, these two characters are both slippery and dangerous. Still, Mr. Bencivenga and associates neglected to discuss their operations or even acknowledge their existence, which is unpardonable because these two fiends cannot be omitted from a complete story of the junk markets. Let's try to make up for this omission. We'll meet the interest pac-man first, a financial Dracula doing business on Wall Street.

THE INTEREST PAC-MAN

I first noted the antics of the pac-man in an article I was asked to write thirteen months before my encounter with the Drexel triplets. In it I warned:

> The interest payment pac-man will gobble up business cash flow to the dismay of analysts and investors. In recession he will trigger widespread defaults.*

That turned out to be an understatement because the pac-man was in no mood to wait for outright recession. Interest charges as a percent of cash flow ran under 10 percent in 1961, but soared to over 40 percent by the time of 1990-91 recession. Net interest for the U.S business system soared to $458 billion in the second quarter of 1989 as against adjusted corporate profits before tax of $309 billion, and adjusted proprietors' income of $355 billion.† That meant net interest had climbed to 69 percent of total earnings of the business sector. In the early 1960s, in contrast, net interest approximated 13 percent of total earnings.

The high leverage was bound to cause great trouble in recession, and it did. The pac-man forced a wide range of well-known and successful companies into default. The fallen included the Cannon Group, Dart Drugs, General Homes, LTV, Maxicare Health Plans, PS New Hampshire, Republic Health, Revco, and Southmark. The pac-man forced a painful restructuring (refinancing) on Griffin Resorts, Integrated Resources, Resorts International, Seaman Furniture, and Bloomingdales. Recognize these names?

The list is far from complete, but illustrative. Were these companies isolated examples of overborrowing, of excessive leverage? No! The unprecedented leveraging of corporate America speeded ahead at a hurricane pace. Nonfinancial corporations, which exclude the banks and financial intermediaries, boosted leverage by borrowing like madmen even as they paid off a large chunk of the existing equity cushion. The Federal Reserve flow-of-funds data tell the story:

---

*Standard and Poor's *CreditWeek* (May 23, 1988).
†*Business Conditions Digest,* Department of Commerce (August 1989), p. 82.

NONFINANCIAL CORPORATIONS:
NET FUNDS RAISED ($ BILLIONS)

YEAR	STOCK FINANCING	DEBT FINANCING
1984	– $ 79	+ $ 188
1985	– 85	+ 161
1986	– 85	+ 225
1987	– 76	+ 141
1988	– 130	+ 201
1989	– 124	+ 186
1990	– 63	+ 101
Total 1984–90	– $642	+ $1,203 (Rounded)

These data show that the biggest leveraging binge in U.S. history occurred in the seven years from 1984 to 1990. Corporate equity fell absolutely by $642 billion even as debt exploded by $1,203 billion. The equity destruction reflected corporate buybacks of their own stock (the equivalent of corporate liquidation of assets) and leveraged buyouts or straight acquisitions of equity. In a leveraged buyout, the moneys raised to pay off (destroy) the equity of the sellers normally came from new junk-bond borrowing. Either the existing management or an outside group would sell junk bonds, then use the borrowed money to secure their own equity ownership with voting stock, thereby gaining control of the companies in play. Prior equity owners were paid off with cash, or securities, or a combination of cash and securities.

MEGALEVERAGING VERSUS TRADITIONAL THEORY

Call this *megaleveraging,* the simultaneous explosion of debt and implosion of equity (see Exhibit 21–1). Megaleveraging contradicted just about everything students of finance ever learned from traditional theory as spelled out in the best textbooks in corporate finance. Sound theory gave way to the junk-bond theorists and practitioners, with dreadful results for corporate America. Historically high interest rates and the huge volume of borrowing combined to catapult net interest payments (interest payments less receipts) to unheard of heights. With the dizzying climb in net interest, just imagine the appetite the interest pac-man had for gobbling up cash flow in recession. And recession is what we got, while bankruptcies soared. That was an easy call. But looking back, I came across this interesting gem that seemed to contradict everything I had forecast. Who do you think wrote this?

I see, therefore, the rentier aspect of capitalism as a transitional phase which will disappear when it has done its work. [This] would mean the euthanasia of the rentier, and, consequently, the euthanasia of the cumulative oppressive power of the capitalist to exploit the scarcity value of capital.

No, it wasn't Marx. It was Keynes. Keynes argued that the rentier (lender) would disappear in *The General Theory.* One thing for sure, you can chalk up this judgment of things to come, made in 1936, as one of the biggest misses of all time. Instead of the euthanasia of the rentier, we witnessed instead a rowdy, loud, theoretically defective, yuppie inspired, government supported, junk rentier boom of unprecedented dimensions. To my knowledge, nobody had the slightest idea of the chaos ahead in corporate finance.

GOVERNMENT SUPPORT FOR JUNK

The sad part about all this was the role of government. Without the tax deductibility of interest, the incentive to raise capital solely through debt as against equity would have been largely ruled out. Without FDIC insurance and the help of Wall Street deposit brokers, it would have been impossible for the thrifts to enjoy, as they did, a huge influx of high-yield deposits to fund an "investment" portfolio of high-yield junk. Without a tax writeoff allowing the scavenger to depreciate newly acquired property at his purchase price, many of the deals would have fallen of their own weight. Who will pay for this? Well, taxpayers will pick up a big part of the bill, of course. (I don't mean to oppose FCIC or other government initiatives. My very point here is to underscore just how government programs can be abused.)

THE CASH-FLOW SCAVENGER

How did this corporate borrowing binge and the simultaneous destruction of equity get started in the first place? Part of the answer can be found in depressed market prices for stock relative to book values or replacement costs. That was surely the case in the first half of the 1980s, and for a while following Black Monday. That part of the story made sense, with little damage. But there's a lot more to the leveraged buyout and acquisition story. I have in mind the role of the *raider, catalyst,* or (euphemistically) *entrepreneurial investor.* I dub them *cash-flow scavengers.* They are the experts who know how to milk cash out of a corporation fast, with immense profit. The scavengers' short-run gain, however, often comes at the cost of capital cutbacks, wholesale job losses; and impaired long-run productivity, competitiveness, and growth.

To understand just how the cash-flow scavenger thinks and calculates, we have to put ourselves in his shoes. We have to understand basic, fundamental valuation theory. We have to see in advance just how and why a corporate raider can buy a corporation, tear it apart, and walk away with a mountain of cash. We need theory for that, good theory. That's why we spent so much time in analyzing income and cash flow theory (chapters 18–20). Let's expand on that analysis in the following exchange with graduate finance students (S):

RH: Do you remember our comments on depreciation?

S1: Depreciation is an accounting allocation of cost, not a cash outlay. It's an implicit cost, not simultaneously involving any cash drain. It's not an explicit outlay.

RH: Of course, just to keep our productive capital intact, we must reinvest revenues covering depreciation. At the same time, corporate property can have great value from cash flow even when the company reports huge losses. Remember, too, that in an inflationary and high-growth economy, the market value of property could skyrocket far ahead of book value. That was the case for many companies in the first half of the 1980s. Stocks were then cheap for many well known and respected companies with a major worldwide franchise and good will, whether from selling soft drinks or cookies. Those intangible values did not show up in recorded book values. Moreover, an unprecedented expansion of credit and money put the economy in a growth mode in the 1980s. That and falling interest rates pushed stocks up, up, up. That spelled Nirvana for the scavenger who bought cheap in a private deal, got control, borrowed a lot of money, then sold his equity, and ran with the money.

Scavenger's Delight: Spotting Cash Cows in Red-Ink Pastures

RH: Even when companies report big losses and stock prices are depressed, the assets can still have immense value. Just so long as revenues exceed *variable* costs, the potential cash flow can literally gush ahead fast. *Cash flow can surge even in a sea of reported red ink* (chapter 18). Remember, too, that any cash available soon is far more valuable than cash due years ahead. That's especially relevant when interest rates are high. Cash-flow scavengers understand much of this, and the public very little. With that in mind, let me read you a poem I wrote. Count the Scavengers' ways to get cash fast:

> Cancel capital outlays
> Reduce inventories to the bone
> Cut dividend payments
> And seek a new loan
> Defer research to lift cash flow
> Fire key employees, just let them go
> Defer interest payments to the last
> Sell corporate assets for quick cash
> Run, run, run, just as fast as you can
> You must keep ahead of the Interest Pac-Man.

The big scavengers were asset players, and the biggest players included existing management and their investment bankers on Wall Street. They would buy control with borrowed money, influence corporate affairs to boost the price of the company's stock, cancel capital expansion plans, fire employees, then sell their stock at the opportune time, and take the money and run. I wonder what all of this has to do with efficient market theories, modern portfolio theory, or the capital asset pricing model. Not much!

The Capital Asset Pricing Model: Flawed and Irrelevant

MM theory sits on the sands of risk-free returns, a fiction without empirical or theoretical support. So does the capital asset pricing model. Just what is that? Well, consider this observation from the seventh edition of *Financial Management* by Eugene Brigham and Louis Gapenski, one of the leading textbooks in finance:

> The expected rate of return on an efficient portfolio in equilibrium is equal to a *risk free return* plus a risk premium (i.e, the expected return on the market portfolio of risky stocks minus the *risk free rate* divided by the *standard deviation of returns* on the market portfolio) multiplied by the standard deviation of the portfolio's returns. (Emphasis added.)*

---

*New York: The Dryden Press, 1994, p. 191.

Did you understand any of that? Well, by now you should understand that there are no risk-free returns. They do not exist! Yet the academic world would have you believe in make-believe models of risk-free rates wrapped in faulty but elegant mathematics. Fortunately, though, the capital asset pricing model (CAPM) has of late come under devastating attack from the academic world itself. My Pace colleagues Professors Bernard Seligman and Maurice Larrain have long described the model as *nonsense*. So have I in "unteaching" MM and CAPM "proofs" the past twenty years. Just count the theoretical and applied flaws of the CAPM:

- *Riskless assets do not exist.* Portfolio managers who stuck with Treasury bills yielding 18 percent in 1981 or 8 percent in late 1990 suffered a massive loss of income. Many lost their clients, then their jobs. Individuals who stuck with Treasury bills yielding 18% in 1981 suffered a major loss of income as rates skidded down, down, down. Any model ignoring income risk and reinvestment risk must be counted as absurd (see chapter 8).

- *Riskless loans do not exist.* The thrifts learned that hard lesson by borrowing in the short term and investing long term just before interest rates exploded upwards in 1981 and, horror of horrors, the yield curve inverted. A comparable hurricane hit the hedge funds in 1994.

- *The CAPM ignores opportunity cost.* Suppose, for example, you own two assets that are negatively correlated, perfectly. One rises from $100 to $110 and the other falls from $100 to $90. According to modern risk concepts, you have suffered no loss because your total valuation remains unchanged. Ha! Tell that to any successful portfolio manager. Tell that to opportunity cost, which demands that money managers consider potential returns and risks wherever they exist (see chapter 22). It will put money managers sporting zero returns out of business.

- *Neither variance nor the standard deviation nor Beta are theoretically satisfactory measures of risk.* These measures pay no attention to the length of the holding period. Is it one quarter? Is it eight years, as with one of my stellar institutional clients, Phil Carret, founder of the giant Pioneer Fund in Boston? Good money managers like Carret try to avoid stocks that trend down even if they drift lower ever so gently. Of first importance to investors is the trend or cyclical thrust of the market, not short-run variance around some mean. How about traders? Yes, they react to almost every blip but have no reliable measures of future dispersion. The CAPM is foreign to trader understanding, properly so.

- *The CAPM model pioneered by economist and Nobel prize winner William Sharpe finds little support in the empirical data.* University of Chicago economists Eugene Fama and Kenneth French, for example, tracked thousands of stocks over five decades but found *no* reliable association between volatility and long-term returns. I couldn't and neither could my colleagues. Why? Well, we know that argument by historical analogy on the fate of individual companies inevitably fails over time in an internationally competitive corporate world marked by perpetual change, upheaval, birth, and death. We know that the past is not an option and, equally important, is not a reliable signal for the future. Opportunity cost, destroyer of the CAPM, taught us that fundamental truth.

- *Institutional money managers who understand the CAPM dismiss it as useless.* I asked forty of my clients, all CIOs or key money managers at Alliance, BEA, Brown Brothers, Carret & Company, Chancellor Capital, Chemical Bank, Citibank, and through the alphabet (Appendix A, Forecast 90). They laughed when I asked about risk-free securities. Is not a test of good theory that it can explain the real world? CAPM fails on that count.

FLAWED THEORY OF RISK IN MM
AND RELATED ACADEMIC MODELS

Let's conclude with some comments from other experts on risk and finance. Let me introduce you to an astute money manager first. Morley Goldberg (MG) manages money for his own investment firm. He telephoned me on June 27, 1989:

MG: The 1929 stock market bubble was largely individual speculation; the Black Monday bubble was mainly institutional speculation, and Wall Street and corporate America manufactured the junk-bond bubble. This latest episode is bound to cripple economic growth. MM theory and the CAPM is foreign to all this.

RH: One thing for sure, the efficient market hypothesis (EMH) can't digest the Parrots and Pros you always find in stock market bubbles, real estate bubbles, and junk-bond bubbles. The real world cannot digest the fictions of risk-free propositions imbedded in MM theory and the CAPM.

MG: They never made sense to me. I don't find any of this stuff useful for investment strategy. Whoever heard of risk-free returns anyway? I wish I could find some.

Consider these comments by Pace Finance Professor Maurice Larrain (ML), American Express International fixed-income manager George Livingston (GL), and former Citibank and Chancellor investment analyst Steve Lewins (SL) on November 18, 1994:

RH: What's your view on the risk-free returns and risk measures in MM theory, modern portfolio theory, and the CAPM?

GL: You can't apply any of this rubbish. Their assumptions destroy the usefulness for any money manager.

SL: They're dead.

ML: Steve's right. Dead, defunct. Did you ever consider that the random walk* view in efficient market theory itself contradicts the idea that corporate financial managers should maximize equity wealth, meaning stock prices? In effect, the best selling texts in finance ask them to maximize random variables. But that's not possible, these same texts then argue. They seem oblivious to their own contradictions.

Shortly after this meeting I received Daiwa Bank Trust Company's 1995 Investment Policy update. Senior Vice President and Chief Investment Officer Paul Travia wrote:

Tons of tomes have been written on modern portfolio theory (MPT) . . . Beta, Alpha, the Sharpe theory, Standard deviation, and so forth—it does not work. We adhere to APT (Ancient Portfolio Theory), which states "buy low—sell high" or "buy high—sell higher."

---

*The random walk argues that in an efficient market individual investors cannot outsmart the market. The idea is that everybody is always perfectly informed and their views are always reflected in market prices. So, dart throwers can do as well as professional money managers in picking stocks. Random walk never made sense to me.

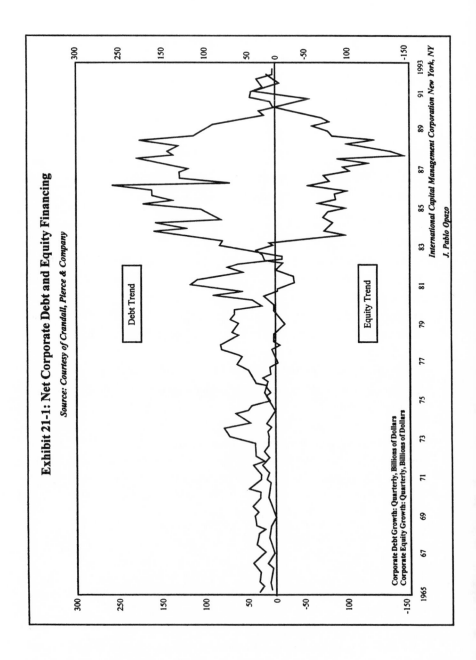

Exhibit 21-1: Net Corporate Debt and Equity Financing

Source: Courtesy of Crandall, Pierce & Company

Debt Trend

Equity Trend

Corporate Debt Growth: Quarterly, Billions of Dollars
Corporate Equity Growth: Quarterly, Billions of Dollars

International Capital Management Corporation New York, NY

J. Pablo Opazo

Part Seven

International Financial Theory, Practice, and Malpractice

22

Parrot and Pro Chatter on
International Finance and Investment

> RH: Howard, my institutional clients don't understand
> that our *current account deficit* is the same as our net
> capital inflow, that the deficit (a debit) and the *net
> capital inflow* (a credit) add up to a *zero* net *inflow.*
> How can I explain that foreigners don't ship us boat-
> loads of dollars from abroad?
>
> HS: Robert, tell those numskulls to call the Justice De-
> partment. Maybe the FBI can nab the foreign coun-
> terfeiters shipping dollars to the United States.
>
> Economist Dr. Howard Sharpe (HS) in a
> conversation with Robert H. Parks in early 1988

Dr. Sharpe's insight and humor worked wonders. He saved me many hours
of telephone time. Still, we must provide a step-by-step explanation of balance-of-payments (BOP) analysis to see how Parrots and Pros operate in international waters. As a start, join me in this exchange with my graduate students in February 1992. (I updated the data to analyze the year 1993.)

RH: The published U.S. balance-of-payments summary statement runs to
seventy small-print rows for each year or quarter in a bewildering maze
of statistics that drives people mad. Focus here on the simplified statement I have prepared. I took each statistic from the Department of Commerce table published quarterly in the *Survey of Current Business.*

U.S. INTERNATIONAL BALANCE-OF-PAYMENTS FOR 1993
(Totals don't match exactly because of rounding.)

($ BILLIONS)	CREDITS +	DEBITS −	NET
a Merchandise	+ 456.8	− 589.2	− 132.5
b Services	+ 186.8	− 131.1	+ 55.7
c Investment Income	+ 110.3	− 110.3	0.0
d Unilateral transfers, net		− 3.25	− 32.5
e CURRENT ACCOUNT DEFICIT			
(a + b + c + d)	+ 753.9	− 863.1	−109.2
f Recorded Capital Flows	+ 226.4	− 143.9	+ 82.5
"Inflows"	"Outflows"		
g Statistical Discrepancy	+ 26.7		+ 26.7
"Inflows"			
h CAPITAL INFLOW			+ 109.2
(f + g)			
i Overall Balance			
(e + f + g + h)	+1007.0	− 1007.0	0.00

Note: The current account deficit ($109.2 billion) is the same thing as the net capital inflow ($109.2 billion), which means one less the other is zero. Economists call these accounting twins *ex post* statistical identities.

Source: Department of Commerce

See the $132.5 billion net deficit on merchandise (or goods) at the top of the third column? That's commonly called the "trade" deficit. While we ran a trade deficit, you can see that we had a surplus on services of $55.7 billion. So, the combined goods and services deficit in 1993 was lower, at $76.8 billion ($132.5 billion less $55.7 billion). Goods include things like automobiles, computers, TV sets, wine, and a wide range of foods; services include insurance, banking, tourism, transportation, and legal and investment consulting activities, to name a few.

One of the most important concepts of all is the balance on current account. That works out to −$109.2 billion in our summary. In addition to goods and services, the current account balance includes investment income flows and "unilateral transfers." You can see that for 1993 the United States received about as much income from investments held abroad as it paid to foreigners who held investments in the United States, both at about $110.3 billion. On the other hand, we ran a net deficit on "unilateral transfers" of $32.5 billion. These are U.S. government grants and payments to pensioners living abroad, along with the gifts and other moneys private citizens send (remit) to people abroad. We sent remittances and monetary gifts abroad by $32.5 billion more than foreigners sent to us.

CURRENT ACCOUNT DEFICIT = CAPITAL INFLOW ON "EX POST" BASIS

RH: Can anybody explain why U.S. capital inflow was $109.2 billion, the same amount as the current account deficit?

S1: You show them both at $109.2 billion, but with different signs. I don't understand any of this.

RH: Capital inflow is simply the other side of the current account deficit. One is the other, but with different signs. Put another way, the current account deficit, the so-called "outflow" of dollars, is the same thing as (mainly) the buildup in foreign claims to dollar assets, and any reduction in U.S. claims to foreign assets. Loosely, you can say the "dollar outflow" is our current account deficit, and "dollar inflow" our capital inflow. But there is no literal outflow or inflow of dollars, with the minor exception of the drain of U.S. currency abroad. We'll return to that. For now, focus on the opposite signs:

Current Account Deficit	− $109.2 billion
U.S. Capital Inflow	+ $109.2 billion

The signs are reversed. True, the official data show recorded capital inflow from foreign investment in the United States of +$226.4 billion, and recorded capital outflow from U.S. investment abroad of −$143.9 billion, or a net recorded capital inflow to the U.S. of +$82.5 billion. Don't despair. We can make one calculation to show the identity of the current deficit with net capital inflow.

"Recorded" Capital Inflow	$ 82.5 billion
Statistical Discrepancy	+ $ 26.7 billion
Corrected Capital Inflow	$109.2 billion

Again, net capital inflow ($109.2 billion) equals the current account deficit ($109.2 billion). The statistical discrepancy equates the two. It tells us that our data are still incomplete, rough. It seems that the recorded inflows were understated, which would mean that foreigners invested more here than we recorded on our books. Maybe though, out-flows were overstated. In any case, *conceptually* the current account deficit is identical to capital inflow. Failure to understand this identity can lead to huge error, as we shall soon see.

S4:   But does that identity hold water? I thought foreign capital was pour-ing into the U.S. to finance our budgetary deficit and our huge trade deficit. I read that every other day in the *Wall Street Journal.*

RH: Look, they are reporters, not experts on arcane BOP accounting. That foreign capital inflow you read about represents a recycling of our own dollars, dollars earned by foreigners that are invested here, whether in securities, time deposits, or even dollar-denominated golf courses. We'll explain and illustrate shortly how recycling works, 100 percent recy-cling. Meanwhile, if you should learn of a *net* influx of dollars from abroad, then turn the counterfeiters in. Call the Justice Department.

S4:   I still don't understand.

Ex Post Accounting Identities Versus *Ex Ante* Demand and Supply

RH: Be patient. To understand, we must first analyze *ex post* and *ex ante* concepts. What are these terms?

S5:   Accounting terms, like debits and credits being equal?

RH: You're correct for *ex post.* Let's explain with a parallel first, and then return to the BOP data. Remember that earlier we had pointed out the obvious, namely, that purchases of goods and services are always equal to sales of goods and services in an accounting or historical sense. That's what is meant by *ex post.* But you know that people can try to buy more at current prices than others are willing to sell at current prices, with the result that prices rise. That's what you mean by *ex ante.* Economists use the jargon *ex ante* to mean the effective demand for and supply of goods and services. If effective demand (*ex ante*) speeds ahead of effective supply (*ex ante*), prices rise, but purchases (*ex post*) must always equal sales (*ex post*).

Now let's apply this distinction to the BOP, and focus first on the *ex post* identities of debits and credits. When the United States exports goods and services, foreigners are obliged to make payment to the United States. This is a U.S. credit transaction, and means either that we increase our claims against foreign exchange, or foreigners decrease their claims against dollars, or a combination of both. When the U.S. imports goods and services, we are obliged to make payments to foreigners. This is a U.S. debit transaction, and means either that we reduce our claims against foreign exchange, or foreigners increase their claims against dollars, or a combination of both.

Let's illustrate what happens when we run chronic deficits with Japan by focusing on just one import transaction. Suppose that you buy a Japanese clock for $10. Assume an exchange rate of 150 yen to the dollar, just for simplicity. Now look at these bank entries:

U.S. BANK

U.S. Bank's Deposits in Tokyo Bank – 1500 yen	Your deposits – $10.

TOKYO BANK

	U.S. Bank Deposits – 1500 yen
	Japanese Exporter + 1500 yen

You ask your bank to sell you a draft for 1500 yen for your $10. The draft *orders* your bank to pay 1500 yen to a Japanese exporter living in Tokyo. Your deposit balance is down $10 because you bought 1500 yen for $10. Your bank, the U.S. bank, now has 1500 less in yen, because you had ordered your bank to pay 1500 yen to the Tokyo Exporter. So, all the Tokyo bank does is to increase the deposit of the Tokyo exporter by 1500 yen in the Tokyo bank, and reduce the deposit of the U.S. bank in the Tokyo bank by 1500 yen. This example is consistent with our statement that when we import from abroad, we reduce our claims to foreign exchange, in this case yen. Thus U.S. bank claims to yen fell by 1500 yen in payment for our imports from Japan.

S6: Yes, but you said that the Japanese were increasing their holdings of dollars as we imported net from them. This example doesn't show that.

RH: You're correct. Let's suppose we have run deficits year after year. Make the assumption too that all transactions are recorded in U.S. dollars, which is mostly the case anyway. In that case, the Tokyo bank could simply instruct the U.S. bank to credit its account in the U.S. bank with dollars. The Tokyo bank, in turn, would (again) credit its exporters with yen. In our example of the clock, the accounts look this way:

U.S. BANK

	Your deposits	−10.
	Tokyo Bank's Deposits	+ 10.

TOKYO BANK

Tokyo Bank's Deposits + $10.	Japanese Exporter + 1500 yen

Again, you bought the Japanese clock for $10, so your account in your bank is down by $10, as before. You're happy because you could pay in dollars. Now the Japanese have your $10. More precisely, the Tokyo bank now has the $10 you formerly owned—in the form of its increased $10 deposit in the U.S. bank. In effect, the Tokyo bank bought the $10 from the Japanese clock exporter. The Japanese clock exporter is happy because he was paid in yen. The Tokyo bank is happy. The U.S. bank is happy. You're happy. Everybody's happy.

RECYCLING DOLLARS

RH: Let's return now to this notion of dollar recycling. I noted that your $10 show up, at least initially, as an increase in Japanese deposits of $10 in the U.S. bank. The Japanese may, of course, later decide to buy U.S. securities or real estate with its increased dollar deposits, in which case the dollar deposits would then be shuffled from the Japanese buyer to the seller of U.S. dollar assets. In any case, the dollars earned by Japanese exporters get recycled one way or the other into U.S. dollar-denominated deposits, securities, apartment buildings, office buildings, golf courses, or other dollar-denominated assets. *Every dollar foreigners as a group earn by exporting to us is recycled here.* Foreigners as a group cannot get out of dollars as long as we run current account deficits.

S7:   Is that true, really?

RH: Yes. If we import more from abroad than we export, that would show up as a practical matter in a pileup in foreign ownership of U.S. dollar-denominated financial and real assets (the counterpart of our current account deficit). That's what has happened. The Japanese could, of course, sell their dollars for other currencies, say British pounds, and in that case the British would own the dollars. But that does not contradict the identity of our current account deficit and net capital inflow.

The BOP statistics, to repeat, confirm this identity. They show that we ran a current account deficit of $109.2 billion in 1993. We know, though, that we cannot have $109.2 billion more debits than credits. Debits must always equal credits in an *ex post* or accounting sense. What gives here? Who can explain why?

S6: Foreigners lent us $109.2 billion as a credit to offset our $109.2 billion net current account debit?

RH: Not bad, but more is involved than lending. As I have just illustrated, foreigners get dollars from us when they export net to us, and they invest those dollars in our corporate bonds, commercial paper, U.S. Treasury securities, stocks, real estate, and other U.S. dollar real and financial assets. These transactions are all counted as credit transactions from the viewpoint of the U.S. Even if foreigners keep the dollars they earn in U.S. bank deposits, that again is counted as a credit transaction for the U.S., as a capital inflow. If the investments here are in credit instruments or deposits under one year in maturity, the net inflow is called short-term capital inflow. Investments beyond one year are called long-term capital inflow. But whether short or long, the inflow is the counterpart of our current account deficit. To repeat, there is no *net* foreign capital inflow into the United States. The *net* is zero. If you really understand this, tell me what you think of this statement attributed to President Lincoln:

If we buy here, we get the goods and keep the money too, but if we buy abroad, we get the goods but lose our money. So we should erect tariffs or quotas to keep foreign goods out of this country.

S7: When we buy goods from abroad with dollars, the dollars have no value to foreign exporters other than to purchase our goods or to invest in U.S. assets. Even if the dollar is used abroad as currency, its ultimate value depends on what it can command in U.S. goods or financial instruments. As you said, our net imports are the same thing as a buildup in foreign claims on us. I guess that's your main point.

RH: Good. Even if we did send a shipload of dollars to a foreign exporter at his request, so that dollars physically went abroad, the only country in which the dollars would have ultimate purchasing power is here. With virtually 100 percent recycling, we don't have to call the Justice Department about any net huge influx of dollars into the United States from Japan. Right? Let me see if you truly understand this. Try to answer this teaser, and be careful: Can foreigners *as a group* get out of dollars or dollar instruments they have accumulated over the years when we run current account deficits?

S7: Why not? Yes, of course.

RH: I said to be careful. They can try to get out as a group, and this has important implications that we shall consider. But can they in fact get out of dollars? The answer is that it is impossible for foreigners as a group to get out of dollars just so long as the United States runs current account deficits. The only way they can get out of dollars is for the U.S. to run current account surpluses. In that case, *our current account surplus* would be exactly offset by our *capital outflow.* If Japanese owners of U.S. Treasury bonds should sell them to Germans, this would entail a swap of deutschemarks payable to the Japanese, and the Germans would end up holding the Treasury bonds. As a group, they are still in dollars. If the Germans were then to sell the bonds to a U.S. bank, the bank would credit the Germans with a dollar deposit, or possibly a marketable certificate of deposit, again denominated in dollars. As a group, foreigners would still own dollars. Try this third teaser. By way of explanation, let me introduce you to Graham Sanders, who is relevant in this discussion. He is a Canadian institutional investment client of mine who headed up the fixed-income operations of C. T. Investment Counsel in Toronto. Here's what he said to me a while back:

> Robert, you say that foreigners as a group cannot get out of dollars. What about this example? Suppose that I sell U.S. Treasury bonds I now own to Chase Manhattan Bank in New York, and ask Chase to pay me in Japanese yen. I have gotten out of dollars. Right? I am a foreigner, and now foreigners as a group are out of dollars. Right?

What's the answer to Mr. Sanders's question?

S8: Chase has to keep an inventory of foreign currencies, including yen, to do business.

RH: Like a grocery store and its inventory of canned peas?

S8: The point is that Chase is now short of yen, the yen it paid to Mr. Graham. So Chase will replenish its holdings of yen, its working inventory of yen. To get yen, it will probably buy yen from the Japanese, paying the Japanese with dollars. That means the Japanese end up holding dollars even though Mr. Sanders, a Canadian, has gotten out of dollars.

RH: My compliments to you. By understanding this, you can protect yourself from turning into an economic schizophrenic. That's someone who holds two contradictory positions at once—like arguing that foreigners would rush out of dollars if they should expect our current account deficits to explode. Again, that's impossible.

S9: Wait a minute. Suppose that Chase bank bought yen from a currency exchange broker. Chase does not have to buy yen from the Japanese.

RH: In that case, the broker may be short of yen and would have to get yen for dollars. Either way, what is involved here is an inventory adjustment. Apart from that qualification, though, we still end up with the accounting identity of the deficit and capital inflow.

EX ANTE PURCHASES AND SALES OF DOLLARS BY FOREIGNERS

RH: This takes us now to *attempts* by foreigners to get into or out of dollars. We have just indicated that foreigners as a group cannot get out of dollars unless, of course, we run a current account surplus. In that case foreigners would reduce their claims to dollars as they incurred current account deficits with us, and paid (net) dollars to buy U.S. exports. True, they can attempt to get out of dollars by selling dollars to each other, by dumping dollars on each other. In that case, the resulting increase in the effective supply of dollars put on the market could very well drive the exchange rate of the dollar down sharply against other currencies. The *ex ante* pressure of increased effective dollar supply could push the dollar way down, but all of the dollars sold would end up *ex post* in the same hands, in foreign hands. They would have showered dollars on each other.

Now, suppose foreigners as a group suddenly tried to get into dollars. They would in that case have to buy dollars from each other. The resulting increase in the effective demand for dollars could very well drive the dollar up sharply against foreign currencies. The *ex ante* pressure of increased effective demand could push the dollar up sharply, but *ex post* foreigners would again end up with the same total of dollars.

S9: But why couldn't a foreign company sell some bonds to U.S. investors, and get dollars that way?

RH: You are correct in a *gross* sense. But you see that a foreign bond sale that generates dollars to foreigners (gross) would mean an exact offsetting increase in their debts in dollars to us (gross). That would not result in a *net* increase in foreign holdings of dollars and dollar-denominated instruments. It would not change by one penny the reported net capital flows between the two countries. Consider another example, one where the U.S. sells bonds to the Italians, denominated in lira. In that case we get immediate lira exchange, but that is offset 100 percent in our debt denominated in lira. Again, there is no *net* increase in U.S. holdings of lira or lira-denominated instruments. Neither example contradicts the basic identity of the current account deficit and foreign capital inflow, otherwise called foreign investment flows into the United States.

S9:   You mean *net* foreign investment.

RH: Yes! Net! I must listen to my own teaching on this. Now, it's often said that the United States is dependent on foreigners to finance its budget and trade deficits. We are warned that the Japanese, for example, might dump all their dollars on the market, and this would send dollar instruments into a tailspin, and push U.S. interest rates up sharply. How about that?

S9:   Well, the Japanese could sell to the Germans, I guess. The *ex ante* pressures could be severe.

RH: Anything else?

S9:   Foreigners own these dollar instruments. If they sell and force dollar prices down, they could be the losers.

RH: Yes. As a practical matter, when Japanese institutions, for example, sell dollars for yen, the buyers are likely to be other Japanese institutions who sell yen for dollars. Their own actions to dump dollars to punish the United States for, say, new trade restrictions could boomerang. Their dollar bonds could plummet. The Japanese know that. They know that to rain dollars on themselves would be tantamount to what I might dub economic *hari-kari*. Even so, whether the dollar would stay down or later rebound in the face of major Japanese sales would hinge on the dollar's real purchasing power against the yen and other currencies, and on the types of economic policies followed by the United States and Japan, among other forces (chapter 23).

THE QUINTESSENTIAL PARROT AT GENERAL MOTORS

Now that we have paved the way with data and theory, let's finally meet the quintessential Parrot I came across at General Motors. This highly perched bird held fast to just about every theoretical error imaginable in the field of international finance, all the while making loud and shrill noises, and with confidence. This is not to suggest that GM's investment staff for its huge pension fund is not first class, relatively speaking. No, my purpose is didactic, educational. I want you to see just how Parrots think, and squawk. I shall refer to our GM-feathered bird as LS, for Loud Squawk, in this exchange that took place on the twenty-sixth floor of the GM building on October 27, 1989:

LS: You can't be serious. How can the dollar move higher when interest rates are falling here, and rising abroad?

RH: Well, forecasting exchange rates is a hazardous business. Still, the dollar is ultra cheap. The bargain dollar shows up in country-by-country purchasing-power-parity (PPP) calculations and in low U.S. exchange-rate adjusted cost and price indexes published by the International Monetary Fund. It shows up in real or inflation-adjusted exchange rates. The United States has a huge price and cost advantage in international markets. Interest-rate differentials here and abroad are narrowing, and . . .

LS: Wait a minute. You economists have been preaching a dollar rebound since 1985, but the U.S. trade deficit is still huge, and dollars pile up abroad. You will see an end to this soon. Foreign investors will sell their dollars. They'll dump dollars for other currencies.

RH: You're right in arguing that economists have been too optimistic, including me. We placed too much confidence in an early and sustained improvement in our trade balance (Exhibit 22–1 on the "J-Curve"). I am puzzled, though, by your second comment. You say foreigners are going to get out of dollars, that foreigners as a group, collectively, will get out of dollars? That's not possible unless . . .

LS: They'll get out, sell, dump, run. That's what I said.

RH: But that would mean a current account surplus for the United States. You just said you looked for bigger current-account deficits, which means foreigners would by definition accumulate even more dollars because . . .

LS: I didn't say anything about a U.S. surplus. Why don't you listen? I said we are headed for bigger deficits, that foreigners will dump their dollars. They will rush out of dollars.

RH: I meant simply that it's impossible for foreigners as a group to get out of dollars unless we run a current account surplus. They can try, but in an *ex post* or accounting sense that's impossible because . . .

LS: Can't get out? Come on! What's this *ex post* crap?

RH: You must distinguish between *ex post* and *ex* . . .

Before I could finish LS stalked out of the conference. He abruptly departed without apology, startling his colleagues.

Highly perched Parrots are quick to anger when cornered. Pros are generally calmer, more persuasive, better educated, often eloquent, and harder to identify. Still, nothing is more dangerous to society than ideologically fired Pros wearing economic blinders. That includes the highly perched Pros in business and government whom we now meet.

Exhibit 22–1: The Esoteric "J-Curve" Effect on Trade

We encountered the quintessential Parrot (Loud Squawk) in this chapter, but failed to give him due credit for his skepticism on the "J-Curve."* Maybe this July 12, 1994, *Monitor* sent to investors can help clear up the mystery:

> The New York Fed deserves kudos for its research on the J-Curve (Spring 1994 *Quarterly Review*). It wrote:
>
>> The Japanese trade surplus has yet to experience the full J-Curve effect. It has not [contracted yet] because the rise in the yen was not a onetime jump.
>
> Onetime jump? Yes, that's the key. What happens with a onetime rise in the yen? Well, the initial effect of yen appreciation is to swell its trade surplus for two reasons. First, importers from Japan do not immediately cut back real purchases in percentage terms by enough to offset the higher percentage climb in prices for Japanese goods when expressed in dollars. Foreign demand is initially inelastic. Second, Japanese importers enjoy immediately lower import costs because, with a rise in the yen, they can buy the same amount of real imports in dollars with fewer yen. Since most transactions are in dollars, their total nominal dollar surplus swells. Over time, though, Japanese exports become so prohibitively expensive that the percentage fall in their real net exports more than offsets the percentage rise in their currency. Foreign demand for Japanese exports becomes elastic, and its trade surplus contracts in dollars.
>
> Here's where the brilliant work of the New York Fed enters the picture. It makes clear that the initial effects of the recent climb in the yen, which swells its trade surplus, has more than offset the lagged effects of earlier advances in the yen, which cut its surplus. The recent initial effects have dominated the lagged earlier effects to date. That cannot continue indefinitely, however, in the absence of a continuing advance of the yen. Given a yen already preposterously overpriced in world markets and the evidence underway now of a fall in its real net exports, a continuing rise of the yen looks like a very low probability. Nothing rises higher and higher forever.
>
> But just suppose the yen moves even higher based, say, on irrational trader fears. Then you would see even larger Japanese surpluses in response to the initial but temporary effect of yen appreciation. In that case, though, we would write a Monitor shifting our focus from the yen bubble to the yen megabubble, foreshadowing an even greater collapse of the yen.

---

*A fall in the U.S. dollar would initially increase its current account deficit. U.S. investors pay higher dollars prices for foreign goods but they don't cut their purchases very much. The percentage increase in price more than offsets their reduced import volume. Over time, though, they do cut back aggressively on imports, and the current account deficit is reduced. When plotted on a graph the relationship of current account surplus to current account deficit looks like a "J," hence the name J-curve.

Based on my conviction that the yen was overpriced, I argued throughout 1995 that the yen was headed for a mighty fall against the dollar (see Appendix A, Forecast 95). The "J-Curve" lagged effects also signaled a fall in the Japanese current account surplus. What happened? The yen fell and Japan's surplus contracted, as predicted.

23

The All-American Protectionists

Delusion Wrapped in Deception

> PETITION FROM THE MANUFACTURERS OF CAN-
> DLES . . . We are subjected to the intolerable competition
> of a foreign rival, who enjoys . . . such superior facilities
> for the production of light that he is enabled to *inundate*
> our market at so exceedingly reduced a price [that] French
> industry . . . is reduced to a state of complete stagnation.
> This rival [is] no other than the sun. [Our] petition is [to]
> pass a law whereby shall be directed the shutting up of
> windows, dormers, skylights, shutters, curtains (and all
> openings) through which the light of the sun is used to pen-
> etrate our dwellings.
>
> Frederic Bastiat (1801–50), *Economic Sophisms**

Economist Frederic Bastiat was a master at spotting economic sophisms, that
is, clever but false arguments. His scorching satire was directed against "protectionists," the intellectual Pros running loose in France in the first half of the
nineteenth century. The candlemakers, he wrote, wanted to save their jobs.
Their solution: Block out the sun! A century and one-half after Bastiat, protectionists still scream that we block out the sun, the Rising Sun that is Japan.

---

*Selections from Bastiat's *Economic Sophism*, in S. Howard Patterson (ed.), *Readings in
the History of Economic Thought* (New York: McGraw-Hill Book Company, 1932), pp.
433–34.

THE RICARDIAN PRINCIPLE OF COMPARATIVE ADVANTAGE

We'll turn to the modern protectionist pitches momentarily, but first we must analyze the case for free trade. Only then can we fully appreciate just how slick but sick these protectionist arguments are. So, please join me in the following exchange, one I have experienced often with graduate students (S) and investment officers:

RH: Have you ever seen the musical *Annie Get Your Gun*? One actress who took the lead role of Annie was Betty Hutton. She sang these words:

> Anything you can do, I can do better.
> I can do anything better than you.

Never heard of her? Well, do you know David Ricardo?

Ss: (No response.)

RH: Ricardo (1772–1823) was a brilliant economist and businessman, as we shall see. Let's turn now to Betty and David. Imagine that they are shipwrecked and stranded on an isolated Caribbean island. Suppose that Betty can do everything better than David except solve economic puzzles. Here are the production possibilities for Betty and David picking coconuts and catching fish:

Output for the Same Hours	Betty	David
either picking coconuts	24	12
or catching fish	12	3

You can see that Betty has an *absolute advantage* in the trees and in the water: she can pick 24 coconuts in the same time it takes David to pick 12, and she catch 12 fish to David's 3. What should Betty propose to David?

S2:   Take a walk.

RH: Ha. She might, but David knows better. He knows that both can benefit by specializing and trading. How so?

S3:   Betty should fish and David pick coconuts.

RH: That's right. Why don't all of you take a few minutes to convince yourself of that before you explain.

S3:   Betty can pick 24 coconuts in the same time it takes her to catch 12 fish. That's a 2 to 1 ratio. David can pick 12 coconuts in the same time it takes him to catch 3 fish. That's a 4 to 1 ratio. So, Betty is twice as efficient in picking coconuts as catching fish, but David is four times as efficient in picking coconuts as catching fish. David has a relative advantage in picking coconuts, and Betty has a relative advantage in catching fish, even though Betty has an absolute advantage in both.

RH: Economists call the relative advantage the *comparative advantage,* after Ricardo. Let's "prove" that Betty and David should specialize and trade.

> Assuming no specialization and no trade,
> Betty forgoes   1 fish for 2 coconuts.
> David forgoes   1 fish for 4 coconuts.

So, how could both Betty and David benefit?

S3:   They would be better off specializing and trading

> 1 fish for 3 coconuts.

RH: Good, assuming specialization and trade

> Betty gives up   1 fish for 3 coconuts.
> David receives   1 fish for 3 coconuts.

Any exchange between the two ratios of 2 to 1 and 4 to 1 would be mutually beneficial, and 3 to 1 falls between the two. At 3 to 1, both end up with one more coconut each by specializing and trading. So, both benefit. The same would hold if Betty gives up 2 fish to get 6 coconuts.

Economists prior to Ricardo, including Adam Smith, ordinarily stressed absolute advantage. No one disputes that all could benefit, for example, when Florida oranges are exchanged for Maine potatoes, an example of absolute advantage. Ricardo's contribution lies in the concept of comparative advantage, the arch-enemy of protectionists.

The Comparative Advantage of Nations

If you couple the genius of Ricardo with the wit of Bastiat, you end up with a powerful case for free international trade. But many analysts question the Ricardian view as being "unrealistic." Consider Harvard economist Michael Porter:

Most important, however, there has been a growing awareness that the assumptions underlying factor comparative advantage theories of trade are *unrealistic* in many industries. The standard theory assumes that there are no economies of scale, that technologies everywhere are identical, that products are undifferentiated, and that the pool of national factors is fixed. The theory also assumes that factors, such as skilled labor and capital, do not move among nations.*

I highlighted *unrealistic*, and bristle at Porter's criticism. Yes, Ricardo was incomplete, but hardly unrealistic. Ricardo created a model the world had never seen before. On that model the rest of us could add our modifications and additions to get closer and closer to the job of explaining the real world. That's the iterative approach, one that is par for the course in sound economic theorizing. On that account, I can see Betty and David picking coconuts on another island, or fishing in better waters. Labor and capital can move, after all, to another island. Call that Ricardian iteration! To be sure, Porter makes a contribution in detailing the many forces that contribute to the growth of individual industries, company-by-company and country-by-country. But Porter is no Ricardo.

DOUBLE-TALK PROTECTIONIST PITCHES

With the principle of comparative advantage as our powerful ally, Porter notwithstanding, let's turn now to the protectionists themselves. We'll first pay attention to the American protectionists who hold high posts in business and government. I'll cite just seven here, but keep in mind that their arguments are widely parroted throughout the realm. Here's my favorite list of All-American protectionists:

- Lee A. Iacocca, former Chrysler Corporation Chairman

- C. Fred Bergsten, Institute for International Analysis

- T. Boone Pickens, Texas Tycoon

- Peter F. Drucker, Professor of the Social Sciences

- Jim Baker, President Reagan's Treasury Secretary

- H. Ross Perot, Texas Billionaire

- President Clinton, Petitioner Against the Rising Sun

The Competitive Advantage of Nations (New York: Free Press, 1990), p. 12.

All seven are protectionists. Iacocca groaned that "we are sitting here going into debt more and more every day, and let the Japanese buy Rockefeller Center." (After leaving Chrysler, he *miraculously* turned up as a born-again free trader supporting the North American Free Trade Agreement [NAFTA].) Economist Bergsten cried that our "dependence on foreign capital has made us hostage to economic events abroad." Pickens wailed for a "six-month moratorium on Japanese investment in the United States."* Clinton, despite his support for NAFTA and the General Agreement on Trade and Tariffs (GATT), repeatedly threatened Japan and China with trade restrictions. He was displeased with our massive import of Japanese goods (of supreme quality) and China's record on civil rights. (Can you imagine China's banning U.S. goods because of its displeasure with Tennessee's record on civil rights?) Perot squealed that NAFTA would kill U.S. jobs, distorting theory and data in his evangelical fever.

Let's turn to an analysis of four pitches of the kind revered by protectionists. Each pitch is riddled with internal contradictions. Each collapses from its own weight. Even so, each is widely touted, accepted, and applauded. Consider these Double-Talk Arguments:

1. Double-Talk on Foreign Capital "Inflow" and "Outflow"

We must lean heavily on the balance-of-payments analysis of chapter 22 to dispense quickly with the confusion involved in capital flows. Protectionists argue that, like it or not, we have become addicted to *foreign capital inflow.* We need the foreigners to finance our "twin" deficits, the internal budgetary and the external trade deficits. Our addiction is so severe that we must guard against *foreign capital outflow.* No hasty withdrawals, please, or all hell could break loose.

Will the real devil stand up? If it's true that foreign capital outflows can sink the U.S. economy, would not foreign capital inflows float the U.S. economy to new heights? Neither is true. Both represent muddled schizophrenia. The protectionist drivel on inflows and outflows is a classic case of confusion (affected confusion by some economists?). An understanding of the identity of the current account with capital flows, and of the difference between *ex post* and *ex ante* concepts is all you need to identify and reject such drivel (chapter 22). With that in mind, let's fire two questions at Iacocca and Pickens:

The New York Times of November 24, 1989 and March 4, 1990.

- Were the Americans, Mr. Iacocca, forced to accept the dollars the Japanese paid—often overpaid—for U.S. investments?

- Is it even possible, Mr. Pickens, to force an investment moratorium on Japan as long as we run current account deficits?

Mr. Pickens's proposal for a moratorium on Japanese investment and Mr. Iacocca's plea for restriction on imports are identical protectionist pitches, pure and simple. If we bar Japanese exports, the Japanese cannot earn dollars. If they are prohibited from earning dollars in the first place, it follows they cannot recycle dollars to U.S. assets in the second place. You can't invest what you don't have.

Just ask yourself what would happen if we were to block Japanese recycling of dollars. Where, then, would the Japanese invest their dollars? Would they not then be pressured to sell their dollars in Germany, in Great Britain, or elsewhere? Would that not send the dollar reeling in foreign exchange markets once we realize that foreigners as a group cannot get out of dollars whenever we run current account deficits? Would not a blockage of Japanese investment in U.S. assets destroy foreign faith in the U.S. dollar? Indeed, why would anyone export to us if they thought for a second that the dollars they earn could not be ultimately spent for our goods and services or invested here? Most important, to block recycling for any major nation would induce other nations to "dump" dollars. The dollar could plunge.

The Bergsten Fallacy on Being Hostage to the Future

What about Mr. Bergsten's notion that we are hostage to the Japanese? Apart from his use of emotionally toned words, economist Bergsten surely must know that our economic fate hinges overwhelmingly on our ability to produce and sell competitively in domestic and world markets. So, using Bergsten's own words, we can say we are hostage to ourselves. Nor is the U.S. hostage to the future, as Mr. Bergsten, Mr. Perot, and others wail. Our payments of interest and dividends to foreigners on their investments here don't simply disappear into thin air. No, interest and dividend dollars earned by foreigners on investments in the U.S. are also recycled into additional dollar-denominated assets, which help to provide jobs and incomes for American citizens.

Relevant here, one of my clients, Daiwa Bank and Trust Company, has its offices at 75 Rockefeller Plaza in New York City. They are proud to be there, as you can imagine. They rent their facilities, as do most foreign firms with offices in the United States. In this instance, American landlords and their employees are the chief beneficiaries. The Japanese pay them in dollars, the very same dollars the Japanese earn through exports and then recycle back as payments to Americans. When you think about it, my Japanese clients recycle U.S. dollars back to me, too. I am an American beneficiary of Japanese export power.

Seldom understood, the billions upon billions of dollars foreigners *as a group* earn in exporting to us are recycled as expenditures or investments in the United States. The one qualification relates to U.S. currency circulating abroad, as in the former USSR. Apart from this, though, we're talking about 100 percent recycling (chapter 22). Foreign held dollars remain here and continue to increase in total here just so long as we run current account deficits. Ah, perhaps I should make a record labeled Dollar Recycling and the U.S. Balance-of-Payments (BOP) deficit. I would try to get Abraham Lincoln's fallacy on international trade into the record. He supposedly said that we lose our money when we buy from abroad, but when we buy at home we keep the goods and the money, too. Lose our money when we buy from abroad? No, not when you factor in dollar recycling:

> A breakdown of Abe's fallacy makes clear
> That the dollars foreigners earn stay here.
> They end up as dollar bonds and dollar stocks,
> Or dollar-denominated apartment blocks,
> Or real estate in Tennessee,
> Or Treasury bills of Washington, D.C.
> They can't escape, you must admit
> When we run a payments deficit.

2. Double-Talk on Infant and Established Industries

This takes us to the second case of double-talk in protectionist arguments. At one extreme, the protectionists argue that young emerging industries need protection. They need to be nourished and cared for, like babies. With protection they can grow strong and compete successfully in the cruel international marketplace. So, raise the tariff walls and increase the import quotas. That's the age-old argument in behalf of "infant industries." At the other extreme, the protectionists argue that we must protect our established industries, our mature industries that have proved themselves to be the backbone of the American economy, and generate employment for millions of American workers. That's the time-worn argument for "established industries."

Candles and Thumbtacks: Essential for National Security?

Protectionist pleading for established defense industries is especially vulnerable to abuse. Listen to Wharton economist Franklin R. Root. I highlighted candles in remembrance of Bastiat:

> In the United States, manufacturers of peanuts, *candles,* thumbtacks, umbrella frames, gloves, and many other products of ordinary consumption have all asked for protection on the grounds of national security.*

The defense argument insists that we need military security to guarantee economic security. Who could ever take issue with that? After all, we cannot afford to let our defenses down, can we? But wait! Consider that nation after nation has accumulated huge stockpiles of nuclear bombs for defense. They have built these bombs for protection. Yes, for *protection.* The problem, though, with military protection is that its logic may be contradictory for the group. As nation A piles up nuclear bombs, this induces nations B and C and D, and throughout the alphabet to do the same, all in the name of protection, of national security. But the arithmetic increase in ownership of nuclear weapons could increase, not decrease, the risk that they might be used, whether by accident, miscalculation, or design. Philosopher Bertrand Russell said as much long ago. Russell's fear complements the fallacy of composition, that what might be true for one could backfire for all. Question: *Does the defense argument fall as a fallacy of composition, possibly the ultimate fallacy of mankind?* We must explore the question further, for it is linked inextricably to the views of scientists on the very nature of economic man. These scientists look with disdain, you know, on economists (see chapters 25 and 26).

3. Double-Talk on Cheap Foreign Labor Costs

Our third case of double-talk protectionists illustrates how easily one can stumble and fall over definitions. I have in mind the cheap foreign labor and capital arguments. Both can be seen as defective once we make explicit just what the word "cheap" means. Let's consider labor costs first. You could define cheap, if you were a protectionist, simply in terms of foreign wage rates compared with U.S. wage rates. But would that be sufficient? Hardly, since relative productivity must be taken into account, too. While U.S. hourly wages, for example, might be double that of foreign wages, so might U.S. pro-

*International Trade and Investment (Cincinnati, Ohio: South Western Publishing, 1990), p. 155.

ductivity measured as output per hour. Take a simple example. If U.S. labor is paid $20 an hour to produce two items and foreign labor $10 an hour to make one item of the same kind, what then would be the *unit* labor cost, the labor cost per item? The answer is $10 an hour, here and there. No difference. No double-talk. The point is that any legitimate comparison of labor costs here and abroad requires that we compare unit labor costs of production, or wages divided by output per hour. We can't leave productivity out of the analysis.

Nor, to repeat, can we leave comparative advantage out of the analysis. *It still pays all nations to specialize and trade even if any individual nation has absolute costs of production far in excess of its trading partners in each and every sector of its economy.* We learned that truth from Ricardo. Make note of this Drucker, Pickens, Perot, Iacocca, Brady, Bergsten, *and* Porter.

We would, of course, have to consider other costs as well as exchange rates before we could even begin to assess the competitive international status of U.S. industry. For example, U.S. exchange-rate adjusted costs and prices in 1995 gave the U.S. a huge competitive cost and price advantage, not disadvantage, in world markets. On that basis, we could see a major reduction ahead in the U.S. current account deficit and a rising dollar, especially against the bubble yen (see chapter 22).

4. Double-Talk on the Cheap Cost Foreign Capital

The argument has been made that the United States was at a huge disadvantage compared to Japan, that Japan could raise capital at much cheaper rates than we could. It's Japanese financial power that underlay the Japanese economic miracle, or so the argument went. Perhaps the strongest statement of this view was set forth by Peter F. Drucker, a revered professor of social sciences.* Drucker concluded that the United States suffered an "enormous competitive disadvantage vis-à-vis the Japanese through our prohibitive cost of capital." Press Secretary Nicholas F. Brady made the same case. Brady added his two cents before the Business Council in Washington, D.C. He declared:

> The cornerstone of any business is capital. In some cases, U.S. companies face capital costs fully twice as high as our foreign competitors. Worse than that, with compound interest at work we fall behind at an ever-increasing rate. The consequence is clear. We simply can't pay more than our competitors for capital,

*Editorial page, *The Wall Street Journal* (January 9, 1990).

which goes into everything we produce, and hope to come out ahead. No one is that good.*

Really? Neither Drucker nor Brady apparently took the time to check their views against the data. The march of events outdated the Brady-Drucker thesis even as they made their pitch. By March 1990 nominal interest rates on long government bonds in Canada, France, the United Kingdom, and Germany had already crossed ours, and they were converging fast in Japan. Japanese ten-year government bonds had shot up to 7.5 percent, only 1 percent below that of U.S. Treasuries. Foreign real interest rates, that is, nominal rates adjusted for inflation, moved higher than ours in Germany, Japan, and in many other industrial nations. Real U.S. interest rates adjusted for taxes in Japan and Germany and in other major industrial nations crossed ours by early 1990. U.S. rates plunged after late 1990 (Appendix A, Forecasts 61–83), contradicting the Brady-Drucker view of high-cost U.S. bond financing even as they proclaimed it with utmost confidence and authority.

What about the alleged cheap cost of stock financing in Japan? The collapse in the Nikkei 225 put an end once and for all to the Brady-Drucker illusion. They, like many others, were simply blind to the Nikkei 225 stock megabubble. That's the way with authorities in power. "Bubble, what bubble?" they asked (see chapter 17).

PROTECTIONIST PARROTS OR PROS?

Let's turn now to several additional instances of protectionism. I invite you to classify.

The General Electric Company

The new protectionists are forever bashing Japan. Indeed, the current hullabaloo reminds me of something I experienced years ago at General Electric. Shortly after I joined GE as an economist in 1958, the company circulated a memorandum asking that its employees not buy foreign cars, appliances, and TV sets. It sent a copy to all of us in the Economic and Industrial Forecasting Operation. GE preached free competition but practiced protectionism abroad to keep foreign products out of the United States. In response to GE's memo, I circulated Bastiat's essay on the petition of the candlemakers to the

---

Treasury News (February 22, 1990), p. 2.

sun. I sent it to the executive offices in New York City. That almost got me fired.

GE officials also practiced a form of protectionism at home. Some entered into secret conspiracies to restrain trade and block competition in everything from light bulbs to steam turbines. Ultimately it was widely reported in the media that the head of the turbine division in Schenectady was sent to prison, but I had no way of knowing that at the time. Relevant here, consider this exchange I (RH) had with a very top manager (TM) of the Schenectady operation for my annual appraisal:

RH: I can't believe you asked us to destroy records on the marketing or sales of steam turbines and light bulbs. I had no records. I have only been here a year. Anyway, that would have been illegal, immoral.

TM: Robert, I did not ask anybody to break the law, but I was concerned about misguided antitrust actions against GE. Nobody else complained about my request. What's your problem? I thought I made myself clear in our meeting with the staff that the executive office wanted those records destroyed. On another matter, the memo you sent around on Bastiat was out of order. You had no business bypassing me. You seem to have trouble adjusting here. Robert, GE is not a university. Be careful.

RH: The other economists have been here forever. They won't speak up. They don't want to jeopardize their promotions, their jobs. But you put them in a terrible bind. If they had had records and handed them over, that would have compromised them. You asked them to put loyalty to GE over everything else. By the way, what did they do?

TM: That's not your business. You're all wet. You make too much of all this. Again, I'm telling you to be careful for your own sake. I have a meeting to attend.

Yes, be careful. Be quiet. I regret I did not shout out the truth about GE's actions at the time. I tried, though, to make up for that lapse of ethical conduct as a straight-shooting Wall Street economist. My aim, the essence of this book, is to explain and document how pressure, insecurity, and selfishness work as a gang on Wall Street to destroy integrity and honor.

GE: Parrot or Pro?

The Youngstown Sheet and Tube Company

I was hired in the mid-1960s to take the superintendents and foremen through a training program in company and national economics. The national economics program proved to be nothing more than a propaganda pitch. Specifically, the glories of competition, dutifully expounded by the rest of Youngstown's teaching staff, went hand-in-hand with the company's propaganda to bar foreign steel from U.S. markets. They set forth every fallacy in the protectionist book. I quit, and returned to Wharton.

Youngstown: Parrot or Pro?

The Ford Motor Company

Ford fired economist Bill Niskanen for daring to talk like a free trader, for having the gall to say something unpleasant about U.S. barriers to imports of foreign automobiles. Bill later became a member of the President's Council of Economic Advisers (1981–85) and was my guest for the institutional forums I hosted in Washington. My compliments go out to Bill Niskanen.

Ford Motor: Parrot or Pro?

The Chrysler Corporation and Autopac

Did you know that Mr. Iacocca had some unpleasant things to say about Autopac, the association for the Auto Dealers and Drivers for Free Trade? As reported by the *New York Times* Iacocca "railed against . . . what he said were 'high-priced Washington lobbyists'" representing Autopac.* As you might guess, Autopac lobbied for lower import barriers to automobiles. You might correctly conclude too that importers of foreign goods are almost universally free traders, while exporters are usually avid protectionists. That figures.

Chrysler: Parrot or Pro?
Autopac: Parrot or Pro?

The United Auto Workers, the American Auto Makers

The two go together. The United Auto Workers stated that they would like to limit imports of Japanese cars to a maximum of 1.5 million in 1990, which compared with the then existing ceiling of 2.3 million. The 2.3 million limit was wrested from Congress by the American Auto Makers in 1982. It was later

---

*December 29, 1989, p. B9.

formalized in a pact between Washington and Tokyo whereby the Japanese agreed to "voluntary" export quotas, a first-rate form of hard protectionism.

The United Auto Workers: Parrots or Pros?

The American Auto Makers: Parrots or Pros?

The European Economic Commission (EEC)

The EEC has asked for limits to Japanese exports of autos to Europe, the objective being to protect mature industries. Suffice it here to say that the pitch may not work. One reason, of all things, is that the U.S. and the Japanese were jointly producing cars in the United States. Because the cars are produced here, they would be considered U.S. exports, not Japanese exports. So the Japanese and the Americans joined together as allies on this issue in potential opposition to the EEC. How nice.

The EEC: Parrot or Pro?

THE QUESTION OF A LEVEL PLAYING FIELD

That's enough of specifics, for the list of Parrot and Pro protectionists is endless. Let's conclude this chapter with two questions. First, who has the better of the arguments, the free traders or the protectionists? Second, if we focus on just two protectionists, the United States and Japan, who is most at fault? You know my answer to the first question. The free traders win hands down, or so I have tried to argue.

I honestly don't have a firm conviction on the second. The United States insists that vested interests in Japan have closed their markets to foreigners. The U.S complaint list runs, for example, from high Japanese tariffs on wood to food to rice; to "Buy Japan" slogans, to mom-and-pop Japanese retail outlets that effectively bar our own mass merchandising retailers; to "Dango," meaning Japanese rigging of bids and contracts to exclude U.S. and other foreign firms from their huge construction industry.

How do we measure and weight these conflicting claims, many of which we have already questioned? Maybe we shouldn't even try. Maybe the question fails to deal with the real issue of just how Americans and Japanese differ in culture, in ethical values, in what is right and wrong, what is moral and immoral. That, at least, is the way Clyde Prestowitz, president of the Economic Strategy Institute, sees it:

[We] have developed the idea that business should be done on the basis of the best offer rather than on the basis of long-term or special relationships. We would think it unfair if a buyer would buy from his fraternity brother or class-mate rather than from a stranger who offered him the same goods for a 20 per-cent lower price. In Japan the opposite is the case. . . . If a buyer turns away from an old friend or relative to do business with a stranger just to get a better price, the buyer is considered unfair. . . . Such behavior is shameful.*

Shameful or not, opportunity cost could not care less. As I write this, Japan's stock market bubble has burst, its economy is in major recession, and the overpriced yen looks vulnerable as net exports measured in real terms and in yen fall hard. To remain competitive, Japanese industrial leaders have sev-ered their long-standing commitments to buy steel exclusively from Japanese producers. Discount stores now boom as low-priced and high-quality imports pour into Japan. To get costs down, lifetime jobs are in jeopardy and bonuses often cut 100 percent. So, the claim that the Japanese were somehow unique made no sense. That was the claim, too, you'll recall, just prior to the fore-cast bursting of the Japanese stock bubble (chapter 17). No, opportunity cost always operates internationally, but you never know just when it will show up with full force.

IDEOLOGICAL SCREAMING ON THE NATURE OF ECONOMIC MAN?

Still, following Prestowitz, you can see that Americans and Japanese may have different ideas about the nature of economic man. So, just what is this complex and extremely controversial being we call economic man? In trying to answer that question, we must now investigate in greater depth the views of economists (chapter 24). Then we will consider the opposing views of psy-chologists, mathematicians, anthropologists, physicists, the new "chaos" the-orists, and other scientists, many of whom are profoundly skeptical of pro-fessional economists (chapter 25). In our continuing inquiry, we will run into ideological screaming at the expense of economic science on all sides.

Swarthmore College Bulletin (February 1990), pp. 13–14.

Part Eight

The Nature of Economic Man—
Theory, Practice, and Malpractice

24

Economists as Preachers

> One of the greatest Reasons why so few people under-
> stand themselves, is, that most Writers are always teaching
> Men what they should be, and hardly ever trouble their
> Heads with telling them what they really are.
>
> Bernard de Mandeville (1670?–1731),
> *The Fable of the Bees* (1705)

Adam Smith borrowed heavily from de Mandeville. Both concluded that economic man was selfish, but that individual selfishness under competition made for group harmony and economic progress. Here we will take a fresh look at the violently conflicting notions we have about economic man. We'll analyze in this chapter the views of economists. Then in chapter 25 we'll investigate anew what various social and physical scientists have to say about economic man. We will consider the views of psychologists, psychoanalysts, anthropologists, natural scientists, mathematicians, and even physicists and related "chaos" theorists, among others. Finally, I'll summarize my tentative findings in chapter 26 drawing heavily on my Wall Street experience in working with this bewildering, complex, and controversial creature we call economic man.

Let's turn to the thinking of the most influential economists and philosophers on economic man. They set forth many of their ideas centuries ago, and their thinking still has great influence on us today. We'll start with Adam Smith. Consciously or unconsciously, Smith had a lot to say about human motivation in his *Lectures* (1748–51) and in his *Theory of Moral Sentiments* (1759). They are required reading for anyone interested in the history of economic ideas. Smith's most complete statement came, however, with the publication in 1776 of *Wealth of Nations*. I can state Smith's conclusion as a paradox:

> Individual "self-love" under competition maximizes income and wealth and progress for society as a whole.

You can quarrel over the words "self-love" (Smith's favorite phrase) versus selfishness or self-interest, but Smith made it clear that by individual self-love he meant filling your own pockets with money, not your neighbors' pockets. Indirectly, though, individual self-love put buying power in the national pockets. That economic conclusion in itself, which Smith documented in great detail, profoundly affected the course of economic theory for centuries to come. At the same time, Smithian economics represented a profound somersault in ethical theory. Many religious teachers, for example, taught that individual unselfishness (indeed, altruism) was the key to the good society, that any society based on individual selfishness was bound to decay and fall over time.

THE SMITHIAN MASTERSWITCH

Selfishness begets selfishness, many religious leaders asserted. Not so, said Smith. Don't confuse what should be with what is, he argued. Take individual selfishness as a given, and build the best of all possible economic worlds on that assumption. Individual selfishness does not produce mass disorder. On the contrary, the result is order, harmony, wealth, and human progress. That's the Smithian paradox, the masterswitch underlying Smith's masterpiece.

Smith drew from many people for his ideas. One was the Scottish philosopher Francis Hutcheson (1694–1746), Smith's teacher at the University of Glasgow. Hutcheson had no trouble at all, as Hutcheson himself saw it, in reconciling self-love for the individual with benevolence and happiness for society as a whole. He put this all down as the "LAW OF NATURE," always written in bold caps, and in "goodness from the effects of Divine Power."* How neat. If things had been as simple as Hutcheson said they were,

---

*S. Howard Patterson, *Readings in the History of Economic Thought* (New York: Mc-Graw-Hill Book Company, 1932), p. 25.

then Smith would not have had to agonize over dogs (always greyhounds) and hearts and invisible hands in trying to discern the true nature of economic man (chapter 2). He could have instead just chalked up everything to Hutcheson's LAW OF NATURE.

Smith leaned also on the writings of de Mandeville, and on the tracts of Jeremy Bentham, an English philosopher and economist (1748–1832). Bentham and de Mandeville could have passed as twin brothers in philosophy. I put their views this way:

> The de Mandeville Paradox: Bad is good, vice is nice.
> The Benthamite Law: Man is base, but that's all right.

Bernard de Mandeville, a native Dutchman who practiced medicine before he went to England, set down his fiery views long before Smith. His *Fable of the Bees or Private Vices Publick Benefits* was published in 1714, and is well known to students of economics. There he praised individual selfishness as a social good. He insisted that he was not really a "bare-faced Champion of Vice," but his own words suggest he protested too much. Nobody anywhere ever put the extreme hedonistic rationale more forcefully than did the wordmaster de Mandeville:

> Thus every part was full of vice,
> Yet the whole Mass a Paradise.*

That language is at once hellish and heavenly, but made to order for Smith's paradox that individual self-love made for group harmony. Now consider this fiery preaching from Jeremy Bentham's *Introduction to the Principles of Morals and Legislation* (1789):

> Nature has placed mankind under the governance of two sovereign masters, pain and pleasure. It is for them alone to point out what we ought to do, as well as to determine what we shall do. . . . The principle of utility recognizes this subjection [and social reformers who try to set up social systems on any other basis] deal in sounds instead of sense, in caprice instead of reason, in darkness instead of light.†

In his *Wealth of Nations*, Smith saw competition as the invisible and beneficial hand guiding and directing prices and output in free markets. The

---

*Patterson, *Readings*, p. 10.
†Ibid., p. 179.

invisible hand was the foundation of his political philosophy *laissez faire,* French for letting things alone, for letting people do as they please with a minimum of government control.

SMITHIAN MICROECONOMICS AND MACROECONOMICS

Smith was a genius in tying loose strings together to explain how free markets work, documenting his research in great depth beyond anything ever done before. His microeconomic analysis of free markets explained what goods were produced, at what prices, and in what amounts. Economists call this *resource allocation theory,* or how resources like land, labor, and capital are put to work to make the goods people want. Smith's macroeconomic theories centered on the savings-investment process in free markets, and how that produced wealth for consumers.

If you will pardon my analogy, you need to step back and use a telescope rather than a microscope to view the vast forces influencing total income, total production, total employment, and the potential for national economic progress. You need a macroeconomic telescope. So, let's peer through the Smithian macroeconomic telescope to spot this economic colossus on the horizon:

6 – STANDARD OF LIVING (WEALTH)
5 – PRODUCTION
4 – PRODUCTIVITY
3 – CAPITAL
2 – SAVINGS
1 – PROFITS AND INTEREST

The six economic building blocks sit one on top of the other. The thrust of Smith's argument was that (1) profits and interest, the key returns to capitalists, would attract (2) savings; which would be invested in (3) capital, that is, plant and equipment and new technology; which would increase (4) productivity, or output per hour; which would lift (5) total production, or output; which would create (6) a higher standard of living and increased wealth for society.

What happens should you kick out the bottom block? According to Smith and other free-market economists, the whole economic colossus could come crashing down. That's why they emphasize that the rewards of profits and interest are absolutely essential in attracting savings, and in motivating investors to forgo current consumption so that real savings can be channeled voluntarily into capital growth.

Take a closer look at "capital," the third building block. Capitalistic production is sometimes called "indirect" or "roundabout" production. That is, instead of producing consumer goods directly and immediately, efforts are directed first to production of the means of production, or capital. Real capital means plant, equipment, machinery, and tools. Financial capital involves money, the circulation of money, and a vast array of financial contracts. A vast and controversial literature exists on the role of financial capital. Not so for real capital! Economists, whatever their political persuasion, have no argument over the astonishing power of real capital in raising the productivity and wealth of society. This is not an issue anywhere.

Let's illustrate the point. Consider my oversimplified fish story, Robinson Crusoe style. You could, of course, catch fish with your hands, without the use of fishing poles, hooks, nets, or boats. That would be a case of direct production. If you first were to take the time and the effort to make fishing tools, that would be a case of indirect, capitalistic production. It doesn't take much imagination to see that indirect or capitalistic production can vastly multiply your catch. No matter, then, what type of economic system you have in mind, there is no argument over the colossal advantage of capitalistic production in a technical sense over direct production. That's not an issue. Economists of all varieties make it clear that nobody other than back-to-nature quacks would oppose capitalistic production and the accompanying division of labor. Who do you guess penned this monumental tribute to capitalism?:

> Capitalism, during its rule of scarce one hundred years, has created more colossal productive forces than have all preceding generations together. Subjection of Nature's forces to man, machinery, application of chemistry to industry and agriculture, steam-navigation, railways, electric telegraphs, clearing of whole continents for cultivation, canalization of rivers, whole populations conjured out of the ground—what earlier century had even a presentiment that such productive forces slumbered.*

Was that Adam Smith? William F. Buckley, Jr.? No, guess again. That is a direct quote from *The Communist Manifesto,* which Marx in collaboration with Friedrich Engels wrote in 1847.

The World's Great Thinkers, The Political Philosophers (New York: Random House, 1947), p. 493.

Economists: Their Debasement of Science on Income Theory

So, just what do economists argue about? It's certainly not over the technical efficiency of capitalistic production and the division of labor. They're matters best left to the engineers, the inventors, the physical scientists. No, the arguments center instead on the forces that (a) motivate economic man to work, save, and invest, and (b) how man should be rewarded for his efforts. That's where the big arguments come. That's where the ideological quarreling takes place on all sides and in all centuries.

It's easy to see why economists would agree to disagree with their fellow economists who hold opposing political views. But even economists of identical political persuasion can find no basis for agreement when it comes to a theory of who is supposed to get what, how much, and why. Instead they fabricate the silliest and most intellectually insulting pap imaginable on how the income pie should be divided up. To compound the internecine warfare among economists on income theory, they have the unmitigated gall to defend their views in the name of science. They bastardize scientific method in the name of economic science.

Economists have no theory of income supported by science. To see why, let's review their pet views one by one with the help of a simple arithmetic example. We'll modify and qualify as we proceed to more complex economic models. Just suppose that you and Lou and Ned go fishing, Robinson Crusoe style. Suppose that (a) all three of you can catch 15 fish a day with your hands, or 5 each, (b) that all three of you working as a team can catch 50 a day with the canoe Lou built, and (c) 200 a day with Lou's canoe plus the net that Ned made. Assume you have no capital tools. Here are the production possibilities:

	TOTAL FISH	ADDITIONAL FISH (Marginal Product)
Direct Production	15 (5 each)	
Capitalistic Production		
Labor + Canoe	50	+ 35 (50 – 15)
Labor + Canoe + Net	200	+ 185 (200 – 15)

You can see that direct production amounts to only 15 fish, and capitalistic production 200 fish, or 185 additional fish. Economists call the 185 extra fish produced with the help of Lou's canoe and Ned's net the *marginal product of capital,* assuming labor is fixed at three men in our example. Now here's my question: How can science help us to divide the incremental catch of 185 fish among Lou, Ned, and you?

Think about that a minute before you read on. Meanwhile, let's sketch the answers economists offer, and you can then compare them with your own. Consider these four arguments on income distribution, the first three from the free-market West, and the fourth from the Marxian East, along with my critical comments on the problems involved.

THE FREE-MARKET MARGINAL PRODUCTIVITY THEORIST

The Argument

Any fool can see that the extra 185 fish belong to capital. Lou should get 35 of that for his canoe, and Ned 150 of that for his net. You get nothing extra.

The Problem

Economists have no way to calculate how much of the additional output can be identified as being produced by any one specific unit of input of labor or capital. Now and then they argue they do, about as regularly as locusts plague the land. The American economist John Bates Clarke is a recent example. He developed the concept *specific marginal productivities* of capital and labor, but no scientists take him seriously today (other than a few preacher economists). The problem, the unsolvable problem, lies in the impossibility of imputation. Science provides us with no basis for dividing up additional output in accordance with the specific contributions of each of the factors of production, land, labor, materials, and real and financial capital. We cannot specifically impute. We cannot measure or justify scientifically just what you, Lou, and Ned contributed to that additional 185 fish.

THE FREE-MARKET COMPARATIVE DISUTILITY THEORIST

The Argument

You have to add up the disutils, or units of pain, that you, Lou, and Ned incurred as labor. Since you all experienced comparable pain as labor, we can assign the same number of disutils. But Lou and Ned, not you, experienced additional pain in building the canoe and net. Their pain took two forms. First, it was hard and disagreeable work. Second, they went without eating the fish they could have caught had they not spent the same time and effort building capital tools. So, both the hard work and the sacrifice of voluntarily forego-ing current consumption of fish add up to a lot of disutils, a lot of pain, and a lot of fish. So, the solution is simple: Add up the total disutils involved for you as labor, and for Lou and Ned as labor and as suppliers of capital, then divide up the fish in proportion to the total disutils assigned each person.

The Problem

Psychologists fall over in laughter on this one. They point out that economists have no measures of utils (units of satisfaction) or disutils (units of dissatis-faction). They make it clear that economists cannot add up things they can't even measure. We reached that conclusion, you may recall, in our discussion of the inability of economists to measure demand and supply (chapter 9). Worse, economists have absolutely no way of making interpersonal compar-isons of disutility. They make believe they do, though, in their carefully con-structed charts of "indifference curves."

Indifference curves represent the height of sterility in economic science. How much pain does a clerk experience, for example, in his eight hours of sort-ing mail as compared with the writer who spends eight hours just to complete a small part of one essay? How many disutils does a ditch digger incur as against the disutils suffered by the bond holder who has provided his capital to others, who must wait for a future reward in interest and return of principal, and who must assume the risk of never getting anything back? Have you any scientific measures for such interpersonal comparisons of pain? If so, would you make any modifications for those who bought their bonds from the money they made as workers as compared with those who inherited the bonds from a rich uncle? Have you some ideas here? I don't. Adding up disutils doesn't help at all.

THE FREE-MARKET TOTAL FACTOR PRODUCTIVITY THEORIST

The Argument

Just add up (a) the wear and tear (depreciation) of capital that is covered by revenues, which represents the return of invested capital plus (b) the net earnings and interest that accrue to investors. Call that the capital input, measured in dollars, for any given production. Now add up the dollars of wages and salaries paid to labor in producing that same production. Call that the labor input. Now add the capital and labor input together, and call that total factor product. Labor is paid what labor produces, and it produces what it's paid. Capital is paid what it produces, and it produces what it's paid. It's that simple.

The Problem

Sounds like a circle to me. What you produce is what you are paid and what you are paid is what you produce.

THE MARXIST LABOR-VALUE THEORIST

The Argument

Let Marx speak for himself:

> The general formula of capital is $M - C - M'$. In other words, a certain quantity of values is thrown into circulation for the purpose of drawing a larger quantity from it.*

Let me try the impossible, that is, to explain in just two paragraphs the essence of *Capital,* which totaled 1048 pages for volume 3 alone. Here we go:

Marx identifies M as the money capitalists spend to buy real capital, that is, the machinery, plant, and materials used to produce final products, and the labor necessary for production. He then traces what he called the "circulation of capital," meaning the circulation of money capital C from the purchase of real capital, through production, to sale of the finished goods. What do you know? At the end of the $M - C - M'$ trail, capitalists end up with more money capital than they started with, or M'. Marx called the extra money surplus value or profits for the economy at large, defined here as M' less M. The question, which so troubled classical economists, remained: Where did this surplus value come from?

A big mystery was involved here. Marx and others contended that the value of products was determined by the average labor time spent in their pro-

---

* *Capital,* Volume III, C. H. Keer & Co., p. 53.

duction. So, the puzzle went, how could you explain surplus value or profits if in fact the equilibrium value of goods exchanged in the market place had to be priced in strict accordance with the average labor time involved in their production? How could you get surplus value out of a product if its total value was explained 100 percent by its labor input? How could you get something more? You probably know the answer Marx gave to this riddle. He said that labor produced more value than it was paid. He argued that capitalists extracted the difference, the surplus value, out of the hides of labor. Moreover, Marx declared, all capital was "congealed labor," for labor was responsible for the production of all the means of production. Capitalists exploited labor, so Marx fumed.

The Problem

Assuming capitalism or socialism or any other type of political economy, we are still back where we started. We still haven't solved in any scientific way just how those extra 185 fish produced with capital and labor should be divided up between you, and Lou with his canoe, and Ned with his net. The introduction of money and money capital does not change the basic problem one bit. Why is that? You know by now:

When income distribution theory marches in, science marches out.

That's true for all political economies. We are left instead with ideological screaming over justice, equity, and ethics. Note that we didn't have to quote a single psychologist in our criticisms of income distribution theory. No, common sense tells you that economists have no sound theory of income distribution supported by science. Whenever, then, you hear an economist talk about how income should be divided up with any precision, or how much such and such income should be taxed, make sure you understand that he has left the economic terrain, and has entered the realm of ethics. He has shifted without telling you from objective scientist to preacher.

SCIENTISTS (AND JOHN AND JANE DOE) VERSUS WARRING ECONOMISTS

Like preachers from competing religions, economists have become infamous for warring with one another. They have gotten away with murderously illegitimate arguments in the name of science, which John and Jane Doe have suspected all along. Lay my fellow witch doctors end-to-end, the public jokes, and they still can't reach agreement.

What's odd, though, is that I could not find in the literature another professional economist who has faulted his colleagues as preachers. Whether on the political left or right or in the middle, economists marched through history mainly as preachers, not objective scientists. To see what I mean, let's turn now to find out why competing scientists view professional economists with such disdain.

25

Scientists on Economic Man

Their Disdain for Economist Preachers

> Psychological hedonism [is] the simple and naive view, so
> popular in the nineteenth century, [that] man always seeks
> to achieve pleasure and avoid pain. Under the influence of
> the [ascetic] motives [man] might just as truthfully be
> called a pain-seeking as a pleasure-seeking animal.
>
> J. C. Flugel, *Man, Morals and Society* (1945)*

> The flapping of a butterfly's wings in Hong Kong could
> explain tornadoes in Kansas City.
>
> James Gleick, *Chaos* (1988)†

Is chaos theory linked with the theory of ascetic man? Yes, on two counts.
First, both views mesh in that they reject the notions of preacher economists
who would have us believe that man's nature is fixed, as though set in hedonistic concrete. Not so, say professional psychologists, natural historians, bi-
ologists, and anthropologists, among other scientists. As a corollary, chaos
theorists are wary of traditional economic theorists and their harmonious
models. Second, they are as worried about man's fired-up ascetic dove as they
are his hedonistic wolf. I'm especially fearful of what I dub "warring ascetics"
in a high-tech world of mass destruction.

---

*New York: International University Press, pp. 88, 93, 94.
†New York: Penguin Books, p. 8.

MATHEMATICIANS AND "CHAOS" THEORISTS ON ECONOMIC MAN

One thing is certain, we must try to decode economic man because that could help immensely in appraising traditional economic theory. With that in mind, let's turn first to chaos theory because it shatters in many respects the assumptions underlying economic man. Chaos theory takes nothing for granted, including the equilibrium and harmony imbedded in traditional economic models. It brings into question the very notion of man as a special creature in the universe. It questions the very idea of human progress as it sheds new light on the prospects for economic man.

Let's begin our analysis with the "butterfly effect" in chaos theory. The idea, as stated by James Gleick, is that the flapping of a butterfly's wings in Hong Kong could produce tornadoes in Kansas City.* Sound far-fetched? Well, chaos theory, or nonlinear dynamics, has intrigued scientists for years. The physical scientists believe they have found chaos just about everywhere. That includes the motion of fluids, the expansion of gasses, the interplay of hydrogen atoms, and vibrating metal strips that suddenly and explosively break in two. Some scientists believe the planets are chaotic. A few scientists think they may have detected elements of chaos in panics, manias, booms, busts, crises, financial crashes, and in the bandwagon effects of the kind I have described.

Just what are the mathematicians saying? They cite two criteria underlying chaotic behavior. The first is that the time path of chaotic behavior is extremely sensitive to the starting point of an initial value (like the stirring of the air from our butterfly). The second is that a chaotic series is "deterministic," not "random." In conflict with the popular meaning of chaotic, they maintain that with any given initial value of a chaotic time series, they can calculate all subsequent values. Edgar Allan Poe said as much long ago:

> We moved our hands ... and gave vibration to the atmosphere. This vibration was indefinitely extended, till it gave impulse to every particle of the earth's air, which thenceforward, and forever, was actuated by the one movement of the hand. [Thus] it became easy to determine in what precise period an impulse of given extent would engirdle the orb.†

---

*Gleick, *Chaos*, p. 8.
†*The Power of Words* (New York: W. J. Black Co., 1927), p. 257.

A TEST FOR IDENTIFYING CHAOS

Scientists, then, say that *if* you can specify precisely the initial value of a chaotic series, you can use an exact mathematical formula to predict all subsequent values. Fascinating! The problem, though, lies in that little word *if.* Who can identify precise starting points? In asking that question, I am reminded of the poet Robert Frost, who said he knew nothing of beginnings and ends. (I'm not sure we know much about the middles, either.) Relevant to all this, let me ask whether you can distinguish between a random variable, one whose values cannot be known with certainty, and a chaotic variable, one whose values can be predicted with complete certainty. Want to try? Then please glance (better, study) the two charts in Exhibit 25–1, which I have taken from the research of the Federal Reserve Bank of St. Louis.* Which one is chaotic?

You can't tell? Neither could I. The variable in the first chart (a) is chaotic; (b) is random. That's the trouble. Indeed, I doubt that we shall ever know the exact beginnings of anything that, according to chaos theory, is necessary for precision in forecasting. Moreover, even if we could precisely define beginnings, intervening events could be expected to alter or even reverse the course of events. A tornado could deflect or even kill Gleick's butterfly. Still, chaos theory is bound to have a profound impact on economic theory. At the very least, chaos theory compels us to question economists who arrive at opposite conclusions from one and the same model. For one example, Smith sees harmony but Marx detects hell in the competitive model. What's the mix of ideology versus science in their views?

As we have seen, the classical economists saw the forces operating in free markets as equilibrating, orderly, and conducive to augmenting the wealth of society. Western economists and neoclassicists argued the same way, as did Smithian economists. Today the neomonetarists, the supply-siders, the expectation theorists, the all-so-efficient theorists of investment markets, and the modern corporate financial theorists following Modigliani and Miller still argue that you find freedom, growth, wealth, and human progress in their models. They do so in the face of a succession of crises and catastrophes running through two world wars; the Great Depression of the 1930s, ethnic and religious fighting; the Holocaust in Germany, recurrent violent booms and recessions in the post-World War II period; deepening poverty and high unemployment throughout Eastern Europe; and rising statistics on rape, murder, and even genocide.

Review (March/April 1990).

But even when equilibrating forces appeared not to work as described, traditional theorists have refused to abandon their models. To explain away "aberrations" in the data, they would insist that either the data were in error, or that we had but to remove statistically the "noise" or "friction" from the data. They have long held to these views despite devastating attacks on classical doctrine by Keynes, who would modify capitalism to save it, and Marx, who would scrap capitalism as being evil, and not worth saving. So, is "noise" in the data an exception to the rule? That's not plausible, say the new chaos theorists, because "exceptions" and "aberrations" came much too often to be dismissed on grounds of faulty data.

Even a few economists, far too few, have swung to that view. They think they may have found chaos in the wild and inexplicable patterns that crop up in commodity prices, exchange rates, stock prices, interest rates, and in the money supply data. One of my colleagues at Pace University, Maurice Larrain, believes he has uncovered chaos in Moody's yields on AA corporate bonds.*

What about chaos among economists? Their consensus forecasts are notoriously more volatile than the data they investigate. Like schools of fish, economists make sharp turns or reverse direction in a fraction of a second, leaving the observer to wonder what goes on. Investors, it is often said, run wild like herds of buffalo. It should come as no surprise, then, that economists like to swim together, like schools of dazed and frightened fish. Pressure and insecurity keep them swimming together. Is it any wonder I keep warning you of consensus economic forecasts, including those of the Blue Chips (see Appendix A and chapter 5).

CHAOS ON WALL STREET?

Can you find chaos on Wall Street? Well, by our own definition of chaos, I cannot know for certain whether I have come across chaotic series or not as a Wall Street economist. I have no way of measuring or detecting the precise beginnings of anything. Even so, I have observed stress and disorder that has often become cumulative and self-reinforcing in major Wall Street firms, often ending in the death of the firm. I have witnessed violent, abrupt, and unpredictable behavior of investors running wild as a herd in the New York and Tokyo stock markets. I have seen instant, abrupt, and wide jumps in foreign exchange and fixed-income prices that have little to do with the smooth equilibrating adjustments incorporated in the models of traditional theorists. What

*Larrain and Pagano, "Nonlinear Dynamics and the Chaotic Behavior of Interest Rates," *Financial Analysts Journal* (September-October 1991).

about chaos among authorities in power? I have tracked closely for over twenty-five years how authorities in power, especially world central bankers, employed the very worst of procyclical policies that just skirted pushing the economy into outright depression between 1973 and 1975 and again in 1981–82. What I have seen firsthand has little to do with the heavenly economic models my fellow economists preach to the world.

BUTTERFLIES: A LINK TO NOBEL PRIZE WINNERS?

I do believe I encountered two chaotic butterflies with Nobel prizes in economics. I mean Franco Modigliani and Merton Miller (see chapters 20 and 21). I argued at length that their view of the cost of corporate capital, one supposedly independent of leverage, found no support in the data. Worse, the arbitrage "proof" they set forth was fatally flawed for the simple reason that it was illogical. Yet the mass of Parrots and Pros in academe and in the applied world of finance bought, sold, and eulogized MM corporate nonsense theory. They still do. But wait! What does bad corporate financial theory have to do with chaos theory? Well, how would you answer this question:

> Would anybody be so rash as to cite the writings of two confused economists in 1958 as the causal spark to the financial tornadoes that swept through the fixed-income markets for junk and trash three decades later?

What about that? Well, I know somebody who might answer yes if he were alive today. I mean George Herbert (1593–1633). Herbert anticipated modern chaos theory by over three centuries. Maybe you have seen his ditty on a butterfly. Pardon, I meant a horse:

> For want of a nail, the shoe was lost;
> For want of a shoe, the horse was lost;
> For want of a horse, the rider was lost;
> For want of a rider, the battle was lost;
> For want of a battle, the kingdom was lost!

PSYCHOLOGISTS ON ECONOMIC MAN

We'll return to chaos theorists in the next chapter, but suffice it to say here that these theories regard the arguments on what makes up economic man as pointless, a waste of time. David Hume, you'll recall, characterized such arguments "a vulgar exercise" (see chapter 3). Even so, we must review the ideas of objective scientists on economic man if for no other reason than to contrast their work with the sloppy work of my fellow preacher economists.

Economic Man as the Ascetic Man?

Just what is meant by the ascetic man? The dictionary defines ascetic man as the self-sacrificing man, one who denies himself the usual pleasures of life for the good of others. That's a 180 degree turn from that of the hedonist, the selfish tag economists put on economic man. Who is correct? Well, Flugel—whom we quoted at the beginning of this chapter—and other psychologists document countless examples across a broad spectrum of society to support their views. Their list includes pain-seeking researchers, doctors, nurses, lawyers, educators, athletes, ministers, soldiers, rulers, writers, explorers, revolutionaries, politicians, and businessmen, among many others. I suspect that even a few economists might one day be included in this long list of self-sacrificing, self-denying, pleasure-avoiding, do-gooder ascetics.

Psychologists argue their case from the history of man, and from psychoanalytical research and experiment. Most important, they insist they can find no scientific evidence supporting the economist's notion of a fixed, unchangeable, and innately selfish human being. Psychologist Erich Fromm has been the most direct. Consider this stinging barb from *The Anatomy of Human Destructiveness*:

> The assumption of a fixed human nature . . . has so often been abused as a shield behind which the most inhuman acts are committed. In the name of human nature, for example, Aristotle and most thinkers up to the eighteenth century defended slavery. Or in order to prove the rationality and the necessity of the capitalist form of society, scholars have tried to make a case for acquisitiveness, competitiveness, and selfishness as innate human traits.*

THE ABUSE OF POSITIVE VERSUS NORMATIVE ECONOMICS

Economists have another defense for their views on the selfish fiend they say is permanently built into the human being. They tell us that they deal in *positive economics*—how economies is actually conducted. They tell us to distinguish

---

* (New York: Holt, Rinehart and Winston, 1973), p. 219.

this from *normative economics*—what economics ought to be. Pick up any modern text in economics, and you will find this distinction hammered away. They infer from all this that they are strictly scientific. "We'll leave the normative economics, the ethics, to you," they seem to say. "Don't mix up one with the other," they solemnly caution. "We just describe what we see," they proclaim.

Nonsense! Economists, whether consciously or unconsciously, put ethics directly into the models they build. The extreme free-market economists are a case in point with their innately selfish *economic man*. When it comes to income distribution theory, economists of all persuasions have their private ethical agenda, whether they be classical, neoclassical, Marxian, Keynesian, neo-Keynesian, monetarist, or supply-sider. You name it. They all bastardize science in the name of ethics (see chapter 24).

Whether on the left or the right, professional economists hold the strangest notions about eternal and fixed natural laws. As a case in point, note here the American philosopher John Dewey's devastating attack on Marx's notion of class conflict as natural law:

> Marx reached the conclusion that all social development comes from conflict between classes, and that class warfare is to be cultivated. Hence a supposedly scientific form of the doctrine of social evolution preaches social hostility as the road to social harmony. It would be difficult to find a more striking instance of what happens when natural events are given a social and practical sanctification.*

Taking my cue from Dewey's assault on Marx, and using Dewey's very words, I could turn natural law against Father Adam Smith himself. I could write:

> *Smith reached the conclusion that economic harmony for society as a whole comes from competition among individuals, and that competition is to be cultivated. Hence a supposedly scientific form of the doctrine of social evolution preaches individual selfishness as the road to social harmony. It would be difficult to find a more striking instance of what happens when natural events are given a social and practical sanctification.*

I doubt that Dewey, who writes of "the exaggeration of harmony attributed to nature," would have objected to my restatement. On the contrary, I believe that Dewey would have shouted out loud that whenever natural law enters into argument over political and social systems, the disputants are forced into interminable and sterile debate. Put it this way:

---

*John Dewey, *Morals and Conduct*, reproduced in *The World's Great Thinkers, Man and Man: The Social Philosophers* (New York: Random House, 1947), p. 465.

When the *LAW OF NATURE* walks into economic and ethical controversy, science walks out.

Naturalists on Economic Man

Who are the most influential of all scientists in explaining the nature of economic man? They are, I would most certainly argue, those versed in natural history, the naturalists. Let's proceed with our inquiry, then, with the best of the lot, Charles Darwin. Consider here Darwin's words in *The Descent of Man*:

> The more important elements [of man] are love, and the distinct emotion of sympathy. The fact that man is the one being who certainly deserves this designation, is the greatest of all distinctions between him and the lower animals.*

Love and sympathy? Yes, Darwin used these two words to describe the chief attributes of man. That hardly sounds hedonistic. What about man's allegedly fixed nature? Darwin's answer is his "main conclusion":

> The main conclusion arrived at in this work, namely, that man is descended from some lowly organized form, will, I regret to think, be highly distasteful to many.†

That will go down as the understatement of all time. Man's nature is not fixed but forever changing! From what I can see, warring economists beset and bedeviled by submerged ideological convictions, have yet to incorporate Darwin's *positive* outlook on man into their own thinking. Instead, they have misinterpreted and bastardized Darwin. They took "survival of the fittest" to mean an innately selfish man. Darwin reached no such conclusion (it was Spencer, not Darwin, who coined the phrase). Just as was the case a century ago under unbridled hedonistic theory, professional economists and religious zealots twist beyond all recognition Darwinian science on the nature of man. Anthropologist Ernest Becker put it precisely in *The Structure of Evil*:

> To use simple hedonism [for] deductive prediction was bound to err because it was based on the shallowest understanding of the complexity of human behavior.‡

Five years after Becker published *The Structure of Evil* he produced his masterwork *The Denial of Death*. Becker concluded that the absolute cer-

---

* (New York: W. W. Norton & Company, 1979), p. 200.
†Ibid., p. 208.
‡(New York: George Braziller 1968), p. 37.

tainty of death was a mainspring of human motivation, a positive force for progress:

> The idea of death, the fear of it, haunts the human animal like nothing else; it is a mainspring of human activity—activity designed largely to avoid the finality of death, to overcome it, by denying in some way that it is the final destiny of man.*

A mainspring? Yes, a noble mainspring for most of society, argues Becker. This places us in a paradox. On the one hand, says Becker, man is narcissistic. Man's love for himself, often above all else, cannot be argued away. Relevant here, Becker cites Aristotle's quip that luck is when the guy next to you gets hit with the arrow. That's self-love, hedonism, narcissism. Call it what you will, this self-directed love of man for himself is understandable; man is determined to survive. On the other hand, writes Becker, man is heroic. He wants to be a hero for society even at the cost of his life. Consider this from Becker's *Denial*:

> We mentioned the meaner side [narcissism], but there is obviously the noble side of man as well. Man will lay down his life for his country, his society, his family. He will choose to throw himself on a grenade to save his comrades; he is capable of the highest generosity and self-sacrifice. But he has to feel and believe that what he is doing is truly heroic.†

So, Becker the anthropologist and Flugel the psychologist see eye-to-eye. Their views could be coupled into one sentence:

> Man is also the ascetic, the pain seeker, who strives to be a hero for society.

NOVELISTS AND SONG WRITERS ON ECONOMIC MAN

Who's your hero in man's ceaseless combat with evil? I have my favorites. One is the protagonist Jean Valjean in Victor Hugo's *Les Misérables,* whom the police imprisoned and hounded until his death for the crime of stealing bread to feed his family. Another is Billy Bigelow, the barker for a carousel, who met death in his attempt to steal money for "his little girl." Recently I

---

*(New York: The Free Press, 1973), p. ix.
†Ibid.

bought the tape for Rogers and Hammerstein's musical *Carousel,* which I had seen many years before. The salesman (S) caught me off guard:

S: *Carousel* is a magnificent musical. But it didn't do that well on Broadway. *Oklahoma,* though, was a smash hit for Rogers and Hammerstein. We have that, too.

RH: What was the problem with *Carousel*?

S: People burst into tears. If you saw *Carousel* and didn't cry, you weren't human. The word got around.

I later listened to the tape, over and over again. Here is the part the salesman had in mind, when Billy learned his wife was pregnant. Billy had no money. He becomes angry, desperate about how to support his "little girl":

> You can have fun with a son,
> But you've gotta be a father to a girl. . . .
> She's gotta be sheltered and fed and dressed
> in the best that money can buy.
> I never knew how to get money,
> but I'll try, I'll try, I'll try.
> I'll go out and make it,
> or steal it, or take it . . . or die.

Billions of Jean Valjeans and Billy Bigelows populate this earth, but you would never know that by squinting through the unsympathetic lenses of economists. Perhaps economists should be required to read *Les Misérables* and listen to *Carousel.* They might also consider how pressure and insecurity are in constant battle with the ascetic and self-sacrificing side of man. Indeed, economists could incorporate Billy Bigelow into their pleasure-pain utility models and indifference curves. It would make a giant difference for the better. Some day economists might even learn to cry.

If many religious leaders treat adults like children with the promise of candy in Heaven or the threat of a whipping in Hell, so do the economists who preach hedonism as the all-motivating force of man. That's not what Charles Darwin, Ernest Becker, Erich Fromm, Victor Hugo, Rogers and Hammerstein, or even many businessmen tell us about economic man. No, they are just as likely to describe economic man as more cooperative than ruthless, more interested in insuring long-run profits by building trust and confidence in others than in deceiving others. They do not, unlike economists of centuries past, appeal to the base side of man.

In pointing up the mainsprings of human motivation—sacrifice, love, sympathy, cooperation, and the *excitement* of tireless research and discovery—our scientists and poets help us to make life worth living. I have highlighted *excitement*. That's my way of paying tribute to bacteriologist Hans Zinsser, who so beautifully though unintentionally documented the thrill of discovery as a powerful force in man.* Zinsser makes mincemeat of the economists' hedonistic models loaded with utils, disutils, and indifference curves.

The Future of Economic Man

So, what do we conclude from these violently conflicting perceptions on economic man? Does harmonious economic theory in fact conflict with chaos theory? I'll summarize my findings in the concluding chapter, borrowing heavily from my experience as a Wall Street economist. I'll also make a tentative projection of economic man, leaning a bit on the new chaos theory.

*Hans Zinsser, *Rats, Lice and History* (Boston: Little, Brown, and Company, 1936), p. 12.

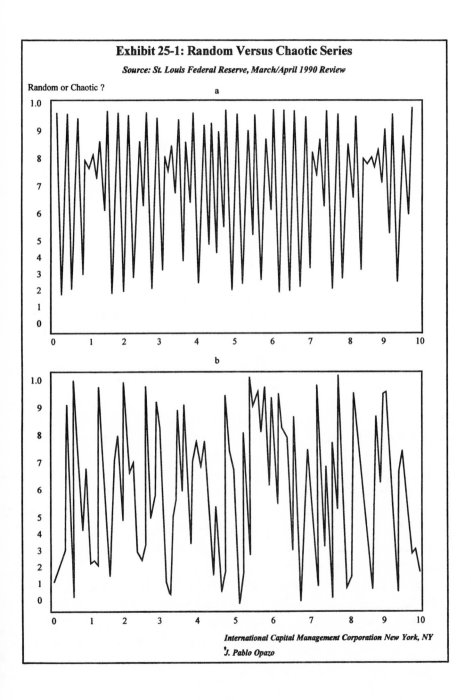

Exhibit 25-1: Random Versus Chaotic Series

Source: St. Louis Federal Reserve, March/April 1990 Review

Random or Chaotic ?

International Capital Management Corporation New York, NY

J. Pablo Opazo

26

The Nature of Economic Man

> Neoclassicists each year expose millions of high school
> and college students to a paradigm (a theory, one that
> teaches selfishness as efficiency). . . . The more people ac-
> cept the neoclassical paradigm as a guide for behavior, the
> more the ability to sustain a market economy is under-
> mined.
>
> Amitai Etzioni, *The Moral Dimension:*
> *Towards a New Economics* (1988)*

Is Etzioni correct? Do economists really undermine society by teaching selfishness as a virtue? Is selfishness itself a threat to the very existence of a free-
market system? I don't have any certain answers. I do know, however, that
science offers precious little support to the view that man is overwhelmingly
selfish or hedonistic. The stereotyped view of man as hedonist hardly debases
him, but it does degrade the economists who have preached such ethical drivel in the name of science during the past three centuries. Economists could
have better spent their time, as did the competing physical and social scientists, in seriously investigating the nature of man.

Even so, are we back where we started? Are we any closer to finding out
just what is the dominant force in man? I believe so, though I doubt we shall
ever know how to weight with any precision our hedonistic as against our ascetic components. That's not the important issue. I'll try my best in this final

---

*New York: The Free Press, pp. 249–50.

chapter to make clear just what the critical issues are with the help of that master teacher and writer Rudolf Flesch and his work *The Art of Clear Thinking.**
Flesch's five-point research outline consisting of the issue or question, existing thinking, thesis, methodology, and conclusions should force me to be brief and stick to the subject.

1. The Question

What is the nature of economic man?

2. Existing Thinking (Review of the Literature)

Just about everybody, it seems, has his pet views. At one extreme, the free-market economists warn against the fallacy of composition in the analysis of economic man. What is true for the part, or the alleged innate selfishness of the individual, is not true for the whole, that is, economic progress, benevolence, and national harmony under competitive capitalism. So they preach. At the other extreme, Marxists contend that what is true for the part, individual selfishness under capitalism, begets a horror story for the whole, or domestic conflict, exploitation, and international war. So they evangelize.

The social and physical scientists other than economists reject both extremes. Man, they argue, is more ascetic than selfish. They believe (hope?) that his ascetic and heroic drives will dominate man's selfish drives. So they contend. Are they correct? Well, that's precisely the most fundamental of questions.

The arguments on economic man go back and forth, round and round. The tracts written over the centuries on the subject now fill our libraries to overflowing. I'm aghast, however, that despite the prodigious quantity of research on the ethical behavior of man, so little of it succeeds in integrating one discipline with another. Becker said it best in his *Denial*: "Knowledge [on the nature of man] is in a state of useless overproduction [and] strewn all over the place, spoken in a thousand competitive voices. Its insignificant fragments are magnified all out of proportion, while its major . . . insights lie around begging for attention."†

---

*(New York, Harper & Row, 1951).
†*Denial,* p. x.

3. The Thesis of This Book

Don't look to economists for straight answers on the nature of economic man. They're wrong in preaching that man is innately and overwhelmingly and permanently selfish. No reputable scientist argues that way. While mainly ignoring the ascetic side of man, which shall shortly command our attention, my fellow economists with very few exceptions have erred in yet another way. They have paid far too little attention to the fear and insecurity that bedevil us. They have neglected the roles of pressure, insecurity, and selfishness *acting as a team* on economic behavior. On that count alone, economists must be faulted for their silly arguments that individual vice produces group paradise, that selfishness begets harmony, that self-love is a virtue. That's economic evangelism. The real story lies in what happens when pressure and insecurity gain control of the individual. In that Jekyll and Hyde metamorphosis, self-interest shows up as selfishness. Deception then rules, deliberate and unconscious, putting all of society at risk.

4. Methodology and Supporting Evidence

I'll note first the evidence on Jekyll-Hyde behavior from my own observations as a Wall Street economist. In chapters 1 through 3, I introduced you to Wall Street's branch managers drunk with rage, investment bankers hell-bent on deception, and executives at the highest level who pressured their chief economics spokesmen to shade, to distort the truth for money, to prostitute their very minds. Their goal first and foremost was to generate commission dollars and related fees. In chapters 4 through 6, we encountered Wall Street's counterparts in Washington D.C., the authorities in power who never admit mistakes of theory or policy, who waltz together in a grand dance of deception.

In chapters 7 through 10 we met the Wealth-Without-Risk Hucksters and Pros, who made fortunes at your expense even as the regulatory authorities imitated Ostriches, each debasing man in his own way. In chapters 11 through 14, we ran into both professional economists and monetary and fiscal quacks, all of whom put ideology over science, and bastardized science for money or heroic status. In chapters 15 through 17 we investigated the role of money managers in bubbles at home and abroad. We found hard evidence of the violent conflict between the harmonious and equilibrating theories of economists, on the one hand, and widespread delusion and deception, on the other, all of which can be taken as a tentative and preliminary support for chaos theory.

In chapters 18 through 21, we came across the very worst of corporate financial theory, which served as a catalyst for junk-bond hucksters and cash-flow scavengers running wild on Wall Street. We learned that theory in the highest citadels of academe stood in violent conflict with any rational notion of economic man, and that Wall Street practitioners used and abused theory and data for their own selfish and despicable ends. The "butterfly" lagged effects, especially in corporate finance, also suggested touches of chaos in the data as economic man joined in the frenzy of rampaging bulls and bears and Parrots and Pros and Ostriches.

In chapters 22 and 23, we presented evidence, both sickening and pervasive, on how influential corporate executives, government officials, and Wall Street's finest distorted and deceived in the name of protectionism even as they wrapped themselves as super-patriots inside the American flag, all the time preaching the wonders of open competition.

In chapters 24 and 25 we vented our wrath on professional economists, on both the political left and right. They proved themselves to be mainly preachers, not objective scientists, in investigating the nature of economic man. They have defaulted to the psychologists; the natural scientists, especially the anthropologists and those versed in natural history; and the physical scientists, especially the mathematicians now investigating chaos theory. Professional economists, we contended, must be counted among the most influential of intellectual Pros, uniquely trained to talk you down and out with their mastery of data, theory, and crooked argument wrapped in unintelligible, formula-laden jargon. Most important, professional economists fight an internecine war. Their often submerged but opposing ideologies dominate their thinking and pervert their science.

There are exceptions to every rule, as witnessed by the respected and honorable economists we have met along the way. Even so, the general rule is to be skeptical of anything and everything economists may say. Always ask yourself what the economist is selling. That includes being skeptical of this economist, for I may be weighted down by repressed biases or exaggerated sympathies that are unknown to me.

EVIDENCE FROM COMPETING SOCIAL AND PHYSICAL SCIENCES

Let me ask what social science should win first prize for overspecialization, isolation from other scientific disciplines, and useless overproduction. You know my answer by now: economics. What tragic irony! How ironic that the economist has fallen victim to specialization. Like Mary Shelley's *Frankenstein* (1817), the economist stands threatened by his own creation. That's my conclusion, one shared in large measure by scientists outside the discipline of economics who have seriously investigated man's economic nature.

On that count, economists would do well to study Sissela Bok's *Lying: Moral Choice in Public and Private Lives* (1978). This Harvard psychologist comes down hard on economists. Indeed, Dr. Bok should be on the required reading list for anybody professing to be an economist, or a professor of ethics, a broker on Wall Street, or even a barker for a carousel. While we're at it, put on the same list Becker's *Denial of Death* (1975), Darwin's *Descent of Man,* Dewey's *Morals and Conduct,* Etzioni's *Moral Dimension,* Flugel's *Morals and Society,* and Fromm's *Anatomy of Human Destructiveness.* Economists in particular, pay heed! Society could benefit immensely once you escape from your prison of specialization, your self-imposed isolation from science.

THE EVIDENCE BEARING ON MAN'S FUTURE

I'm sure you will agree, following Becker, that any worthwhile investigation of economic man demands that we look at the consequences to society of man's actions, whatever his motives may be. Even unselfish drives can cause great troubles. The age-old saw that the road to Hell is paved with good intentions comes to mind. If there's any truth to that, then we may be wasting our time in trying to determine just how selfish or unselfish man is. That's not the big issue. No, the issue lies elsewhere. Put it this way:

> David Hume was right. We're still not even close to calculating the proportions of the dove in man as against the wolf and serpent in him. That's a sterile exercise. What's important is to be wary of any parallel to man from the animal world. There is nothing more dangerous in this world than the fired-up ascetic in pursuit of what he feels to be a noble cause, but possibly at the risk of your life and mine.

Let's conclude with the frightening views of two senior Soviet economists. On February 14, 1991, I hosted a colloquium for students and faculty at Pace University. Our speakers were Dr. Lev Karpov (LK), Head of the Institute of the USA and Canada, Academy of Sciences of the USSR and Dr. Katya Shevleeva (KS), an economist and daughter of Dr. Stanislav Shatalin. Dr. Shatalin, you may remember, was President Gorbachev's principal economic adviser who resigned in protest in 1990. What these two economists said at the colloquium bore intimately on my concern over the risks of civil war, chaos, nuclear proliferation, and the nature of economic man:

RH: Katya, why did your father resign?

KS: In protest that his plan for free markets was shelved. My father also expressed his fears, his protest, over the drift of our country to dictatorship.

RH: Dr. Karpov, I hear of the risks of civil strife, dictatorships, race conflicts, and of nuclear bombs ending up in the hands of warring republics in the wake of the disintegration of centralized authority from Moscow. Do you share these concerns?

LK: Life is not black and white, it's technicolor. But I'm concerned most over nuclear devices falling into the wrong hands, especially criminals. They're getting easier and less expensive to produce. It's getting late in the game for *homo sapiens*.

How late? Well, I don't pretend to have any final answers. Like the chaos theorists, I don't pretend to understand the beginnings of anything. Yet according to them, we must understand more about the beginnings before we can forecast with any confidence the future. Even so, I would like to make one final observation, and one final forecast. The questions I directed at these Soviet economists, which we later discussed at great length, had nothing to do with the merits or demerits of Marxist theory. (Bewildering to me, most of the Russian economists I met over the years had read little of Marx, and remembered virtually nothing of what they had read. They had no knowledge of Western Marxists.)

The questions I posed had a lot to do, however, with the guiding forces for any economic system. To illustrate my point, please glance at these two exhibits, one for the United States and the other for the former Soviet Union:

THE UNITED STATES	THE FORMER SOVIET UNION
Standard of Living (Wealth)	Standard of Living (Wealth)
Production	Production
Productivity	Productivity
Capital	Capital
Savings	Savings
Profits and Interest	The Nomenklatura

With the collapse of the nomenklatura (Soviet economic command structure), what are the risks facing another economic and political system? Economic chaos? Civil War? Nuclear bombs falling into "unauthorized hands"? Renegade computer experts breaking into the secret files of the military? I

don't know, but these are all real risks according to Drs. Karpov and Shevleeva. Even so, their caustic and damning critique of the nomenklatura went
far beyond anything I have ever heard. That includes even the bellicose raving of American political thinkers on the extreme righteous right. Just yesterday, it seems, many of them wanted to blast my Moscow colleagues and
friends out of existence. These were highly motivated ascetics!

Now, suppose ascetic revolutionaries were to kick the bottom pillar from
under capitalism. The capitalistic colossus would collapse, too, if nothing
were put in its place. We would all suffer, possibly moving through chaos to
dictatorship. Nobody wants that either. Even so, that doesn't argue against taking steps to modify capitalism, to exercise control and regulation over the pure
play of free and unbridled markets. Put it this way:

> Economic man still has far too much of the dog, the serpent, and the wolf
> in his makeup to be set totally free, unregulated. That's one hard lesson
> I learned from a street called Wall, and from the physical and social sci-
> entists who do serious research on the nature of economic man.

At the other extreme, I also learned from serious students of human nature, whether scientists or poets, to fear the raving of ascetic heroes, whether
on the economic left or right, whether from the liberal or the conservative
camp. Sir William S. Gilbert (1836–1911) put it this way:

> I often think it's *comical*
> How nature always does contrive
> That every boy and every gal,
> That's born into this world alive,
> Is either a little Liberal,
> Or else a little Conservative!*
> (Emphasis added.)

5. Conclusion

Comical? I'm more frightened than amused over warring ascetics, whether
they be on the political left or right, whether liberal or conservative. Each can
bastardize science in promoting his special ideology. Still, let me conclude
with a positive forecast, one I believe is consistent with nature as an evolv-
ing, forever changing, and progressive force for economic man:

*From *H.M.S. Pinafore,* Act 1, quoted in John Bartlett's *Familiar Quotations,* 15th edition (Boston: Little, Brown and Company, 1980), p. 627.

As the centuries pass, the notion of man as innately selfish, hedonistic, narcissistic, combative, or even ascetic but destructive, will pass. Economic man will evolve into a higher being, a rational hero at peace with himself and society. Man in the countless centuries to come will evolve into a physical and social being unrecognizable to the witch doctors of this century. He will progress without limit even as he wrestles daily with new moral, religious, political, and economic issues. (One colossal issue, certainly, will be the role of genetic engineering in man's destiny.)

What could go wrong with my happy prediction? What's my biggest caveat? My fear is that warring ascetics, heroes in pursuit of "noble" causes no matter what the cost, could annihilate themselves and all of us. They would trip on the oldest of fallacies, the fallacy of composition, a fallacy that appears across most of the chapters of this book. The fallacy tells us that self-styled and self-appointed do-gooders pursuing contradictory goals can put all of mankind in jeopardy by generalizing from their own limited circumstances to project their views on the whole of humanity. True, risks abound in the struggles of hedonist versus hedonist, or hedonist versus ascetic. But the greatest peril comes from warring ascetics who would risk human extinction for their special faith, god, or country.

Is it possible, though, that the very threat of global destruction has unified mankind? Novelist Milan Kundera asks that very question in *The Art of the Novel*: "The modern era has nurtured a dream in which mankind . . . would someday come together in unity and everlasting peace. Today, the . . . planet has finally become one indivisible whole, but it is war, ambulant . . . war, that embodies and guarantees this long-desired unity of mankind. Unity of mankind means: No escape for anyone anywhere."* Modifying Kundera, I would put the risk this way:

Guarantees don't exist. Indeed, man's very existence is in peril from warring ascetics in a high-tech world.

What, then, are the odds for mutual destruction of the human race from the warring ascetics? I don't know. Nobody knows. I suspect, though, that what I shall dub the *ascetic risk* poses by far the greatest risk to humanity. *The Economist* worries that such a risk may lie, for example, in war between Islam and the West.† It calls that "The Fundamental Fear." Maybe, but as I write this

*(New York: Grove Press Inc., 1988), pp. 11–12.
†August 6–12, 1994.

I count not one but some seventy wars, revolutions, and insurrections taking place across the globe. That's quite enough to frighten any good probability theorist over the risk of nuclear war through accident or design. But what about the plundering hedonists? Well, they may be easier as a rule to spot and to control than warring ascetics. Hedonists are not likely to sacrifice their lives for anything (like running a truck full of explosives into certain death to attack their perceived enemy). Unlike Mahatma Gandhi, a preeminent apostle of nonviolence, *far* too many self-appointed ascetics will fight to their death (and ours) for their beliefs. I'm far more frightened of warring ascetics than I am of killer asteroids, though either could smash the earth and mankind into nothingness.

A POSTSCRIPT ON THE PRO

Perhaps you noticed that I failed in twenty-six chapters to find an animal that would match the Pro, the human intellectual prostitute. I tried hard enough but was unsuccessful, even after long search. I asked money manager Morley Goldberg, whom we met earlier, about this many years ago in July 1982:

RH: Morley, I can't find a convincing analogy in the animal kingdom for the Pro, the human intellectual prostitute. I have asked my students, my institutional clients, my friends, my fellow economists, everybody. They have yet to come up with anything convincing. I need an animal that is smart, sophisticated, alert, attractive, affable, and clever enough to deceive without being detected or even suspected. I need an animal that deceives himself, unconsciously, and one who feels righteous in his zeal to convert you and me to his special brand of everlasting truth. I need an animal made up of ascetic dove and hedonist wolf, the way David Hume described man. I'm worried most about ascetics—the highly motivated economic, political, or religious zealots. They now have the doomsday weapons to blow themselves and everybody else off this planet. I need another animal to go with my Parrots and Ostriches. Any ideas?

MG: Robert, there is no such animal outside of man. The Pros exist only among humans; man is the worst of the lot in the animal kingdom. The Pro on Wall pretends to be upstanding, righteous, like the preacher. But he is worse than the street mugger. You're right in saying the Pro may not even realize what he's doing. He represses the dark side of his actions. Ask any good psychologist.

Yes, ask the psychologist about the nature of economic man. Ask the psychiatrist, the natural scientist, the anthropologist, the physicist, the medical researcher, the mathematician, and the poet who does serious thinking on the mystery of economic man. Make sure you ask the chaos theorist, and even the myrmecologist. Who? The myrmecologist, a student of ants, is a specialist in change. This scientist reminds us that humans, which number just one species, are recent arrivals on this earth. Ants, though, have been around for 100 million years and account today for an estimated 15,000 extant species. Maybe we can learn about man and human survival from the myrmecologists and the ants.

Someday you might even ask and get straight answers from the professional economist on the nature of economic man, but only after he evolves from preacher to scientist.

Appendix A

The Danger of Consensus Forecasting

1970–1995

> THE PROPHET: A Wizard, sitting in the marketplace, told the fortunes of the passers-by. A person ran up in great haste, and announced to him that the doors of his house had been broken open, and that all his goods were being stolen. He sighed heavily, and hastened away as fast as he could run. A neighbor saw him running, and said, "Oh! you fellow there! You say you can foretell the fortunes of others; how is it you did not foresee your own?"
>
> Aesop (Sixth Century B.C.E.)

A HISTORY OF FORECASTS AND CONTROVERSY: 1970–1995

The Danger of Consensus Forecasting

Do you know anybody who has prescience or knowledge of things before they happen or come into being? I don't. Still, all planning requires forecasting, whether it be sloppy or thorough. Being thorough means (a) that you must not only pay attention to sound theory but also actively look for new data and new developments that may contradict your most precious convictions, (b) that you must be skeptical of authorities in power, always checking what they say against relevant data and sound theory, (c) that you not rely on luck, a fickle ally, (d) that you be wary of projecting ahead the most recent experience, the equivalent of betting on the horse out front no matter how long the race, and most important (e) that you extract yourself from the consensus herd that seldom sees a financial bubble until it has burst. To be thorough is to be scientific. *Economic forecasting is hardly an exact science, but economists can at least try to be scientific. Many don't even try.*

A Wall Street economist must have a thick skin. He knows the press will track his errant ways. He knows that selective reporting can be highly entertaining (chapter 12). He knows that psychology cannot be separated for short periods from data and sound theory on the fundamentals. The year 1994 will go down as a classic case: Inflation fears fanned by wolf calls of the Fed itself suddenly rocketed interest rates higher even as the actual pace of inflation continued down. *There are no market timers in the short run.*

The following are direct quotes from the press and other published reports. Each of my forecasts is followed by an explanation of subsequent events. Assuming we can learn from our errors, I have tried to explain what I think went wrong with my worst projections, numbered 12, 25, 28, 32, 34, 39, 70, and 86. I did, though, manage to spot the developments listed here. Luck was my consort in spotting Black Monday (35, 38, 41, 42) and the Nikkei 225 crash (40, 42, 58, 59) and the fall of the yen (95). My list of publications and their related forecasts are as follows:

The 1969–70 Recession	1
Economic Recovery, Blue Skies after 1970	2
"King Gold is Dead" (1973 comment on Gold)	3
The 1973–75 "Maxi-Recession, Mini-Depression"	4–9
Predicted Collapse of Wage and Price Controls	13, 18
Predicted Soaring Inflation and Interest Rates in Late 1970s	14–17, 18, 19
Emergency Bailouts of Financial Institutions	20
The Achilles Heel of "Reaganomics": Signals for the 1981–82 "Mini Depression"	21–24
The Folly of Jimmy Carter and Chairman Paul Volcker (1980)	21, 22
Collapse of Interest Rates and Oil (1981–82)	23
King Dollar's Rise, Fall, Rise (1980–95)	31, 46–49, 52, 62, 95
The "Black Monday" Stock Crash (10/19/87)	35, 38, 41–42
Bad Omens for Junk Bonds (1988–89)	43, 53
The Plunge in the Nikkei 225 (1990)	40, 42, 58, 59
Disinflation and "Growth" Recession (1990)	53

Global Slump, Lower Interest Rates (1990–93)	61, 62, 87, 89
Japan in Recession, Megabubble Yen (1993–94)	84, 87
Disinflation, End of Mutual Fund Boom	89–94
Gingrich's Contract with (on) America (1995)	93
Predicted plunge in long treasury bond yields (1995)	94
Predicted the Fall of the Yen	95
Predicted declining bank reserves risks recession or subpar growth	96

FORECASTS

1. *The Commercial and Financial Chronicle,* January 22, 1970, p. 1.

"The economist for one of Wall Street's largest firms (Robert H. Parks, Francis I. duPont & Co.) foresees a significant decline taking place in interest rates, particularly in shorter maturities, and concludes some sort of recession is now underway (and that) a serious and prolonged recession should not be entirely overlooked."

Fact: The economy entered a serious recession; rates fell.

2. *Wharton Quarterly,* University of Pennsylvania, Fall 1971.

"With excess demand eliminated from the economy, with ample labor and capital resources, and with governmental policies designed to lift demand, the likelihood is that we shall see a vigorous recovery of the economy in the two-to-three years ahead."

Fact: The economy did enjoy a vigorous recovery until late 1973 but both inflation and interest rates started to climb rapidly.

3. *The Wall Street Journal,* August 20, 1973, p. 1.

"King Gold is dead."

Fact: My focus was not on the price of gold. I argued rather that we should not and would not revert to some kind of gold standard, that the merits of gold were more myth than fact. I still hold to that view, detailed in chapter 12.

4. *The Times Picayune,* November 24, 1973.

"Robert H. Parks (Blyth Eastman Dillon) sums up: 'Even a fairly optimistic assumption on the Mideast and oil would require a revised forecast of minirecession.' "

Fact: The economy entered into what I characterized at the time as a maxi-recession (mini-depression). See (8).

5. *Curriculum, 24th Annual University for Presidents,* Acapulco, Mexico, March 31–April 6, 1974, p. 22 (Debate between Robert H. Parks and Eliot Janeway)

"According to Robert H. Parks, if neither happens (oil spigots turned back on or oil prices reduced), the United States is headed for recession, with corporate profits falling by 10–15%, unemployment advancing to 7%, and a zero growth in real GNP for 1974. The likelihood is that the United States will run surpluses in net trade and capital accounts."

Fact: We did fall into recession, but I grew progressively negative, as indicated in subsequent forecasts, especially forecast (8). The U.S. ran surpluses on its trade and current accounts in the 1973–75 recession.

6. *New York Post,* September 24, 1974.

"Robert H. Parks, Chief Economist of Advest Inc., an institutional services firm, maintains that 'the price boom for industrial materials has just about run its course.' "

Fact: Industrial prices continued downhill.

7. *The Wall Street Journal,* September 30, 1974.

"Robert H. Parks, Chief Economist of Advest Co., is worried that 'the ongoing government restriction of demand may lead to economic overkill.' "

Fact: Government policy overkill pushed the economy into a major recession.

8. *Christian Science Monitor,* November 18, 1974.

"Mr. Parks expects that real gross national product will decline 1.5 to 2 percent (as opposed to a conventional prediction of a flat GNP) and that unemployment will rise to 8 percent or higher."

Fact: Real GNP fell 1.2% in 1975 and unemployment averaged 8.5% for the year.

9. *New York Post,* January 24, 1975.

"Calling it a mini-depression, Robert H. Parks said it will be short-lived in contrast with the protracted economic earthquakes of the 1930s. Parks said his turn to guarded optimism is based on 'new governmental stimulus not yet announced and a slowing of inflation.' "

Fact: Government policy shifted from restraint to stimulus, and overall inflation topped out a few months later.

10. *The Wall Street Journal,* May 23, 1975.

"Robert H. Parks, Executive Vice President of Advest Institutional Services, was even more outspoken: 'The financial markets can easily handle the upcoming Treasury financing provided (a) the Federal Reserve is sufficiently accommodative and (b) Treasury Secretary Simon gets more professional counsel on elementary economic and financial matters.' "

Fact: Treasury Secretary Simon was worried, prematurely, about Treasury borrowing pushing interest rates up. Interest rates in fact declined through 1976.

11. *Business Week,* April 12, 1976.

"The simple fact, as Robert H. Parks, Chief Economist of Advest, puts it, is that 'business is not yet in a borrowing mood,' and 'the inventory reductions last year and the profits surge in the last half permitted companies to rebuild their liquidity bases.' "

Fact: That helped to explain the fall in interest rates in 1976.

12. *Money,* August 1976.

"Another pessimist, Robert Parks, says: 'Gary Shilling and I are from different planets. I think he is on Mars.' Parks thinks inflation will be back up over the 7% level by the middle of next year or earlier."

Fact: I was early because inflation did not climb that high until the first quarter of 1978.

13. *The Wall Street Journal,* January 23, 1977.

"Robert Parks, executive vice president of Advest Co., believes the President's proposal for a voluntary wage and price control program is 'a folly and a farce—it simply wouldn't work.' "

Fact: It didn't work.

14. *The Wall Street Journal,* March 22, 1977.

"In the view of Robert H. Parks (Advest Co.), he sees Treasury bill yields rising almost two percentage points later this year."

Fact: Three-month bills rose from 5.3% from the end of 1977 to 7.2% at the end of 1978.

15. *Business Week,* April 11, 1978.

"Mr. Parks is in a good position to assess the new state of psychology. He runs a roundtable for money managers [and] listening to what they say has convinced him of two things, both of them bad. The first dark prospect is inflation controls. The second grim prospect is tightness of money to fight inflation."

Fact: We got both.

16. *The Wall Street Journal,* August 22, 1978.

"The Fed has a tiger by the tail (fast money growth of its own making and fast inflation), and the probability that it can live with fast money growth will approach zero in the next six months," asserted Robert H. Parks (Advest).

Fact: In November the Federal Reserve shifted gears to a sharp reduction in money growth.

17. *The Wall Street Journal,* October 18, 1978.

"Mr. Parks predicts that 'when the Fed finally tightens, you'll see interest rates soar; you could get an increase of 1.5 to 2 points while you're having lunch.' "

Fact: The prime rate rocketed from 10% on November 1 to 11–3/4% by year-end. Branch managers wanted me fired for my extremely pessimistic forecast.

18. *The Wall Street Journal,* November 6, 1978.

"The voluntary [price restraint] program 'will self-destruct within three to five months,' contends Robert H. Parks, Chief Economist at Advest Co."

Fact: It did just that as inflation soared in 1979 to high double-digit land.

19. *The New York Times,* February 9, 1979.

"This combination of inflationary devils should lift the inflation rate from 12 percent to 15 percent, possibly even higher."

Fact: The inflation rate referred to was the producer price index. The index was later reported for January at a 15.6% annual rate.

20. *Journal of Commerce,* May 9, 1979.

" 'That's why we look for more headline news on emergency financial bailouts of the savings banks. First Pennsylvania, a commercial bank, is a mere prelude to the troubles ahead,' according to Robert H. Parks, who heads up Robert H. Parks and Associates."

Fact: That was one grand understatement.

21. *The Wall Street Journal,* October 20, 1980.

" 'Look for a post-election blowoff in interest rates as the Fed is finally forced to restrict the explosive growth of money and credit,' said Robert H. Parks, head of Robert H. Parks & Associates. 'The delayed monetary restraint will collide head-on with an inflation-fired climb in credit demands. The result will be to abort recovery and produce a deepening recession in 1981.' "

Fact: We got all that.

22. Portfolio Letter (Institutional Investor Publication) April 27, 1981.

"To pave the way for long-run sustainable growth, Parks believes the monetarist quintet is willing to risk recession."

Fact: By monetarist quintet I meant Sprinkel, Roberts, Ture, Kudlow, and Jordan, all key administration officials. But it was Fed extreme monetary restriction colliding head-on with massive public and private borrowing that (a) pushed interest rates to the heavens, (b) crowded out private spending, and (c) produced recession.

23. *Bondweek* (Institutional Investor Publication) July 20, 1981.

The following quote from the publication focused on the July 9, 1981, *Monitor* entitled "In Recession," which I have reproduced in Appendix B. "Parks told *Bondweek* that 'the four major interest-rate bears, including economists Philip Braverman, Chase Manhattan; Henry Kaufman, Salomon Bros.; Sam Nakagama, Kidder Peabody; and Albert Wojnilower, First Boston [were wrong].' The message to investors is clear, says Parks: Buy long, prime-quality bonds. The worldwide recession will represent the first crack in the stranglehold of the oil cartel."

Fact: Recession brought interest rates and oil prices down hard.

24. *The Wall Street Journal,* April 29, 1982.

"Disinflation and recession are now coming on top of a dangerously overborrowed economy. This . . . should produce a record post-World War II fall in profits."

Fact: Profits fell hard.

25. *Business Week,* July 25, 1983.

"Indeed, in recent issues of his letter, *The Money and Capital Markets Monitor,* Wall Street economist Robert H. Parks—who had been a steadfast bull on bonds before and after their advance—has switched sides. He says flatly that interest rates will go up."

Fact: Interest rates did climb later, but I overstated the rise.

26. *The Wall Street Journal,* April 18, 1984.

"Robert H. Parks of Robert H. Parks & Associates agreed that the pace of recovery probably will slow, but he contended that this doesn't necessarily mean that interest rates will decline."

Fact: Interest rates had a little further to go up, but then peaked around mid-year.

27. *The New York Times,* April 27, 1984.

"But the market also listens to Robert H. Parks . . . who says 'Drs. Death, Doom, and Gloom are understating the likely rise in interest rates this year.' "

Fact: Interest rates rose rapidly from April for several months, then turned down in the second half of 1984.

28. *Barron's,* November 5, 1984.

"Another reason for listening to some current contrarians is that they also went against the crowd three years ago—and won. Then, with interest rates at record highs, they beat the drums for bonds—something Dr. Doom didn't get around to doing until almost a year later. Two notable voices among them: Fred D. Kalkstein . . . and Robert H. Parks."

Fact: That was a nice compliment, but the fact is that I should have turned bull once again, then and there, on bonds. As it turned out, I waited until the next spring, and missed part of the long-bond rally.

29. Standard & Poor's *CreditWeek,* April 29, 1985.

"Fed policy has been expansionary—extremely expansionary—all along. That's a key reason now for ruling out early recession."

Fact: No early recession materialized, but economic growth slowed.

30. *The Bond Buyer,* May 25, 1985.

"Our own view is that Gramm-Rudman is a placebo, an unmedicated political pill given to the economic body merely to humor."

Fact: The budget cutting requirements were largely circumvented via accounting smoke and mirrors.

31. *Money and Capital Markets Monitor,* October 9, 1985.

"Until the March 27, 1985, *Monitor* we had been a persistent bull on the dollar. But we then warned that King Dollar may yet imitate Humpty Dumpty in the second half of this year. We switched completely in the May 3 *Monitor,* titled "Sell King Dollar NOW" (Appendix E).

Fact: The dollar came down sharply.

32. Standard & Poor's *CreditWeek,* July 8, 1985.

"Coming on top of extreme fiscal and monetary stimulus already in place, this third stimulus (i.e., a lower dollar) would push up interest rates sharply during the second half of 1986 or later."

Fact: Interest rates went down in the second half of 1986, but did move up in the first half of 1987. I underestimated the weight of global excess supply and underestimated the extent of foreign competition as a continuing force working against inflation. Put another way, the United States is not a "closed economy" but operates in an open and intensively competitive international world.

33. Standard & Poor's *CreditWeek,* February 3, 1986.

"But, the strong domestic fiscal/monetary forces are currently being subjected to huge offsets. This accounts for the sluggish economy over the last year and more."

Fact: A high-priced dollar in world markets, intense international competition, restrictive governmental policies abroad, and worldwide gluts all contributed to a sluggish U.S. economy.

34. *Business Week,* June 29, 1986.

"(Recession) will drive down interest rates on long-term Treasury bonds from the current 7.5% to 5% by spring."

Fact: There was no recession, and my forecast of rates was dead wrong. I overestimated government restraint.

35. *The Market Chronicle,* February 26, 1987, p. 15.

"Stock market bulls could profit by reading Charles Mackay's classic treatise on speculation. The title: *Extraordinary Popular Delusions and the Madness of Crowds.*"

Fact: That was good advice because world stock markets did fall hard. The U.S. stock market peaked in August, then suffered a record one-day decline on Black Monday, October 19, 1987.

36. Standard & Poor's *CreditWeek,* March 7, 1987.

"Developing economies are without the means to generate the income even to service their debts. Put another way: revulsion + austerity + debt drag = default."

Fact: Brazil's recent suspension of interest payments on commercial foreign debt is an example of true default. (**Revulsion** means an abrupt cutback of lending by the industrial world to the third world. **Austerity** means a suppression of demand and spending and borrowing, a restrictive policy imposed on the third world by the International Monetary Fund acting for the industrial lenders.)

37. *Barron's,* June 8, 1987, p. 1.

"Robert Parks, a certified practitioner of the dismal science, Wall Street division, remarks on Mr. Volcker's adrenaline-codeine prescription for monetary policy and notes that the Fed's attempt to repair the damage wrought by overkill in '81-'82 resulted in an enormous explosion in credit, from $500 billion in 1982 to over $1 trillion last year."

Fact: Volcker's God-like image is overdone, as I have argued.

38. *Barron's,* September 21, 1987, p. 79.

"On a similar tack, Robert H. Parks, director of the Moore & Schley research unit bearing his name, also concludes that bonds' huge advantage over stocks' earnings and dividend yields makes prime fixed-income instruments 'attractive in the extreme.' "

Fact: Yes, indeed. Bond prices and long CATS (long zero-coupon bonds) soared following the stock market crash of Black Monday, October 19, 1987.

39. *Barron's,* November 30, 1987, p. 73.

"Right after the stock market crumbled, economist Robert Parks proclaimed in these pages that the phantom of inflation was dead. But Bob should have known better. Phantoms, alas, never die."

Fact: Yes, I should have known better. I was wrong.

40. S&P's *CreditWeek,* November 30, 1987, p. 1.

"Investor irrationality in U.S. and Japanese stock markets lies in the failure to heed basic stock market theory. Investors are ignoring [stock valuation models] and their three crucial variables: interest rates, corporate income and dividend trends, and the cost of capital [the required rate of return that would rationally compensate investors for holding stocks]."

Fact (and a warning): My contention was that the Japanese stock market was for gamblers, not prudent investors responsible for other peoples' money.

41. *New York Post,* February 9, 1988, p. 33.

"I have not written much about Bob Parks's ideas because of the extremely secretive, even furtive, manner he has developed. He has an exasperating habit of issuing press releases that tell about all his interesting and influential clients and advisers who are going to hold secret meetings the press cannot attend. I find this sort of posing extremely irritating, and an obnoxious form of boasting. Nevertheless, Bob's ideas are logical and forceful. He was for long a lonely voice (for which he has my sympathy) in stating that the 1987 stock market boom in America was an insane development and would leave much pain and disaster behind. He was right."

Fact: Post Economics Editor Maxwell Newton wrote this. Was I obnoxious? Perhaps. But all meetings were advertised. Many (not all) were kept off-the-record for a good reason. With the press in attendance, government officials and investment heads tended to imitate clams. Max's death saddened me, and I'll always remember his irreverence to "the high and mighty." He had no patience for Parrots and regularly crucified Pros.

42. *Barron's,* February 15, 1988, p. 102.

On this scale, [Parks] recently told clients, Tokyo is flashing 'red, red.' Parks rated the U.S. (stock market) red-and-yellow on August 18, 1987, red-red on October 7."

Fact: The U.S. stock market crashed as predicted. We had to wait until 1990 to get a major plunge in the Japanese market.

43. *The Market Chronicle,* March 31, 1988, p. 6.

"Corporate comptrollers . . . had the opportunity to raise capital through stock financing prior to Black Monday at skyhigh prices, at dirt cheap rates. They blew it."

Fact: Yes, they blew it. They overloaded themselves with debt, including junk bond financing.

44. Standard & Poor's *CreditWeek,* May 23, 1988, p. 45.

"A flight to quality has already begun. In the last quarter of 1987 individual investors abandoned their DOGS [dangerously-overpriced-gung-ho-stocks]and fled to CATS [certificates of accrual on Treasury securities] and other fixed-income vehicles."

Fact: Individual investors did begin to lighten holdings prior to Black Monday but, like institutional investors, they failed to get out early enough. The flight to quality dollar-denominated bonds accelerated in 1989, as forecast below.

45. *Barron's,* July 4, 1988, p. 2.

Barron's noted that (a) my forecast of interest rates "was the lowest of a group of financial economists [it] polled [for its] July 4, 1988 issue [p. 52]," and (b) I was extremely positive on the stock market.

Fact: Long rates came down, and short rates went up. My switch to a bull on U.S. stocks and bonds proved timely even though the stock market had already recovered somewhat from its Black Monday lows by July.

46. *Business Week,* September 12, 1988, p. 26.

"The consensus outlook these days is that the big improvements in the trade deficit this year lie behind us. Don't bet on it, advises economist Robert H. Parks of Moore & Schley."

Fact: The first quarter 1989 trade deficit dropped sharply.

47. *The Market Chronicle,* November 17, 1988, p. 1.

"Professor Martin Feldstein and other academics set off their own false alarms (on the dollar). A good case can be made that these alarm bells are false alarms."

Fact: They were false alarms; the dollar rose as forecast until mid–1989.

48. Standard & Poor's Credit Week, November 21, 1988, p. 1.

"Major and sustained cuts in the trade deficit will occur in 1989 in lagged response to the dollar's massive fall. . . . The improvement is likely to bring about a buying frenzy for the dollar."

Fact: The trade deficits fell sharply, but the dollar slumped in 1989, and did not rebound until 1990–91.

49. *The New York Post,* January 17, 1989.

"The consensus of Wall Street firms, including several of the giants, is to diversify out of the dollar and into key foreign-denominated securities. This will prove to be one giant error for the New Year. The United States now represents a prime investment market."

Fact: U.S. dollar-denominated securities outperformed most world markets.

50. *The Market Chronicle,* February 23, 1989, p. 1.

"Stock Valuation Models Flash Amber to Bright Green: The Advance Strike Against Accelerating Inflation." (Headlines of the editor for article they requested.)

Fact: It was all go. What a contrast with the "red, red" signals incorporated in the October 7 and 14, 1987, *Monitor* (see chapter 9 and forecasts 35, 40–43).

51. Standard & Poor's *CreditWeek,* May 8, 1989, p. 48.

"Tighter money since early 1988 will also have a lagged impact and show up in a pronounced slowing of economic growth and inflation in the second half of this year, with long U.S. Treasuries trading in the 8.0% to 8.5% range. The Fed should shout victory and ease, here and now."

Fact: Luck must have been my ally, for real GNP growth slowed to about 1 percent in the fourth quarter and long Treasury yields declined to trade between roughly 8 percent and 8.5 percent. But real growth, inflation, and interest rates all climbed sharply in the first quarter of 1990 to the surprise of just about everybody, including this startled economist.

52. *Business Week,* June 5, 1989, p. 27.

"Late last summer, economist Robert H. Parks . . . began advising his clients that some surprising drops in the trade deficit lay ahead (*BW*—September 12). He also advised his clients that neither world central bank chiefs nor King Canute will be able to hold back the return of King Dollar and that U.S. securities markets would rally sharply over the next 12 months. So what does Parks see ahead now that his earlier predictions have apparently borne fruit? In four words, more of the same."

Fact: The results were a bit mixed. Interest rates fell, stock prices rose (but not "sharply,"), the dollar soared against the yen, but fell against other key industrial currencies.

53. *The Tampa Tribune-Times,* August 20, 1989, p. 2E.

"This soft landing stuff . . . what they're talking about is 1 percent growth, and that is going to raise holy hell with a lot of nonfinancial corporations, corporations so overloaded with junk bonds that this is going to produce (for them) a hard landing."

Fact: With this forecast of a "growth recession," revenues and cash flow fell short of the funds required to pay interest on many junk bonds, with the result that defaults soared (see chapter 20).

54. *Barron's,* September 18, 1989, p. 71.

" 'The proceeds of Treasury and [Resolution Trust Corp.] borrowing siphons money from the credit stream, but puts it into the hands of depositors or new thrift managers, who then return it to the credit stream. That's a wash, a net zero for new money and credit growth,' Parks asserts."

Fact: That's the way it is, something not generally understood by the markets.

55. *Bond Week,* September 25, 1989, p. 8.

"Parks predicts the ascendance of 'King Dollar.' "

Fact: I turned from bear to bull in early 1988, and have kept that bullish stance ever since. The dollar fell against major currencies in 1989, then rose in 1990–91, but not as much as I had forecast.

56. *Bond Week,* November 6, 1989, pp. 10–11.

"The monetarists still scream recession, asserting that once again the Federal Reserve has pursued monetary overkill. The recession-depression bears could be right, of course, but I hardly think a case can be made on their monetary calculations."

Fact: The monetarists were wrong, again. They failed to recognize the defect in "total adjusted reserves," which went nowhere. In fact, however, we experienced a de facto cut in legal reserve requirements that was the basis for the rebound in money broadly defined as M2.

57. *Business Week,* December 25, 1989, p. 77.
     Barron's, December 25, 1989, p. 32.

In a poll of economists on the 1990 economic outlook, I forecasted generally higher real growth, lower interest rates, and less inflation than the consensus.

Fact: My inflation forecast and interest rate projections were far too low.

58. Standard & Poor's *CreditWeek,* January 29, 1990, "Cost of Capital Crossover," p. 1, 39.

"Perceptions that the U.S. suffers an intractable competitive disadvantage vis-à-vis the Japanese from prohibitive capital costs are incorrect. Differential costs of debt are narrowing between the two countries as Japanese interest rates surge. Meanwhile, equity costs are converging, too, and they could cross at any time, especially if the Japanese stock market megabubble collapses. . . . [The Japanese] should run from yen to dollars."

Fact: A bull's eye hit on this bear forecast. The Japanese stock market collapsed and the yen simultaneously weakened.

59. *Bond Week,* March 19, 1990, p. 13.

"The Japanese, who have a money growth rate of 10–11%, are now in the Catch–22 situation of tightening monetary policy and watching the stock market go down, perhaps even crash, or allowing inflation to run amok."

Fact: What's new? All bubbles burst, but who can know just when? My early warning (Forecast 39) was followed by a still substantial climb in the Japanese stock market. So, you would have profited—as a reckless gambler, not a prudent investor—to have stayed in the Japanese market until late 1989 (see chapter 17).

60. *The Wall Street Journal,* October 10, 1990, p. A12.

"Robert H. Parks, an economic consultant in New York, believes that the Fed has been too slow to adopt an easier monetary policy and, as a result, he now fears a 'major recession' instead of the mild one he previously predicted."

Fact: The recession was characterized as mild. I should have stuck with my earlier forecast. However, the recovery from recession after March 1991 was unusually slow.

61. *The Dow Jones News,* Ticker-Tape Release 12 Noon, October 26, 1990, by Candace Cumberbatch.

"While Parks has a sunny forecast for the dollar, he sees very stormy times for global economies. . . . The economy is being strangled by influences including the Federal Reserve's reluctance to ease more forcefully, fiscal restrictiveness and the oil shock caused by the Mideast turmoil, Parks says, adding that any Fed easing done now will likely be too little and too late."

Fact: The Fed pursued overkill once again and pushed the economy into the 1990–91 recession, as in 1973–75 and 1981–82. The Fed seldom learns from its mistakes.

62. *Barron's,* November 12, 1990, p. 60.

"'The dollar will be hit again the moment we get a couple of interest rate cuts,' predicts economist Robert Parks. 'But the huge interest differentials between the U.S. and its trading partners will be short-lived.' Parks thinks the dollar (is) extremely undervalued on the basis of purchasing power parity (and) once the economies of our trading partners start to sag, interest rate differentials will implode and bargain hunters will start snapping up dollar-denominated assets."

Fact: The dollar did rebound. (See Forecast 68.)

63. *Business Week,* December 3, 1990, p. 24.

" 'Once the gulf crisis is resolved,' Parks says, 'oil prices will collapse in the context of a worldwide cyclical decline. . . . 'Ironically,' says Parks, 'the darkest economic times are often the most promising for the financial markets. I am advising my clients to purchase long bonds now, and the highest quality stocks in the months ahead, when the recession hits with full force.' "

Fact: The stock market climbed, far more than I had expected, oil prices fell, and interest rates declined. Luck was with me on this.

64. *Barron's,* January 21, 1991, p. 56.

"Economist Robert Parks, who recorded Kindleberger's prognostications in an interview published in the May 1978 Pace University *International Newsletter,* believes the three Rs have come back with a vengeance."

Fact: That was revelry (stock market overspeculation), revulsion (an abrupt cutback in lending and Fed monetary overkill) and restriction (protectionism) as signals for recession. I have reviewed Dr. Charles P. Kindleberger's views throughout this volume and note the forums and interviews I conducted for this most distinguished and prescient economist. (For example, see chapter 5.)

65. Standard & Poor's *CreditWeek,* January 28, 1991, page 1.

"Interest-rate targeting required the Fed to strip reserves from the financial system to brake the decline in interest rates. That procyclical policy is akin to monetary overkill, which led me to shift my forecast from a mild recession to a major one."

Fact: The recession was mild but not major, though the recovery from recession proved to be the slowest in post-World War II history. See chapter 5 for an explanation of the folly of interest-rate targeting.

66. *The Christian Science Monitor,* February 7, 1991, p. 8.

" 'If the Fed does not soon . . . start pushing liquidity into the system, I may change my forecast from major recession to depression,' says Robert Parks, an economic consultant to institutional investors. 'It is a dangerous situation.' "

Fact: The Fed shifted to an easier stance, but too late to avoid recession and post-recession anemia.

67. *Business Week,* May 13, 1991, p. 20.

"The most important leading indicator for the economy, insists economic consultant Robert H. Parks, is real private domestic borrowing—that is, borrowing by consumers, businesses, and state and local governments. He points out that such credit fell in real terms in the fourth quarter for the first time since the Great Depression and appears to be still declining—indicating 'no letup in the recession.' "

Fact: The recession was officially over by spring 1991 but subpar recovery followed. I was wrong again.

68. *The Wall Street Journal,* May 28, 1991, p. C10.

"Among factors working in the dollar's favor are the current 'ultra cheap' dollar levels that will likely attract bargain hunters, the possibility of 'dramatic continued improvement' in the U.S. trade performance, and the likelihood of diminishing U.S. inflationary pressures, Mr. Parks says."

Fact: Despite trade gains and lower inflation, the dollar weakened after mid-year.

69. *Christian Science Monitor,* May 31, 1991, p. 4.

"By contrast [to those expecting early economic recovery], New York economic consultant Robert Parks [said] 'We have yet to see the full impact of restrictive credit and monetary policies.' "

Fact: The economy moved from recession to "growth" recession (subpar growth).

70. *Business Week,* December 31, 1991, p. 63.

"What economists are predicting for 1992." Of fifty economists polled, I was one of the most pessimistic on the economy for 1992.

Fact: Far too pessimistic! I was way off base.

71. *Barron's,* December 30, 1991, pp. 36, 37.

"Adds Robert H. Parks, who heads his own consulting firm, lower rates in and of themselves merely cut one borrower's expense and one lender's income. The economic stimulus comes from expanding the supply of money and credit, which he contends Greenspan & Co. have been loathe to do."

Fact: The Fed was too tight.

72. *The Christian Science Monitor,* January 28, 1992, pp. 1 and 2.

"Mr. Parks argues that the sharp decline in interest rates last year was the result of a declining demand for money, rather than an aggressively stimulative monetary policy. Don't confuse Fed leadership with Fed 'followship,' he says."

Fact: The Fed did follow rates down, and was far too restrictive.

73. Standard & Poor's *CreditWeek,* February 3, 1992, p. 1, 4.

"An overly restrictive monetary policy has helped cause a severe recession, already the longest and potentially the meanest since the 1930s."

Fact: My forecast of recession was correct, but it turned out to be a fairly mild slump.

74. *Barron's,* June 29, 1992, p. 38.

Survey of twelve economists forecasting interest rates, with my numbers being among the lowest.

Fact: Rates fell but less than I had expected.

75. *Business Week,* July 20, 1992, p. 20.

"Economic consultant Robert H. Parks has long insisted the Fed has been far too cautious. . . . Increases in currency in circulation and required reserves over the past year have almost completely offset soaring reserve growth, leaving 'almost nothing' to support credit growth."

Fact: The Fed habitually swings from monetary overstimulus to overkill.

76. *The Christian Science Monitor,* October 23, 1992, p. 8

"Robert Parks, a Wall Street economist, worries about a repeat next year of the 1981 situation . . . when the Federal Reserve kept a tight monetary policy, refusing to finance the deficit with new money."

Fact: Yes, I worried that huge *nonmonetized* Treasury borrowing would "crowd out" private borrowing and demand. This made for subpar growth (see chapter 6).

77. *Barron's,* December 28, 1992, p. 31.

"Among the bond bulls in this survey, only Robert H. Parks, who heads a New York economic consultancy, doubts the economy is headed for a sustained expansion. Constrictive policies, combined with a global recession, will push Treasury yields lower, while the Fed's misplaced inflation fears will induce it to push short-term rates higher next year."

Fact: Growth but most anemic recovery since 1945.

78. Standard & Poor's *CreditWeek,* January 25, 1993, p. 1.

"What worries me the most is the conspicuous absence of inflation-adjusted private credit growth and broad money M2. . . . The good news will show up in continued disinflation and much lower yields on long prime dollar-denominated corporate bonds and Treasuries."

Fact: That bond-bull stance was on target for 1993.

79. *Business Week,* April 19, 1993, p. 22.

" 'The broad weakness in the monetary aggregates is definitely clouding the near-term economic outlook,' warns Parks."

Fact: Yes, insufficient stimulus was signaling subpar growth.

80. The Christian Science Monitor, April 9, 1993, p. 8.

"Parks asks whether the combination of tight money (falling money aggregates), government spending cuts, and higher taxes will choke off business, depress money velocity, and send the economy back down again."

Fact: Real GDP dropped to a minuscule 0.7% advance in the first quarter of 1993.

81. Pace University, Center for Applied Research, February 1993, p. 1.

"[Note the] parallels today with the haywire theories, policies, and forecasts of 1981–82."

Fact: See chapter 6 on the brake of huge *nonmonetized* Treasury deficits.

82. *Barron's,* July 5, 1993, pp. 58–59.

"The biggest bull on bonds is the most bearish on the economy. Parks sees higher unemployment and lower bond yields [resulting] from a wrong-headed Fed [and] contractionary fiscal policy."

Fact: I had forecast a 5.9% yield on long Treasuries, the lowest of fifty-five economists polled by Barron's (and the *Wall Street Journal*). Yield's in fact fell to about 5.8 percent. The consensus was far too high.

83. *Christian Science Monitor,* October 28, 1993, p. 9.

"Dr. Parks argues that U.S. monetary and fiscal policy is overly restrictive and that interest rates will be forced to decline [reflecting] slow economic growth."

Fact: Woe is for me and just about everybody else forecasting interest rates. The economy spurted strongly in the fourth quarter. Despite a continued downtrend in inflation, inflationary psychology dominated. Interest rates soared, bankrupting some hedge funds and others who borrowed heavily to invest in fixed-income derivatives. (See Appendix I for a short primer on derivatives.) Psychology blew me and just about everybody else out of the water.

84. *Barron's,* December 6, 1993, p. 15.

" 'Proposed fiscal measures to boost the Japanese economy mean little because they won't take early action to speed money growth,' says Robert H. Parks."

Fact: Their economy and markets are still struggling as of late 1995.

85. *Business Week,* December 27, 1993, p. 69.
86. *Barron's,* December 27, 1993, p. 38.

Parks is concerned over "the delayed impact of contractionary fiscal and monetary policies. . . ."

Fact: My low inflation forecast was on target but interest rates surged anyway. Fear dominated markets. Psychology lifted rates even as the economic fundamentals keep disinflation (lower inflation) on track. End 1994 recorded the lowest inflation rates in three decades. Can anybody show me how to track, measure, and forecast psychology?

87. Standard & Poor's *CreditWeek,* January 29, 1994, p. 1.

"[The] yen [bubble will] burst."

Fact: Nobody knows when.

88. *Institutional Investor,* January 1994, p. 66.

"Even if [projected] earnings and dividends were to exceed the historical norms, [U.S.] stocks are overpriced now. . . . Money managers run in herds like buffalo, and they will be caught this time, too."

Fact: Stocks went just about nowhere in 1994 but rose sharply in 1995.

89. *Business Week,* June 20, 1994, p. 121.

Polled by *Business Week,* I forecast the slowest GDP growth for the first half of 1995.

Fact: Too low.

90. *Barron's,* July 4, 1994, p. MW8.

"Parks . . . insists that tight money and fiscal policies assure [economic slow-down]."

Fact: The data by year-end 1994 signaled a slowing in autos and housing, and a disturbing pileup in inventories.

91. *The Christian Science Monitor,* November 18, 1994.

"Parks, a Pace University Professor who also advises forty major financial in-stitutions, expects velocity to reverse, slowing down the economy."

Fact: The unheralded surge in interest rates in 1994, I argued, would slow ve-locity, kill the bond funds, and slow the growth of stock funds. We got most of that. (See chapter 11 for historical parallels.)

92. *The Wall Street Journal,* December 5, 1994, p. C2.

"The very forces that led to a massive buildup of stock funds . . . have re-versed themselves. I expect to see a shift away from stocks into bond funds again. . . ."

Fact: All the facts are not in yet, but see chapter 11 and exhibit 11–1 on his-torical parallels focusing on money turnover and mutual funds.

93. *The Christian Science Monitor,* January 6, 1995, p. 13.

"That's why Wall Street economist Robert Parks terms the Republican promise a Contract 'on' America. 'If Newt Gingrich gets his way, big Al

Greenspan will not sit idly by,' says Mr. Parks. '[Mr. Parks calls the budget estimates in the Contract] ideological screaming. It has nothing to do with economic science.' "

Fact: We saw this voodoo-economics before in 1981–82 (chapter 6 and Forecasts 30 and 94).

94. Standard & Poor's *CreditWeek,* January 23, 1995, p. 1.

"Fed-manufactured inflation phantoms . . . will evaporate as long as Treasury yields skid abruptly below 7 percent."

Fact: "A bull's eye, thirty-year Treasuries plunged from almost 8 percent in January to below 6.4 percent by October."

95. *Barron's,* March 17, 1995, p. 42.

"Manic thinking now rules crowd behavior. . . . The coming resurgence of the dollar and descent of the yen will spark a boom in dollar-denominated long bonds."

Fact: U.S. bond prices rose sharply and the yen descended abruptly against the dollar, as predicted. The dollar bought about 80 yen, its low in April 1995, but soared to 104 by September of that year. The hot-air mania supporting the yen reminded me of comparable mania preceding our forecasts of Black Monday and the Nikkei 225 crash (chapters 15–17).

96. *The Christian Science Monitor,* November 3, 1995, p. 8.

"A decline in commercial bank reserves since the start of 1994 troubles Robert Parks, a New York economic consultant. Similar declines, he says, signaled previous post World War II declines. This time falling reserves will result in either very slow growth in the economy or another recession, he predicts."

Fact: See chapter 11, p. 169, for documentation of how Fed constriction of "adjusted" reserves regularly precipitates economic slumps.

Appendix B

In Recession

Seven Financial Fallacies of Four Bond Bears

The Money and Capital Markets Monitor (Excerpts)
July 9, 1981
(This *Monitor* was also published in *Bondweek,* July 20, 1981.)

In the August 6, 1980, *Monitor* we cautioned: "Given the hard evidence of an emerging worldwide recession, we expect to see ... the first crack in the stranglehold of the oil cartel. ... The United States is now in its eighth post-World War II recession. [The] four bond bears may be right, but we don't think so. The essence of their analysis can be put forth in seven propositions, none of which is convincing:

3. "The tax cut in October, or whenever, will lift rates higher." No, not unless excessively monetized. Nonmonetized tax cuts add not one penny to the money stock ... and are unlikely to fuel an excessive increase in *total* demand.

4. "Higher military spending will push rates up." No, not unless excessively monetized.

6. "Funding will push long rates back up." This waiting-in-the-wings argument has limited validity, but overlooks the fact that funding (a) entails no net demand for credit, (b) pushes short rates down, and (c) entails a reduction in bank loans and the money stock, hence can be perceived as disinflationary (positive for bonds).

Conclusion: Now is the time to make major commitments [to] long prime bonds.

Appendix C

Two Deflationary Shocks

Oil Plus Monetary Overkill?

A Double Tax on A Sagging Economy Signals Recession
The Money and Capital Markets Monitor (Excerpts)
August 24, 1990

The oil shock has brought with it poor theory, the mother of disastrous policy. This is the third time around, and it suggests a policy strikeout. . . . The dollars ripped out of business and consumer pockets to pay for higher energy would cut into real income, hence depress demand. Higher oil-induced costs would depress earnings of most of the nonoil sectors of the economy, hence depress capital outlays. To repeat, an oil-induced commodity inflation is a one-shot surge in prices, not a force for a sustained acceleration in inflation. . . .

Suppose the Fed were to constrict credit and money in response to higher oil prices. Why, that would be the equivalent of slapping one tax on top of another. That's what happened in 1973–75 and 1981–82.

Conclusions: The risks of recession have soared.

Appendix D

Stock Valuation Models Flash Red, Red

The Money and Capital Markets Monitor (Excerpts)
October 7, 1987

STOCKS VERSUS BONDS

In the August 18, 1987 *Monitor* we concluded: "Stock Valuation models are flashing yellow and red." . . . If you expect dividend growth to fall below a 7.5% average annual advance, be cautious. If you (a) think that the relatively optimistic assumption of a 7.5% annual dividend growth is too high and (b) are not satisfied with the historically low 2.78% current dividend yield on stocks, then you should be doubly cautious. . . . If you feel current inflationary fears are overblown, as we do, you might well start jettisoning high PE stocks for low-priced prime long bonds here and now.

Conclusion: Stock valuation models now flash red, red.

The Money and Capital Markets Monitor (Excerpts)
October 14, 1987

STOCK VALUATION MODELS STILL SIGNAL RED, RED

Even with optimistic dividend growth projections and a ludicrously low required return (cost of capital) assumed for equity investment, the stock market models still flash red, red (*Monitor,* October 7). . . . The present yields on
long PRIME bonds and their first-cousin CATS and STRIPS are now extremely attractive. Consider making massive commitments to these investment jewels now.

Conclusion: Be wary of gold bugs. Be alert to worrisome stock valuation
models. Go for CATS (long zeros).

Appendix E

Sell King Dollar

The Money and Capital Markets Monitor (Excerpts)
May 3, 1985

We have been a persistent bull on the dollar. In the September 20, 1984, *Monitor* we wrote that "the dollar is headed higher for the next six-to-nine months." In the February 21, 1985, *Monitor* we maintained that it was too early to dump the dollar, that "the time is not ripe." In the March 27, 1985, *Monitor,* however, we concluded that "King Dollar may yet imitate Humpty Dumpty in the second half of this year."

THE CAUSAL FORCES FOR A
MAJOR FALL IN THE DOLLAR

Imminent Recession? We just made forty-five telephone calls to institutional clients here and in Canada. About one-fifth are looking for recession. Our view: Forget it. Giant domestic stimulus rules that out.

A Dollar-Denominated Debt Glut? This prospect is generating enormous worry among institutional investment officers. Our view: Yes the time to worry is now. Our reasoning is fairly straightforward. It is this:

No corrective mechanism is in place to bring the giant U.S. current account deficit down. Its mirror image, the pileup in foreign-held dollars, will continue unchecked. Why? The reason lies in . . . unprecedented U.S. stimulus that (1) propels domestic buying power forward and (2) . . . further speeds imports.

Conclusion: The time to start diversifying out of the dollar is now.

Appendix F

Buy King Dollar

The Money and Capital Markets Monitor (Excerpts)
January 6, 1989

THE PARKS FORUMS FOR INSTITUTIONAL INVESTORS

We are making arrangements with senior officers of the new administration, the Congress, the IMF, World Bank, and the FDIC for forums to be held Tuesday evening, April 18 and Wednesday, April 19. One important item on our agenda will be the prospects for the dollar.

BUY KING DOLLAR!

The consensus of Wall Street firms, including several of the giants, is to diversify investments out of the dollar and into key foreign-denominated securities. This will prove to be one giant error for the New Year. . . . The dollar is undervalued, whether measured via IMF exchange-rate-inflation adjusted cost and price indexes or purchasing-power-parity estimates. . . . Dollar-denominated bonds and stocks sport yields generally greater than those of most foreign instruments. The United States now represents a prime investment market as contrasted, for example, with the gamblers market in Tokyo with much lower yields on bonds and minuscule-to-invisible yields on stocks . . .

Conclusion: Commit now to the very highest quality dollar-denominated long bonds and U.S. equities.

Appendix G

Consensus Misreading of Yield Curves

The Money and Capital Markets Monitor (Excerpts)
November 17, 1992

The bond-bear consensus missed badly on yet another count: they misread yield curves. True, the slope of the curve does reflect market expectations, *but consensus expectations can be wrong.* For example, consensus expectations as reflected in the yield curve were wrong, predictably, in late 1990 (*Monitor,* October 24, 1990) and, again, in 1991 and 1992. To bond-bear consternation, the yield curve fell across its entire spectrum. Despite temporary rebounds, the 1990–92 trend of yields has been down, down, down, with each upturn followed by new lows.

So, what explains bond-bear failure? Let's try to answer that question with a simplified example of the meaning behind yield curves. Suppose we restrict our initial example to just one-year and two-year contracts, and assume initially that both present yields and expected future yields are at 6 percent. In that case, the investor would be indifferent as to either contract, and the yield curve would be flat. Suppose, however, the expected yield one year out rises to 12 percent. In that case, arbitragers would sell the two-year contract, buy the one-year contract, and produce a new equilibrium. One possibility is that yields would fall to 4 percent on one-year bonds, and rise to 8 percent on two-year bonds. So, you could (a) buy a two-year bond at 8 percent or (b) buy a one-year bond at 4 percent, reinvest in one year at 12 percent, and earn 8 percent for the two years. Thus, $\frac{(4\% + 12\%)}{2} = 8\%$. These are equivalent options, and define the upsweeping curve, with the forward rate at 12 percent.

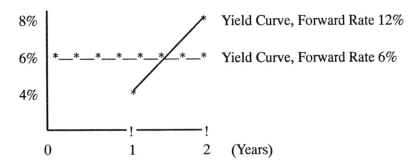

We can see that the two-year rate is simply the average of current and expected (forward) rates. More precisely, the long rate is the *geometric* average of current short-term rates and a series of expected short-term forward rates. To repeat, though, the slope of the curve can seriously mislead. It did just that to the 1990–92 bond-bears. In many cases, however, the slope can help. For example, the steeply inverted slope in 1981 was one major factor that induced us to forecast recession and lower rates (*Monitor,* July 9, 1981).

Postscript (November 22, 1994): Yields continued down contrary to expectations well into 1993, then exploded in 1994. Fears of inflation and economic recovery prompted hedge funds and others to dump their bonds, a classic case of psychology dominating fundamentals. Just about everybody was caught flat-footed, including me. So, I must remember to add psychology to my other two gods—data and theory—at least for short-run projections. If only I had a science of tracking, measuring, and forecasting psychology. Sigh.

Appendix H

Historical Perspective on Bubbles

MACKAY, KENNEDY, AND KINDLEBERGER ON BUBBLES

Consider here, as an extension of chapters 15 through 17, the bubbles that intrigued Charles Mackay, Charles Kindleberger, and Paul Kennedy. Note the ingredients common to all bubbles.

Mackay on Bubbles

Mackay emphasized in his *Extraordinary Popular Delusions and the Madness of Crowds* that all bubbles collapse, sooner or later, generally sooner than the crowd expects. This is what Nobel Prize winner John R. Hicks said (chapter 15). Mackay tells us that the Mississippi bubble in France in 1719–20 had many variants, one being that of a trading monopoly with Louisiana that would tap the resources of the great Mississippi River, including all its supposed riches in precious metals. Investors, dreaming of unlimited profits, bid share prices of the Mississippi Company to celestial levels. Promoters and speculators made quick fortunes, then got out. Prices collapsed when the dream collapsed. That's all the Mississippi Company was, a highly promoted dream.

He cites John Law's Land Bank in France as a second variant of the Mississippi scheme. The idea was to issue money against land pledged as security, the amount of the issue never to exceed the *market value* of the land. Investors interpreted that qualitative limit to mean sound finance. It wasn't. The fallacy, of course, lay in the absence of any quantitative limit to money creation. So, what happened? Rapid money growth spurred inflation, which lifted land prices, which speeded the money printing presses ever faster, which catapulted land prices higher and higher. Predictably, John Law's Land Bank also collapsed.

Does not Law's bank scheme remind you of the Tokyo market in which stock prices pushed real estate and land prices higher, which lifted stock prices, which pushed real asset prices yet higher, and so on in one grand circle? Does it not remind you of the Fed chasing its own tail in "targeting" interest rates (chapter 5)?

A third bubble that caught Mackay's eye was the South Sea Bubble in England in the 1720s. This produced visions of great riches to be made by investing in stock of the South Sea Company. The company was supposed to be involved in all kinds of profitable ventures, including the exploitation of vast gold mines in Mexico and Peru. Gold was supposed to make the country rich, reminding one of the crazy notions of the modern gold bugs (chapter 12). The bubble burst, of course, when speculators realized finally that deceit and fraud were the principal products of the South Sea promoters.

Mackay's account of the tulipomania craze of the 1630s that swept through all of Holland is unforgettable. Its promoters infected the Dutch with a mad, speculative fever, whatever their background and intelligence, their position, their education. Mackay wrote (page 91) that a single tulip bulb, the Semper Augustus, "was thought to be very cheap at 5,500 Florins." That amounted to a good fortune when translated into land, cattle, real estate. When prices started to retreat, Mackay wrote (page 95): "It was seen that somebody must lose fearfully in the end." Lose they did.

Does this remind you of anything recent? Of course. Mackay made plain that what I have dubbed Parrots and Pros and Ostriches have been around for centuries, that they swell mightily in numbers in times of bubbles (see the concluding sections of chapters 16 and 17).

Kennedy on Bubbles

Paul Kennedy stressed that the world's economic powers wax and wane, rise and fall, live and die.* Explosive one day, and down the next. That's history, and that's the future. That's true for everything, including Japan. Kennedy is

---

The Rise and Fall of the Great Powers (New York: Random House, 1987).

no stranger to the Gompertz curve, our life-and-death curve that dominates markets, institutions, and everything else including you and me (chapter 8). That becomes immediately apparent in the very title of his masterpiece *The Rise and Fall of Great Powers*. We quote here Kennedy's comment on the "Japanese miracle":

> [Japan's] very success is already provoking a scissors effect reaction against its export-led expansion. The one blade of those scissors is the emulation of Japan by other ambitious Asian NICS (newly industrialized countries) . . . not to mention China itself. . . . The second even more worrying blade of the scissors has been the increasingly hostile reaction of Americans and Europeans to the seemingly inexorable penetration of their domestic markets by Japanese products.*

Hostile? That's no exaggeration (see chapter 22).

Kindleberger on Bubbles

Dr. Charles Kindleberger, whom we earlier met, stressed the fallacy of composition as being a constant companion of all bubbles.† The attempt of the crowd to get out of the market together, to squeeze through the little door all at once, is an example of that fallacy. It just doesn't work, not for the crowd.

---

*The Rise and Fall of Great Powers, pp. 459–60.
†*Manias, Panics and Crashes* (New York, Basic Books, 1978).

Appendix I

A Short Primer on Derivatives

A derivative is a security that derives its value from an underlying security. Derivatives can be extremely volatile and their *percentage* price gains or losses are a multiple of the *percentage* price gains or losses of the underlying contract. I'll illustrate the basic ideas and arithmetic (oversimplified) in the case of bond futures, currency puts, the forward versus the spot market in currencies, collateralized mortgage obligations, and put and call options on individual stocks. The extreme volatility attracts, of course, speculators as well as hedgers, as we'll see. Volatility and enormous potential rewards also attract Parrots, Pros, and Ostriches.

David Hume Versus Regulatory Ostriches

Day-after-day, headline news tells us of the many rouge traders in derivatives who have chalked up enormous losses for themselves and their firms while allegedly engaging in conspiracy, fraud, the falsification of records, and other activities. Recognize these names?: Nicholas Leeson, who allegedly lost $1.33 billion for Barings PLC; Joseph Jett, who was accused of comparable unauthorized losses at Kidder Peabody, a brokerage firm; Toshihide Iguchi, who is now under indictment for having cost Daiwa Bank Ltd. $1.1 billion; Mr. Citron of Orange County, California; and the alleged activities of Piper Jaffrey Company, Paine Webber, Prudential Securities, Askin Capital Management, BankAmerica Corporation, and on and on. The list swells even as I write.

We have just touched the tip of derivative loss and bankruptcy. I wrote of security regulators as ostriches in their blindness to the megabubble Nikkei 225 (chapter 17). Ostriches dominate, too, in their regulation of derivative madness. Is it possible that the 1995 Republican controlled Congress truly believes that man is comprised of 100 percent dove and zero percent wolf and serpent? What would David Hume have said about Republican proposals to deregulate the securities industry to expel even the ostriches (chapter 3)?

Bond Futures

You know that when market interest rates rise sharply market prices of already issued and outstanding bonds fall. Just suppose that Fred Futures Seller expects interest rates to rise (bond prices to fall) and that Bill Futures Buyer expects interest rates to fall (bond prices to rise). Now consider these initial trades and the results.

INITIAL TRANSACTION

Fred Futures Seller   Sold futures at price of 90*
Bill Futures Buyer   Bought futures at price of 90

Fred Futures Seller sells his contracts because he wants to lock in the price of the bonds before they fall. Bill Futures Buyer believes the bonds won't fall in value (interest rates will stay the same or fall) so he's willing to buy based on future higher values. Bill looks for a profit on rising futures prices.

Suppose that six months later interest rates in fact are lower (bond prices higher), and that futures prices also rise from 90 to, say, 92 on the contracts sold to Fred Futures Seller and Bill Futures Buyer (again reflecting the fall in interest rates). How do Fred and Bill fare?

FUTURES PRICES

Fred Seller   Futures price at 90
               Futures price six months later   92
Bill Buyer   Futures Price at 90
               Futures price six months later   92

Assuming that futures prices in fact rise to 92, Fred loses 2 (or 90 – 92) and Bill gains 2 (or 92 – 90). For Fred and Bill considered as a duet, it's a wash. What Fred loses, Bill gains. Actually, though, when Fred and Bill orig-

*A quote of "90" means 90 percent of par, or 90% x $1,000 = $900.

inally entered into the futures contracts, both had to deposit money (initial margin requirement) with a futures exchange to assure that each would keep his side of the contract. The exchange would in this case credit Bill with 2 and simultaneously reduce Fred's account by 2. If Fred gets worried about interest rates continuing to fall, he may buy a futures and in effect get out of the market, after having lost 2. Bill, if he so desires, can sell a futures contract, pocket his gain of 2, and be out of the market.

In the jargon of the financial markets, Fred Seller is *short* futures and Bill Buyer is *long* futures. *They don't actually buy or sell the underlying bonds but instead make pure bets as to the direction of futures prices.* To see just how much leverage is involved, consider that the initial margin (cash deposit) is but a small fraction of the price of the underlying asset. The initial margin might run, for example, only 2 percent on Treasury bonds, or $2,000 for every $100,000 of market value. That's a high leverage! If, say, futures prices soar and wipe out Fred's initial cash margin, the broker is sure to call Fred for more cash. Fred Seller could lose mightily on soaring futures prices (and Bill Buyer could lose mightily on falling futures prices).

Hedging Versus Speculating with Bond Futures

What is hedging? Suppose that Jim Worry had a portfolio of bonds but was afraid interest rates just might rise (bond prices would fall). He wants to avoid loss even though the market value of his bond portfolio is assumed to fall. In that case Jim Worry would *sell* bond futures. With a perfect hedge (unlikely, because cash and futures prices do not move precisely together), if interest rates rise, he would lose 2 each on the bonds he holds (cash bonds) but gain 2 each on the bond futures contracts. Jim Worry has hedged.

Suppose, on the other hand, that Robert Risk wants simply to speculate and make a lot of money on bond futures. He could buy futures in expectation that interest rates would fall and, if he's right, make a bundle of money because he could cash in his futures at a higher-than-market price. If he's wrong and interest rates rise, making the price of his futures fall, then he could lose mightily. If he sells futures in expectation that interest rates will rise, and he's right, he could make a huge profit. If he's wrong and interest rates fall and fall and fall, he could suffer heavy losses.

Collateralized Mortgage Obligations (CMOs)

CMOs are mortgage-backed securities (bonds), which we touched on in chapter 21. The standard contract is subject to price risk, reinvestment risk, and prepayment risk. Assume, for example, that you own CMOs, expect interest rates to continue falling but, horror of horrors, they surge much higher, as they did in 1994. You suffer a double whammy. First, as interest rates rise, the price of long-duration debt contracts falls the most. That hits hard the prices of your long-dated CMOs. Second, the effective duration of the CMO lengthens, which also means lower market prices (Exhibit 10-1: A Technical Note on Duration). Duration lengthens because mortgage borrowers decide to postpone any early prepayments. On the other hand, suppose interest rates fall, as expected. If you held long-dated CMOs, the fall in rates would translate into higher CMO prices. Also, happily for you, early prepayments to refinance mortgages would effectively reduce the average duration of your CMO portfolio, and CMO prices would rise even more. So, you can enjoy a big capital gain under these circumstances of falling rates, especially if you had purchased the CMOs at big discounts just before rates plunge and mortgages are prepaid.

With falling interest rates, though, reinvestment risk can cost you. If rates have plunged and your CMOs paid off in cash because of early prepayments, you now have to reinvest that cash at lower interest rates. The reinvestment risk at lower rates can offset partly or completely any capital gain you may have enjoyed on falling interest rates, early prepayment, and the cut in duration.

What happened in 1994? You know by now. CMO prices plunged (as market interest rates soared). They plunged even more as an echo of the effective lengthening of duration, the so-called extension risk. Why? Mortgage borrowers elected to postpone prepayments. A number of major investment organizations lost heavily as a result. Some fell into bankruptcy.

Hedging and Speculating against the Japanese Yen

In the *Money and Capital Markets Monitor* dated July 17, 1995, which I sent to institutional money managers, I developed the basic theory and mechanics of spot and forward currency markets. As I'll explain in detail, the spot market is the actual or cash market. The forward market is the cash price stipulated now on a contract to buy or sell currency at a future date. I was worried about an overpriced Japanese yen, and suggested the following hedge for U.S. investors heavily invested in yen-denominated securities:

> Let's put the conclusion first and then explain. We'll focus on the yen and the dollar. Note first that interest rates in the U.S. are much higher than in Japan. Take three-month bills as an example, with the arithmetic and mechanics and theory spelled out in the exhibit below. You see that the percentage spread in interest rates of the United States over Japan roughly matches the percentage spread be-

tween spot and forward rates. You also see that the forward rate sells at a premium over the spot rate for a country with the lower interest rates, like Japan. The forward rate sells at a discount from spot for a country with the higher rates, like the United States. Why? A fast answer is that currency arbitragers make it so. A more detailed answer tracks the actions of arbitragers and others step-by-step in plain English using simple arithmetic (exhibit).

You see there (exhibit) how you can borrow U.S. dollars at higher interest rates than in Japan, buy yen at spot, invest yen at the much lower interest rates of Japan, but still just break even. What? Yes, you still break even because you probably sold (simultaneously with your spot purchase) the yen back for dollars at a forward premium over spot. Now reverse the mechanics. That is, you borrow yen at low interest rates, buy dollars spot, invest those dollars at the higher interest rates offered by U.S. bills, and still just about break even. What? Yes, you break even because you probably entered into a forward contract when you bought spot to simultaneously sell your dollars back for yen at a discount from spot. Arbitragers got there before you to rule out a risk-free profitable ride around the currency market.

Most important is the simple mechanism involved in protecting against a plunging foreign currency, a high risk here and now for the yen. Hedging in the forward markets may be your answer. . . .

EXHIBIT: SIMPLE ARITHMETIC AND THEORY OF FORWARD MARKETS

In the *New York Times* of July 13, 1995, you can find these quotes for July 12 on page D7:

	$ Price of 1 Yen	Yen Price of $1.00
Spot	.011422	87.55
90-day fwd	.011569	86.44

You see that one yen sells on July 12 in the immediate or spot (cash) market for $.011422. So $\frac{\$1.00}{\$.011422}$ means you can buy wholesale 87.55 yen for $1.00. You also see that the ninety-day forward dollar price of the yen is higher (priced at a premium over the spot price). We used interest rates for June 28 reported by the Federal Reserve's Division of International Finance. The differential interest rates between countries roughly match the premiums or discounts. . . . Now follow this arbitrage to see if you can catch a free ride starting on July 12, 1995:

(1) Borrow $1.00 at 5.89% annual rate, 1.4725% rate (or .0147) for three months. To break even you must make enough to pay back almost $1.015 principal plus interest ($1.00 x 1.0147).

(2) Buy yen with your $1.00 at $.011422 spot (87.5503 yen per dollar). Thus $\frac{\$1.00}{\$.011422} = 87.5503$ yen.

(3) Invest 87.5503 yen for three months in Japanese bills yielding a low 1.16% annualized [interest rate], 0.29% for three months. Total receipts are: 87.5503 yen x 1.0029 = 87.8042 yen.

(4) Sell back your 87.8042 yen for dollars at the three-months forward $.011569 per yen (86.44 yen per $1.00). You get back $1.0158, or 87.8042 yen x .011569. Great, but under Step (1) you paid just about the same amount, or $1.015. (The slight discrepancy reflects rounding and the small differences in interest rates in late June versus the exchange rates we cited for early July.)

So, arbitragers beat us to it. You can also see the importance of hedging against wildly overpriced currencies. Suppose, for example, that you hedge 1,000,000 yen forward for three months at the forward rate of .011569. Then you're assured of $11,569 of dollar receipts. If the dollar spot rate should fall three months hence to $.01 per yen (100 yen to the dollar), your dollar receipts (unhedged) would total only $10,000, or below the value at spot on July 7 of $11,422. You lose $1,422 unhedged. Of course, if the spot yen appreciates, you miss out on potential profit. Since nobody knows when a bubble will pop, you're better off with longer hedges (next *Monitor*). We used three-month rates merely to illustrate. Check us against the interest-parity formula:

$$\text{Forward} = \text{Spot} \quad x \left(\frac{1 + \text{US Interest}}{1 + \text{Japan's Interest}}\right)$$
$$.0116 \quad = .011422 \ x \left(\frac{1.0147}{1.0029}\right)$$
$$.0116 \quad = .011422 \ x \ 1.01177$$

So, the interest spread ($\frac{1.0147\% - 1.0029\%}{1.0147\%}$ = .012%) about matches the spread of the reported forward over spot rates ($\frac{.011569 - .011422}{.011569}$) = .0127%. Eureka! You have deciphered the arcane interest-parity theorem.

Japanese Yen Put Warrants

Consider now the mechanics of a currency put, a contract to sell the yen with the expectation that the yen would fall against the dollar. The following is taken from the August 1, 1995 *Money and Capital Markets Monitor* sent to institutional managers. As you can see, I was worried about U.S. investors in major *unhedged* yen-denominated securities:

The yen is a bubble and [only] Lady Luck, Mistress of Short-Run Market Timing, knows just when the bubble will burst. It could burst tomorrow. To be conservative, though, we'll assume the bubble yen bursts sometime between now and December 1996. That rules out put options on yen futures with expiration dates in August, September, and October this year [1995]. Yen currency futures have expiration dates through March 1996, still too short under our assumption but perhaps not yours (next *Monitor*). But Japanese yen put warrants are now available from several brokerage houses. While most of them have early (too early) expiration dates, the Bear Stearns "Japanese Yen Put Warrants" are exercisable until December 12, 1996. Yes, all currency warrants involve a high degree of risk, including the risk of expiring worthless. With that caveat, here are details on these Yen Put Warrants:

Strike Price in Yen Per Dollar	95.53 Yen
Price of Warrant as of July 28, 1995, in Dollars	$2.75
(Quotes: American Stock Exchange Composite Listing)	

Cash Settlement Value (CSV) = $50 − [$50 x $\left(\frac{\text{Strike Rate}}{\text{Spot Rate}}\right)$]
where Spot is Yen Per Dollar

If Spot is 95.53,	CSV = $50 − [$50 x $\left(\frac{95.53}{95.53}\right)$]	
	= $50 − $50 =	$0.00
If Spot is 100,	CSV = $50 − [$50 x $\left(\frac{95.53}{100}\right)$] =	$2.24
If Spot is 110,	CSV = $50 − [$50 x $\left(\frac{95.53}{110}\right)$] =	$6.58
If Spot is 140,	CSV = $50 − [$50 x $\left(\frac{95.53}{140}\right)$] =	$15.88

So, where is the yen headed? It has trended up, up, up for a long time, but recently has faltered against the dollar. So, if the value of the yen trends higher once again relative to the dollar, you lose. If yen volatility decreases, the trading price of the warrant would likely fall, other things being equal. As the time remaining to the expiration date of the warrant decreases, the trading price of the warrant will likely decrease, other things being equal. Other risks abound, but we shall not discuss them here. Any serious speculator or hedger, though, would surely take the time to study the Bear Stearns Prospectus Supplement to the Prospectus of 10/7/94. Finally, with the exchange rate as of 7/28/95 at 88.17 yen to the dollar, note that the warrant was out-of-the-money by $4.17 even though it traded at $2.75 on the same date (reflecting mainly time value to expiration):

$$\text{CSV} = \$50 - [\$50 \text{ x } \left(\tfrac{95.53}{88.17}\right)] = -\$4.17.$$

Conclusions: The out-of-the-money Bear Stearns Japanese Yen Put Warrants expiring December 1996 are made in Heaven for those who, like us, expect the bubble yen to burst. What's the Devil's catch? The warrants [if I'm wrong] could expire worthless.

Stock Derivatives: Puts and Calls

Stock derivatives are the easiest to understand. The fundamental idea is simple. A put, for example, gives you the right but not the obligation to sell stock at the strike price. You would buy a put at a strike price of, say, 100 if you expected the market to fall to, say, 80. If the market does fall to 80, your put would soar in price to reflect your contractual right to sell for 100 something now valued in the market at only 80. The premium (price) you paid for the put would soar. Since the premium is but a fraction of the price of the stock itself, your potential *percentage* price gains on the put can be huge.

Of course, if the market price of the stock rises above your strike price on the put, your put would be out-of-the-money. It might still have some "time value" provided buyers believe the market might still be headed for a fall before the expiration date of the put. If the market price for the stock remains above the strike price of the put at expiration, then the put would expire worthless. That's why economists call the put a "wasting" asset.

So, you can make big bucks on puts. But losses are limited to the price (premium) of the put. You can lose the premium (price) you paid for the put, and that's all. It's this big potential gain (a mighty leverage as compared with buying the stock itself) with a limited and stipulated potential loss that is so attractive to many speculators and hedgers. (Just reverse this example of a put for a *call,* an option to buy stock at a price stipulated now, the strike price, in expectation that market prices will rise along with a *magnified* rise in the market price of the call option.)

That's the basic idea of puts and calls, but you might want to check into any good investment text for the mechanics and details. That's the easy part. The hard part is to forecast the market, a most difficult and time-consuming task stressed throughout this book.

Glossary

Absorption thesis (tax incidence). The argument is that the final burden (incidence) of the corporate income tax reduces corporate cash flow and net profits, hence it rests on corporate shareholders. This is the opposite of the shifting thesis, which argues that higher income taxes are shifted backward to suppliers or labor in lower prices or wages, or forward into higher consumer prices, or both. *See* shifting thesis.

Arbitrage. The simultaneous purchase and sale of two securities that are essentially identical in order to profit from a disparity in their prices. The law of one price is that identical assets in the same market command identical prices.

Bears. Investors who expect securities prices to fall.

Black Monday. The October 19, 1987 stock market decline, the biggest one-day fall ever for the Dow Jones industrial index.

Blue chip economists. Consensus forecasts of some fifty economists, published by a private organization.

Building permits. Authorization by local governments to begin construction on houses, apartments, etc.

Bulls. Investors who expect securities prices to rise.

Capacity utilization. Labor and capital (plant, equipment, and other facilities) employed as a percentage of the labor force and potential output. Below-capacity operation is characterized by unemployed labor and idle factories.

Capital Asset Pricing Model (CAPM). An equilibrium investment model stating that the expected and required return on a portfolio of securities is the risk-free rate plus a premium for portfolio (unsystematic) risk and market (systematic) risk. Among other problems, the CAPM assumes risk-free lending, risk-free borrowing, and risk-free arbitrage, all pure fictions (see chapter 21). So does the parallel MM model in corporate finance (see chapter 20).

Capital inflow. In international finance, capital inflow is identical to the current account deficit. When, for example, the United States runs a deficit, foreigners increase their net claims against the United States, which is called net capital inflow to the United States. The ex post identities, the current account deficit and capital inflow, are widely misunderstood and account for serious errors of analysis (see chapter 22).

Capitalized value. The present value calculated by discounting all projected future net receipts at the required return (cost of capital). The rational and well-informed investor may, of course, come up with higher or lower values than that of the market. Markets can go haywire (see chapters 15–17).

Capital investment. In real terms, investment in plant and equipment and other productive facilities.

Carrying costs. Out-of-pocket costs incurred in holding an inventory of goods or property, e.g., insurance and financing (interest) charges. It's also the difference between the futures and spot prices of an asset or security, and can entail interest income foregone in order to invest in spot (cash) assets. *See* opportunity cost.

CATS. Certificates of accrual on Treasury-backed zero-coupon securities sold at a deep discount from face value. CATS pay no interest at any time but return the full face value at maturity.

Chaos. Confusion and disorder. Mathematicians, though, define a chaotic series as one that can be predicted with precision provided (a) you can define the beginning of the series and (b) you assume no intervening events will alter your prediction. Economists, needless to say, have no such power. Still, chaos theory now challenges conventional theory (see chapters 25 and 26).

Checkable deposits. Accounts at banks and other financial institutions against which you can draw checks for payment without prior notice. You can also withdraw cash from your checkable (demand) deposits using automatic teller machines.

Chief economist. The top economist and normally the economic spokesperson for a company or other organization. His/her job may include analysis and forecasting, and managing others on staff, including junior economists.

Circuit velocity of money. As an extension of Irving Fisher's concept of velocity, I mean the turnover of money as it circulates within the complex of commercial banks and nonbank financial intermediaries. Circuit velocity is little understood among economists and Fed policymakers (see chapter 11).

Classical preachers. Contemporary economists who misunderstand the views of classical economists set forth two centuries ago. They apply the classical solutions of the eighteenth century, which focused on long-run trends, to short-run cyclical swings of the twentieth century—a mighty error. Key Federal Reserve officers often do just that (see chapter 5).

CMO. A collateralized mortgage obligation, that is, a bond backed by a portfolio of mortgages, with the mortgages separated into short-term, medium-term, and long-term portfolios (also called tranches) to meet different investor tastes. Each CMO bond is paid a fixed interest stream derived from the interest earned on the underlying mortgages. CMOs can be extremely risky investments (see chapter 20 and Appendix I).

Coincident indicators. Economic series like income, production, employment, sales, and Gross Domestic Product (GDP) that rise and fall at roughly the same time the overall economy rises and falls. These "rear-view mirror" data are among the most popular but the very worst forecasting tools (see chapter 1).

Conglomerates. A corporation involved in a number of unrelated businesses (see chapter 1).

Consensus forecast. Just add up and rank the forecasts of Gross Domestic Product (GDP) or other economic series, and calculate the arithmetic mean or median to represent consensus thinking. Consensus forecasts can be dangerous to your financial health (see chapter 5 and Appendix A).

Cost of debt capital. The required return for investing in any given debt security reflecting the multiple risks that could be involved. *See* risk components of interest rate.

Cost of equity capital. The required return for investing in stock calculated as the return on the highest grade corporate bonds (sometimes U.S. Treasuries) plus an additional return, the equity premium, for any additional risk. The premium would reflect company risk, the risk of the individual stock, plus the risk of overall stock market fluctuations. Despite the claims of modern portfolio theory, no satisfactory measure of risk exists now; it never has and never will (see the final pages of chapter 21).

Cost of capital (composite or weighted average). The average cost involved in raising, say, debt and equity with the weights defined as the market values of the debt and equity (see chapters 19 and 20).

Countercyclical policy. Policies designed to offset cyclical swings in the economy to provide sustained and satisfactory economic growth.

Coupon (zero) strips. Zero-coupon bonds using Treasuries.

Crowding in. *Monetized* government tax cuts or expenditures that increase private income, financing, spending, and output in an economy operating below capacity (see chapter 13). *See* monetized borrowing.

Crowding out. Government deficits via *nonmonetized* tax cuts and higher spending that displace or depress private financing, income, spending, and output to cause recession (see chapter 6). *See* nonmonetized borrowing.

Current production. Consumption, investment, and government goods and services measured in current prices. *See* gross domestic product (GDP).

Cyclicals. Stocks or other assets that fall or rise sharply with the cyclical fall and rise of the economy.

Default. Failure to pay contractual payments of principal and interest.

Demand deposits. *See* checkable deposits.

Demand elasticity. The percentage change in quantity associated with any percentage change in price.

Demand for money to hold. The reciprocal of the velocity of money (see chapter 7. *See* velocity of money.

Demand-pull inflation. Price rises resulting from growth of demand faster than the supply of goods or services that are offered to the market.

Derivative. A financial instrument whose value is derived from the value of expected fluctuations in an underlying financial instrument, with percentage fluctuations in the underlying asset reflected in magnified percentage fluctuations in the value of the derivative (see Appendix I for examples).

Direct (private) placements. Sale of debt or equity securities to professional investors such as life insurance companies or pension funds.

Discounted value. The present value of future receipts discounted at the required cost of capital. *See* cost of capital.

Disinflation. A slower rate of inflation.

Dividend irrelevancy theorem. Other things being equal, the idea that the market price of stock should rise to reflect the plowback of earnings, the same earnings that otherwise might have been paid directly as dividends. (See chapter 16 for pitches based on deliberate or affected confusion.)

DOGS. Dangerously overpriced Gung-Ho stocks. I argued that investors should avoid DOGS in favor of lovable CATS prior to Black Monday (see chapter 15).

Duration of a bond. That point in time between the purchase and the maturity of a bond when swings in interest income received from reinvestment of the coupon interest just offset the opposite swings in price so that the realized yield approximates the initially computed yield to maturity. Thus if interest rates were to fall, the lower interest stream from reinvestment of coupon income at lower rates would just offset at the point of duration the higher price of the bonds. Also a measure of potential price volatility of a bond (see chapter 10).

Earnings ratio. Earnings, either those for the past twelve months or those projected for the next twelve months, divided by the present market price of a stock. Turned upside down, the earnings ratio becomes the price/earnings multiple.

EBIT. Earnings before interest and taxes.

Econometrician. An economist whose statistical model is based mainly on past correlations of economic series. These models rarely if ever take note of a cyclical turn in the economy.

Economic Man. Those attributes of human beings which explain economic decision making and overall conduct in society. The focus of this book chapter-by-chapter highlights the opposing views of economists and competing scientists (see especially chapters 24–26).

Equity premium. The extra return investors require and expect over and above the stated return on, say, low-risk, high-grade corporate bonds or Treasury securities.

Ex ante. Expected. Also effective demand and supply, meaning, for example, the desire and ability to buy or sell a commodity at a given price. Often confused with *ex post* statistical identities.

Ex post. Historical accounting identities like purchases and sales, borrowing and lending, the current account deficit and capital inflow in international finance, terms often confused with effective demand and supply (see chapters 7 and 22).

Fixed cost. Costs that remain unchanged as a function of sales and output (see chapter 7).

Fixed income group. Money managers of fixed-income securities like bonds, Treasury bills, and mortgages.

Forward investment commitments. Contracts to provide financing in the future with terms stipulated at the time the contracts are drawn. *See* direct (private) placements.

Four bond bears. In 1981 they included top Wall Street economists: Henry Kaufman (Dr. Doom), Al Wojnilower (Dr. Death), Phil Braverman, and Sam Nakagama (see chapter 6 and Appendix B).

Fundamental (equilibrium) value. The present value of all future receipts discounted at a required discount rate (cost of capital) by well-informed analysts who pay strict attention to good theory and data. The actual market price may be far above or far below the fundamental value.

Gold bugs. The quintessence of naive but highly motivated and often highly emotional analysts who see heaven in gold and the old gold standards, while paying no attention to sound theory, history, and data. Deeply conservative, they have strong convictions on how government is supposedly stripping our freedoms away and debasing the currency (see chapter 12).

Gompertz curve. A plotted curve depicting rates of percentage change on the vertical axis and time on the horizontal axis. See the Gompertz variation of our life-death curve in chapter 8.

Growth recession. Anemic growth of the economy below its potential, signaling rising unemployment.

Gross domestic product (GDP). Total value of goods and services produced within the United States.

Gross national product (GNP). Total value of goods and services produced in the United States *minus* (roughly) our imports from abroad *plus* our exports to foreign nations.

High-grade bonds. High-quality bonds with a high-probability that all contract terms for repayment will be kept.

Idiocy Circle. The attempt by the Federal Reserve, for example, to keep interest rates from rising by greatly expanding the supply of reserves and money and credit, but with the result that excessive and continued monetary easing unintentionally backfires to produce accelerating inflation and higher interest rates (see chapter 5).

Implied (internal) rate of return. That rate of return which equates the present price of an investment with the discounted value of all projected future receipts.

Incidence (tax). The final resting place or burden of the tax, or who ultimately pays the tax.

Income velocity. Spending for current production divided by the money stock. Income velocity now exceeds 6 times for the narrowly defined money stock, or M1. That is $\frac{GDP}{M1}$ = 6x (see chapter 7 and Exhibit 7–1).

Inflation. A rise in the general price level, the same as a fall in the real purchasing power of the monetary unit for goods and services (see chapter 7).

Institutional investor. Investors such as banks, insurance companies, pension funds, etc.

Interest-sensitive stocks. Stocks, like high-grade utility stocks, that tend to move up when interest rates fall, and vice versa. Any major cyclical fall in the stock market, though, could send interest-sensitive stocks down, too (see chapter 2).

Inverse correlation. Things that move in opposite directions. For example, throughout most of the post-World War II period, interest rates generally declined or softened when the size of the federal budget deficit increased, and interest rates generally rose when the budgetary deficit contracted. With few exceptions, the magnitude of the deficit and interest rates went their opposite ways, a fact almost universally misunderstood (see chapter 6).

Inverted yield curve. A plot of yields on the vertical axis and time to maturity on the horizontal axis such that short-term rates are higher than intermediate-term rates, which are higher than long-term rates. See chapter 9 on the widespread misreading of the slope of yield curves as forecasting tools.

J-curve. The initial versus the lagged impact of, say, a fall in the value of the dollar in foreign exchange markets. See Exhibit 22-1 on the J-curve and the Japanese yen.

Lagging indicators. Economic series like plant and equipment expenditures and commercial and industrial loans that tend to continue to rise after the overall economy has moved into recession. They are unreliable indicators of the future.

Liquidity. The ability to sell any asset at a price close to the current market.

Long run. That period of time when all costs are variable, when business wants to generate revenues that cover all costs plus a normal (satisfactory) profit at the minimum.

Long Treasury bonds. Any Treasury bond with a maturity beyond ten years.

Loose quantity theorist of money. The smart analyst who always pays attention to money, money velocity, and output.

Market period. Economic time frame in which goods are already produced. Past costs of production may be irrelevant to your decision to hold or sell (see chapter 18).

Market weights. The proportions using market values in, say, calculating the average composite cost of raising both debt and equity capital (see chapters 19 and 20).

Microeconomic focus. A thorough analysis of the individual parts or components of the economy, which can be highly misleading (see chapter 1).

MM arbitrage "proof." The risk-free borrowing and lending proof offered by economists Modigliani and Miller. They contend that the average weighted cost of capital of a corporation is independent of leverage. See chapter 20 for our view that the MM thesis violates both good theory and the data, and chapter 21 on the CAPM, which also founders on the academic fictions of risk-free borrowing, risk-free lending, and risk-free arbitrage. *See* capital asset pricing model (CAPM).

Monetarist. A monetary theorist following the views of Nobel Prize winner Milton Friedman. See chapter 11 for our criticism of monetarist theory and practice.

Monetary aggregates. Various measures of the money supply (see chapter 7 for details on M1, M2, and M3).

Monetized borrowing (deficits). Borrowing and simultaneously printing money to finance the borrowing. The Federal Reserve and the Treasury define monetization as direct Federal Reserve purchases of Treasuries, but that concept is far too narrow (see chapter 6).

Near money. Close money substitutes like mutual funds.

New stock issues. Stock offerings just brought to the market such as IPOs (initial public offerings) to raise capital.

Nominal interest rate. Actual or current rate, unadjusted for inflation.

Nonmonetized borrowing (deficits). Borrowing existing money (no increase in the existing money supply). A money shuffle, as explained in chapter 11 and Exhibit 11–1.

Opportunity cost. The income or rewards foregone. If you invest in a Japanese bond at 5 percent but could earn 9 percent on a British government bond, your gross opportunity cost is 9 percent, and your net opportunity cost is 4 percent. Investors frequently overlook the dominion of opportunity cost, to their sorrow. See especially chapter 17 on the collapse of the Nikkei 225.

Par. Stated value of stock or bond at issue.

Parrot. Naive investors who repeat what others have to say without understanding. They populate both the buy side and sell side of Wall Street in great numbers.

Parrot circle. Chasing your tail by confusing definitions with analysis (see chapter 8).

Perpetual bonds. Bonds with no maturity but with a fixed stream of interest payments.

Portfolio. The mix of investment securities held.

Present value. Future receipts discounted to the present.

Pros. The despicable intellectual prostitutes (including top Wall Street executives as well as senior government and corporate officials) who rampage throughout the pages of this book. They represent the very worst features of "economic man."

Procyclical fiscal and monetary policy. Policies that make a bad situation worse. (Examples would include increasing interest rates or sharply cutting federal expenditures in time of recession, thus deepening the recession.) See chapters 3–6.

Productivity (economic). Output per hour of all workers. See also the composite index of productivity in chapter 24, one that presumes to measure the individual contributions to total output of labor and capital.

Progressive tax. A graduated tax system in which higher incomes pay higher tax rates than lower incomes.

Protectionists. Parrots and Pros who would keep us from importing foreign goods by, for example, raising tariffs. See chapter 23. Their naivete and self-serving arguments almost match those of gold bugs. *See* gold bugs.

Purchases (MV). Money times the income velocity of money, or total spending for current production.

Pure interest rate. That rate you demand for waiting for your interest and principal to be returned to you even with no risk of nonpayment. It is a volatile rate widely misunderstood, and influenced mightily by fluctuations in the demand for and supply of credit (see chapter 9).

Random. Each item of a given set has an equal probability of being chosen.

Reaganomics. Supply-side economic theory associated with President Ronald Reagan. It argued for tax cuts as a panacea to spur incentives, productivity, and economic growth. The theory was (is) seriously flawed (see chapter 6).

Real gross national product (GNP). Inflation adjusted GNP.

Real interest rate. Inflation adjusted nominal rate. *See* nominal interest rate.

Recession. A cyclical fall in the economy.

Reference (cyclical) dates. Peaks and troughs of the business cycle as estimated by the National Bureau of Economic Research.

Registered representatives (RRs). Brokers with security firms.

Required investment return. The return you demand to compensate you for investment in any given alternative. *See* cost of capital.

Reserves. Mainly the vault cash or deposits held at the Federal Reserve of banks and other financial institutions who are members of the Federal Reserve System.

Reverse-yield gap. The yield on AAA bonds less the dividend return on stocks (see chapters 15 and 17).

Risk (components) of an interest rate. We noted eleven components in chapter 10: credit risk, inflation risk, capital risk, marketability risk, reinvestment risk, liquidity risk, pure-rate risk, call risk, event risk, prepayment risk, and exchange-rate risk.

Sales (PT). Index of prices P times an index of output T in the Fisherian equation of exchange $MV = PT$. Simply put, P is the average price paid for current production (T), where PT = GDP. Money (M) times the turnover of money or velocity (V) is the total expenditure (MV) for current production. So, $MV = PT = GDP$.

Security analyst. A researcher who focuses on a company's future prospects by analyzing its debt and equity contracts.

Shading (painting to the bright side). Euphemism for deception and deceit, conscious or unconscious. One example is that of a government official who publicly talks about bright economic prospects while privately forecasting recession. Another example is that of economists who dare not forecast recession for fear of antagonizing their employers. See chapters 1, 2, and 3.

Shadow open-market committee. A private group of economists made up of monetarists who track and appraise Federal Reserve policies (see chapter 11).

Shifting thesis (tax incidence). The view that the burden of a corporate tax (who ultimately pays) is shifted either forward to consumers in the form of higher prices or backward to suppliers and labor in the form of in lower prices paid for wages or raw materials.

Short run. Period of time analytically when fixed (sunk) costs have already been incurred.

Stagflation. Recession combined with higher inflation, as occurred in 1973–75.

Stimulate an economy. To lift private spending, output, and employment via expansionary fiscal and monetary policies.

Stock market bubble. A greatly overpriced market.

Stocks. Equity ownership in a corporation.

Subpar growth. Growth below potential.

Time preference theory. A theory of interest in which the equilibrium rate just matches (a) the demand for credit for those who want to borrow in order to consume now rather than later with (b) the supply of credit provided by those who forego current consumption by lending from current income.

Transactions velocity. Spending for all purposes (current production plus purchases and sales of financial instruments, foreign exchange, second-hand goods, etc.), which means a much higher velocity. For example, the turnover of demand deposits runs now at about 4,000 times a year for large New York City banks (see chapter 7 and Exhibit 7–2). *See also* income velocity.

Underwriting. Sales of newly issued securities by a brokerage firm to raise debt or equity capital for corporations, either through a best-efforts basis (for a commission fee as agent) or through buying the issue outright from the corporate issuer and selling it to investors (acting as a principal) with the hope of making a profit on the resale.

Upsweeping yield curve. A chart depicting short-term rates below intermediate rates, which are below long-term rates, with the vertical axis representing yields and the horizontal axis representing time to maturity.

Variable labor costs. Labor and materials and other costs that fluctuate with the volume of output.

Velocity of money. The turnover or rate of speed at which money is spent. *See* income velocity *and* transactions velocity.

Zero-coupon bonds. Bonds with no interest payments, but a single sum (principal) payable at maturity. These bonds are sold at deep discounts from maturity value. *See* CATS.

Bibliography

Bastiat, Frederic. "Economic Sophisms," in S. H. Patterson (ed.), *Readings in the History of Economic Thought*. New York: McGraw Hill Book Company, 1932.

Batra, Ravi. *Regular Economic Cycles*. New York: St. Martin's Press, 1985.

Becker, Ernest. *Denial of Death*. New York: The Free Press, 1973.

———. *Structure of Evil*. New York: George Braziller, 1968.

Bloom, Allan. *The Closing of the American Mind*. New York: Simon and Schuster, 1987.

Bok, Sissela. *Lying: Moral Choice in Public and Private Lives*. New York: Random House, 1978.

Brigham, Eugene F. *Financial Management: Theory and Practice,* Fourth Edition. New York: Dryden Press, 1985.

Brigham, Eugene, and Louis Gapenski. *Financial Management: Theory and Practice,* Seventh Edition. New York: The Dryden Press, 1994.

Buckley, William F., Jr. *Right Reason*. New York: Doubleday & Company, 1985.

Colton, Caleb C. Quote from Tyron Edwards, *Useful Quotations*. New York: Grosset & Dunlap, 1938.

Darwin, Charles. *The Descent of Man*. New York: W. W. Norton & Company, 1979.

deMandeville, Bernard. "Fable of the Bees," in S. H. Patterson (ed.), *Read-*

441

ings in the History of Economic Thought. New York: McGraw Hill Book Company, 1932.

Dewey, John. *Morals and Conduct,* in Sax Commins and Robert N. Liscott (eds.), *The World's Great Thinkers, Man and Man: the Social Philosophers.* New York: Random House, 1947.

Dickens, Charles. Quote from Tyron Edwards, *Useful Quotations.* New York: Grosset & Dunlap Publishers, 1934.

Epictetus. "The Manual," in Sax Commins and Robert N. Liscott (eds.), *The World's Great Thinkers, The Social Philosophers.* New York: Random House, 1947.

Etzioni, Amatai. *Moral Dimension: Towards a New Economics.* New York: The Free Press, 1988.

Federal Reserve Bank of New York. *Quarterly Review* (Fall 1988 and Spring 1994).

Federal Reserve Bank of Richmond. *Economic Review* (March/April, May/June, and July/August 1990).

Feldstein, Martin. *Capital Taxation.* Cambridge, Mass.: Harvard University Press, 1983.

Fisher, Irving. *Why the Dollar Is Shrinking.* New York: The Macmillan Company, 1914.

Flesch, Rudolf. *The Art of Clear Thinking.* New York: Harper & Row, 1951.

Flugel, J. C. *Man, Morals, and Society: A Psychoanalytical Study.* New York: International Universities Press, 1945.

Friedman, Milton, and Anna J. Schwartz. *Monetary History of the United States.* Princeton, N.J.: Princeton University Press, 1963.

Fromm, Erich. *Anatomy of Human Destructiveness.* New York: Holt, Rinehart and Winston, 1973.

Givens, C. J. *Wealth without Risk: How to Develop a Personal Fortune without Going Out on a Limb.* New York: Simon and Schuster, 1988.

Gleick, James. *Chaos.* New York: Penguin Books, 1988.

Holland, Daniel. "Effect of Taxation on Compensation and Effort: The Case of Business Executives." *Proceedings of the National Tax Association,* 1969.

——. *Dividends Under the Income Tax.* Princeton, N.J.: Princeton University Press, 1962.

Hume, David. Selections from *Inquiry Concerning the Principles of Morals,* in *Hume Selections,* edited by Charles W. Hendell. New York: Charles Scribner's Sons, 1927.

James, William. *Pragmatism.* Cambridge, Mass.: Harvard University Press, 1975.

Kennedy, Paul. *The Rise and Fall of the Great Powers.* New York: Random House, 1987.

Keynes, John Maynard. *General Theory of Employment, Interest, and Money.* New York: Harcourt Brace and Company, 1936.

———. *How to Pay for the War.* New York: Harcourt Brace and Company. 1940.

———. *A Tract on Monetary Reform.* London: Macmillan and Co., Ltd., 1923, p. 80.

———. *Treatise on Money,* Volume II. Cambridge, England: The Royal Economic Society, 1930.

Kundera, Milan. *Art of the Novel.* New York: Grove Press, Inc. 1988.

———. *Book of Laughter and Forgetting.* New York: Penguin Books, 1981.

Larrain, Maurice, and J. Pagano. "Nonlinear Dynamics and the Chaotic Behavior of Interest Rates," *Financial Analysts Journal* (September/October 1991).

Lerner, Abba. *The Economics of Control.* New York: The Macmillan Company, 1959.

Mackay, Charles. *Extraordinary Popular Delusions and the Madness of Crowds.* New York: L. C. Page and Company, 1852, reprinted in 1932.

Marx, Karl. *Capital,* Volumes I, II, and III. New York: Charles Keer & Company, 1906, reprinted in 1932.

———. *The Communist Manifesto,* in Sax Commins and Robert N. Liscott (eds.), *The World's Great Thinkers: The Political Philosophers.* New York: Random House, 1947.

Miller, Merton H. "The Modigliani-Miller Propositions After Thirty Years," *Journal of Economic Perspectives* (Fall 1988).

Mitchell, David. *Introduction to Logic.* Garden City, N.Y.: Doubleday & Company, Inc., 1970.

Modigliani, Franco, and Merton H. Miller. "The Cost of Capital, Corporation Finance, and the Theory of Investment," *American Economic Review* (June 1958).

Parks, Robert H. "The Cost of Capital Crossover [and the Nikkei 225 Mega-bubble]," *Standard & Poor's CreditWeek* (January 29, 1990).

―――. "Fed 'Targeting' Risks Economic Anemia or Full Recession," *Standard & Poor's CreditWeek* (November 13, 1995).

―――. "Monetarist Mania," *Standard & Poor's CreditWeek* (April 29, 1995).

―――. "Monetary Policy and the Creation of Near-Money," *Financial Analysts Journal* (September/October 1965).

―――. "Portfolio Operations of Commercial Banks and the Level of Treasury Security Prices," *The Journal of Finance* (March 1959).

―――. "The Theory of Tax Incidence: International Aspects," *National Tax Journal* (June 1961).

―――. "Trouble with M1," *Banking, Journal of the American Bankers Association* (November 1970).

―――. "Use and Abuse of Financial and Monetary Data," *Journal of Portfolio Management* (Spring 1975).

Parks, Robert H., and Murray E. Polakoff, et al. *Financial Institutions and Markets.* New York: Houghton Mifflin, 1970.

Patterson, S. H. (ed.) *Readings in the History of Economic Thought.* New York: McGraw Hill Book Company (1932), pp. 39 and 45.

Poe, Edgar Allen. *The Power of Words.* New York: W. J. Black Company, 1927.

Porter, Michael. *The Competitive Advantage of Nations.* New York: The Free Press, 1990.

Prestowitz, Clyde. *Swarthmore College Bulletin* (February 1990).

Riley, William B., and Austin H. Montgomery. *Guide to Computer-Assisted Investment Analysis.* New York: McGraw Hill Book Company, 1982.

Root, Franklin R. *International Trade and Investment.* Cincinnati, Ohio: South Western Publishing Company, 1990.

Schienemann, Gary S. "Japanese P/E Ratios," in *Prudential-Bache Securities Investment Report* (June 20, 1988).

Shakespeare, William. Quotation from *Measure for Measure,* in John Bartlett's *Familiar Quotations.* Boston: Little, Brown & Company, 1980.

―――. *Tragedy of Macbeth,* Act IV, Scene I, New York: Lancer Books, 1968.

Smith, Adam. From *The Wealth of Nations* and *Lectures on Justice, Police, Revenue and Arms,* in S. H. Patterson (ed.), *Readings in the History of Economic Thought.* New York: McGraw Hill Book Company, 1932.

Sprinkel, Beryl W. *Money and Markets: A Monetarist View.* Homewood, Ill.: Richard D. Irwin, Inc., 1971.

Strunk, William, and E. B. White. *Elements of Style.* New York: Macmillan Company, 1959.

Strachey, John. *The Nature of Capitalist Crisis.* New York: J. J. Little and Ives Company, 1935, p. 7.

Thouless, Robert H. *How to Think Straight: The Technique of Applying Logic Instead of Emotion.* New York: Simon & Schuster, 1947.

Weston, J. Fred et al. Articles by prominent economists on Modigliani-Miller Cost of Capital Theory. The Financial Management Association (Summer 1980).

Zinsser, Hans. *Rats, Lice, and History.* New York: Little, Brown and Company, 1936.

Index